The *Mathematica*® Graphics Guidebook

The *Mathematica*® Graphics Guidebook

Cameron Smith

and

Nancy Blachman
Variable Symbols, Inc. and Stanford University

Addison-Wesley Publishing Company
Reading, Massachusetts • Menlo Park, California • New York
Don Mills, Ontario • Wokingham, England • Amsterdam • Bonn
Sydney • Singapore • Tokyo • Madrid • San Juan • Milan • Paris

This book was reproduced from text and illustration files supplied by the authors.

Material in Chapter 4 on plotting functions in two dimensions and Chapter 5 on using the standard packages is reproduced courtesy of *The Mathematica Journal*.

Library of Congress Cataloging-in-Publication Data
Smith, Cameron. 1959--
    The Mathematica graphics guidebook / by Cameron Smith and Nancy Blachman.
        p.   cm.
    Includes bibliographical references and index.
    ISBN 0-201-53280-8
    1. Computer graphics. 2. Mathematica (Computer file)
  I. Blachman, Nancy. II. Title.
  T385.S622 1995
  510´.285´5369--dc20   92-23215
                                                                    CIP
                                                                     r93

Package ISBN   0-201-53280-8
Book ISBN   0-201-82656-9
Disk ISBN   0-201-82655-0

1 2 3 4 5 6 7 8 9 10-CRW-9897969594

Contents

Preface

Mathematica is an exceptionally flexible and powerful tool for producing mathematical graphics. *Mathematica* makes it easy to create graphs of functions, plots of data, pictures of geometrical solids, and other mathematical illustrations either with built-in functions or with simple programs of your own. This book tells you what you need to know to make the most of the graphics capabilities of *Mathematica*. Whether you are a beginner, an experienced user of *Mathematica*, or even someone who doesn't use *Mathematica* at all but wants to use pictures produced by *Mathematica* in your publications, you will find information in this book that will help you. This Preface will help you figure out which parts of the book to read to find the information you need.

This book describes Version 2.2 of *Mathematica*, which is the current version at the time of this writing. Early versions of *Mathematica* (1.03, 1.04, 1.1, and 1.2) had much more limited graphics capabilities than Version 2 and later versions. The differences are great enough that we decided it would not be practical to try to describe all versions in this book. If you are using any level of Version 1 of *Mathematica*, we recommend that you switch to the current version.

- Why Cameron Wrote This Book

I worked for Wolfram Research, Inc., for about two years, beginning in the spring of 1988 when the first version of *Mathematica* was in its final stage of beta-testing, shortly before it was released to the public. My job was to get information about *Mathematica* out to people who needed it, and to that end I gave presentations at conferences and trade shows, wrote technical reports and other end-user documentation, and provided technical support to developers of *Mathematica* packages and other *Mathematica*-related software. I was privileged to get glimpses of the exciting ideas that hundreds of creative and enthusiastic people were rushing to put into practice, but I also saw at first hand how the lack of complete, detailed documentation could hamper a promising project.

During my tenure at WRI I also did a great deal of *Mathematica* programming, and I really came face-to-face with the information gap in the spring of 1989 when I was asked to produce about 150 illustrations for a calculus textbook. The authors wanted to create a visually engaging text, and the publisher had agreed to use four-color printing, not just for a few plates, but for the entire book. This was a new idea in calculus textbook design, and the authors had many ideas for ways to use photographs, diagrams, and other visual aids to communicate the ideas of the calculus. They needed dozens of attractive and accurate figures depicting plots of functions, curves, and surfaces, solids of revolution, and other mathematical objects. *Mathematica* was an obvious choice to make these illustrations, and the then-new version 1.2, with many new graphics features, promised to make the job easy and fun.

Well, parts of it were fun, but none of it was easy! Even though I had by then read Stephen Wolfram's book, *Mathematica: A System for Doing Mathematics by Computer*, from cover to cover several times, I found that there were many features of *Mathematica* graphics that I just didn't understand until I tried to use them. Stephen couldn't document every feature of every function without bloating his book to the size of the Manhattan telephone directory, but keeping the book to a manageable length forced him to leave some odd corners of *Mathematica* graphics unexplored, and I found that I needed to explore them if I wanted to produce publication-quality graphics. If I hadn't had access to the developers of *Mathematica* to get questions answered (and, occasionally, to get workarounds for bugs) I don't know whether I could have finished the project.

When the idea of writing a book about *Mathematica* graphics was presented to me, I thought of that textbook project, and I determined to write the kind of book that I wished I had had then. Given a function to plot or an object to draw, it's easy to get *Mathematica* to produce *some* graphical representation, but to get a particular image that makes a particular point you must simultaneously control coloring, lighting and shading, sampling, scaling, labeling, and all the other factors that go into producing an image with *Mathematica*. To do that you need a thorough understanding of how *Mathematica* graphics are produced, and a complete and detailed reference guide with plenty of practical examples to follow. That's what I've tried to give you in this book.

■ Why Nancy Wrote This Book

I developed an interest in computer graphics when I took a graduate-level course on this topic from Leo Guibas at Stanford University during the winter of 1986. In the summer of 1988 I taught that course. At the end of the summer I went to the computer graphics conference SIGGRAPH, where I saw Stephen Wolfram demonstrate *Mathematica*. I was favorably impressed with the software, and subsequently went to work for Wolfram Research, Inc., the developer of *Mathematica*.

In 1989 I left Wolfram Research to start my own company, Variable Symbols, Inc., to provide consulting and training in mathematical software. In 1991 I wrote the tutorial book *Mathematica: A Practical Approach* to help people learn to use *Mathematica* effectively. This book has been well received. Though I was already familiar with *Mathematica*, I learned more about this software package when writing the book.

When Cameron asked me in the fall of 1992 to join him as co-author of the *Mathematica Graphics Guidebook*, I was delighted. Writing this book has given me an opportunity to learn more about *Mathematica*'s graphics capabilities. I hope this book enables you to take better advantage of *Mathematica* and spend less time fighting it.

- How This Book Was Written

Since the original reason for writing this book was the lack of documentation for many features of *Mathematica* graphics, you won't be surprised to learn that we didn't write the book simply by referring to other printed sources. We started with Stephen Wolfram's book, but whenever it was vague or unclear, or whenever we saw *Mathematica* producing results that differed from what Stephen's book led us to expect, we pursued other sources of information in an attempt to understand fully what was happening so that we could explain it to you. We interviewed the developers at Wolfram Research who write and maintain the graphics code in *Mathematica*, and we are grateful to them (especially Henry Cejtin and Tom Wickham-Jones) for their assistance in puzzling out the rationale underlying *Mathematica*'s graphics features. In a few cases we were even vouchsafed a glimpse of *Mathematica*'s source code!

We didn't stop there, either. All the information we include in this book has been substantiated by extensive testing; on average, we created a dozen or more trial graphics for each one that appears in the book. We exercised some hitherto unexplored aspects of *Mathematica*'s graphics, including some undocumented features; in fact, we uncovered a few bugs in the program (or discrepancies in the documentation, depending on how you look at it) in the course of doing experimental research for this book.

For this reason, the information here records the performance of *Mathematica*: what actually happened, whether or not we thought that was what was *supposed* to happen. If this book disagrees with other references on some point, it is safe to assume that the other book is describing what *Mathematica* was intended to do and this book describes what *Mathematica* actually does. This means, of course, that some of the odd phenomena documented here will (we hope) disappear in future versions of *Mathematica*, as enhancements and bug fixes bring the performance of the program closer into line with the design specifications. As *Mathematica* evolves, this book may fall out of step with future versions, but for now, it is as accurate and complete a description of *Mathematica*'s graphics as you will find anywhere.

▪ Who Should Read This Book

Anyone who uses *Mathematica* can benefit from the information in this book. For example, scientists and engineers who work with large data sets find that a single well-designed plot is far more informative than a huge table of numbers. Teachers attempting to convey complicated ideas can capture students' attention by using still and animated displays to enliven lectures, handouts, and textbooks. Researchers can turn abstruse concepts into pictures that make mathematics almost tangible, stimulating the imagination in ways that symbol manipulations never could. One of *Mathematica*'s greatest strengths is its smooth integration of symbolic, numerical, and graphical capabilities. Even if your work is primarily involved with numbers or formulas you will quickly come to appreciate the ability to translate your ideas into vivid and accurate images.

Of course, some people's primary reason for using *Mathematica* is its graphical abilities. To be useful, a book or journal that treats topics in the sciences must have illustrations that not only are appealing to the eye but also are faithful to the concepts they illustrate. Professional technical illustrators and production specialists find *Mathematica* valuable for producing diagrams of geometric figures, graphs of functions, plots of data sets, and other mathematical illustrations that are both beautiful and accurate. And it is not only publishing professionals who need these capabilities. As desktop publishing systems become more versatile and more faithful to the standards of fine publishing, more and more authors (including the authors of this book) are electing to compose and typeset their own work. *Mathematica* is an excellent tool for preparing technical illustrations for publication, but anyone who uses it for that purpose will need the information in this book.

Perhaps you've never used *Mathematica* before — maybe it was the prospect of drawing beautiful mathematical graphics that attracted your interest, and this book is your first exposure to *Mathematica*. Graphics programming is a good introduction to *Mathematica*, or to programming in general, because there's a special satisfaction in getting a program correct and being rewarded with a beautiful picture. You can skim this book to get an idea of what you can accomplish with *Mathematica*, but before you begin programming you should read the introductory chapters and try out some of the examples in Stephen Wolfram's book, *Mathematica: A System for Doing Mathematics by Computer*, which we refer to as "The *Mathematica* Book." You should keep The *Mathematica* Book at hand as you read this one so you can look up any non-graphics-related *Mathematica* keywords and concepts you don't understand. (The graphics-related ones are all explained here, of course!) You may also want to look at Nancy Blachman's tutorial book *Mathematica: A Practical Approach*, which was written especially to introduce newcomers to *Mathematica*.

■ What's Where in This Book

In attempting to make this the one book a *Mathematica* user needs in order to learn about graphics, we've included material at many levels. Not every reader will need to read every chapter right away. Here's a survey of the contents so you can figure out where to begin.

This book begins with a chapter that discusses the design of *Mathematica*'s graphics capabilities; it describes the issues that the developers considered when developing *Mathematica*'s graphics commands. The second chapter describes the building blocks or *graphics objects* that are supported in *Mathematica*. Chapter 3 contains a survey of the commands or graphics primitives for producing graphics objects (points, lines, polygons, circles, arcs) and directives for specifying attributes (colors, thickness, line style). The commands for plotting functions are described in Chapter 4. Examples of many of the functions that are included with packages (files containing functions defined in *Mathematica*'s programming language) distributed with *Mathematica* can be found in Chapter 5. Chapter 6, which is about the coordinate systems in *Mathematica*, is intended for users who want to understand why the graphics commands were designed to work as they do. The final chapter describes all of *Mathematica*'s graphics options.

If you're eager to get going you can run the examples in this book and experiment with them by changing numerical parameters or substituting one function for another. These examples are included on the disk in the back of this book. If you want to produce a certain kind of graphic, you can skim the book for a similar one and then alter the commands to produce a graphic that suits your needs. Code for graphics that are not included in the body of the text can be found in the appendix.

■ Other Information You Should Have

You should have a copy of the book *Mathematica: A System for Doing Mathematics by Computer*,[1] by Stephen Wolfram, the principal author of *Mathematica*. This is the reference manual for *Mathematica*, and it explains the details of the *Mathematica* language: when to use what kinds of brackets, in what order to specify the arguments to

---

[1] Bibliographic information for this and other references can be found in the list of Suggested Readings at the end of this book.

a function, how to insure that a function's local variables will not interfere with global ones, and so forth. We will explain all the graphics-related *Mathematica* operators in this book, but for other detailed points of the *Mathematica* language we will refer you to "The *Mathematica* Book," as Stephen Wolfram's book is commonly called. Be sure to get the latest edition, which describes Version 2 of *Mathematica*.

The *Guide to Standard Mathematica Packages* is part of the documentation that is shipped with each copy of *Mathematica*. It describes the *Mathematica* commands that are not built into the *Mathematica* kernel but are nonetheless part of every version of *Mathematica* because they are defined in program packages that are part of the *Mathematica* distribution. Many useful graphics functions are defined in packages, and we give an overview of the most commonly used ones in Chapter 5. But whereas the kernel of *Mathematica* is fairly stable and commands are rarely added or redefined, Wolfram Research adds new packages to each new release of *Mathematica*. This means that the present book can be definitive as regards the built-in commands, but not as regards the packages, so it is well worth your while to own a current copy of the *Guide to Standard Mathematica Packages*. If several users are sharing a single copy of *Mathematica*, each user should have his or her own copy of this guide, which can be ordered from Wolfram Research, Inc. for a nominal fee (US$10 at this writing).

You should also get a copy of the machine-specific documentation for the particular version of *Mathematica* that you are using. *Mathematica* is available on more than thirty different computer systems, which differ in both hardware and software. *Mathematica*'s programming language was designed to work the same way in all implementations, but some differences from one version to another are unavoidable. This is especially true of graphics display, which depends on features of the operating system your computer runs as well as the physical characteristics of the terminal you are working at. (Do you use a "graphical user interface," such as NeXTStep, the X Window System, or the Macintosh Finder? Does your computer have a mouse? How many bit planes does your monitor provide?) Both this book and The *Mathematica* Book present information that is (as much as possible) the same for all versions of *Mathematica*, but there are a few things you will want to know that are necessarily different from machine to machine, such as how to stop a runaway calculation, or how to produce animated graphics (assuming that your version of *Mathematica* supports them; not all versions do). Even as basic a matter as how to print your graphics on your computer's printer will be system-dependent. (Is it a laser printer, an ink jet printer, or a dot matrix printer? Does it use an imaging language such as PostScript or PCL, or must its hardware be driven more directly?)

It seems that most users of Macintosh or MS-DOS versions of *Mathematica* regard their computers as "personal." They purchase and install their own copies of the software they use, and they keep the software manuals in their own custody. It also seems, however, that most people who use *Mathematica* under UNIX, VMS, and other "big-computer" operating systems regard *Mathematica* as part of the "system software" of which one copy is provided for many users of a single machine. Since "system software" is usually ordered by, delivered to, and installed by a system administrator, manuals tend to end up in the system administrator's office. The result: many users of *Mathematica* are not even aware that a User's Guide for their version of *Mathematica* exists. *Please* don't be one of these users. Borrow the User's Guide, read it, and, if you're going to do any programming of your own, get your own copy. Extra sets of documentation can be ordered from Wolfram Research, Inc.

If you're just beginning to learn *Mathematica*, you may want to consult Nancy Blachman's book *Mathematica: A Practical Approach*. Nancy developed this book as a text for the *Mathematica* training courses offered by her company, Variable Symbols, Inc. The presentation was refined by the experience of teaching many dozens of classes, and feedback from hundreds of students helped shape it into an excellent introduction to *Mathematica*.[2]

If you are going to write *Mathematica* "packages" to distribute to others, you may want a copy of *Programming in Mathematica*, by Roman Maeder, one of the co-authors of *Mathematica*. This book concentrates on the subtleties of *Mathematica* programming, with extensive and detailed discussions of the risks and benefits of local variables, named options, default settings, and other issues of software design. The discussion is not merely theoretical: several useful packages are developed from scratch, with explanations of why things were done in certain ways. Although we both had extensive experience programming in *Mathematica* before Roman's book appeared, we learned some new and useful techniques from reading it, and we recommend it to anyone who wants to develop code of sufficient quality to distribute.

- How to Read This Book

This book is about programming in *Mathematica*, and it contains a great deal of *Mathematica* input and output. The input is typeset in `a bold typewriter face, like this,` and the output is in a `light typewriter face, like this`. *Mathematica* keywords in the text are also set in the `upright typewriter type`. When we want to show you the result of executing a particular piece of *Mathematica* code, we will display it like this:

---

[2]Cameron wishes to note that he has taught several *Mathematica* tutorials from this book, and recommends it highly and without reservation.

```
Integrate[ 1/(1+x^3), x ]
        -1 + 2 x
ArcTan[--------]                              2
       Sqrt[3]     Log[1 + x]   Log[1 - x + x ]
---------------- + ---------- - ---------------
    Sqrt[3]            3               6
```

Sometimes, we will show you a piece of "generic" *Mathematica* code, as a pattern to follow when writing *Mathematica* programs of your own. Here is an example of such a pattern:

Plot[*function*, { *variable*, *start*, *end* }]

The words and symbols in typewriter type must be typed exactly as shown, but the words in *slant roman type, like this,* must be replaced by actual *Mathematica* expressions. One way of making replacements in the pattern above would be

Plot[Sin[x], { x, 0, 2Pi }]

Here Sin[x] is the *function,* x is the *variable,* 0 is the *start* value, and 2Pi is the *end* value. When the result of executing a command includes a picture (the typical case in this book), it will be typeset like this:

Plot[Sin[x], { x, 0, 2Pi }]

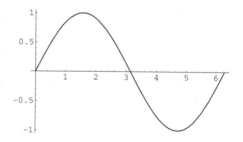

-Graphics-

In the first parts of this book, we assume that you are already familiar with the basic syntax of *Mathematica*, and with some of the *Mathematica* operators such as Transpose, Map, Apply, Table, and Range. You should already know how to define a "function" (actually, a rewriting rule) in *Mathematica*, know what an "option setting" is, and know the differences between the four kinds of bracket pairs: (and), [and], [[and]], and { and }. Throughout the book we have tried to keep the level of mathematical sophistication as low as possible but some mathematical knowledge is required to fully understand the material on adaptive sampling.

Sections and subsections are numbered: 2, 3, 3.1, 3.2, etc. We've tried to keep cross-referencing to a minimum in this book, even at the cost of some redundancy between chapters, because both authors dislike having to flip from section to section in a book to track down the information we need.

- The Accompanying Disk

All the input statements in this book are on the accompanying disk. There are files containing the inputs from the chapters, the appendix, and the color plates. Files with names that terminate in ".ma" are intended to be opened with the *Mathematica* Notebook Front End.

```
chapter1.ma   chapter3.ma   chapter5.ma   chapter7.ma   appendix.ma
chapter2.ma   chapter4.ma   chapter6.ma   color.ma
```

Start up the Notebook Front End and then open up a file by selecting the menu item *Open* in the *File* menu. Graphics are included in the files appendix.ma and color.ma. You can generate or regenerate a graphic by putting your cursor in an input line or cell and (1) hitting the enter key, (2) depressing the shift and return keys simultaneously, or (3) selecting the menu item *Evaluate Selection* from the *Action* menu.

Files with names that terminate in ".m" are intended to be used on systems running *Mathematica* without the Notebook Front End, such as MS-DOS or Unix. These files are in the directory or folder named "dos-unix."

```
chapter1.m   chapter3.m   chapter5.m   chapter7.m   appendix.m
chapter2.m   chapter4.m   chapter6.m   color.m
```

Start up *Mathematica* and then read a file by invoking the command "<< *filename*," where *filename* is one of the files in the directory called "dos-unix."

You may need to resize the graphics to make them resemble the images in the book. If you have a small amount of RAM, you may not be able to run all the inputs on this disk during a single *Mathematica* session.

When an input does not produce the results shown in the book, we recommend that you start a new *Mathematica* session and re-execute the input. If you still have problems, please send your input together with the result you obtained to Nancy Blachman.

Nancy Blachman
Variable Symbols, Inc.
6537 Chabot Road
Oakland, CA 94618-1618
Email: nb@cs.stanford.edu
Fax: 510-652-8461

- The Four-Color Insert

In the middle of this book are color versions of some of the graphics shown in this book. The inputs for producing these graphics are included in the files named color.ma and color.m on the disk that accompanies this book.

- The Philosophy of This Book

This book discusses combinations of features in addition to documenting them one by one. Other books tend to present each feature in isolation and show how that feature works. The goal of our book is to show you how to create useful and beautiful graphics, using whatever features or combinations of features may be necessary. For that reason, you will find that although most of the examples in this book are narrowly constructed to illustrate particular points, every so often we make an example more elaborate than strictly necessary, to show you how *Mathematica*'s graphics commands can be used in realistic ways to construct publishable graphics. We also point out what combinations of features do not work well together, so that you will know what works and what to avoid.

In this book we present a great deal of computer code, but few large programs and no complete *Mathematica* packages. Instead we provide short sample calculations, which illustrate the ideas and the steps involved in making elaborate mathematical graphics. It is our experience (and the lesson of UNIX) that large programs that attempt to anticipate all needs and serve many functions at once are difficult to write, difficult to debug, and difficult to use—and suffer from the added drawback that the one option you need in any given circumstance is the option that the author failed to anticipate and therefore didn't provide. We have found it far more useful to keep a large collection of small parts, which we can assemble in different configurations to solve a variety of problems. Besides, large programs in *Mathematica* really ought to be structured as *Mathematica* "packages", and make use of *Mathematica*'s contexts for data hiding and localization. These concepts are important, but they have little to do with mathematical graphics, and so we chose to avoid dealing with them. We suggest that you consult Nancy's book or Roman Maeder's book if you want to know more about this aspect of *Mathematica* usage.

Acknowledgments

The authors wish to thank the people who have helped us to write this book. Any flaws or shortcomings are solely our responsibility, but this book owes many of its virtues to the support and assistance we received from others.

Naturally, we thank the creators of *Mathematica*, which we have found to be a powerful and well-designed system for calculating and programming. The following people have been especially helpful in providing detailed information about the system: Stephen Wolfram, Dan Grayson, Roman Maeder, Steve Omohundro, Henry Cejtin, Jerry Keiper, David Ballman, Theodore Gray, Igor Rivin, Dave Withoff, Bruce Smith, and Tom Wickham-Jones.

Special thanks go to Donald Knuth, Leslie Lamport, Tomas Rokicki, Trevor Darrell, and Pehong Chen. Donald Knuth created the TeX typesetting system, and Leslie Lamport built the LaTeX document preparation system over TeX. By creating this beautiful software and placing it in the public domain, they have made huge steps toward changing computer-assisted, book-quality typesetting from a prohibitively expensive and esoteric craft, practiced and understood only by specialists, to something that every author can use. We relied on Tomas Rokicki's TeXview and dvips programs, which allow previewing of TeX documents on a computer screen and printing them on a laser printer or phototypesetter, to bridge the gap between TeX's "device-independent" page descriptions and the realities of getting print on paper. Trevor Darrell's psfig/TeX macro package made the inclusion of *Mathematica*'s PostScript illustrations in the manuscript completely painless, and Pehong Chen's makeindex program relieved us of a great deal of drudgery in preparing the index. Without these five pieces of software we would never have been able to typeset this book ourselves, which means we would have lost a deeply satisfying part of the creative experience.

We could not have completed this book without access to certain computer network resources: electronic mail, USENET newsgroups, and "anonymous ftp" software archives. Our gratitude goes to those organizations that provided us with guest access to their computer systems while we worked on the book: Wolfram Research, Inc.,

Middlebury College, Stanford University, Wright State University, and the Mathematics Department of the University of Illinois.

Thanks also to the many people who reviewed intermediate versions of the manuscript and provided valuable comments and criticisms, including Nelson Blachman, Dave Burmaster, Henry Cejtin, Mike Hess, Silver Jones, Lew Lefton, Silvio Levy, Paul McGill, Michael Mossinghoff, Troels Petersen, Chris Reed, Marcel Richter, Susumu Sakakibara, Steve Scherr, Dana Scott, Julie Simon, Enid Steinbart, and other anonymous reviewers.

We are also indebted to the membership of the Info-TeX and mathgroup mailing lists and the comp.text.tex and sci.math.symbolic USENET newsgroups for some extremely helpful comments and questions and some fruitful discussions. Many exchanges resulted in substantial improvements to both the content and the appearance of this book. The following people (listed in alphabetical order) probably didn't realize how important their contributions were to us: Steve Christensen, Victor Eijkhout, George Greenwade, Joe Grohens, Joe Kaiping, Silvio Levy, Frank Mittelbach, Art Ogawa, Tom Rokicki, and Rainer Schöpf.

The support and encouragement we received from the people at Addison-Wesley knew no limits. Everyone we dealt with was warm, cooperative, and enthusiastic. Allan Wylde, whose enthusiastic support for *Mathematica* brought many important *Mathematica* resources into print, conceived the idea of a *Mathematica Graphics Guidebook* and encouraged Cameron to undertake the project. Peter Gordon shepherded and sustained us through the completion of the manuscript. Both of them exhibited unheard-of patience and understanding in the face of innumerable delays. Helen Goldstein, Associate Editor, and Juliet Silveri, Production Supervisor, also gave us guidance and assistance. We would also like to thank Lyn Dupré, who did an excellent job of copyediting drafts of this manuscript, and Ann Knight, who patiently supervised production.

On a personal note, Cameron would like to thank his parents, Cameron Smith and Beverly Cearley, who always believed, and made him believe, that he could accomplish anything he set his mind to, and who taught him to value knowledge. He also thanks Ellen Cotman, Carol Conrad, and Patricia Gibson, three of his early teachers who helped him to discover the beauty of mathematics, and George Francis, who encouraged him as a graduate student to learn about computer graphics and to "get his hands dirty" with computer code, thus learning practice as well as theory. Finally, his most important thanks go to his wife, Julie Simon, who never flagged in her understanding, patience, and support during the writing of this book.

Nancy would like to thank her parents, Nelson and Anne Blachman, and her sister Susan Blachman, for their support and encouragement. She also thanks Helen Chernicoff and Alesia Bland for handling Variable Symbols business while she was working on this book. Finally, she thanks Henry Cejtin for filling us in on the history and design of many of *Mathematica*'s graphics capabilities.

Cameron Smith
Beavercreek, Ohio

Nancy Blachman
Oakland, California

November, 1994

Chapter 1

The Design of *Mathematica's* Graphics Commands

Mathematica's versatile graphics capabilities have contributed greatly to its success. You can use *Mathematica* to plot functions and data in two and three dimensions, produce contour and density plots, and draw arbitrary figures. This chapter discusses the design of *Mathematica*'s graphics commands, explaining how the creators of *Mathematica* decided what features to implement and pointing out some of the decisions and compromises they had to make. Understanding the underlying design of *Mathematica*'s graphics will give you a mental model that will make it easier for you to learn and remember the ins and outs of the graphics commands.

Wolfram Research, Inc. (WRI) had to make tradeoffs when designing *Mathematica*'s graphics capabilities. They wanted the graphics commands to be easy to use but also flexible and powerful, and they wanted the graphics *Mathematica* produces to be accurate but also able to be rendered quickly. Since it is nearly impossible to design algorithms that have all of these properties, the designers of *Mathematica* had to set priorities among their goals. In general, they gave higher priority to ease of use and rapid results, so that a user who knows little about *Mathematica*'s way of doing things can get satisfactory results quickly. They concentrated on providing built-in commands to produce the kinds of graphics people want most often, such as graphs of functions, and they designed these commands to require minimal user input to produce reasonably accurate graphs showing interesting regions of a curve or surface, within a short time. They also made the graphics commands flexible and powerful by designing them to accept dozens of optional arguments, giving fine control to users who need it. In the tradeoff between accuracy and speed, the designers gave priority to producing results within a short time to minimize the frustration that comes from waiting for a response. Optional arguments can be used to instruct the sampling algorithms to do a more thorough job when necessary (at the cost of a longer delay before a picture is displayed).

The designers at WRI also wanted *Mathematica* graphics to be completely general. Since they knew that they couldn't anticipate all the types of graphics users would need, they provided drawing capabilities enabling *Mathematica* to draw anything at all. Thus, a user can enter a simple graphic containing a few geometric objects directly from the keyboard, using graphics primitives like `Point`, `Line`, `Circle`, and `Polygon`. More complicated graphics can be created by *Mathematica* programs that compute the position and appearance of graphical elements. In fact, many of *Mathematica*'s graphics capabilities are implemented in just this way: not in compiled code built into the *Mathematica* kernel but in programs written in *Mathematica*'s programming language. Wolfram Research includes dozens of so-called packages of functions with each copy of *Mathematica*; once a package is loaded, its functions behave just like those built into the kernel. Many of these packages were written in response to requests from users long after the original design of *Mathematica*'s graphics was completed. Because the graphics were designed to be general, WRI was able to add functionality to *Mathematica* without having to redesign the program's inner workings. If you need a kind of graphic for which there is still no predefined command, you too can write a program or package to create it, and your program can fit in as a seamless extension of *Mathematica*'s graphics capabilities.

Wolfram Research also wanted *Mathematica*'s graphics to be capable of display on as wide a range of graphics devices as possible. They chose the PostScript language as the external medium for *Mathematica* graphics because it was designed to be device independent. When *Mathematica* was designed, PostScript was already supported on many output devices, from laser printers to high-resolution imagesetters. Moreover, Adobe Systems, Inc., was developing Display PostScript and Level 2 PostScript to support interactive use in windowing environments. Because PostScript is a high-level programming language, it was possible to implement some of the graphics support routines in PostScript procedures instead of in the *Mathematica* kernel, allowing the graphics to adapt themselves to the printing environment in certain ways without requiring regeneration by *Mathematica*. For example, you can enlarge a graphic by 20 percent without increasing the height and width of the text labels, because the text placement calculations are carried out largely in PostScript code at the time the graphic is rendered. If you have installed special fonts on your system, you don't have to go through any configuration process to be able to use them in *Mathematica* graphics, because it is the PostScript interpreter, not the *Mathematica* kernel, whose job it is to know about fonts. In fact, *Mathematica* doesn't have to know anything about the physical characteristics of an output device, so the same *Mathematica* graphic can be rendered on any PostScript device with no custom programming inside *Mathematica*. Using PostScript also allows *Mathematica* graphics to be exported to graphic design applications such as Adobe Illustrator, so that design features not supported by *Mathematica* can be added manually. In short, the choice of PostScript has made *Mathematica* graphics more portable and more powerful than they could have been if they had been implemented in any other form.

1.1 Easy to Use

The most commonly needed tasks are designed to be the easiest to specify. To plot a function or expression in one variable, you simply specify the expression and the interval over which the plot should be made. For example, the following input instructs *Mathematica* to plot $\sin x$ for values of x between 0 and 2π:

```
Plot[ Sin[x], { x, 0, 2Pi } ];
```

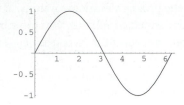

Although many decisions have to be made when a function is plotted, you need not concern yourself with them unless you are dissatisfied with the plot that *Mathematica* produces. *Mathematica* decides how frequently to sample a function, where to position the axes and tick marks, what range of values to display, and how to shade or color the graph. The choices that *Mathematica* makes depend on the settings of the *options*. If you do not specify an option, a default setting is used. Consequently, you need only to provide a minimal amount of information to produce a graph.

Let's look at another function, $f(x) = \frac{\sin \pi x}{\pi x}$, known as the *sinc* function, which is used in the theory of Fourier transforms. The *sinc* function takes on values between $-.218$ and 1. Notice that *Mathematica* doesn't show the entire range of values.

```
Plot[ Sin[Pi x]/(Pi x), { x, -4, 4 } ];
```

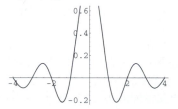

By default, *Mathematica* decides the range of values to show. It attempts to show the most interesting parts of the graph clearly, even if that requires it to cut off extreme values.

■ Options

Sometimes *Mathematica* doesn't show you what you want to see. In such cases, you can take the driver's seat and specify optional additional arguments that affect what *Mathematica* displays. You can control most aspects of drawing a graph through options. An option setting is a rule of the form *name->value* or *name:>value*, where *name* is the name of the option and *value* is the value it is assigned. (The difference in meaning between -> and :> is explained in The *Mathematica* Book.) Option settings must follow required arguments, with multiple settings separated by commas. Optional arguments may be given in any order, since each option setting specifies the *name* of the option being set. Here is the previous example, but this time the entire range of values is shown because we specified the option setting PlotRange->All. The graph is also drawn with a thicker line because of the PlotStyle setting.

```
sincGraph = Plot[ Sin[Pi x]/(Pi x), {x,-4,4}, PlotRange->All,
                 PlotStyle->Thickness[0.008] ];
```

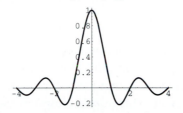

A graphics command such as Plot returns a result that you can use as input to another command. We assigned the name sincGraph to the preceding graph. With the Show command, we redisplay the graph with grid lines to simulate graph paper. (See Section 2.6 on page 25 for more information on the Show function.)

```
Show[ sincGraph, GridLines->Automatic ];
```

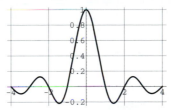

You can use the double-question-mark command, ??, which gives online help, or the Options function to see what options a command accepts. Here are the options accepted by the Plot command:

```
Options[Plot]
                          1
{AspectRatio -> -----------, Axes -> Automatic, AxesLabel -> None,
                GoldenRatio
  AxesOrigin -> Automatic, AxesStyle -> Automatic, Background -> Automatic,
  ColorOutput -> Automatic, Compiled -> True, DefaultColor -> Automatic, Epilog -> {},
  Frame -> False, FrameLabel -> None, FrameStyle -> Automatic, FrameTicks -> Automatic,
  GridLines -> None, MaxBend -> 10., PlotDivision -> 20., PlotLabel -> None,
  PlotPoints -> 25, PlotRange -> Automatic, PlotRegion -> Automatic,
  PlotStyle -> Automatic, Prolog -> {}, RotateLabel -> True, Ticks -> Automatic,
  DefaultFont :> $DefaultFont, DisplayFunction :> $DisplayFunction}
```

This list also shows the options' default settings. When an option is not specified, its default is used. For example, the output for Options[Plot] shows that the option PlotPoints assumes the default setting 25 if you don't specify its value. For descriptions of all the options for the graphics operators, see Chapter 7.

1.2 General Purpose

Mathematica provides a complete set of primitives for drawing arbitrary pictures in two and three dimensions. Using these primitives, you can write a program to prepare any kind of graphics you need, so you are not limited to the features that the designers of *Mathematica* thought to provide. This graphic illustrates many of the two-dimensional shapes that are available in *Mathematica*:[1]

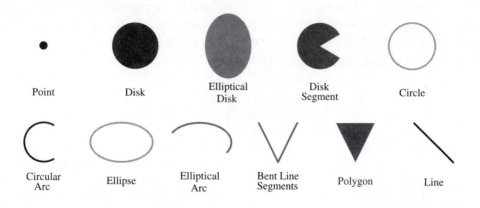

With these primitives, you can draw almost any figure. A similar set is available for 3D graphics.

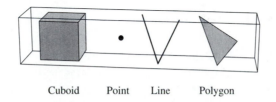

---

[1] For most of the illustrations in this book, we have given the *Mathematica* commands to produce the graphic where the graphic appears in the text. In the few cases where the code is too unwieldy or is irrelevant to the discussion, we have moved it to the Appendix.

▪ Resizing *Mathematica* Graphics

One basic assumption about the graphics produced by *Mathematica* is that they can be resized. Attributes such as dot size and line thickness are specified as fractions of a graphic's overall width, so that they scale up or down proportionally when the graphic is rescaled.

1.3 The Evolution of *Mathematica*'s Graphics

The original design of *Mathematica*'s graphics centered on function plotting in two and three dimensions using the `Plot` and `Plot3D` commands, and the original capabilities were sparse. It has always been the goal of WRI that *Mathematica* become the standard tool for preparing scientific and mathematical graphics. *Mathematica*'s original graphics capabilities were not adequate for this objective; they lacked many features that are necessary for preparing publication-quality graphics. For example, many scientific journals have standards dictating how data plots and other graphics must appear. These standards specify such details as where the axes are placed, how they are labeled, where major and minor tick marks must appear, and what fonts may be used for titles and legends.

As *Mathematica* has come into wider and wider use, WRI has received feedback indicating what features users want and need if they are to use *Mathematica* graphics in their books, articles, and other presentations. These suggestions have influenced the evolution of *Mathematica*'s graphics capabilities. Major enhancements were made in the passage from Version 1.1 to Version 1.2, and again from 1.2 to 2.0. In Versions 2.1 and 2.2, minor bug fixes were applied to the built-in commands and new graphics packages have been created. The result is that *Mathematica* is now a robust system for producing technical illustrations and other scientific and mathematical graphics.

Still, because so many improvements have been "retrofitted" into the original design, features do not always work together as you might hope. Some combinations produce unappealing results, as, for example, when frame labels collide with axis labels and plot labels. In this book, we point out which combinations of features work well and which do not, so that you will know what produces worthwhile results and what to avoid.

Chapter 2

Data Types

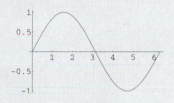

-Graphics-

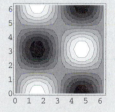

-ContourGraphics-

-Graphics3D-

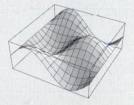

-SurfaceGraphics-

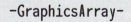

-GraphicsArray-

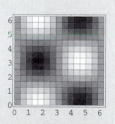

-DensityGraphics-

Mathematica has built-in graphics-building commands (such as ListPlot, Plot3D, and ContourPlot) for making the most common types of mathematical graphics: graphs of functions and plots of data sets. We call them "graphics-building" commands because they do their work by constructing and displaying graphics objects. A graphics object is a *Mathematica* expression containing information about how to draw a picture. *Mathematica* draws a picture by translating the information in a graphics object into instructions in the PostScript programming language and then passing those instructions to a PostScript interpreter, which executes the instructions and creates an image. In this book, we refer to the *Mathematica* expression that represents an image as a graphics object and to the image itself as a graphic The process of executing PostScript code to produce an image is called rendering a graphic.

Mathematica has several kinds of graphics object, which you can think of as separate data types for representing different kinds of two- and three-dimensional graphics. This chapter explains the overall structure of the different types of graphics objects and why there are many types. It focuses on what the types are for rather than on how to use them. Chapter 3 will present in detail the elements from which graphics objects are assembled.

Graphics objects can be discarded after display, or they can be saved in variables and redisplayed with different option settings to adjust such parameters as viewpoint and scaling. In this chapter, we explain how to use the Show command to display graphics objects, and in Chapter 7, we will examine the complete list of *Mathematica*'s graphics option settings.

2.1 Two-Dimensional Graphics Objects

There are two kinds of two-dimensional graphics objects in *Mathematica*: Graphics and GraphicsArray. Graphics objects represent any two-dimensional graphics (including plots of functions as well as geometrical figures that you create yourself). GraphicsArray is a composite data type whose elements are other graphics objects.

2.1.1 Graphics

A Graphics object is an expression of the form[1]

$$\text{Graphics[} \textit{list of elements, option settings } \text{]}$$

A graphics element in the *list of elements* can be a graphics primitive or a graphics directive. Graphics primitives are expressions such as Point, Line, and Polygon that

---

[1] If you are uncertain about the meaning of this example, or the significance of the typefaces, refer to the section "How to Read This Book" in the Preface.

represent shapes to be drawn, while graphics directives are expressions such as RGBColor and PointSize that affect the way the primitives are drawn: what color they are, how thick the lines are, how large the dots are that represent points, and so on. The *option settings* are specifications such as AspectRatio->1 and AxesOrigin->{0,0}. You can use option settings like these to specify scaling and other parameters that affect how a graphic is displayed. The complete lists of graphics elements and options are given in Chapters 3 and 7; for now, it is enough to know that they exist and to be able to recognize an option setting when you see it.

Here is an example of a Graphics object built from scratch. The *list of elements* in this example consists of a point, a bent line connecting three points, and a solid rectangle. The *option settings* include commands for axes to be drawn, with automatic choice of scaling and tick marks and the title "My First Picture" to be drawn over the plot.

```
mypic = Graphics[ { PointSize[.03], Point[{1/5,3/4}],
                Line[{{0,0},{1/2,1},{1,2/3}}],
                Rectangle[{1/2,1/3},{3/4,1/2}]
            },
            {  Axes->Automatic, PlotLabel->"My First Picture" }
        ];
```

Executing this command builds a graphics object and stores it in the variable mypic, but does not display it. The command to display a graphics object is Show. (Plotting functions such as ListPlot and Plot3D call Show implicitly.)

```
Show[mypic];
```

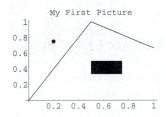

Function plots created by the Plot command are Graphics objects just like mypic. When you use Plot to graph a function, it samples the function at many points (using an adaptive algorithm described in Section 4.1.3), and builds a Graphics object. The *list of elements* of this Graphics object includes a Line object that draws a line connecting the points obtained by the sampling algorithm. The *option settings* are set up to reflect the appropriate scaling, labeling of axes, and so forth, for that plot. Here is an example:

```
Plot[ Sin[x], {x,0,2Pi}, PlotStyle->RGBColor[1,0,0] ];
```

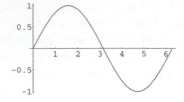

The sine curve (which is shown in red on a color monitor or in a shade of gray on a black-and-white display) is drawn by a single Line primitive just like the one in the example we built from scratch. The only difference is that in the example, we made a Line that connected only three points, whereas in the plot, the Line connects about 80 points on the graph of the equation $y = \sin(x)$.

Like Plot, the built-in functions ParametricPlot and ListPlot produce Graphics objects as their results. So do many functions defined in packages that are distributed with *Mathematica*, such as MultipleListPlot, BarChart, and WorldMap. We will discuss *Mathematica*'s built-in plotting functions in Chapter 4 and its graphics packages in Chapter 5. Other graphics data types can also be converted to Graphics form, as explained in Section 2.7 on page 31.

2.1.2 GraphicsArray

The GraphicsArray data type is intended to make it easier to display many graphics objects together by combining them into a single object. It has the form

GraphicsArray[*array of graphics objects*, *option settings*]

The *array of graphics objects* can be either a one-dimensional array (i.e., a list) or a two-dimensional array (i.e., a list of lists). If it is a list, the graphics objects are displayed side by side in a row. If it is a list of lists, each sublist makes a row of the combined display and the rows are stacked to form columns. The sublists in a list of lists need not be of the same length; short lists are filled with blank space at the right. Each graphics object is drawn independently of the others in its own rectangular subregion of the whole plotting area, according to its option settings. Options in the *option settings* of the GraphicsArray object affect the array as a whole — for example, specifying Frame->True causes a frame to be drawn around the entire array, not around each individual graphic.

Here is an example showing the use of GraphicsArray to present a table of scatter plots for multivariate data:

```
pts = Block[ { x, randomdigits = N[Pi,500] - 3 },
        Table[ ( x = 10^6 randomdigits; randomdigits = Mod[x,1]; x/10^6 ), {60} ] ];
pts = Transpose[Partition[pts,3]];
```

Why didn't we simply use *Mathematica*'s Random function to cook up random numbers for this example? Because we wanted to generate numbers in a reproducible way, so that if you try this example yourself, you will get the same results that we got.[2] Now that we have our data, the next step is to construct the Graphics objects that make up the individual cells of the scatter plot table.

```
grarray = Table[ ListPlot[ Transpose[{pts[[j]],pts[[i]]}],
                   PlotStyle -> {PointSize[.03]},
                   DisplayFunction -> Identity,
                   AspectRatio -> 1, PlotRange->{{0,1},{0,1}},
                   Ticks -> None, Axes -> False,
                   Frame -> True, FrameTicks -> None ],
              {i,3}, {j,3} ];
```

We have used several option settings here to get the cells to look the way we want them to. In particular, we used the DisplayFunction option to prevent ListPlot from displaying each plot as it was created; we use this technique throughout the book to display objects side by side instead of one at a time. Finally, we put the array of Graphics objects inside a GraphicsArray and use Show to display it, as shown here:

```
Show[GraphicsArray[Reverse[grarray]]];
```

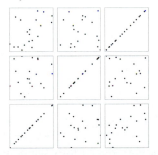

We used the Reverse function here to reverse the rows in order for the ascending diagonal to appear as a straight line. Try executing this example without the Reverse to see why we did it this way. Incidentally, the composite GraphicsArray was displayed even though its component Graphics objects were not, because the GraphicsArray object has its own DisplayFunction setting that is unaffected by the DisplayFunction->Identity settings in the individual Graphics objects.

GraphicsArray is especially well suited to displaying the frames of an animation sequence in a context in which animation is not possible (on the pages of this book,

---

[2]You might think that we should have used SeedRandom[] to guarantee reproducible results. Unfortunately, changes in *Mathematica*'s random number generator from version to version mean that not even the use of SeedRandom[] guarantees that Random[] always generates the same sequence of numbers. At least the digits of π don't change.

for example). Here is a command that defines anim to be a list of 18 plots showing stages in the generation of a Lissajous curve:

```
anim = Table[ ParametricPlot[ {Sin[3t],Cos[5t]}, {t,0,n}, DisplayFunction->Identity,
        PlotRange->{{-1.1,1.1},{-1.1,1.1}}, Ticks->None, AspectRatio->1 ],
      {n,Pi/9,2Pi,Pi/9} ];
```

The option setting DisplayFunction->Identity tells *Mathematica* not to display the plots as they are generated; the other options control the appearance of the plots. On most systems that run *Mathematica*, there is a way to display a sequence of graphics like anim in quick succession to form an animation; the method varies depending on the operating system and user interface. In this book, we use GraphicsArray to display such sequences:

```
Show[GraphicsArray[Partition[anim,6]]];
```

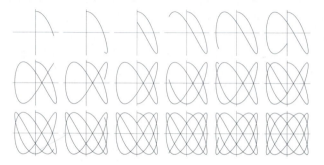

Many versions of *Mathematica* are capable of displaying animations, but on those that aren't, or when you want a printed representation, GraphicsArray is very useful. In Section 5.2.1 on page 149 we present code to convert animations to graphics arrays automatically.

The GraphicsArray type was introduced into *Mathematica* in Version 2.0. In Versions 2.0 and 2.1, it was a built-in data type, implemented in C code, but in version 2.2, it was removed from *Mathematica*'s kernel and implemented instead in *Mathematica*'s own programming language. The structure of a GraphicsArray object is the same as before, but now when *Mathematica* is asked to display a GraphicsArray, instead of invoking special-purpose C code, it simply converts the GraphicsArray object to a Graphics object in which the cells of the array are represented by Rectangle objects (which are described in Section 3.2.4). This is an excellent example of *Mathematica* programming done right. The new version of GraphicsArray behaves in all respects as if it were a built-in part of *Mathematica*, but the code is much easier to understand and maintain than the C version was. (In fact, the C version had bugs in the code that laid out graphics inside a GraphicsArray; these bugs are no longer present in Version 2.2.) The *Mathematica* code for GraphicsArray is less than two pages long and is well worth studying, especially if you are thinking of trying to write functions of your own that you want to act as much as possible like *Mathematica*'s built-in features. The commands

```
Begin["Graphics`Private`"];
Save["GAdef.txt",GraphicsArray];
End[];
```

cause the definition of GraphicsArray (and the functions that GraphicsArray calls) to be written to the file GAdef.txt. On some systems, you may also be able to find the file GraphicsCoercion.m in a directory called Preload; this file contains the definition of GraphicsArray and is loaded when a new *Mathematica* kernel is initialized.

Unfortunately, there is still a bug in the treatment of the PostScript clipping path in GraphicsArray objects. Use of the option setting PlotRange->All can trigger this bug when text strings spill outside the display area. Consider the following example:

```
gr1 = Graphics[{ Point[{6,3}], Point[{0,0}], PointSize[.04], Point[{4,1}],
        Text[ FontForm["A VERY LONG TEXT STRING",{"Courier",12}], {4,1} ] },
        Frame->True, FrameTicks->None, Background->GrayLevel[2/3], PlotRange->All ];
gr2 = Graphics[{ Point[{6,3}], Point[{0,0}], PointSize[.04], Point[{4,2}],
        Text[ FontForm["ANOTHER LONG STRING",{"Courier",12}], {4,2} ] },
        Frame->True, FrameTicks->None, Background->GrayLevel[2/3] ];
Show[gr1];
Show[GraphicsArray[ { gr2, gr1, gr2 }, GraphicsSpacing->.2 ]];
```

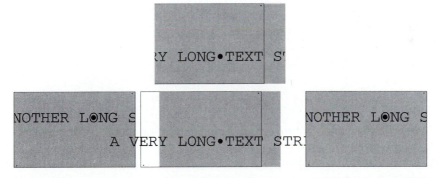

First, we display the graphics object gr1 by itself. It contains a text string so long that even with the setting PlotRange->All, the string does not fit within the display area, and so is clipped. However, when we display gr1 as one subgraphic in a GraphicsArray, the text is able to spill outside the area allotted for gr1 and into the graphic to the left. In fact, it also spills into the space of the graphic on the right, but this is not obvious because the graphic on the right is drawn last and so covers up the spilled part of the center graphic's text. Even the frame drawn by the Frame option is not properly clipped in the center graphic. In the graphics on the left and right, the setting PlotRange->All is not used, and the graphical elements are clipped correctly. We expect this to be fixed in future releases of *Mathematica*.

2.2 Three-Dimensional Graphics Objects

Graphics3D is the most general type of 3D graphics, in that any three-dimensional scene, whether it represents, say, a solid object, or the graph of a function, may be depicted as a Graphics3D object. Graphics3D is similar to Graphics: A Graphics3D object has the form

Graphics3D[*list of elements*, *option settings*]

Of course, the points, lines, polygons, and so forth, in a Graphics3D *list of elements* must be specified with three coordinates instead of two. User-written packages that extend *Mathematica*'s 3D graphics capabilities almost always produce Graphics3D objects (rather than SurfaceGraphics, which we will look at next). A complete list of the graphics elements that can appear in Graphics3D objects is given in Chapter 3.

Here is a simple example of a Graphics3D object, in which we display one point, one line, and one polygon:

```
boxpic = Graphics3D[{ PointSize[.04], Point[{1/2,1,1/3}],
                      Line[ { {0,0,0}, {1,1/2,1/3}, {1/2,1,1} } ],
                      Polygon[ { {1,1/5,0}, {0,1,0}, {0,0,1/2} } ] }];
Show[boxpic];
```

The first thing to notice about this example is the cube: It wasn't one of the objects that we asked *Mathematica* to display, so where did it come from? *Mathematica* displays 3D graphics in a viewing region in space, which has the form of a rectangular box. *Mathematica* automatically scales 3D graphics to fit inside this box. You can specify a setting for the BoxRatios option to determine the shape of the bounding box and thus control how the graphics are scaled. *Mathematica*'s default for displaying 3D graphics is to draw the edges of this box to give you a frame of reference for the scene. The option setting Boxed->False displays the graphics without the box, but notice how this scene appears to lose its "three-dimensionality" without the box for reference.

```
Show[boxpic,Boxed->False];
```

Another thing to notice about this scene is that the line pierces the polygon and that the part of the line that passes behind the polygon is not displayed. Here is another example, in which each of two triangles obscures part of the other:

```
Show[Graphics3D[{ Polygon[ { {0,0,1}, {1/2,1,0}, {1,1/2,0} } ],
                  Polygon[ { {2/3,0,1/3}, {1,1,2/3}, {0,2/3,1/3} } ] },
                  ViewPoint -> {2,2,3} ]];
```

Figuring out what parts of a scene hide other parts, and drawing only the parts that are supposed to be visible, is the most complicated and time-consuming aspect of displaying three-dimensional graphics. In a scene involving hundreds of elements, the time required to eliminate hidden features can far outweigh the time to compute the positions of the elements in the first place. The SurfaceGraphics data type, discussed in the next section, was introduced into *Mathematica* to optimize hidden-feature removal in a special case.

The function ParametricPlot3D can be used to plot parametrized curves and surfaces; it constructs a Graphics3D object in much the same way that the two-dimensional plotting functions Plot and ParametricPlot construct Graphics objects to represent their results. Here is an example:

```
ParametricPlot3D[ { s, Exp[-s^2] Cos[t], Exp[-s^2] Sin[t] }, {t,0,2Pi}, {s,-2,2} ];
```

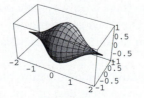

Many packages distributed with *Mathematica* define additional commands for constructing Graphics3D objects. Here, for example, are some familiar mathematical shapes:

```
Needs["Graphics`Polyhedra`"];  Needs["Graphics`Shapes`"];
Show[GraphicsArray[{ Graphics3D[Dodecahedron[]], Graphics3D[Torus[]],
                              Graphics3D[Stellate[Icosahedron[]]] }]];
```

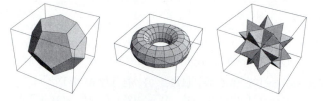

2.3 Optimized Surface Graphics Objects

The other principal 3D graphics type besides Graphics3D is SurfaceGraphics. To understand why the SurfaceGraphics type is useful, consider that a general surface in three dimensions, like the one depicted here, can have complicated folds and self-intersections.

Structures like these make the problem of hidden-line and hidden-surface removal for general three-dimensional scenes difficult and time-consuming. But there is one important kind of three-dimensional scene that never exhibits this kind of self-intersection — namely, a surface defined as the graph of a function $z = f(x, y)$. Such a surface can't loop back upon itself because two different points on the surface can't have the same x and y coordinates. After all, for any given values of x and y, the expression $f(x, y)$ defines only a single z value, so there is only a single point on the surface corresponding to that choice of x and y. Expressed geometrically, no point on the surface can lie directly above another point on the surface (which is exactly what happens in the loop above).

If you know that certain kinds of hidden-feature problems (such as the loop) cannot occur in a scene, you can save a great deal of time in drawing the scene simply by not bothering to check for those problems and not keeping track of the information that you need to solve them. Because surfaces defined by functions $f(x,y)$ occur so frequently, and because they are guaranteed to be free of certain kinds of complications, *Mathematica* includes the special type SurfaceGraphics to handle them efficiently. Graphics3D objects can represent any kind of three-dimensional scene, but may require a long time to render; SurfaceGraphics objects are more restricted in what they can represent, but where they can be used, they can be rendered much faster than a corresponding Graphics3D object can. For this reason, *Mathematica*'s Plot3D and ListPlot3D functions produce SurfaceGraphics objects rather than Graphics3D objects.

A SurfaceGraphics object has the form

$$\text{SurfaceGraphics}[\textit{ array of z values, option settings }]$$

The *array of z values* is a rectangular array of real numbers representing the heights of an array of points on the surface. Only the z coordinates of the points are specified; *Mathematica* infers the x and y coordinates from the MeshRange option setting. The *option settings* include most of the same options as those available for Graphics3D, including settings for BoxRatios and ViewPoint. An important point to note is that the *array of z values* is *transposed* from what you would ordinarily expect: The x coordinate of the surface corresponds to the second coordinate of the array, and the y coordinate of the surface corresponds to the first coordinate of the array. For example, if you construct a SurfaceGraphics object whose *array of z values* is a, then the height of the surface at the third value of x and the fifth value of y is given by a[[5,3]], *not* by a[[3,5]].

It is uncommon for users to construct SurfaceGraphics objects by any other means than the use of the Plot3D and ListPlot3D functions, which are discussed in Chapter 4. User-written programs almost always construct Graphics3D objects, which display more slowly but are more general and usually easier to use.

■ Combining SurfaceGraphics Objects

To understand the limitations in the use of SurfaceGraphics objects, consider a situation in which you have separately plotted two functions $f(x,y)$ and $g(x,y)$ and want to display the two surfaces in a single picture. If the surfaces are represented as SurfaceGraphics objects, they cannot be combined. The reason is that when you display two surfaces together, you are reintroducing the general hidden-feature-elimination problem whose absence SurfaceGraphics was designed to exploit. (That is, there can once again be two different points in the scene that have the same x and y coordinates but different z coordinates — namely, $f(x,y)$ and $g(x,y)$.) The special, fast algorithm used to display SurfaceGraphics objects does not work on arbitrary 3D graphics scenes. To display two surfaces in a single picture, *Mathematica* must convert the SurfaceGraphics representations to Graphics3D form. Applying the Graphics3D function to a SurfaceGraphics object performs this conversion, but even if you don't do this explicitly, *Mathematica* does it automatically whenever you ask it to display two or more SurfaceGraphics objects in a single graphic.

Here's an example. First, we plot two functions, saving the SurfaceGraphics objects in two variables.

```
Block[{ $DisplayFunction=Identity },
      sincos = Plot3D[ Sin[x] Cos[y], {x,0,2Pi}, {y,0,2Pi} ];
      coscos = Plot3D[ Cos[x] Cos[y], {x,0,2Pi}, {y,0,2Pi} ]    ];
Show[GraphicsArray[ { sincos, coscos }, AspectRatio->1/3 ]];
```

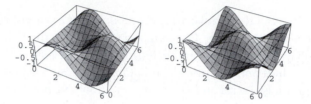

(Resetting $DisplayFunction inside the Block statement is a way of suppressing the display of the individual graphics so that we can display them side by side in a GraphicsArray.) Applying the Graphics3D function to the SurfaceGraphics objects converts them to Graphics3D forms, which take considerably longer to display but can be combined in a single picture.

```
Show[Graphics3D[sincos], Graphics3D[coscos]];
```

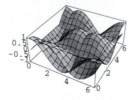

Even if we had simply said Show[sincos,coscos], *Mathematica* would have performed the same conversion and produced the same graphic. For more information about converting graphics from one data type to another, see Section 2.7 on page 31.

▪ Erroneous Values

The entries in the *array of z values* of a SurfaceGraphics object are supposed to be real numbers. Floating-point numbers, integers, and rational numbers are permitted, but values of other types interfere with the display of the surface. Here is an example to show what happens:

```
tbl1 = tbl2 = Table[ y-x, {y,16}, {x,16} ];
tbl2[[3,5]] = Indeterminate;  tbl2[[14,3]] = 3 + 5 I;
tbl2[[12,12]] = Infinity;    tbl2[[6,9]] = unknown;
```

First, we make a table of values, which we store in the variables tbl1 and tbl2. We preserve the copy in tbl1 for reference, but we "poke holes" in the copy in tbl2 by assigning strange values to various positions in the table. We use a complex number, the two quasi-numerical values Indeterminate and Infinity, and the symbol unknown as examples. Here is what happens when we try to display this mess:

```
Show[GraphicsArray[{SurfaceGraphics[tbl1],SurfaceGraphics[tbl2]}]];
```

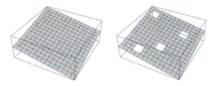

```
Plot3D::gval: Function value 3 + 5 I at grid point xi = 3, yi = 14
    is not a real number.

Plot3D::gval: Function value Indeterminate at grid point xi = 5, yi = 3
    is not a real number.

Plot3D::gval: Function value unknown at grid point xi = 9, yi = 6
    is not a real number.

General::stop: Further output of Plot3D::gval
    will be suppressed during this calculation.
```

The graphic on the right has holes in the surface where the strange values were inserted, and *Mathematica* issues error messages to complain about them. *Mathematica* tolerates such values, however, because they could easily be generated by accident — for example, if Plot3D were used to plot a function over a region containing a singularity. (This is presumably the reason for having the messages refer to Plot3D even though these particular surfaces were not generated with Plot3D.) More serious errors in the *array of z values* can prevent the display altogether. For example, suppose we now execute these commands:

```
tbl2[[10,14]] = {1,2,3};
Show[SurfaceGraphics[tbl2]];
```

Mathematica simply does not know what to do with the list we inserted into tbl2, so it is unable to display the surface. In fact, it attempts to generate PostScript code for this graphic, but gives up when it encounters the bad element. This leaves you with a half-constructed PostScript file that will cause errors if you attempt to import it into another application.

- Surface Shading

There is one more thing to know about SurfaceGraphics objects. By default, they are colored by simulated illumination: Each of the polygons that make up the surface is colored according to the light it would reflect to the viewer's eye from the light falling on the surface (as specified by the LightSources and AmbientLight options). But SurfaceGraphics objects can also take an optional additional argument that specifies explicit colors for the patches on the surface. A SurfaceGraphics object that includes coloring information has the form

SurfaceGraphics[*array of z values*, *array of colors*, *option settings*]

If the array of z values has m rows and n columns, it defines an array of $(m - 1)$ rows and $(n - 1)$ columns of rectangular patches on the surface, so the *array of colors* must be an $(m - 1)$-by-$(n - 1)$ array of color (or gray scale) specifications.

Coloring by simulated illumination or by an explicit *array of colors* is controlled by the Lighting option, which is True by default. If you set Lighting to False instead, the surface is colored according to height: The highest points on the surface are colored white, the lowest black, and those in between intermediate shades of gray. (This scheme can be modified by the setting of the ColorFunction option.)

Incidentally, there is no way to alter the reflection characteristics of a surface represented as a SurfaceGraphics object; the simulated illumination model always treats the polygons in a SurfaceGraphics surface as diffuse white reflectors. If you convert a SurfaceGraphics object to Graphics3D form, however, you can use SurfaceColor directives to change the way the surface reflects light, so that, for example, you can depict specular highlights. For more information on the simulated illumination model, see the discussion in Section 7.4.2, which starts on page 254.

2.4 Mixed 2D and 3D Graphics Objects

ContourGraphics and DensityGraphics are special-purpose data types. They produce two-dimensional representations of the graphs of functions of the form $z = f(x, y)$, which can also be represented as three-dimensional surfaces. The format of ContourGraphics and DensityGraphics is similar to that of SurfaceGraphics:

ContourGraphics[*array of z values*, *option settings*]
DensityGraphics[*array of z values*, *option settings*]

The only basic difference is in the "head" of the expression, which tells how the information is to be displayed: as a surface, as a contour plot, or as a density plot. (The different kinds of object do use different option settings, however, as explained in Chapter 7.)

To give you an idea of the similarities and differences in these representations, here is the same function displayed three times, once as a SurfaceGraphics object, once as a ContourGraphics object, and once as a DensityGraphics object:

```
Block[{ $DisplayFunction=Identity },
    gr1 =     Plot3D[ Sin[x] Cos[y], {x,0,2Pi}, {y,0,2Pi} ];
    gr2 = ContourPlot[ Sin[x] Cos[y], {x,0,2Pi}, {y,0,2Pi} ];
    gr3 = DensityPlot[ Sin[x] Cos[y], {x,0,2Pi}, {y,0,2Pi} ];  ];
Show[GraphicsArray[ {gr1,gr2,gr3} ]];
```

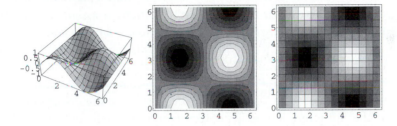

ContourGraphics and DensityGraphics, like SurfaceGraphics, usually are not created by user programs but only by their respective built-in plotting commands (ContourPlot and ListContourPlot, and DensityPlot and ListDensityPlot).

2.5 Print Forms of Graphics Objects

Mathematica's built-in plotting functions construct and display graphics objects. From the point of view of *Mathematica*'s evaluator, the graphics objects are the results of, or returned values from, the graphics-building functions, and the pictures displayed are merely side effects. However, we humans almost always care only about the pictures; to us, the graphics objects are usually irrelevant. For example, looking at an array of dozens or hundreds of numbers that forms part of a SurfaceGraphics object is almost never as instructive as looking at the picture of the surface it represents. For this reason, *Mathematica* by default prints graphics objects in abbreviated forms. A graphics object prints simply as the name of its data type, surrounded by hyphens. For example,

```
sincos = Plot3D[ Sin[x] Cos[y], {x,0,2Pi}, {y,0,2Pi} ]
```

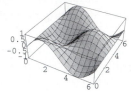

```
-SurfaceGraphics-
```

The `-SurfaceGraphics-` line indicates that the result of the `Plot3D` command was a `SurfaceGraphics` graphics object. You can suppress this line by appending a semicolon to the command, since it is a convention of *Mathematica* that a command ending with a semicolon does not display its result. (This is useful any time a *Mathematica* command is being executed primarily for its side effects, as when an assignment statement is being used to store an unwieldy array under a convenient variable name.)

When you interact with the *Mathematica* kernel through a Notebook Front End, both the formatted and unformatted forms of most computation results are stored in the Notebook, and you can use the Formatted/Unformatted toggle in the Cell menu or Style Inspector panel to switch back and forth between the display of each form. But because the full forms of graphics objects tend to be large and useless, Notebook Front Ends have a special switch, usually found in the Action Settings dialog box, that prevents the full forms from being generated and stored. By default, this switch is on, which means that if you unformat an output cell containing an abbreviated graphics result (such as the -SurfaceGraphics- cell above), you see not the full textual form of the graphics object but another abbreviation. Depending on the version of *Mathematica* you are using, you see either a message similar to this:

```
The Unformatted text for this cell was not generated.
Use options in the Actions Preferences dialog box to
control when Unformatted text is generated.
```

or a skeletal representation such as this:

```
SurfaceGraphics["<<>>"]
```

If you want to see the complete structure of a graphics object, you can ask for the object's `InputForm`. This is the form that you have to type into *Mathematica* from your keyboard to recreate the object. Since the full input form of a complicated graphics object may stretch over dozens or even hundreds of lines, you probably aren't going to want to re-create a plot of, say, the sine function by typing its specification at the keyboard. If what you really want is a general idea of the structure of a graphics object, the safest thing to do is to ask for its `InputForm` enclosed in `Short`. Here is an example;

the 3 in the Short command tells the print formatter not to print more than three lines of output.

Short[InputForm[sincos], 3]

SurfaceGraphics[{{0., 0.4338837391175582, 0.7818314824680299, 0.974927912181824,
    0.974927912181824, 0.78183148246803, 0.4338837391175583, <<5>>, -0.78183148246803,
    -0.4338837391175584, -(2.449212707644754*10^-16)}, <<14>>}, <<1>>]

The full 15-by-15 array of numbers has been abbreviated, so only a few of its characteristic parts are shown. The <<5>> indicates that 5 real numbers were omitted in the first row of the array of z values that makes up the first part of the SurfaceGraphics object. The <<14>> means that 14 rows laid out just like the first were suppressed. The <<1>> represents the list of graphics options. With the abbreviated forms, the output of Short was printed in three lines.

2.6 Displaying Graphics Objects

Show is the command that displays graphics, usually to the screen. We have already seen several examples of the use of Show, the syntax of which is

$$\text{Show[} \textit{graphics object(s)}, \textit{ option setting(s) } \text{]}$$

The first arguments to Show must be one or more graphics objects (or one or more lists of graphics objects, nested into sublists in any way). If several graphics objects are specified, they are combined and displayed in a single graphic. Depending on the types of the graphics objects, combining graphics may require conversion; for example, if you Show a ContourGraphics object with a Graphics3D object, both are converted to Graphics objects and then displayed together as such. See Section 2.7 on page 31 for more information about converting graphics from one data type to another. If option settings are supplied, they are applied to the graphics object displayed by Show.

2.6.1 Graphics Option Settings and Show

Graphics option settings provided as arguments to Show take precedence over any settings already present in the graphics object or objects Show is being asked to display. For example, *Mathematica*'s default scaling for graphics generated by the Plot command gives a potentially misleading scale in this plot:

```
sinpic = Plot[ Sin[3x], {x,0,4Pi} ];
```

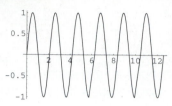

You can use the Show command to override the default and force *Mathematica* to display the graph with a 1-to-1 scale. That would make the unit lengths in x and y the same, giving a somewhat more realistic picture of the function (and, in this case, incidentally making some undersampling problems near $x = 6$ and $x = 10$ more evident).

```
Show[ sinpic, AspectRatio->Automatic ];
```

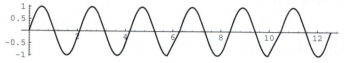

Using Show to redisplay an object you have already created is more efficient than using Plot to re-create the object.

Be aware, however, that not every option setting that can be used with a plotting function like Plot makes sense to Show. In general, option settings that control viewing parameters such as scaling, viewpoint, axes labeling, and so forth, can be altered, but options that control how a list of plotting points was computed — how many sample points to take, for instance — cannot be changed by Show because any change involves reevaluating a function, and the information about the function is not stored in the graphics object. For example, the command

```
sincos = Plot3D[ Sin[x]Cos[y], {x,0,2Pi}, {y,0,2Pi},
                    ViewPoint->{1,1,1}, PlotPoints->{12,10} ];
```

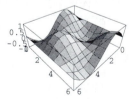

causes *Mathematica* to produce a SurfaceGraphics object that represents a graph of the equation $z = \sin(x)\cos(y)$, with the function sampled at 12 points in the x direction and 10 points in the y direction, and with the surface displayed as if seen from the viewpoint $(1, 1, 1)$. By redisplaying the object with Show, you can override the ViewPoint setting but not the PlotPoints setting, so this works:

```
Show[ sincos, ViewPoint->{4,8,0} ];
```

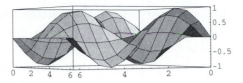

but this doesn't:

```
Show[ sincos, PlotPoints->{15,20} ];

SurfaceGraphics::optx: Unknown option PlotPoints in -SurfaceGraphics-.
```

The PlotPoints option controls not how a surface is displayed but how the points on the surface are computed. Changing the number of PlotPoints requires more points on the surface of the graph of $z = \sin(x)\cos(y)$ to be computed, and Show cannot do this. You have to give a new Plot3D command to obtain a new SurfaceGraphics object if you want a picture of the surface with finer plot divisions.

2.6.2 What Show Really Does

In reality, Show itself does little computation and no displaying, only a bit of bookkeeping. Show accumulates graphics objects and option settings into a single graphics object; then it invokes the function designated by the current setting of the DisplayFunction option to determine how to display that object. The setting of the DisplayFunction option should always be a function (that is, either a "pure function" object or the name of a function); the function is expected to take a graphics object as its argument and cause that object to be displayed.

The default setting of DisplayFunction causes graphics to be directed to the screen. (This is explained at length under the entry for DisplayFunction on page 233 in Chapter 7.) By using a different setting of DisplayFunction, you can cause graphics to be written to a file instead or to be "piped" into another process (if you are using a version of *Mathematica* that runs under UNIX or another operating system that supports pipes). This capability can be useful if you have a program of your own that reads graphics specifications and displays them. Suppose you have a ray-tracing program. You could reset the DisplayFunction for Graphics3D objects, so that, instead of displaying a PostScript version of graphics objects, the DisplayFunction fed them (in an appropriate format) to your program. You could then create ray-traced pictures of mathematical objects, using *Mathematica* to create the objects and your program to do the display.

2.6.3 What Show Returns

The result of Show is whatever is returned by the DisplayFunction that Show invokes. The default DisplayFunction returns unaltered the graphics object it receives from Show (displaying a graphic is a side effect that doesn't alter anything). A simple way to combine several graphics objects into one without displaying the composite is to give a command such as

```
gmany = Show[ g1, g2, g3, DisplayFunction->Identity ];
```

The Show command combines the graphics objects g1, g2, and g3 into a single object, which is then passed to the function named by the DisplayFunction option. However, in this example, the DisplayFunction is set to the Identity, which is a *Mathematica* function that simply returns its argument without doing anything to it (in particular, it doesn't display it). So the combined graphics object is returned unchanged as the result of Show, and this result is stored under the name gmany, but no picture is displayed.

In principle, the DisplayFunction can perform any manipulation whatever on the graphics objects it receives from Show. In practice, it is a bad idea to use DisplayFunction for complicated computations with graphics objects, because it gets called "invisibly." It is better to have DisplayFunction simply return its input as its output and to make explicit calls to graphics-building functions if you need to transform graphics objects.

2.6.4 How Show Combines Objects

The simplest combinations are of Graphics with Graphics or Graphics3D with Graphics3D. When several Graphics objects are combined, the resulting combined Graphics object has a list of elements containing the original objects' lists as sublists. However, the option settings for the combined object are those of the first object only, together with any options specified directly to Show. Option settings from objects after the first are discarded. Here is an example:

```
g1 = Graphics[ { RGBColor[1,0,0], Polygon[{ {0,3}, {3,2}, {0,2} }] },
                          AspectRatio->1/4, Background->GrayLevel[0] ];
g2 = Graphics[ { Thickness[.03], Line[{ {3,1/2}, {1/2,0}, {0,1} }] },
                          Frame->True, FrameTicks->None ];
g3 = Graphics[ { Circle[{2,2}, 1], Rectangle[ {4,1}, {5,3} ] },
                          AspectRatio->2 ];
Show[GraphicsArray[{ g1, g2, g3 }]];
```

```
g4 = Show[ g1, g2, g3, Axes->True, Background->GrayLevel[.8] ];
```

```
InputForm[g4]
```

```
Graphics[{{RGBColor[1, 0, 0], Polygon[{{0, 3}, {3, 2}, {0, 2}}]},
   {Thickness[0.03], Line[{{3, 1/2}, {1/2, 0}, {0, 1}}]},
   {Circle[{2, 2}, 1], Rectangle[{4, 1}, {5, 3}]}},
  {Axes -> True, Background -> GrayLevel[0.8], AspectRatio -> 1/4,
   Background -> GrayLevel[0]}]
```

Because the elements from each original object are confined within a sublist for that object, directives like RGBColor and Thickness affect only the primitives to which they originally applied. For example, the RGBColor[1,0,0] directive from g1 caused the Polygon from g1 to be red, but it didn't change the colors of the Circle, Line, and Rectangle from g2 and g3; similarly, the Thickness[.03] directive from g2 made the Line from g2 thick but not the Circle from g3. The combined graphic g4 has an aspect ratio of $\frac{1}{4}$ because of the setting from g1, but it doesn't have a frame because the Frame and FrameTicks options from g2 were discarded. The background of the combined graphic is light gray, not black, because the Background setting given directly to Show overrode the setting from g1; in fact, both settings were retained in the option list of g4, but the one specified to Show comes first and so it is the one obeyed.

Show combines Graphics3D objects in the same way it combines Graphics objects: The result is a new Graphics3D object whose list of elements has a sublist for each original object but whose option settings are those of the first object only, preceded by options specified directly to Show.

The only combinations of graphics objects that produce meaningful results are Graphics with other Graphics and Graphics3D with other Graphics3D. All other combinations require type conversions. Show determines a suitable type (either Graphics or Graphics3D), converts all the objects to that type, and then combines them in the manner already described. SurfaceGraphics are converted to Graphics3D when they are combined with other SurfaceGraphics or Graphics3D objects; we saw an example of this in Section 2.3 on page 20. In all other combinations, the objects are converted to Graphics form. Section 2.7 gives the details of how such conversions are performed.

When Graphics objects are combined, they are drawn one atop the other in the order in which they were specified to Show. Therefore, you must specify objects in the appropriate order, or the interesting features of one object may be obscured by a later one. For example, suppose you want to produce a graph of a function $y = f(x)$ that shows contour lines as they would be drawn by ContourPlot, but shades the surface in patches the way DensityGraphics does instead of using the usual contour shading algorithm. You can achieve this effect by combining a contour plot with a density plot, but you have to do it in the right order.

```
Block[ { $DisplayFunction = Identity },
    cg = ContourPlot[ Sin[x] Cos[y], {x,0,2Pi}, {y,0,2Pi}, ContourShading->False ];
    dg = DensityPlot[ Sin[x] Cos[y], {x,0,2Pi}, {y,0,2Pi}, Mesh->False ];
    gr1 = Show[dg,cg];
    gr2 = Show[cg,dg];
];
Show[GraphicsArray[{ gr1, gr2 }]];
```

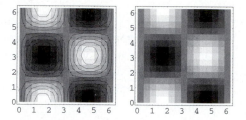

The variable cg contains a ContourGraphics object in which the contour shading has been suppressed, and the variable dg contains a DensityGraphics object in which the mesh lines have been suppressed. These objects are converted to Graphics form when they are combined. In the graphic on the left, we laid the contour plot atop the density plot and obtained a useful result. In the graphic on the right, we laid the density plot atop the contour plot, and the shading of the density plot obscured the contour lines. This overlaying effect does not occur when Graphics3D objects are combined; in that case, the graphics elements are combined into a single scene and *Mathematica* performs hidden-feature elimination on the whole scene at once.

Some combinations, although technically possible, do not produce useful results. Here is an example:

```
Block[ {$DisplayFunction = Identity },
    cg = ContourPlot[ Sin[x]Cos[y], {x,0,2Pi}, {y,0,2Pi}, ContourShading->False ];
    sg = Plot3D[ Sin[x]Cos[y], {x,0,2Pi}, {y,0,2Pi} ];
    gr1 = Show[cg,sg];
    gr2 = Show[gr1, PlotRange->All];
];
Show[ GraphicsArray[{ gr1, gr2 }] ];
```

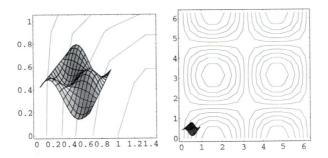

The SurfaceGraphics object sg, created by Plot3D, and the ContourGraphics object cg, created by ContourPlot, were both converted to Graphics form when combined, but differences in scaling in the resulting Graphics objects make the surface small in relation to the contour lines. The Graphics object created from the SurfaceGraphics object uses a range of [0, 1] in each coordinate, whereas the Graphics object created from the ContourGraphics object uses the range specified by the ContourGraphics object's MeshRange setting.

2.7 Graphics Type Conversions

Sometimes it is desirable to convert one graphics data type to another. There are two principal reasons to do this: to combine graphics objects to display them in a single graphic, as discussed in the preceding section, or to save time by avoiding unnecessary recalculation. When you use Show to combine objects for display, *Mathematica* performs any necessary conversions automatically. To convert a graphics object manually to a desired type, you use the name of that type as a function. For example, if g3D is a Graphics3D object, the assignment statement

```
g2D = Graphics[g3D];
```

converts g3D to a Graphics object and stores it in the variable g2D. Note that conversion is not performed in place; each conversion creates a new graphics object. In our example, g2D contains a Graphics object but g3D still contains the original Graphics3D object.

When you convert an object from one graphics data type to another, option settings that are not appropriate for the new data type are discarded. Thus, if you create a contour plot using the Contours option and then convert it to a density plot, the Contours setting is dropped when the ContourGraphics object is converted into a DensityGraphics object. In fact, when you convert Graphics3D to Graphics, *all* option settings are discarded, even options like Background and PlotRegion that are equally appropriate for 2D and 3D graphics. Furthermore, only the graphics elements explicitly listed in the Graphics3D object are converted; features such as axes labels, tick marks, grid lines, and the bounding box are not represented in the resulting Graphics object.

Here is a table summarizing the conversions that can be performed:

Make this type of graphic:	From these types of graphics:
Graphics	GraphicsArray, Graphics3D, SurfaceGraphics,
	DensityGraphics, ContourGraphics
Graphics3D	SurfaceGraphics
SurfaceGraphics	ContourGraphics, DensityGraphics
ContourGraphics	SurfaceGraphics, DensityGraphics
DensityGraphics	SurfaceGraphics, ContourGraphics

2.7.1 Conversion Quirks

Converting a Graphics3D object to a Graphics object may appear to distort the graphic. This is not a bug; it is a natural consequence of the different ways that 2D and 3D graphics are scaled by default. Consider this example:

```
Block[ { $DisplayFunction = Identity },
  g3D = ParametricPlot3D[ {u,Cos[u]Cos[v],Cos[u]Sin[v]}, {u,-Pi/2,Pi}, {v,0,2Pi},
                Axes->False, Boxed->True, ViewPoint->{2,-.4,1} ];
  g2Da = Graphics[ g3D ];
  g2Db = Show[ g2Da, AspectRatio->Automatic ];
];
Show[GraphicsArray[{ g3D, g2Da, g2Db }]];
```

The graphic on the left is a Graphics3D object, and the other two graphics are Graphics objects created from it. The center graphic appears distorted, not because the conversion mispositioned the polygons but because the default AspectRatio setting of Graphics objects forced the graphic to be rendered in a rectangle of a predetermined shape. This shape happens not to match the "natural" shape of the original graphic in this particular case. In the graphic on the right, we explicitly specified the setting AspectRatio->Automatic, which instructed *Mathematica* to display the Graphics object with its natural shape. Specifically, the graphic is scaled so that the unit lengths in x and y are equal, which restores the original appearance of the 3D graphic (except that it is slightly enlarged because space in the drawing area is no longer being occupied by the bounding box).

When a Graphics3D object is converted to Graphics, polygons keep their colors. RGBColor directives are inserted into the list of graphical elements in the Graphics object, so that each polygon retains the color it would have had when the Graphics3D object was displayed. If the Lighting option was set to True in the Graphics3D object, indicating that polygons in the three-dimensional scene should be displayed with simulated illumination, the RGBColor directives inserted into the Graphics object give polygons the colors assigned to them by the illumination model. If Lighting is set to False, the colors of polygons are determined by explicit color directives in the Graphics3D object's list of graphics elements.

When a SurfaceGraphics object is converted to Graphics3D, the list of elements in the Graphics3D object contains Polygon primitives for the polygons that are drawn when the SurfaceGraphics object is displayed. The z coordinates of the corners of these polygons come from the array of z coordinates stored in the SurfaceGraphics object, while the x and y coordinates come from the object's MeshRange option setting. If the SurfaceGraphics object contains a coloring array, or if it has an explicit ColorFunction setting specifying how the surface is to be colored, the colors are copied into the Graphics3D object, so that displaying the Graphics3D object produces the same picture as displaying the SurfaceGraphics object.

When SurfaceGraphics are converted to Graphics, the result is the same as if the conversion had been performed in two stages: First the SurfaceGraphics object is converted to Graphics3D; then the Graphics3D object is converted to Graphics.

One perhaps unexpected consequence of the foregoing information is this: Suppose a SurfaceGraphics object's ColorFunction option is set to Automatic (which is the default) and its Lighting option is set to False, and suppose you convert this object to Graphics or Graphics3D form. All of the polygons that make up the surface will be colored black, and the converted object will display as a big black blob. This might be surprising, but it is not technically a bug because black is the default drawing color for polygons and other objects in Graphics3D and Graphics. Nevertheless, this result is not very useful. Instead, you probably want the polygons colored according to the usual algorithm used for SurfaceGraphics when Lighting is False, that is, gray levels running from black to white with polygons at the bottom darker than those at the top. Fortunately, you can achieve this result easily by giving an explicit setting for the ColorFunction option.

```
Block[ { $DisplayFunction = Identity },
    sg1 = Plot3D[ Sin[x]Cos[y], {x,0,2Pi}, {y,0,2Pi} ];
    sg2 = Show[ sg1, Lighting->False ];
    sg3 = Show[ sg1, Lighting->False, ColorFunction->GrayLevel ];
    sg4 = Show[ sg1, Lighting->False, ColorFunction->(GrayLevel[1-#]&) ];
];
```

```
Show[GraphicsArray[{ Graphics[sg1], Graphics[sg2], Graphics[sg3], Graphics[sg4] }]];
```

In the first graphic, the Lighting option has its default setting of True, and the conversion from SurfaceGraphics to Graphics works as expected — the polygons have the colors assigned by the simulated illumination model. In the second graphic, Lighting is set to False and the surface comes out entirely black. In the third and fourth graphics, the use of an explicit ColorFunction setting works around this problem. The setting ColorFunction->GrayLevel in the third graphic colors the surface with the default coloring scheme, while the setting in the fourth graphic inverts the graphic by exchanging black and white. The default setting of ColorFunction in SurfaceGraphics objects is Automatic, which has the same effect as the setting GrayLevel when SurfaceGraphics are displayed, but the Automatic setting is ignored in the conversion to Graphics3D or Graphics.

The preceding example also illustrates that the bounding box and axes are lost when a SurfaceGraphics or Graphics3D object is converted to Graphics form; that is, Line and Text primitives to represent the axes, tick marks, and tick labels are not included in the list of elements in the Graphics object created by the conversion.

2.7.2 Saving Time

Converting graphics objects from one data type to another can save time that would be spent repeating calculations unnecessarily. For example, suppose you have used Plot3D to construct a surface plot of a function $f(x, y)$ and you decide you also want a contour plot. You could use ContourPlot, but *Mathematica* would start from scratch, resampling the function to obtain an array of z values that Plot3D has already calculated. You can avoid this recalculation by converting the SurfaceGraphics object produced by Plot3D to a ContourGraphics object, as in this example:

```
Block[ { $DisplayFunction = Identity },
    sg = Plot3D[ Sin[x^2 - y^2], {x,-1,3}, {y,-2,2} ];
    cg = ContourGraphics[ sg ];
    dg = DensityGraphics[ sg ];
];
Show[GraphicsArray[{ sg, cg, dg }]];
```

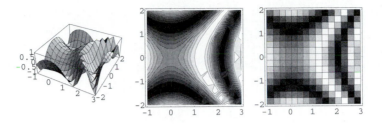

In this example, we used `Plot3D` to create a `SurfaceGraphics` object, which we saved in the variable `sg` and then converted to `ContourGraphics` and `DensityGraphics` form. Any of these types can be converted into any of the other two in this way. This is not surprising because all three types have the same structure: an array of z values followed by a list of options.

This conversion really does save time, as this example shows:

```
Block[ { $DisplayFunction = Identity },
    sg = Plot3D[ Sin[x^2 - y^2], {x,-1,3}, {y,-2,2} ];
    Print[ "Time to create a new contour plot: ",
        First[Timing[ cg1 = ContourPlot[ Sin[x^2 - y^2], {x,-1,3}, {y,-2,2} ]; ]] ];
    Print[ "Time to convert surface plot to contour form: ",
        First[Timing[ cg2 = ContourGraphics[ sg ]; ]] ];
    If[ First[cg1] === First[cg2], Print[ "Both plots have the same data points." ] ];
];
```

```
Time to create a new contour plot: 0.233333 Second
Time to convert surface plot to contour form: 0.05 Second
Both plots have the same data points.
```

It took nearly five times as long to create a contour plot from scratch as it took to convert an equivalent surface plot to a contour plot.

2.8 Summary

In this chapter, we have seen the data structures that *Mathematica* uses to represent graphics in the computer's memory. Understanding how *Mathematica* stores graphical objects is important in being able to work effectively with *Mathematica*'s graphics. Knowing how an object is represented can help you understand what happened when you get an unexpected result, and knowing how graphics objects are built up allows you to write programs to create pictures that go beyond the predefined graphical functions of *Mathematica*.

Chapter 3

Graphics Primitives and Directives

In Chapter 2 we saw that Graphics and Graphics3D objects represent scenes as lists of expressions. These expressions represent the elements (points, lines, polygons, ...) of the scenes and the attributes (color, thickness, ...) of those elements. This chapter explains the elements that can be used in building up Graphics and Graphics3D data structures. Some elements can be used only in 3D graphics, some can only be used in 2D, and some can be used in both.

3.1 Localization

Mathematica has two types of graphics element: those that draw objects, which we call *graphics primitives*, and those that do not draw anything themselves but affect the appearance of objects drawn by other elements, which we call *graphics directives*. In a 2D graphics object, for example, the primitive Point[{2,3}] causes a filled disk representing a point to be drawn with its center at the point (2, 3) in the drawing's coordinate system. The directive RGBColor[1,0,0] doesn't draw anything, but it does dictate that graphics objects that follow it in a graphics list be drawn in red.

An important fact about *Mathematica* graphics is that the effects of graphics directives, such as drawing color, line thickness, and point size, are localized within sublists. The list of graphics objects that is the first argument to Graphics can contain sublists and sub-sublists, and if you reset a graphics attribute within one of these sublists, the attribute reverts to its previous setting at the end of the sublist.

This behavior is illustrated in the following code, which draws two black triangles and one gray one. The color specification that causes the middle triangle to be gray "expires" at the end of the inner sublist, so the last triangle is black instead.

```
Show[Graphics[
  {
    GrayLevel[0],
    Polygon[{ {0,0}, {1,2}, {2,0} }],
    {
      GrayLevel[.8],
      Polygon[{ {2,2}, {3,0}, {4,2} }]
    },
    Polygon[{ {4,0}, {5,2}, {6,0} }]
  }
]];
```

Three-dimensional graphics in *Mathematica* (as represented by Graphics3D objects) also have localization in sublists. Thus the following code, which has the same structure as has the code above, also draws two black triangles and one gray triangle.

```
Show[Graphics3D[
 {
    GrayLevel[0],
    Polygon[{ {0,0,0}, {1,2,0}, {2,0,0} }],
    {
       GrayLevel[.8],
       Polygon[{ {2,2,2}, {3,0,2}, {4,2,2} }]
    },
    Polygon[{ {4,0,0}, {5,2,0}, {6,0,0} }]
 },
    Lighting->False
]];
```

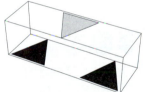

Versions of *Mathematica* prior to 2.0 did *not* have localization in sublists in Graphics3D objects. Adding this feature made it much easier to create 3D graphics that look the way you want them to.

3.2 Primitives and Directives for 2D Graphics

In this section, we describe the graphics primitives that may be used in 2D graphics environments. These include not only Graphics objects, but also the Prolog and Epilog option settings in 3D graphics, which provide backgrounds or overlays. (The Prolog and Epilog options are explained in Chapter 7 on pages 219 and 221.)

3.2.1 Colors

When a color specification appears in a list of graphics elements, all graphics primitives following it in the list (such as Point, Line, and Polygon) will be drawn in that color, until either the list ends or another color specification appears.

There are four built-in color specification directives in *Mathematica*: GrayLevel, RGBColor, Hue, and CMYKColor. GrayLevel specifies shades of "pure" gray, and is useful for creating graphics to be rendered on black-and-white devices. The other three systems specify colors that are appropriate for different color devices.

- GrayLevel

GrayLevel[*n*] specifies a shade of gray, with *n* ranging from 0 (black) to 1 (white). Values of *n* smaller than 0 or larger than 1 produce errors.

```
Show[Graphics[{ PointSize[.2],
    GrayLevel[0],   Point[{0,0}],
    GrayLevel[.25], Point[{.25,0}],
    GrayLevel[.5],  Point[{.5,0}],
    GrayLevel[.75], Point[{.75,0}],
    GrayLevel[1],   Point[{1,0}]
}, Frame->True, FrameTicks->None ]];
```

The last point is not visible because it is drawn in white. The first and last points are cut off because *Mathematica*'s automatic scaling algorithm does not take the PointSize (i.e., the radius) of a point into account when it determines cutoff values. The fact that the frame is interrupted on the right shows that the frame is drawn before (i.e., beneath) the points—the white point on the right is drawn on top of the frame, and the part of the frame it overlaps is "whited out."

- RGBColor

RGBColor[*r*,*g*,*b*] specifies a color in the RGB color system. Each of *r*, *g*, and *b* must be a number between 0 and 1 inclusive, representing fractional intensity of red, green, or blue, respectively. For example, a pure red at full intensity would be specified as RGBColor[1,0,0], whereas a half or 50 percent intensity yellow would be RGBColor[.5,.5,0] (because yellow light may be thought of as a mixture of equal parts of red and green, with no blue component). If the red, green, and blue components are equal, then a shade of gray results. Thus RGBColor[.3,.3,.3] produces the same effect as GrayLevel[.3] (although it does *not* cause *Mathematica* to generate the same PostScript code, because the setrgbcolor operator is used instead of setgray). RGBColor[0,0,0] is black, and RGBColor[1,1,1] is white.

```
Show[Graphics[{ PointSize[.15],
    Table[ {RGBColor[i/5,0,0],Point[{i,6}]}, {i,5} ],
    Table[ {RGBColor[0,i/5,0],Point[{i,4}]}, {i,5} ],
    Table[ {RGBColor[0,0,i/5],Point[{i,2}]}, {i,5} ]
}],PlotRange->{{0,6},{1,7}}, Frame->True, FrameTicks->None ];
```

In this picture, the top row of points runs from black to red, the middle row from black to green, and the bottom row from black to blue. Since the picture is printed in shades of gray in this book, this illustration gives you an idea of how colors are converted to gray levels for printing. If you executed this example on a computer with a color monitor, or printed the picture on a color printer, the points would be colored appropriately.

The color model used by the RGBColor directive is called "additive color" because increasing the inputs (the settings of the R, G, and B parameters) increases a color's brightness and intensity. The natural state of the image surface of an additive color device, when no inputs are being delivered, is assumed to be black; other colors are produced if the level of input is increased. This corresponds to the physical characteristics of devices like computer monitors, whose phosphors emit colored light when excited by an electron beam. The stronger the excitation, the brighter and more intense the light emitted. Additive color models are generally appropriate for devices that emit light rather than reflect it from an external source.

▪ CMYKColor

The CMYKColor directive is similar to the RGBColor directive, in that it specifies colors as mixtures of basic components. The component colors in the CMYK system are cyan, magenta, yellow, and black ("K" is used to represent black because "B" represents blue in the RGB system). However, this system is subtractive, so increasing the cyan, magenta, yellow, or black setting makes the color darker. In a subtractive color model, the natural

state of the image surface is assumed to be white, and an increase in input absorbs or
inhibits light, thus darkening the color. This corresponds to the physical characterstics
of ink applied to white paper — the ink absorbs light, thus darkening the paper, and
the more ink applied the darker the paper gets. For this reason, a subtractive color
model is appropriate for describing colors in an image that will be reproduced in print.
Indeed, the component colors of the CMYK system (cyan, magenta, yellow, and black)
correspond to the ink colors used in standard four-color printing.

In the following example, the colors run from white to cyan in the top row, white
to magenta in the second row, white to yellow in the third row, and white to black in
the fourth row.

```
Show[Graphics[{ PointSize[.12],
    Table[ {CMYKColor[i/5,0,0,0],Point[{i,8}]}, {i,5} ],
    Table[ {CMYKColor[0,i/5,0,0],Point[{i,6}]}, {i,5} ],
    Table[ {CMYKColor[0,0,i/5,0],Point[{i,4}]}, {i,5} ],
    Table[ {CMYKColor[0,0,0,i/5],Point[{i,2}]}, {i,5} ]
}],PlotRange->{{.3,5.7},{.5,9.5}}, Frame->True, FrameTicks->None ];
```

- Hue

The Hue directive represents points in the HSB (hue, saturation, brightness) color model.
The arguments of Hue should be real numbers between 0 and 1. You can specify Hue with
one argument, which determines the color but uses default values of 1 for saturation
and brightness, or you can specify all three components.

```
Show[Graphics[{ PointSize[.08], Table[ {Hue[i], Point[{i,1}]}, {i,0,1,.1} ] },
    PlotRange->{{-.05,1.05},{0,2}}, AspectRatio->1/8,
        Frame->True, FrameTicks->None ]];
```

This example shows the effect of varying the hue parameter. A hue of 0 or 1 represents
red, $\frac{1}{3}$ represents green, and $\frac{2}{3}$ represents blue. Since we called Hue with only one
argument, the saturation and brightness values were given their default values of 1,

indicating maximum saturation and brightness. In the next example, we see the effect
of varying these parameters.

```
gr1 = Graphics[{ PointSize[.1],
        Table[ {Hue[i/5,j/4,1],Point[{i,j}]}, {j,0,4},{i,0,5} ] },
            Frame->True, FrameTicks->None, PlotRange->{{-.5,5.5},{-.5,4.5}} ];
gr2 = Graphics[{ PointSize[.1],
        Table[ {Hue[i/5,1,j/4],Point[{i,j}]}, {j,0,4},{i,0,5} ] },
            Frame->True, FrameTicks->None, PlotRange->{{-.5,5.5},{-.5,4.5}} ];
Show[GraphicsArray[{gr1,gr2}]];
```

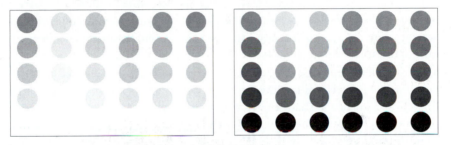

In the graphic on the left, saturation increases from the bottom row to the top row,
with brightness fixed at a maximum setting. In the graphic on the right, saturation is
at the maximum setting, whereas brightness increases from bottom to top.

- Other Color Specifications

Other color specification systems are defined in a package called Graphics`Colors`, described on page 142 in Section 5.2.1. The color specifications defined in this package
include YIQColor (the form used for NTSC video signals) and HLSColor (the hue-lightness-
saturation system). You have to load this package if you want to specify colors in one
of these systems using the command

```
Needs["Graphics`Colors`"];
```

Graphics`Colors` also contains definitions allowing dozens of colors to be specified by
name, such as Aquamarine, HotPink, and ForestGreen.

- Why So Many Systems?

In principle, one color system should be adequate for specifying colors. In practice,
however, display devices with different physical characteristics are not equally faithful
in all regions of the color spectrum. For example, the inks used in four-color printing
don't mix uniformly, so certain colors are hard to print even though they are easy to

display on a color monitor. The software that drives a device can better compensate for the device's idiosyncrasies if the colors to be rendered are specified in a system that corresponds closely to the way the device actually creates colors. We have already mentioned that a computer video monitor is an additive color device, so the RGBColor model is appropriate for specifying colors when a graphic is to be rendered on a screen. But the subtractive color used in four-color offset lithographic printing makes CMYKColor a better choice for creating graphics that are ultimately destined for that medium.

The PostScript language supports the RGB and CMYK color systems directly via the setrgbcolor and setcmykcolor operators, and gray scales via the setgray operator. The Post-Script code that *Mathematica* generates for the RGBColor directive uses the setrgbcolor operator; the code for the CMYKColor directive uses setcmykcolor; and the code for GrayLevel uses setgray. You are free to use any form of color specification on any device — for example, setcmykcolor on an RGB device or a black-and-white device, or setrgbcolor on a CMYK device — and the PostScript interpreter will use an internal algorithm to translate that color specification into the appropriate form. But if you want an exact color match, to a particular shade of ink, for example, you are likely to get better results by specifying the color in the display device's "native" color system rather than by relying on internal conversions. Level 2 PostScript supports user-defined color spaces, so you may even want to define a coloring function of your own that uses the PostScript primitive to invoke custom PostScript color operators, if you are generating images to be displayed to a device with unusual color characteristics.

3.2.2 Points

▪ Point

Point[{x, y}] specifies that a round dot of the current color is to be drawn centered at the point (x, y).

▪ PointSize

PointSize[n] specifies the diameter of points drawn by the Point primitive. The argument n is interpreted as a fraction of the width of the picture; typical values for n are in the range .001 to .02. This means that when a graphic is resized larger or smaller, the dots representing points grow or shrink proportionately. This example illustrates the effect of different PointSize settings. As you can see here, a setting of .25 specifies a point whose diameter is one-fourth of the total width of the picture.

```
Show[Graphics[
    Table[ {PointSize[i],Point[{(1+4.8i)^2,0}]}, {i,.05,.25, .05} ],
        Frame->True, FrameTicks->None,
        PlotRange->{{1.1,5.5},{-.7,.7}}, AspectRatio->Automatic ]];
```

- AbsolutePointSize

AbsolutePointSize[n] is a later addition to *Mathematica*, having first appeared in Version 2.0. Like PointSize, it specifies the diameter of points drawn by the Point primitive, but its argument n is interpreted as an absolute size in PostScript points (72 points equal 1 inch). Points drawn within the scope of an AbsolutePointSize specification do not change size when a graphic is enlarged or shrunk.

In the example below, we create a graphics object containing two points and display it three times at different sizes. The size of the point on the left is specified with PointSize; the size of the point on the right is specified with AbsolutePointSize. The dot representing the point specified with PointSize gets bigger or smaller when the graphic is resized, whereas the one representing the point specified with AbsolutePointSize always remains the same size.

```
Show[Graphics[{ PointSize[.05], Point[{3,1}], AbsolutePointSize[8], Point[{6,1}] }],
    PlotRange->{{0,9},{0,2}}, AspectRatio->Automatic, Frame->True, FrameTicks->None ];
```

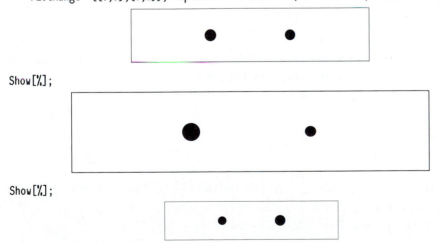

```
Show[%];
```

```
Show[%];
```

How you resize a graphic depends on the version of *Mathematica* you are using. In a Notebook Front End, you can resize a graphic by clicking on it with the mouse and dragging the corner of its bounding rectangle to the size desired. If you are using the psfix utility to print a graphic, you specify the size with the command-line arguments -width and -height. In any case, the *Mathematica* kernel knows nothing at all about resizing, treating all graphics as arbitrarily scalable. Consult the user's guide for your computer's version of *Mathematica* for details.

3.2.3 Lines and Curves

▪ Line

Line[{ $\{x_1,y_1\}$, $\{x_2,y_2\}$, ..., $\{x_n,y_n\}$ }] specifies that line segments are to be drawn in the current color beginning at *{x1,y1}* and connecting the points in the order specified. If you want to draw a closed line, you must use a list in which the last point is equal to the first point; otherwise, an open line is drawn.

```
gr1 = Graphics[Line[{   {0,0},{1,2},{2,1}   }]];
gr2 = Graphics[Line[{   {0,0},{1,2},{2,1},{0,0}   }]];
Show[GraphicsArray[ {gr1, gr2} ]];
```

▪ Circle

Circle[$\{x,y\}$, *r*] specifies that a circle of radius *r* centered at the point (x,y) is to be drawn in the current color at the current thickness. Circle is a misnomer, since Circle more generally draws arcs of ellipses. Circle[$\{x,y\}$,$\{rx,ry\}$] specifies that an ellipse is to be drawn centered at (x,y) with axes parallel to the x and y axes, and semiaxis lengths *rx* in the x direction and *ry* in the y direction. Circle[$\{x,y\}$,r,$\{t1,t2\}$] draws an arc of a circle, with endpoints at the points whose radii make angles *t1* and *t2* to the positive x axis. Circle[$\{x,y\}$,$\{rx,ry\}$,$\{t1,t2\}$] draws an arc of an ellipse.

Observe that because of the effects of *Mathematica*'s automatic scaling, circles often do not appear circular:

```
circpic = Show[Graphics[{ Circle[{1,1},1], Circle[{3,1},1] }], Axes->Automatic ];
```

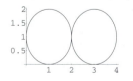

In this case, you can work out that the aspect ratio of the graphic needs to be 1/2 (i.e., one unit on the y axis for each two units on the x axis) in order for circular circles to result.

```
Show[circpic,AspectRatio->1/2];
```

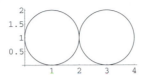

In general, however, you don't have to calculate the necessary AspectRatio setting by hand; you can simply use the setting Automatic to tell *Mathematica* to compute the aspect ratio that makes a unit in y the same length as a unit in x. Doing so guarantees that circles will be circular, however they happen to be distributed.

```
bubbles = Table[ Circle[{5 Random[],3 Random[]},Random[]], {10} ];
Show[Graphics[bubbles],AspectRatio->Automatic];
```

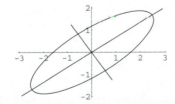

Note that you cannot use the Circle command to draw an ellipse whose axes are not parallel to the x and y axes of the graphic. Use a Line primitive instead.

```
theta = 34 Degree;
m = { {Cos[theta], -Sin[theta]}, {Sin[theta], Cos[theta]} }; (* rotation matrix  *)
pts = Table[ m . { 3 Cos[t], Sin[t] }, {t,0,2Pi,Pi/24} ];   (* multiply by m to *)
a = m . {3.5,0} ; b = m . {0,1.5} ;                         (* rotate elipse    *)
Show[Graphics[{ Line[pts], Line[{a,-a}], Line[{b,-b}] }, Axes->Automatic ]];
```

The expression {3 Cos[t], Sin[t]} is a parametric representation of an ellipse whose semiaxes are 3 and 1; multiplying by the matrix m rotates the ellipse 34 degrees around the origin. We used the Table command to generate a list of points on this ellipse and a Line primitive to connect the points, drawing the ellipse. We also used Line primitives to represent the axes of the ellipse.

▪ Thickness and AbsoluteThickness

Thickness[*n*] specifies the width of a curve drawn by a Line or Circle primitive. The argument *n* is a fraction of the total width of the graphic, so the thickness varies in proportion to overall size when the graphic is resized. AbsoluteThickness[*n*] specifies a thickness in PostScript points that does not vary as the graphic is resized.

This example, we draw two thin lines and a thick circle to show the effects of Thickness.

```
gr1 = Graphics[{
    Thickness[0.02], Line[{{0,0}, {1,1}}], Line[{{1,0}, {0,1}}],
    Thickness[0.15], Circle[ {1/2,1/2}, 1/2 ]
}, AspectRatio->Automatic, DisplayFunction->Identity ];
gr2 = Show[ gr1, PlotRange->All ];
gr3 = Show[ gr1, PlotRange->{{-.2,1.2},{-.2,1.2}} ];
Show[GraphicsArray[{ gr1, gr2, gr3 }]];
```

We drew the same figure three times to make a point about how Thickness interacts with the PlotRange option. *Mathematica*'s automatic scaling algorithm, which is used if no explicit PlotRange is specified, does not take Thickness into account; rather, it treats lines and circles as ideal objects having zero thickness. This means that thick lines passing near the edges of an automatically scaled graphic are clipped; we see this in the graphic on the left, where the outer edge of the thick circle is noticeably flattened along the edges of the graphic. The setting PlotRange->All instructs *Mathematica* to take Thickness settings (among other things) into account when scaling graphics, so that all the features of a graphic will appear in full without being clipped. The righthand graphic shows that the same thing can be accomplished by an explicit PlotRange setting, if the range specified is large enough.

The following example shows the use of Thickness in the PlotStyle option of Plot to distinguish between two curves being plotted on the same axes.

```
Plot[{Sin[x], Cos[x]}, {x, 0, 2Pi},
     PlotStyle -> {{Thickness[0.02]}, {Thickness[0.08]}}];
```

- Dashing and AbsoluteDashing

Dashing[{ l_1, l_2, ..., l_n }] specifies a dashing style with which a Line or Circle primitive is to be drawn. The l's are lengths, each specified as a fraction of the total width of the picture. Each time a new curve is drawn, it is dashed as follows: First a segment of length l_1 along the curve is drawn, then a segment of length l_2 is not drawn, then a segment of length l_3 is drawn, then a segment of length l_4 is skipped, and so on. If the end of the list of lengths is reached before the entire curve has been drawn, the next segment is of length l_1, and the process is repeated until the full length of the curve has been drawn. In the simplest case, the specification Dashing[{l}] instructs *Mathematica* to draw curves with alternating segments and gaps of length l. Dashing[{}] turns off dashing, so that solid lines are drawn.

```
Show[Graphics[{
    Dashing[{0.07}], Line[{{-1,-1/2},{1,1/2}}], Line[{{-1,1/2},{1,-1/2}}],
    Dashing[{0.07,0.03}], Circle[{0,0},1/2],
    Dashing[{0.07,0.03,0.01,0.03}], Line[Table[{x,(x-x^3)/2},{x,-1.2,1.2,.1}]]
}, AspectRatio->Automatic ]];
```

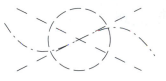

```
Plot[{Sin[x], Cos[x]}, {x, 0, 2Pi},
    PlotStyle -> {{Dashing[{0.07}]}, {Dashing[{0.07, 0.03}]}}];
```

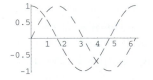

There is also an AbsoluteDashing specification that gives the on/off lengths in printer's points. Like AbsolutePointSize and AbsoluteThickness, it guarantees that a certain feature (in this case, the lengths of the dashes) will remain the same when a graphic is resized.

3.2.4 Filled Regions

- Polygon

Polygon[{ $\{x_1,y_1\}$, $\{x_2,y_2\}$, ..., $\{x_n,y_n\}$ }] specifies that a filled polygon (i.e., the interior, not just the boundary) with vertices at the (x,y)s is to be drawn in the current color. (It is *not* necessary for the last point in the list to be equal to the first; an edge joining the last point to the first is assumed and is automatically included.) The Polygon primitive draws the interior, but does not highlight the boundary in any way. Highlighting is easy, however, as this example shows:

```
leftpoly = { {0,0}, {1,0}, {0,1} };
rightpoly = ( # + {2,0} )& /@ leftpoly;
rightboundary = Append[ rightpoly, First[rightpoly] ];
Show[Graphics[{
    GrayLevel[.8], Polygon[ leftpoly ], Polygon[ rightpoly ],
    GrayLevel[.4], Thickness[.02], Line[ rightboundary ]
}], AspectRatio->Automatic ];
```

In the lefthand copy of the triangle, only the interior is filled. In the righthand copy, we first use a Polygon to draw the filled region, and then a Line to trace around it. You could easily assemble this into a handy function:

```
LimnPolygon[points:{__},linestyle___] :=
    { Polygon[points],
        Flatten[{ linestyle, Line[ Append[points,First[points]] ] }] }
```

The specification LimnPolygon[*points,style commands*] draws the polygon specified by the *points* exactly as the Polygon primitive would, but it outlines the polygon with a line drawn in the style specified by the *style commands* (which may be given as separate arguments or in a list). The *style commands* are placed within a sublist with the Line object that outlines the polygon, so that they will affect only that object and not any other part of the scene. For most purposes, LimnPolygon can now be treated as if it were a primitive graphics object.

```
Show[Graphics[ {GrayLevel[.7],
    LimnPolygon[ { {0,0},{1,0},{1,1} }, Thickness[.03], GrayLevel[.4] ]
}]];
```

Here is a more involved example, which uses the fact that the complex n^{th} roots of unity are the vertices of an n-gon in the complex plane:

```
primroot5 = Exp[ 2 Pi I / 5 ];
pts = {Re[#],Im[#]}& /@ (- I N[ primroot5 ^ Range[5] ]);
pts2 = Join[pts,pts][[ 2 Range[5] ]];
Show[Graphics[{
    PointSize[.05], Point/@pts,
    Line[ Append[pts,First[pts]] ],
    { GrayLevel[.8], LimnPolygon[pts2,GrayLevel[0]] },
    Circle[{0,0},1]
}], AspectRatio->1];
```

This example raises an interesting question. If the points specified in a Polygon primitive outline a convex polygon, then there is no ambiguity about what is meant by the "interior" of the polygon. But consider an example like the following:

```
pts = { {0,0}, {0,1}, {1,1}, {1,0}, {.2,.2}, {.2,.8}, {.8,.8}, {.8,.2}, {0,0} };
Show[Graphics[Line[pts]]];
```

Is the center region in the interior of the polygon? *Mathematica* uses a convention called the "nonzero winding number" rule: Any region of the plane that is encircled a nonzero number of times by tracing along the edge of a polygon is considered to be in the interior of that polygon. Therefore *Mathematica* displays the polygon with the center region filled, as here:

```
Show[Graphics[Polygon[pts]]];
```

See Section 3.2.6 on page 69 on the use of PostScript for more on this example, however.

• Rectangle

In its simplest form, Rectangle[{*xmin*, *ymin*}, {*xmax*, *ymax*}] may be regarded as an abbreviation for Polygon[{ {*xmin*, *ymin*}, {*xmax*, *ymin*}, {*xmax*, *ymax*}, {*xmin*, *ymax*} }]. The PostScript code generated for these two primitives is essentially the same.

```
Show[Graphics[{
    Rectangle[{0,0},{1,1}], Rectangle[{1,2},{2,4}],
        Rectangle[{3,1},{7,2}], Rectangle[{5,3},{6,5}]
}]];
```

However, the Rectangle primitive accepts as an additional argument an arbitrary graphics object, which it uses to fill the rectangle. You can thus assemble any collection of *Mathematica* graphics into a single picture in a completely general way. This capability is similar to what you can do with GraphicsArray, but more flexible. For example, in preparing one of the illustrations for this book, we wanted to display three contour plots together, but we wanted to group two of them more closely than the third in order to stress their similarities. We used the following code:

```
gr1 = ContourPlot[ Sin[x^2 - y^2], {x,-1,3}, {y,-2,2}, ContourLines->False,
            Contours->30, DisplayFunction-> Identity ];
gr2 = Show[ gr1, ContourLines->True ];
gr3 = ContourPlot[ Sin[x y], {x,1,7}, {y,1,7}, ContourLines->False,
            Contours->40, DisplayFunction-> Identity ];
Show[Graphics[ { Rectangle[{0,0},{5,5},gr1], Rectangle[{6,0},{11,5}, gr2],
        Rectangle[{14,0},{19,5},gr3] } ], AspectRatio->Automatic ];
```

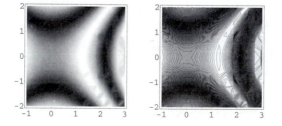 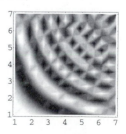

If we had used GraphicsArray to display the plots, we would have had to use equal spacing:

```
Show[GraphicsArray[{gr1,gr2,gr3}]];
```

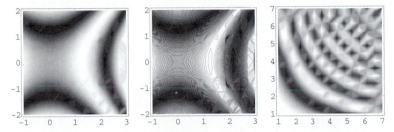

In fact, beginning in Version 2.2, *Mathematica* has implemented the GraphicsArray data type internally by translating it into a collection of Rectangle primitives.

There is one tricky point you should keep in mind when using Rectangle to display a graphics object. The object is always drawn with its own AspectRatio setting. If the aspect ratio of the rectangle, defined by the corners you give as the first two arguments to Rectangle, is not the same as the AspectRatio setting, the graphic is drawn inside the rectangle specified by Rectangle but does not fill it. To illustrate this, we will use Rectangle to make several copies of the following graphic:

```
circles = Graphics[ Table[ Circle[{i,j}, 1/8], {i,0,1,1/8}, {j,0,1,1/8} ],
          Frame->True, FrameTicks->None ];
Show[circles];
```

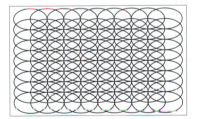

And we will use the function rect to draw a graphics object inside a Rectangle primitive together with a Line primitive that outlines the edges of the Rectangle:

```
rect[ {llx_,lly_}, {urx_,ury_}, gr_ ] := {
    Line[ { {llx,lly}, {urx,lly}, {urx,ury}, {llx,ury}, {llx,lly} } ],
    Rectangle[ {llx,lly}, {urx,ury}, gr ]
}
```

Now we will use rect to make a graphic containing three copies of the graphics object circles:

```
Show[Graphics[{
    rect[ {0,0}, {1,1/GoldenRatio}, circles ],
    rect[ {2,0}, {4,3}, circles ],
    rect[ {5,1}, {9,2}, circles ]
}], Frame->True, AspectRatio->Automatic ];
```

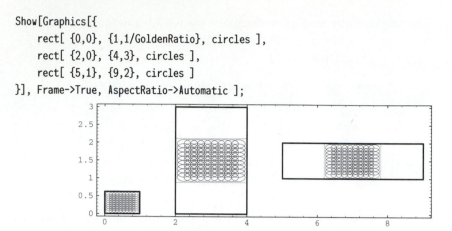

We drew the first copy of circles inside a rectangle that runs from 0 to 1 in x and from 0 to 1/GoldenRatio in y. The aspect ratio of this rectangle is 1/GoldenRatio, which exactly matches the AspectRatio setting of circles, so the graphic entirely fills the rectangle. In the second copy, the rectangle runs from 2 to 4 in x and from 0 to 3 in y, so its aspect ratio is $\frac{3}{2}$, which is much larger than that of circles. The rectangle is proportionally taller and thinner than the circles graphic, so the circles graphic does not fill the rectangle but leaves open space above and below. In the third copy of circles, the enclosing rectangle runs from 5 to 9 in x and from 1 to 2 in y, producing an aspect ratio of $\frac{1}{4}$, which is much smaller than that of circles. The rectangle is short and wide, and again the circles graphic does not fill it, but this time the empty space is at the left and right.

In general, if a Rectangle primitive specifies a graphics object g to be drawn inside a rectangle r, then the rectangle s that g actually occupies is characterized as follows:

- s has the same center as r.

- s is contained entirely within r.

- s has the aspect ratio specified by the AspectRatio option of g.

- s is the largest rectangle that meets the preceding conditions.

▪ Raster

Raster[*array*] represents an array of rectangles shaded gray. The *array* must be a matrix of real numbers, with an m-by-n matrix representing an m-by-n array of adjacent rectangles. By default, the i, j^{th} entry of the matrix corresponds to a rectangle whose color is the gray level specified by the entry, whose lower left corner is at the point

$(j - 1, i - 1)$, and whose upper right corner is at (j, i). (That is, row indices of the matrix correspond to y coordinates, and column indices correspond to x coordinates.) The complete form of the Raster primitive is

$$Raster[array,\{\{xmin, ymin\}, \{xmax, ymax\}\}, \{zmin, zmax\}]$$

which means that the values in the array are linearly rescaled before being converted to GrayLevel specifications, so that *zmin* corresponds to a gray level of 0 (black) and *zmax* to 1 (white), and that the array is mapped into the rectangle whose lower left corner is at the point (*xmin,ymin*) and whose upper right corner is at (*xmax,ymax*). If you omit *zmin* and *zmax*, the entries in the array are not rescaled, and if you omit the lower left and upper right corners, the array is scaled from $(0, 0)$ to (n, m) in graphics coordinates, where m is the number of rows and n is the number of columns in the *array*. Here is an example showing the effect of the arguments to Raster:

```
m = { {0., .1, .2, .3, .4 },
      {.2, .3, .4, .5, .6 },
      {.4, .5, .6, .7, .8 } };
Show[GraphicsArray[{
    Graphics[ Raster[m], Axes->Automatic ],
    Graphics[ Raster[m,{{2,4},{12,16}}], Axes->Automatic ],
    Graphics[ Raster[m,{{2,4},{12,16}},{0,2} ], Axes->Automatic ]
}]];
```

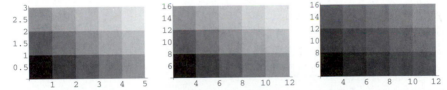

In the first two examples, the entries in the array m are interpreted as GrayLevel values without rescaling, because *zmin* and *zmax* were not specified. In the third example, the raster cells are only half as light because the range of possible values is specified as {0,2} instead of the default {0,1}, and we have only specified values between 0 and 0.8. In the first example, the axes run from 0 to 5 in x and 0 to 3 in y because the matrix m has five columns and three rows. In the second and third examples the axes run from 2 to 12 in x and 4 to 16 in y because we specified the rectangle with lower left coordinate $(2, 4)$ and upper right coordinate $(12, 16)$ as the region into which we wanted the Raster to be mapped.

Notice also that the bottom row of the matrix m corresponds to the top row of the raster. That is because row coordinates in an array increase from the top down, but y coordinates in a graph increase from the bottom up. (For example, the third row in a matrix is counted from the top down, while the line $y = 3$ is located three units up from the x axis.) The result is a top-to-bottom inversion that you should keep in mind when you are using the Raster primitive.

An important use of the Raster primitive is as a means of importing digitized gray-scale images into *Mathematica* graphics. The following image was rendered by being read into a Raster object from a GIF file. (GIF is a file format developed by CompuServe for storing multicolor digitized raster images.)

The Raster primitive is different from all other graphics primitives in one important respect: It accepts an option setting. The ColorFunction option specifies a function that can be used to convert the numerical entries in the *array* argument to color specifications. In this way, the Raster primitive can be used to specify color as well as black-and-white images. Here are some simple examples:

```
m = { {0., .1, .2, .3, .4 },
      {.2, .3, .4, .5, .6 },
      {.4, .5, .6, .7, .8 } };
Show[GraphicsArray[{
    Graphics[ Raster[m, ColorFunction->Hue] ],
    Graphics[ Raster[m, ColorFunction->GrayLevel] ],
    Graphics[ Raster[m, ColorFunction->(GrayLevel[1-#]&)] ]
}]];
```

In the first example, the Hue function converts the numerical entries in the array m to color specifications. In the second example, the function GrayLevel is converts numbers to gray levels (which is the same as the default behavior of Raster). And in the third example, the image is inverted by subtracting the entries in m from 1 to exchange white and black. For more information about how to use the ColorFunction option setting, see Section 7.5.2 on page 269. The RasterArray primitive, described in the next section, gives you a more direct and more flexible way of representing digitized color images.

- RasterArray

The RasterArray primitive is almost identical to the Raster primitive, but the entries in the matrix are color specifications instead of real numbers. Thus this primitive gives you a way to represent digitized color images as well as black-and-white images. The general form of RasterArray is

$$\text{RasterArray}[\ array,\ \{\{xmin,ymin\},\{xmax,ymax\}\}\ ]$$

As with Raster, the array is mapped into the rectangle whose lower left corner is at the point ($xmin,ymin$) and whose upper right corner is at ($xmax,ymax$). If you omit these arguments, the array is scaled from $(0,0)$ to (n,m) in graphics coordinates, where m is the number of rows and n is the number of columns in the $array$. Here is an example similar to the ones shown above for the Raster primitive:

```
m = Table[ RGBColor[ i/5, j/3, 0 ], {j,1,3}, {i,1,5} ];
Show[GraphicsArray[{
    Graphics[ RasterArray[m], Axes->Automatic ],
    Graphics[ RasterArray[m,{{2,4},{12,16}}], Axes->Automatic ]
}]];
```

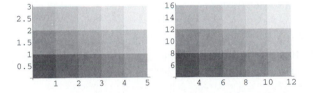

Using RasterArray to represent color images is more versatile than using Raster with the ColorFunction option because you can use RGBColor, CMYKColor, Hue, and GrayLevel settings directly without having to concoct a ColorFunction setting to translate numbers into colors.

- Disk

Disk[$\{x,y\},\{rx,ry\},\{t1,t2\}$] takes the same parameters as Circle, with the same interpretations, but it draws a filled region:

Disk[{x,y},r]	draws a circular filled disk
Disk[{x,y},{rx,ry}]	draws a filled ellipse
Disk[{x,y},r,{t1,t2}]	draws a filled circular sector
Disk[{x,y},{rx,ry},{t1,t2}]	draws a sector of an ellipse

Here's an example showing the four kinds of Disk. Note that the aspect ratio of the plot can cause a circular Disk not to appear circular. The setting AspectRatio->Automatic will correct this.

```
gr1 = Graphics[{ Disk[{0,0},   1 ],
                 Disk[{0,4},{1,2}],
                 Disk[{2,0},   2, {-Pi/8,2Pi/3}],
                 Disk[{2,4},{1,2},{-Pi/8,2Pi/3}] }, Frame->True, FrameTicks->None ];
gr2 = Append[ gr1, AspectRatio->Automatic ];
Show[GraphicsArray[{gr1,gr2}]];
```

3.2.5 Text

Text[expr,{x,y}] draws text representing the expression expr in the default font (usually a fixed-width font such as Courier), positioned so that the center of a rectangle enclosing the text is at {x,y}. If expr is a string, its characters are drawn—on multiple lines if the newline character (represented as "\n") is included. If expr is another kind of expression, its OutputForm is displayed, unless another formatting wrapper (such as InputForm) is explicitly requested.

```
Show[Graphics[{
    Text["     2\n    x\nCos[--]\n     4",{0,0}],
    Text[Cos[x^2/4],{1,0}],
    Text[InputForm[Cos[x^2/4]],{2,0}],
    Text[TeXForm[Cos[x^2/4]],{3,0}]
}],AspectRatio->1/10,PlotRange->All];
```

$$\text{Cos}[\tfrac{x^2}{4}] \qquad\qquad \text{Cos}[\tfrac{x^2}{4}] \qquad\qquad \text{Cos}[\text{x}^2/4] \qquad\qquad \backslash\cos\ (\{\{\{x^2\}\}\backslash\text{over }4\})$$

If you want the text positioned some other way than centered—if, for example, you want the text placed so that its lower left corner is at {x,y}—you can use text coordinates. Each text string in a graphic carries its own coordinate system, in which the left edge of a rectangle enclosing the text is at x coordinate -1, the right edge is at x coordinate $+1$, and the bottom and top edges are at y coordinates -1 and $+1$, respectively. Text["*string*",$\{x,y\}$,$\{dx,dy\}$] positions the text so that the point $\{dx,dy\}$ in text coordinates is attached to the point $\{x,y\}$ in graphics coordinates.

```
Block[ { $DefaultFont = {"Courier",12} },
    Show[Graphics[{ PointSize[.02],
        Point[{4,1}], Text["CENTERED",{4,1}],
        Point[{4,2}], Text["LOWER LEFT",{4,2},{-1,-1}],
        Point[{4,3}], Text["UPPER RIGHT",{4,3},{1,1}]
    }], Frame->True, FrameTicks->None,
        PlotRange->{{-2,10},{0,4}}, AspectRatio->Automatic ]
];
```

- A Quirk in Text Offsets

Examine the following graphic carefully:

```
Show[Graphics[{
    Line[{ {0,0}, {0,3}, {4,3}, {4,0}, {0,0} }],
    {GrayLevel[.7],
        Line[{ {0,2}, {4,2} }], Line[{ {1,0}, {1,3} }],
        Line[{ {2,0}, {2,3} }], Line[{ {3,0}, {3,3} }]  },
    PointSize[.015],
    Point[{1,2}], Text[ "text", {1,2}, {0,2} ],
    Point[{2,2}], Text[ " two\nlines", {2,2}, {0,2} ],
    Point[{3,2}], Text[ "this\nis a\nmuch\ntaller\nlabel", {3,2}, {0,2} ]
},
    AspectRatio -> Automatic
]];
```

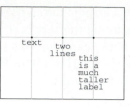

Why is the text in the center lower than the text on the left, and the text on the right lower yet? The answer is that because text coordinates are relative to the bounding box of the text, the specification {0,2} in text coordinates represents a greater vertical displacement in a text that is five lines tall than in a text that is only one or two lines tall.

You must be alert to this if you try to position text by attaching it to a point outside its bounding box. For example, this quirk is responsible for a bug in the positioning of tick mark labels on horizontal axes when the labels consist of more than one line. (See Section 7.1.3 on page 228, which describes the Ticks option.)

▪ Text in Different Directions

The Text primitive also accepts a fourth argument, specifying the direction in which the text should run. This argument has the form $\{mx, my\}$, interpreted as follows:

- The text runs from left to right if mx is positive and from right to left if mx is negative.

- The text runs from bottom to top if my is positive and from top to bottom if my is negative.

- The text follows a line that has direction vector (mx, my).

Here is an example illustrating some of the possibilities:

```
Block[ { $DefaultFont = {"Courier",8} },
    Show[Graphics[{ PointSize[.03],
        Point[{-1,2}], Text["BOTTOM TO TOP",{-1,2},{0,0},{0,1}],
        Point[{5,-2}], Text["RIGHT TO LEFT",{5,-2},{0,0},{-1,0}],
        Point[{5,6}], Text["LEFT TO RIGHT",{5,6},{0,0},{1,0}],
        Point[{2,2}], Text["SLOPE UP",{2,2},{0,0},{2,1}],
        Point[{8,2}], Text["SLOPE DOWN",{8,2},{0,0},{2,-1}],
        Point[{11,2}], Text["TOP TO BOTTOM",{11,2},{0,0},{0,-1}]
    }], Frame->True, FrameTicks->None,
        PlotRange->{{-2,12},{-4,8}}, AspectRatio->1/2 ];
]
```

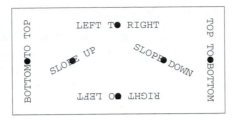

Note that the Text primitive uses its *fourth* argument to specify the orientation of the text, so you must specify all of the first three arguments. In the preceding example, we specified {0,0} to center strings on their anchor points, even though centering is the default. If we had omitted the {0,0}, the Text primitive would have had only three arguments, and so the last argument would have been interpreted as specifying an offset rather than a direction.

Unfortunately, text rotated to orientations other than horizontal or vertical doesn't always work the way you might expect when it is combined with an offset. Here is some code to make pictures containing rotated strings:

```
degstr[th_] := StringJoin[ToString[th]," DEGREES"]
str[ th_, offset_ ]:= { Point[{th,1}],
        Text[ degstr[th], {th,1}, offset, {Cos[th Degree],Sin[th Degree]} ] }
ClearAll[pic]
pic[ offset_, plotrange_, angles_ ] :=
    Show[Graphics[{ PointSize[.015], str[#,offset]& /@ angles },
            PlotRange->plotrange, AspectRatio->.2,
            Frame->True, FrameTicks->None, DefaultFont->{"Courier",10} ]];
```

We will use the function pic to make several pictures containing rotated text. The first picture shows perfectly acceptable results, because the offset is specified as {0,0}, which corresponds to the center of the text.

```
pic[ {0,0}, {{-10,95},{-.1,2.1}}, Range[0,90,10] ];
```

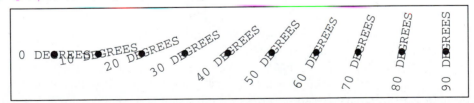

In the next two pictures, the offsets are {0,1} and {0,-1}, which specify text anchored respectively below or above its center. The text at 0 degrees and 90 degrees is positioned as expected, but the text at other rotations is not.

`pic[ {0,1}, {{-10,95},{-.1,1.1}}, Range[0,90,10] ];`

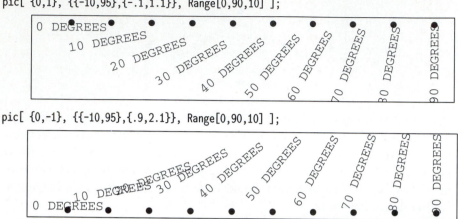

`pic[ {0,-1}, {{-10,95},{.9,2.1}}, Range[0,90,10] ];`

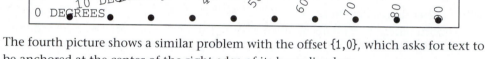
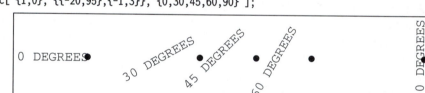

The fourth picture shows a similar problem with the offset {1,0}, which asks for text to be anchored at the center of the right edge of its bounding box.

`pic[ {1,0}, {{-20,95},{-1,3}}, {0,30,45,60,90} ];`

This unfortunate interaction appears to result from the fact that the PostScript operator `pathbbox` produces a bounding box whose edges are horizontal and vertical in device coordinates rather than in user coordinates. The edges of the bounding box of a rotated string are not parallel to the reading direction of the string unless the string is horizontal or vertical. Here is a picture illustrating this situation:

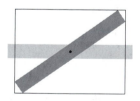

The light gray rectangle represents a piece of unrotated text, the dark gray rectangle represents the same text rotated about its center through an angle of 35 degrees, and the black outline represents the bounding rectangle of the rotated text. Since text offsets are given relative to the bounding rectangle, they produce unfortunate results when the rotation angle is not a multiple of 90 degrees.

This problem is overcome to some extent if the offset parameter is adjusted. The function RotatedText given here is intended to be used similarly to how the Text primitive is used, but its fourth argument is given as a rotation angle in degrees rather than as a vector. RotatedText generates a Text primitive in which the offset parameter has been rotated by the same angle as the text itself (adjusted by a fudge factor, explained below).

```
RotatedText[str_,pt_,offset_:{0,0},angle_:0,fudge_:1] :=
    Block[ {t = N[angle Degree],c,s},
            {c,s} = {Cos[t],Sin[t]};
            Text[ str,  pt,  offset . {{c,s},fudge{-s,c}},  {c,s}  ]
    ]
```

This example shows the effects of RotatedText:

```
Show[Graphics[{
        PointSize[.015],
        Point[{-6,-8}],Point[{4,0}],Point[{14,8}],Point[{18,2}],
        (* These work OK: *)
        RotatedText[degstr[#],{-6,-8},{-1,0},#]& /@ {0,30,60,90},
        RotatedText[degstr[#],{4,0},{0,0},#]& /@ {0,30,60,90},
        RotatedText[degstr[#],{14,8},{1,0},#]& /@ {0,30,60,90},
        (* This doesn't: *)
        RotatedText[degstr[#],{19,2},{0,1},#]& /@ {0,30,60,90}
}],
        Frame->True, FrameTicks->None, DefaultFont->{"Courier",10},
        PlotRange->{{-8,24},{-10,10}}, AspectRatio->.2
];
```

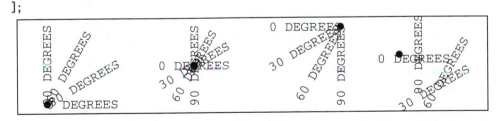

The strings with offsets {0,0}, {1,0}, and {-1,0} are drawn correctly. Unfortunately, the strings drawn with offset {0,1} in orientations other than horizontal and vertical are still positioned strangely, which happens because the text is much wider than it is tall. The fudge factor argument to RotatedText can compensate for this, but it can't be computed from within *Mathematica* because it depends on the particular font and point size being used; *Mathematica* has no information about the actual shapes and sizes of the characters that make up the text.

Text involving strings of more than one line is affected by similar problems when displayed in orientations other than horizontal and vertical:

```
twolines[th_] := StringJoin[ ToString[th], " DEGREES\nABCDEFGHI" ];
Show[Graphics[{
    RotatedText[twolines[#],{#,1},{0,0},#]& /@ {0,30,60,90}
}],
    Frame->True, FrameTicks->None, DefaultFont->{"Courier",10},
    PlotRange->{{-20,100},{0,2}}, AspectRatio->1/3
];
```

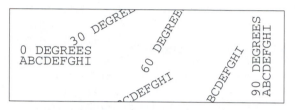

Until the handling of rotated text is improved (in some future version of *Mathematica*), we recommend that you restrict yourself to horizontally or vertically running text. If you need to label a *Mathematica* graphic with text running at angles, export the graphic to a drawing program such as Adobe Illustrator and use that application to add text.

- Text in Different Fonts

FontForm[*string*, {*font spec*, *size*}] is a special form that may be used in place of a string as the first argument to the Text primitive. The *font spec* should be the name of a PostScript font; the *size* is a font size in printer's points, with a typical value of 10 or 12. Not all *Mathematica* PostScript interpreters support variable font sizes, but the code to resize a font is included in the PostScript for a picture, regardless. This means that variable font sizes print correctly on a PostScript printer even if they all show in one size on the screen.

```
Show[Graphics[{
        Text[FontForm["Times Bold",{"Times-Bold",12}],{1,1}],
        Text[FontForm["Helvetica",{"Helvetica",15}],{1,2}],
        Text[FontForm["Courier Oblique",{"Courier-Oblique",10}],{1,3}]
}], Frame->True, FrameTicks->None, PlotRange->{{0,2},{0,4}} ];
```

You can use any font name in the FontForm specification. Text can be drawn in any font known to the PostScript interpreter that is rendering the graphic. Usually, this PostScript interpreter is the one used by *Mathematica*; however, if you are preparing a graphic to be written to a file and sent to a service bureau for printing, you might want to specify a font that is available on the service bureau's printer even if it is not known by *Mathematica*'s own PostScript interpreter. Text in such a font will appear in Courier when *Mathematica* displays the graphic (because Courier is the default used by a PostScript interpreter when it can't find a requested font), but the true font name will be recorded in the PostScript code generated by *Mathematica*, and the correct font will be used when the graphic is printed at the service bureau.

Unfortunately, there is no way to mix text in several fonts within a single Text primitive, even if you use FontForm. For example, it might be nice to label a plot with a title printed mainly in Times but with one or two special symbols drawn from the Symbol font:

Rate of β emission as a function of diffraction angle ϕ

But there is no way to specify such a title with the PlotLabel option because the setting for PlotLabel must be a single object, and even if you wrap the object in FontForm, you can specify only a single font. Ideally, you would define functions like these:

```
times[s_] := FontForm[s,{"Times-Roman",10}];
symbol[s_] := FontForm[s,{"Symbol",10}];
```

and then be able to specify

```
SequenceForm[ times["Rate of "], symbol["b"], times[" decay"] ]
```

as your PlotLabel. However, this doesn't work with *Mathematica*'s present handling of FontForm. The best you can do is position separately each piece of text that needs to be in a different font, which can be tedious. Here is an example:

```
label = Show[Graphics[{ Text[times["Rate of "],{2,1},{1,0}],
                        Text[symbol["b"],{2.2,1}],
                        Text[times[" decay"],{2.4,1},{-1,0}] },
                    AspectRatio->1/4, PlotRange->{{0,4},{0,2}} ]];
```

Rate of βdecay

```
Plot[ CosIntegral[x], {x,.25,15}, PlotRange->{{0,15},{-.5,.5}},
      Epilog->{Rectangle[Scaled[{.5,.8}],Scaled[{1,1}],label]} ];
```

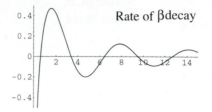

We created a Graphics object called label to contain the text requiring multiple fonts, then used a Rectangle primitive in the Epilog option to overlay label onto a plot. This approach allowed us to experiment first with the coordinates in label to get the text positioned properly (a tedious trial-and-error exercise), and then experiment separately with the coordinates of the Rectangle to get the completed label positioned properly on the plot (more tedium). Clearly, this is not the best way to label your *Mathematica* graphics. If you need text in multiple fonts in your graphics, we recommend that you export your graphics to a graphic design program such as Adobe Illustrator and use its text manipulation capabilities.

- Multiple Lines of Text

The text display routines in *Mathematica* were designed for use with monospaced fonts, and they support nonmonospaced fonts imperfectly at best. Consider this example:

```
expr = Cos[x^2/4];
Show[Graphics[{
        Text[ expr, {0,0}],
        Text[ FontForm[expr,{"Helvetica",8}], {1,0} ],
        Text[ FontForm[InputForm[expr],{"Helvetica",8}], {2,0} ]
}], PlotRange->All, AspectRatio->1/6];
```

$$Cos[\frac{x^2}{4}] \qquad\qquad Cos[\frac{x^2}{4}] \qquad\qquad Cos[x^2/4]$$

The same expression expr is displayed as text three ways. In the first example, we see that the OutputForm of the expression is used by default. In the second example, we instruct *Mathematica* to set the text in 8-point Helvetica type, but this choice doesn't work well with OutputForm because Helvetica is not a monospaced (fixed-pitch) font. When *Mathematica* formats multiline fractions and exponents, it relies on the assumption that all characters (including spaces) have the same width; when this is not true, the horizontal spacing is inconsistent and multiline expressions are displayed incorrectly. In the third example, the label is again set in Helvetica, but this time it is formatted in InputForm, which is a linear rather than a two-dimensional format. Since InputForm does not rely on consistent spacing across multiple lines, the label is typeset acceptably. We can correct the problem in the center example by changing the setting of the flag Mfixwid in the PostScript code generated for the graphic. This flag is true by default, which tells *Mathematica*'s PostScript procedures for text manipulation to assume that they are working with fixed-width fonts. Editing the PostScript code for a graphic to change the Mfixwid setting to false tells the text procedures not to assume that the fonts in the graphic are monospaced; instead, the procedures apply an adjustment to each text string to compensate for variable character widths. Here is how the same graphic looks after this adjustment is made:

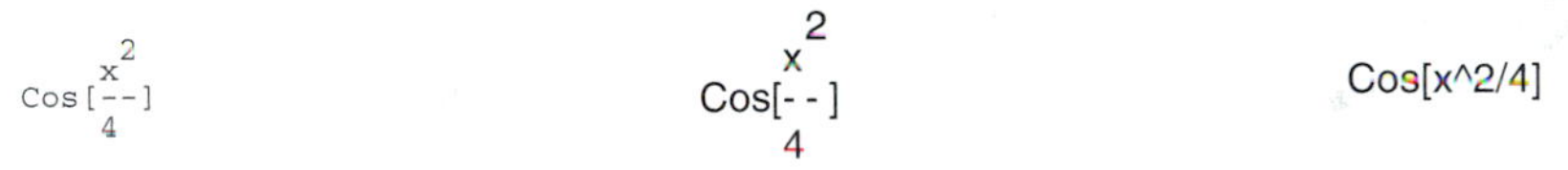

$$\text{Cos}[\frac{x^2}{4}] \qquad\qquad \text{Cos}[\frac{x^2}{4}] \qquad\qquad \text{Cos}[x\text{^}2/4]$$

The adjustment forces the text to be treated as an array, with characters arranged not only in rows but in columns as well. In a monospaced font, characters in lines of text fall into columns naturally, as long as the lines all have the same left margin. Resetting the Mfixwid flag causes a PostScript procedure to be invoked that forces all multiline text into columns by padding character widths so that, say, the fourth character in any line is as wide as the fourth character in any other line.

Mathematica cannot determine for itself when the adjustment is needed, since it has no way of knowing which fonts are monospaced. Furthermore, the cure is sometimes worse than the disease, as in the following example:

```
Show[Graphics[{
    Text[FontForm["Elliptical\n    Disk",{"Times-Roman",12}],{0,0}],
    Text[FontForm["Circular\n  Arc",{"Times-Roman",12}],{1,0}]
}], AspectRatio->1/7, PlotRange->All];
```

Elliptical   Circular
Disk   Arc

Here is the same text with the spacing adjustment applied:

Ellip ti cal   Cir cular
Disk   Arc

The gap after the "p" in "Elliptical" is the result of padding the "p" to have the same width as the "D" in "Disk." Other gaps in the text appear for similar reasons. In general, you don't want to perform the width adjustment on text labels in nonmonospaced fonts if you can avoid it. The operation is time consuming and slows down the rendering of graphics, and its effect is useful only when you need columns of letters to align (as when printing the OutputForm of a *Mathematica* expression). It is better simply to restrict yourself to monospaced fonts when you want column alignment, and let nonmonospaced fonts typeset at the widths their designers intended.

Note that there is no way to specify the spacing adjustment from within *Mathematica*, either in the Text primitive, with option settings, or by setting switches in a Notebook Front End. The psfix procedure provides the -stringfix option to specify that the adjustment should be performed, but for versions of *Mathematica* that do not include psfix (such as the Macintosh version), the only way to perform the adjustment is to edit the setting of the Mfixwid variable in the PostScript code for a graphic. The setting is global, so there is no way to specify that some text in a graphic should be adjusted.

▪ Truncated Text

The automatic scaling algorithm that *Mathematica* uses to supply a PlotRange setting when none is given does not take text labels into account. This oversight can cause text near the edges of a graphic to be truncated. The setting PlotRange->All forces *Mathematica* to rescale the graphic so that all text labels fall entirely within the plotting region; however, this rescaling does not change the way axes or frames are drawn, as the following example demonstrates.

```
gr1 = Graphics[{
      Text[FontForm["Times Bold",{"Times-Bold",12}],{1,1}],
      Text[FontForm["Helvetica",{"Helvetica",15}],{1,2}],
      Text[FontForm["Courier Oblique",{"Courier-Oblique",10}],{1,3}] },
        DisplayFunction->Identity, Frame->True, FrameTicks->None ];
gr2 = Show[ gr1, PlotRange->All ];
gr3 = Show[ gr1, PlotRange->{{0,2},{0,4}} ];
Show[GraphicsArray[{gr1,gr2,gr3}]];
```

In the graphic on the left, no PlotRange is specified and the text at the top and bottom gets clipped. In the center graphic, the setting PlotRange->All causes the graphic to be scaled slightly smaller so that the text fits within the plotting region, but the frame drawn by the Frame option maintains its same position in graphics coordinates and so cuts through the text labels at the same place as in the first graphic. In the graphic on the right, we specified an explicit PlotRange large enough that the points (in graphics coordinates) to which the text labels are anchored fall well inside the plotting rectangle.

3.2.6 PostScript

PostScript[*string*] inserts the PostScript code in the *string* verbatim in a *Mathematica* 2D graphic. You should use this feature only with the greatest caution, and only if you are a knowledgeable PostScript programmer.

Bear in mind that the PostScript interpreters included with most versions of *Mathematica* do not implement the full PostScript language but only a subset sufficient to represent *Mathematica*'s graphics primitives. On these system, some valid PostScript code will cause errors if included in a *Mathematica* graphic. Only in versions of *Mathematica* that are built over a full PostScript interpreter (such as the Sun NeWS versions, the versions for Silicon Graphics IRIS workstations running 4Sight, and the version for the NeXT computer, which uses Display PostScript) can completely general PostScript be displayed on the screen. The Macintosh version in particular does not support the full PostScript language, so in this version, raw PostScript code can safely be included only in graphics intended for printing on a PostScript device (such as an Apple LaserWriter) and not for display on the screen.

With these caveats in mind, we present an example showing one useful way of including user-defined raw PostScript code in a graphic. The graphic below consists of three parts: The left part shows the boundary of a nonconvex polygon with self-intersections, and the middle and right parts are two copies of the filled polygon. The copy on the right is drawn according to the PostScript "nonzero winding number" filling rule, which *Mathematica* always uses (because the PostScript code that *Mathematica* generates for a Polygon primitive invokes the PostScript fill operator, which uses this rule). The middle copy is drawn according to the "even-odd" filling rule, which is implemented by the PostScript eofill primitive. This fill is accomplished with the eoPolygon function, which expands to an ordinary Polygon primitive surrounded by code that temporarily re-defines *Mathematica*'s filling command to mean eofill. The polygons were drawn in the given order as evidence that the save / restore pair did in fact save and restore the original definition of the polygon-filling operator.

```
ClearAll[eoPolygon];
eoPolygon[ vlist_ ] := {
    PostScript["save"],
    PostScript["/F { eofill } def"],
    Polygon[vlist],
    PostScript["restore"]
}
vertices = { {0,0}, {0,1}, {1,1}, {1,0}, {.2,.2}, {.2,.8}, {.8,.8}, {.8,.2} };
Show[Graphics[{
    Line[ Append[vertices,First[vertices]] ],
    eoPolygon[({1.5,0}+#)& /@ vertices],
    Polygon[({3,0}+#)& /@ vertices]
}]];
```

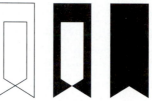

If you try this example with a version of *Mathematica* older than 2.1, use the string
"/fill { eofill } def" rather than "/F { eofill } def". Older versions of *Mathematica*
generated PostScript code that used the fill operator directly, but newer versions use
abbreviations like F to reduce the amount of PostScript text that has to be written to
a file and sent to a screen or a printer. Abbreviating saves many thousands of bytes in
large, complicated graphics.

3.3 Primitives and Directives for 3D Graphics

Most of *Mathematica*'s 3D graphics primitives and directives are straightforward generalizations of the two-dimensional versions described in the Section 3.2. Here is an
example that illustrates the three-dimensional primitives and some of the directives:

```
Show[Graphics3D[{
    Cuboid[{0,0,0},{1,1,1}],
    PointSize[.02], Point[{2,.5,.5}],
    RGBColor[0,0,1], Line[{ {2.5,1,1}, {3,0,0}, {3.5,.5,1} }],
    Polygon[{ {4,1,1}, {4.5,0,0}, {5,.5,.5} }]
},
```

```
PlotRange->{{-.5,5.5},{-.1,1.1},{-.1,1.1}}, BoxRatios->Automatic,
ViewPoint->{0.293, -2.824, 0.767}, Ticks->None, Axes->{True,False,False},
DefaultFont->{"Times-Roman",8},
AxesLabel->
    {"    Cuboid          Point         Line              Polygon",None,None}
]];
```

Cuboid   Point   Line   Polygon

The following sections document these features in more detail, concentrating on the differences between two dimensions and three dimensions.

3.3.1 Colors

Color specifications in 3D graphics work the same as in 2D graphics: You can use the built-in functions GrayLevel, RGBColor, CMYKColor, or Hue, and if you load the Graphics`Colors` package, you can also use CMYColor, YIQColor, and HLSColor, as well as named colors. As in 2D graphics, a color directive affects any Point or Line objects that follow it in a graphics list until the list ends or another color directive appears. Polygon objects, however, are colored differently if the simulated lighting model (controlled by the Lighting option) is used. See the description of the FaceForm and SurfaceColor directives for more details.

3.3.2 Points

Point, PointSize, and AbsolutePointSize function exactly as in 2D graphics, except that a list of three real numbers (instead of two) must be specified to position a point in three-dimensional space.

3.3.3 Lines

Line, Thickness, Dashing, AbsoluteThickness, and AbsoluteDashing also work the same way in 3D as in 2D graphics, except that three coordinates are needed to specify the points joined by a Line. There is no three-dimensional analogue of the two-dimensional primitive Circle.

3.3.4 Cuboids

The graphics primitive Cuboid is, in a sense, the three-dimensional counterpart of the two-dimensional primitive Rectangle. A "cuboid" is a right rectangular parallelepiped oriented with its edges parallel to the coordinate axes. Cuboid[$\{x_1,y_1,z_1\},\{x_2,y_2,z_2\}$] represents a cuboid with one vertex at (x_1,y_1,z_1) and the diagonally opposite vertex at (x_2,y_2,z_2). The special case Cuboid[$\{x,y,z\}$] places one vertex at (x,y,z) and the opposite one at $(x+1, y+1, z+1)$. Here is example of a cube made of Cuboids:

```
ClearAll[f,g,h]
g[l_,d_] := Cuboid[l,l+d]
h[m_,l_] := g[ Insert[l,#,m], -.08 ]& /@ Range[0,1,.1]
f[l_] := h[#,l]& /@ {1,2,3}
Show[ Graphics3D[ f /@ { {0,0}, {0,1}, {1,0}, {1,1} } ]];
```

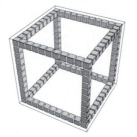

3.3.5 Polygons

Drawing polygons in three dimensions is more complicated than in two dimensions, primarily because of *Mathematica*'s simulated illumination model. This section explains the details of drawing and coloring polygons in three dimensions.

▪ Polygon

Syntactically, the three-dimensional Polygon primitive, like the Point and Line primitives, is a simple extension of its two-dimensional counterpart. The expression

$$\text{Polygon[} \{ \{x_1,y_1,z_1\}, \{x_2,y_2,z_2\}, \ldots, \{x_n,y_n,z_n\} \} \text{]}$$

specifies that a polygon with the given vertices is to be drawn. However, as just mentioned, drawing polygons in three dimensions is more complicated than drawing them in two dimensions, because the given points might not all lie in a plane (although, of course, they should). Early versions of *Mathematica* handled this situation effectively by dissecting the polygon into a collection of triangles and drawing each triangle separately (but highlighting only the edges that were edges of the original polygon). Here is an example of a nonplanar "polygon" as Version 1.2 of *Mathematica* drew it:

```
Show[Graphics3D[
  Polygon[{ {0,0,0}, {1,0,0}, {1,1,0}, {1/2,1,1}, {0,1,1}, {-1,1,1/2}, {-1,0,0} }]
]];
```

The current version of *Mathematica* follows the same procedure, but it uses the same color for all subtriangles, so that the nonplanarity of the polygon is not evident:

```
Show[Graphics3D[
  Polygon[{ {0,0,0}, {1,0,0}, {1,1,0}, {1/2,1,1}, {0,1,1}, {-1,1,1/2}, {-1,0,0} }]
]];
```

Mathematica now computes the color only for the subtriangle formed by the first three vertices, and it uses that color for the entire polygon. For purposes of hidden-feature elimination, however, polygons are still decomposed into triangles. As in two dimensions, polygons in three dimensions are assumed to be convex, and nonconvex polygons are "convexified" when they are displayed, as shown here:

```
Show[Graphics3D[ Polygon[{ {0,0,0}, {0,1,0}, {1,1,0}, {1,0,0},
    {.2,.2,0}, {.2,.8,0}, {.8,.8,0}, {.8,.2,0} }] ]];
```

Note that in this example, part of the edge of the polygon has been obscured because of the way the "convexification" was carried out. Wolfram Research has not documented the algorithm it uses for this process, and we recommend that you not try to display nonplanar or nonconvex polygons in three dimensions. The Polygon primitive was not implemented for this purpose.

- EdgeForm

EdgeForm[*spec*] specifies the drawing style for the edges of polygons. Once an EdgeForm has been specified, all Polygon objects following it in the list are displayed with that EdgeForm style (until another EdgeForm setting is specified or the list ends). The specification *spec* can be either a single directive or a list of directives; the directives that are meaningful in an EdgeForm specification are colors (given with RGBColor, CMYKColor, GrayLevel, or Hue) and Thickness. (You may also use a Dashing directive, but it is ignored.) As a special case, you can use EdgeForm[] (i.e., no arguments to EdgeForm) to indicate that you do not want the edges of polygons to be drawn.

```
Show[Graphics3D[{
    EdgeForm[ {RGBColor[1,0,0], Thickness[.02] }],
    Polygon[{ {0,0,0}, {1,2,0}, {2,0,0} }],
    { EdgeForm[ {RGBColor[0,0,1], Thickness[.04] }],
        Polygon[{ {2,2,2}, {3,0,2}, {4,2,2} }] },
    Polygon[{ {4,0,0}, {5,2,0}, {6,0,0} }]
}]];
```

- Lighting and SurfaceColor

The faces of a polygon are colored in one of two ways, depending on whether simulated lighting (as specified by the Lighting option) is used. If simulated lighting is not used, each face is colored according to the most recently specified color directive, just as with Line and Point objects (except that different colors may be specified for the front and back faces by means of the FaceForm directive, described below). If simulated lighting is used, the color is computed by adding together the diffuse and specular reflections from the ambient light (specified by the AmbientLight option setting) and the light rays incident on the face (where the light rays have the colors and directions specified by the LightSources option setting). The SurfaceColor directive allows you to specify the reflection characteristics of polygon faces. The setting `SurfaceColor[d]` specifies no specular reflection and a diffuse reflection with albedo given by the color directive *d*. The default is `SurfaceColor[GrayLevel[1]]`, which means that polygon faces reflect as if they were modeled from a matte white substance (such as plaster of Paris). The setting `SurfaceColor[GrayLevel[.6]]` specifies that all colors of light are reflected equally, but with albedo 0.6 (so that only 60 percent of incident light is reflected).

The setting `SurfaceColor[RGBColor[.1,.6,.4]]` specifies that colored light is reflected so that the reflected color contains 10 percent of the incident light's red component, 60 percent of its green component, and 40 percent of its blue component. "Diffuse reflection" means that the color and intensity of the light reflected from the surface depend only on the angle that the surface presents to the incoming light (i.e., the angle between the surface normal and the direction of the light rays). Light from each point on the surface is in effect radiated with equal intensity in all directions, so that the surface appears to be the same color when viewed from any angle (as long as the angle between the surface and the light source does not change).

You can use a setting of the form `SurfaceColor[d,s]` to specify that, in addition to diffuse reflection with albedo *d*, the surface provides specular reflection with albedo *s*. "Specular reflection" means that a point on the surface does not reflect light equally in all directions, so that the appearance of the surface depends not only on the angle at which the light meets the surface but also on the angle from which the surface is viewed. The greater the angle between the direction of mirror-image reflection and the viewer's line of sight, the less light will be reflected to the viewer. The intensity falls off as a power of the cosine of this angle; the default value of this power (or "specular exponent") is 1, but you can use the setting `SurfaceColor[d,s,n]` to specify that a specular exponent of *n* should be used. The higher the value of *n*, the more "mirror-like" the reflection will be (because a perfect mirror reflects an incoming ray in only one direction).

In summary, suppose that light rays with color *c* and direction *L* are incident upon a polygon face F, whose reflection characteristics are given by `SurfaceColor[d,s,n]`, and suppose that F has surface normal vector *V* and is being viewed along the line-of-sight vector *S*. Let α be the angle between *V* and *L*, and let θ be the angle between *S* and the vector that is the mirror reflection of *L* in F. The light reflected to the viewer has color $c(d \cos \alpha + s \cos^n \theta)$. The sum and product in this expression are componentwise; that is, the reflected light's red component is determined by the red component of the incident light multiplied by the sum of the red components of the surface's diffuse and specular albedoes, and the same holds for the green and blue components.

Here is an example showing how artificial lighting affects the colors of polygons:

```
a = { {0,0}, {0,1}, {1,1}, {1,0} };
gr0 = Graphics3D[ { GrayLevel[.8],
        SurfaceColor[GrayLevel[.4],GrayLevel[1],4],
        Polygon[ Insert[#,0,1]& /@ a ],
        Polygon[ Insert[#,1,2]& /@ a ],
        Polygon[ Insert[#,0,3]& /@ a ],
        Thickness[.06],
        Line[{ {0,0,0}, {1,1,1} }]
    }, DisplayFunction -> Identity ];
gr1 = Show[ gr0, Lighting->True ];
gr2 = Show[ gr0, Lighting->False ];
Show[GraphicsArray[{ gr1, gr2 }]];
```

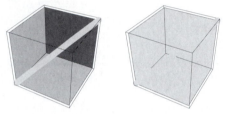

Three mutually perpendicular surfaces are specified with the same color and SurfaceColor characteristics. In the graphic on the left, artificial lighting is used. Therefore the GrayLevel setting determines the color of the Line primitive but has no effect on the coloring of the Polygon primitives, whose appearance is determined by the SurfaceColor directive. In the graphic on the right, artificial lighting is turned off, so the SurfaceColor directive has no effect and the Polygon primitives are drawn according to the GrayLevel setting (so the Line primitive, which has the same color, seems to vanish).

The next example illustrates the difference between diffuse and specular reflection. The same sphere, illuminated by the same light sources, is displayed three times. Only the reflection characteristics of the surface are changed.

```
Needs["Graphics`Shapes`"];
s = Sphere[1];
opts = Sequence[ Lighting -> True, Boxed -> False,
    LightSources -> { {{1, 0, 1}, GrayLevel[1]}, {{-1,-.3,0},GrayLevel[.7]} },
    Background -> GrayLevel[0], PlotRegion -> {{-.25,1.2},{-.25,1.2}} ];
gr1 = Graphics3D[ s, opts ];
gr2 = Graphics3D[ {SurfaceColor[RGBColor[1, 0, 0], GrayLevel[1], 4],s}, opts ];
gr3 = Graphics3D[ {SurfaceColor[GrayLevel[0], GrayLevel[1], 4],s}, opts ];
Show[GraphicsArray[{ gr1, gr2, gr3 }]];
```

In the graphic on the left, the default reflection characteristics are used, so the sphere has a diffuse albedo of 1 and performs no specular reflection. In the center graphic, the diffuse albedo is 1 for red light and 0 for green and blue light, so only red light is reflected diffusely. However, specular reflection with an albedo of 1 and a specular exponent of 4 is now performed. In the graphic on the right, all diffuse reflection is eliminated, so we can clearly see which part of the middle sphere's appearance is due to specular reflection.

- FaceForm

FaceForm[*front color*, *back color*] allows you to specify separate colors for the front and back faces of a Polygon. The front face, by definition, is the one you see when the vertices of the polygon appear to have been specified in counterclockwise order. If the vertices appear to be in clockwise order, you are looking at the back face. The *front color* and *back color* may be color directives (GrayLevel, RGBColor, CMYKColor, or Hue) or SurfaceColor directives. Here is an example of the use of FaceForm:

```
p = Graphics3D[{ FaceForm[ GrayLevel[2/3], GrayLevel[1/3] ],
        Polygon[{ {0,0,0}, {1,0,0}, {1,1,1}, {0,1,1} }] }, Lighting->False ];
vwpts = { 1.5 Cos[#], 1.5 Sin[#], .4 }& /@ ( Range[-80, 95, 25] Degree );
grlist = Append[ p, ViewPoint-># ]& /@ vwpts;
Show[GraphicsArray[grlist]];
```

For simplicity, we have specified Lighting->False to turn off the simulated illumination model, so that the two faces of the polygon appear with the exact colors specified by the FaceForm directive. We have displayed the polygon from several different viewpoints, so that the front face gradually turns away from the viewer and the back face comes into view. As you walk around the polygon, you can see that the front face is light gray (GrayLevel[2/3]) and the back face is dark gray (GrayLevel[1/3]).

3.4 Summary

In this chapter, we have seen the structure of graphics objects in *Mathematica*. Graphics and Graphics3D objects are actually "containers" that hold lists of graphical elements that make up a scene. We have also seen the kinds of elements *Mathematica* offers. In the next chapter, we will finally be able to start producing complicated graphics, confident that we understand how each feature of a graphic is represented internally.

Chapter 4

Commands for Producing Graphics

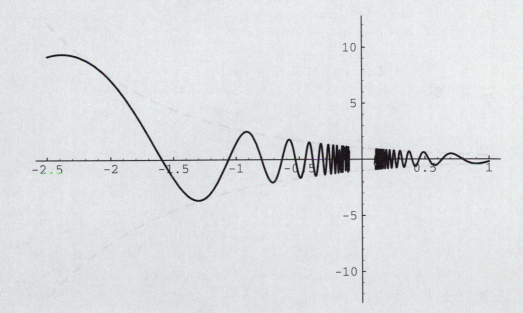

You could use the graphics data types and graphics primitives described in Chapters 2 and 3 to write *Mathematica* programs to plot expressions (or functions). However, doing so is usually unnecessary because many commands for plotting functions are built into *Mathematica*. This chapter describes and illustrates these commands, which build 2D and 3D graphics objects and display them, typically on the screen. Sometimes you *will* need to write your own programs, because you want an effect that isn't provided by the built-in plotting commands. Even in those cases, though, you will find it useful to know how the built-in commands work and why they work that way, so that you can get an idea of the best way to produce your desired graphics with *Mathematica*.

4.1 Two-Dimensional Function Plotting

Mathematica has commands that make it easy to produce graphs of expressions. If you want a two-dimensional plot, commands such as Plot, ParametricPlot, LogPlot, LogLogPlot, PolarPlot, and ImplicitPlot may interest you. The first two functions (Plot and ParametricPlot) are built into *Mathematica* and are described in this chapter. The other four functions (LogPlot, LogLogPlot, PolarPlot, and ImplicitPlot) are defined in packages distributed with *Mathematica* and are described in Chapter 5.

The Plot and ParametricPlot commands are designed for producing curves in two dimensions. Here is an example showing graphs produced by Plot and ParametricPlot:

```
Block[ { $DisplayFunction = Identity },
    gr1 = Plot[ Sin[x], {x,0,2Pi} ];
    gr2 = Plot[ Sec[x], {x,0,2Pi} ];
    gr3 = ParametricPlot[ {(1+Sin[5t]/5)Cos[t], (1+Sin[5t]/5)Sin[t]}, {t,0,2Pi} ]
];
Show[GraphicsArray[{ gr1, gr2, gr3 }]];
```

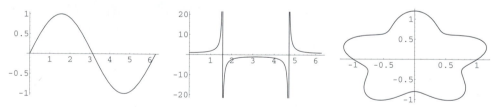

In the sections that follow, we describe the capabilities of Plot and ParametricPlot in more detail.

4.1.1 Plot

The `Plot` command makes a two-dimensional plot of a well-behaved function of the form $y = f(x)$. To graph such a function, call `Plot` with two arguments: an expression representing $f(x)$ and the interval over which the plot should be made. The template is

`Plot[ expression, interval ]`

The *expression* can be any *Mathematica* expression, but it must simplify to a real-number-valued expression involving one real-number variable. The *interval* specification has the form {*variable, min, max*}, where *variable* is the name of the independent variable in the *expression*. The arguments *min* and *max* must be numerical expressions — that is, they can be explicit numbers (integer, rational, or floating-point constants), symbolic numbers (like `Pi` and `E`), or numerical functions of these (like `Sqrt[5]` or `Log[Pi]`). In short, an expression is numerical if it can be converted to a real number with the function `N`. The command `Plot[ - Sum[(-x)^i,{i,3}], {x,-1,2} ]` tells *Mathematica* to plot the expression $x^3 - x^2 + x$ for values of x between -1 and 2. When you enter this command, *Mathematica* produces this graph:

`Plot[ - Sum[(-x)^i,{i,3}], {x,-1,2} ];`

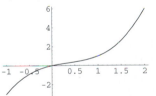

When you plot a function of the variable x, the argument of the function is x, not x_ or #. If the plotting variable x has been assigned a value, this value is temporarily "hidden" while the `Plot` command uses the variable to construct the plot. After the `Plot` command finishes executing, the variable's value is restored, as this example illustrates:

`x = 5; Plot[ (x+1)(x-3), {x,-2,4} ]; Print["The value of x is ",x]; Clear[x]`

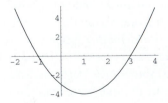

`The value of x is 5`

In older versions of *Mathematica*, the Plot command would fail if a value were assigned to x. If this happens, use Clear[x] to remove the value of x and then reissue the Plot command.

▪ Plotting More Than One Function

What if you want to plot more than one function on a graph? In Chapter 2, we saw that you can use the Show command to combine several plots into one, but doing so assumes that you have already created the plots as separate graphics objects. If you are not interested in seeing the individual functions before plotting them together, you can specify a list of expressions as the first argument to the Plot function. All the expressions are plotted over the interval specified by the second argument.

Plot[{Exp[x-1], Exp[1-x]}, {x, 0,2}];

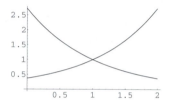

You can plot one, two, ten, or more functions on the same graph; *Mathematica* does not place a limit on the number. You are limited only by the amount of memory you have on your system and the amount of time you are willing to wait for the graph to be rendered.

▪ Taking Control of Plot

The Plot command allows you to specify additional arguments besides the plotting interval and the expression to be plotted. The complete template for Plot is

Plot[*expression, interval, option settings*]

You can use these *option settings* to control *Mathematica*'s plotting algorithm by specifying certain values that *Mathematica* would otherwise derive for itself.

Here is an example showing one reason that you might want to take control of the plotting process. By default, *Mathematica* suppresses extreme values in favor of more interesting and more typical values. (For a description of how *Mathematica* does this, see pages 214–217.) However, sometimes *Mathematica*'s algorithm for deciding which values to include goes awry. In the following graph, for example, the y intercept has been chopped off so that points near the x axis can be displayed.

```
Plot[ 3^(-x^2), {x, -5, 5} ];
```

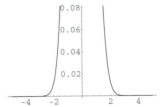

This truncation might lead an unwary user to conclude that the function hurtles to infinity. In fact, nothing about this graph prevents *Mathematica* from showing all the points, and you can instruct it to do so by setting the PlotRange option. When we specify the option setting PlotRange->All, *Mathematica* displays all the sampled points on the curve.

```
Plot[ 3^(-x^2), {x, -5, 5}, PlotRange->All ];
```

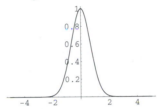

Another plotting feature you might want to control is labeling. By default, *Mathematica* labels some of the tick marks on a graph. It provides the PlotLabel option for specifying a label for an entire plot, the AxesLabel option for labeling the axes, the Ticks option for controlling the locations and labels of tick marks, and the DefaultFont for specifying the font used for these labels. These options give you complete control over the way plots are labeled, as you can see in this example:

```
Block[ { $DisplayFunction = Identity },
  grarray = {
    { Plot[ Sin[x], {x,0,2Pi}, PlotLabel->"sin(x)" ],
      Plot[ Sin[x], {x,0,2Pi}, PlotLabel->FontForm["sin(x)", {"Times-BoldItalic",10}] ],
      Plot[ Sin[x], {x,0,2Pi}, AxesLabel->{"x","sin(x)"} ]},
    { Plot[ Sin[x], {x,0,2Pi}, Frame->True,
        FrameLabel->{"x",FontForm["sin(x)",{"Times-Italic",8}]} ],
      Plot[ Sin[x], {x,0,2Pi}, DefaultFont->{"Times-Italic",8} ],
      Plot[ Sin[x], {x,0,2Pi}, DefaultFont->{"Symbol",8},
        Ticks->{{0,{Pi/2,"p/2"},{Pi,"p"},{3Pi/2,"3p/2"},{2Pi,"2p"}}, {-1,-.5,0,.5,1}}]]}
};
Show[GraphicsArray[ grarray ]];
```

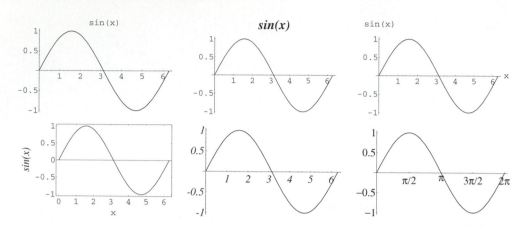

For more information on and examples of labeling a plot, see Section 7.1.2 on page 222; for labeling axes, see Section 7.1.3 on page 224; and for controlling the tick marks and tick labels, see Section 7.1.3 on page 226.

When you plot several curves on the same set of axes, you can use the PlotStyle option to draw the curves in different colors or styles to make them distinguishable. The setting for the PlotStyle option should be a list of lists of style commands. The first list of style commands specifies the style for the first expression, the second list specifies the style for the second expression, and so on. PlotStyle uses a list of lists (rather than a single list) so that you can specify more than one attribute for each curve.

Here we plot sin x with a thick red line, cos x with a dashed dark gray line, and $1/(x + 1)$ with moderately thick purple line:

```
Plot[ { Sin[x], Cos[x], 1/(x + 1) }, {x, 0, 2Pi},
        PlotStyle->{ { Thickness[.02],RGBColor[1,0,0] },
                     { Dashing[{.05,.02}],GrayLevel[.25] },
                     { Thickness[.01],RGBColor[.5,0,.5]} } ];
```

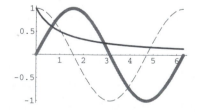

These examples show only a few of the possibilities for using optional arguments to control the appearance of a graph. The Options command allows you to see all the options accepted by the Plot command together with their default values:

```
Options[Plot]

                           1
{AspectRatio -> -----------, Axes -> Automatic, AxesLabel -> None,
                  GoldenRatio
  AxesOrigin -> Automatic, AxesStyle -> Automatic,
  Background -> Automatic, ColorOutput -> Automatic, Compiled -> True,
  DefaultColor -> Automatic, Epilog -> {}, Frame -> False,
  FrameLabel -> None, FrameStyle -> Automatic, FrameTicks -> Automatic,
  GridLines -> None, MaxBend -> 10., PlotDivision -> 20.,
  PlotLabel -> None, PlotPoints -> 25, PlotRange -> Automatic,
  PlotRegion -> Automatic, PlotStyle -> Automatic, Prolog -> {},
  RotateLabel -> True, Ticks -> Automatic, DefaultFont :> $DefaultFont,
  DisplayFunction :> $DisplayFunction}
```

See Chapter 7 for descriptions and permissible values for all of the plotting options.

4.1.2 ParametricPlot

The command `ParametricPlot` produces a curve described parametrically—that is, a curve whose points (x, y) are specified by two functions of another variable, such as t. The form of the command is

ParametricPlot[*list of two expressions, interval, optional arguments*]

`ParametricPlot` is similar to `Plot` in most respects and accepts all the same graphics option settings. In fact, you can think of

Plot[*f[x]*, {*x, min, max*}]

simply as a shorthand form of

ParametricPlot[{*x, f[x]*}, {*x, min, max*}]

Here we draw the curve whose abcissa is $x = \cos 7t \cos 11t$ and whose ordinate is $y = \cos 7t \sin 11t$ for t in the interval $[0, 2\pi]$:

`ParametricPlot[{ Cos[7t] Cos[11t], Cos[7t] Sin[11t] }, {t, 0, 2Pi} ];`

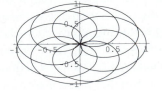

You can use the AspectRatio option to override *Mathematica*'s choice of axis scaling. With the setting AspectRatio->Automatic, the graph is drawn to scale. In other words, one unit in the x direction is drawn the same size as one unit in the y direction. Setting the Axes option to False causes no axes to be drawn.

```
ParametricPlot[ { Cos[7t] Cos[11t], Cos[7t] Sin[11t] }, {t, 0, 2Pi},
    AspectRatio->Automatic, Axes->False ];
```

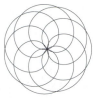

Like Plot, ParametricPlot can plot many curves at once:

```
ParametricPlot[{
    (0.5 + Cos[x]) { Cos[x], Sin[x] }, { Cos[x], Sin[x] }, { Sin[2x] Cos[x], Sin[2x] Sin[x] } },
    {x, 0, 2Pi},
    PlotStyle->{
        { Thickness[.002], RGBColor[1,0,0] },
        { Dashing[{.05,.02}], GrayLevel[0] },
        { Thickness[.01], RGBColor[0,1,0] }
    },
    AspectRatio->Automatic ];
```

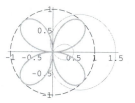

Without the use of AspectRatio->Automatic in this plot, the circle would not have appeared circular.

4.1.3 Sampling

The commands Plot and ParametricPlot graph an expression or function by sampling it at many points and joining the points with line segments. In this section, we discuss some of the issues that arise in selecting points at which to sample the function. Some of these issues are machine dependent (e.g., roundoff error in machine floating-point operations), some are theoretical (e.g., aliasing in periodic functions), and some have to do with the particular algorithm that *Mathematica* uses to choose sampling points.

- Using Caution with the Sampling Algorithm

When *Mathematica* samples a function to construct a graph, it doesn't always display all the sample points it has computed. It might seem strange that *Mathematica* computes points only to discard them later, but in many cases, this strategy leads to a more useful graph than one would get if all the points were displayed. This is especially true when the sampling algorithm hits extreme values.

In this example, we plot the function $\cot x$ over the intervals $[1, 10]$ and $[1, 9.75]$, using the default setting PlotRange->Automatic, which discards extreme values.

```
gr1 = Plot[ Cot[x], {x, 1, 10}, DisplayFunction->Identity ];
gr2 = Plot[ Cot[x], {x, 1, 9.75}, DisplayFunction->Identity ];
Show[GraphicsArray[{gr1, gr2}, DisplayFunction:>$DisplayFunction ]];
```

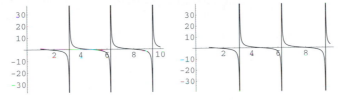

You can override the default by specifying PlotRange->All, which instructs *Mathematica* to display all the sample points it computes. Oddly enough, this setting does not produce more accurate renditions of $\cot x$.

```
gr1 = Plot[ Cot[x], {x, 1, 10}, PlotRange->All, DisplayFunction->Identity ];
gr2 = Plot[ Cot[x], {x, 1, 9.75}, PlotRange->All, DisplayFunction->Identity ];
Show[GraphicsArray[{gr1, gr2}]];
```

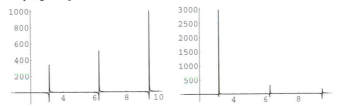

Because the cotangent function takes on such a wide range of values, *Mathematica's* plotting algorithm selects quite a different set of sample points for one interval than it selects for the other. Looking at either plot by itself, you might draw some false conclusions about the cotangent; for example, you won't see its periodicity, or its quasisymmetry around the x axis. Looking at both plots side by side is even more confusing. The graphs appear so different because *Mathematica's* sampling algorithm was tuned for plotting smooth curves, not curves with discontinuities like those in the graph of the cotangent.

Mathematica's default is to discard extreme values so that undue emphasis is not placed on atypical features of a graph, especially when those features may be artifacts of the sampling algorithm that are not truly representative of the function being graphed. You can override this default and take control of this part of the graphing procedure, but you have to be careful in doing so. Knowing how the sampling algorithm works will help you understand why the defaults were chosen and help you decide when it is appropriate to override the defaults in order to get a better plot.

- Graphing the Same Function on Different Machines

When you graph the same expression on a Macintosh and on a Sun or other workstation, why don't the graphs look the same? Isn't the kernel, the computational engine of *Mathematica*, essentially identical on different machines? Not entirely. For efficiency, *Mathematica* uses the floating-point hardware of the computer to perform calculations with real numbers within the machine's precision. Different computers calculate real numbers to different levels of precision. Since plotting functions use machine arithmetic, this difference in precision can cause *Mathematica* to draw a function differently on different computers. The expression x + Sin[2Pi x] is shown below. The first graph was produced on a Macintosh with version 2.0, and the second was produced on a NeXT workstation with version 2.2.

```
Plot[ x + Sin[2Pi x], {x, 0, 24}, PlotPoints->19 ];
```

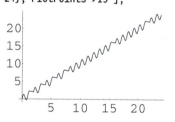

```
Plot[ x + Sin[2Pi x], {x, 0, 24}, PlotPoints->19 ];
```

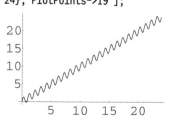

The coordinates of the points sampled depend on the floating-point hardware of the computer and the release (version number, such as 2.0 or 2.2) of *Mathematica* that you are using.

- Adaptive Sampling

Mathematica graphs a function or an expression by sampling the expression at points along the plotting interval and connecting the sampled points with straight line segments. In the graph on the left, the vertical lines show where *Mathematica* takes samples when plotting the expression $(x - 1)(x - 3)(x - 4)$ over the interval $[0.5, 4.5]$, while the graph on the right shows the curve as *Mathematica* draws it.

Mathematica does not attempt to fit curves or splines through the sample points; it simply connects them with straight lines. Using splines would require assumptions about the graphs being plotted that would be beneficial in some cases and harmful in others.

Computing the value of an expression at many points can be time consuming. To avoid computing more points than necessary, *Mathematica* uses a sampling algorithm that adapts itself to the shape of the graph it is drawing. The algorithm starts sampling on a set of x values equally spaced along the interval over which the function is being plotted. The option PlotPoints specifies the number of initial samples. In intervals where the graph is essentially linear, the initial sample points are sufficient, but in curved sections of the graph, *Mathematica* computes additional sample points. In this way, the algorithm spends extra computing time on the parts of the graph that require it, but does not waste time computing points that are not needed.

How does *Mathematica* decide when it needs to compute additional points? It works across the plotting interval from left to right, taking the sample points three at a time. Each group of three points defines two line segments having a common endpoint. *Mathematica* computes the "bend angle" between these two line segments, and computes an additional sample point if the bend angle is larger than the cutoff specified by the MaxBend option setting. To see how this works, look at the following diagram, in which *A*, *B*, and *C* are the three sample points already known to be on the graph.

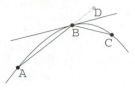

The bend angle that *Mathematica* works with is the angle by which the secant line *BC* bends away from the direction of the secant *AB*; in the diagram, this is the angle *CBD* formed by *BC* with the segment *BD*, obtained by extending *AB* through *B*. This bend angle is a measure of how well the bent line *ABC* approximates the curve, in the following sense: If the function being graphed had a continuous derivative, the secants *AB* and *BC* would approach the tangent line at *B* as the points *A* and *C* approached *B*. In the limit, the bend angle between *AB* and *BC* would become 0. In a finite approximation, there is usually a nonzero bend angle, but the smaller the angle the more closely the secants approach the tangent and the better the approximation. Therefore it is reasonable for *Mathematica* to use the bend angle to decide if it needs to improve its graph by sampling at additional points.

If the bend angle exceeds the `MaxBend` specification, the adaptive sampling algorithm bisects the interval on the x axis corresponding to the longer of *AB* and *BC*, and computes the function value at that midpoint, giving it an additional sample point. (If *AB* and *BC* are of equal length, the algorithm picks *AB*.) Now *Mathematica* has four points where it previously had three. It repeats this procedure with the leftmost three of these points, subdividing again and again until the bend angle is smaller than the `MaxBend` cutoff, however, it will not subdivide the same interval more than the number of times specified by the `PlotDivision` option setting. This limit ensures that the plotting algorithm will terminate even if *Mathematica* is asked to plot a function that has a jump discontinuity (since no amount of subdivision will reduce the bend angle in that case). When *Mathematica* decides that it need not or should not compute an additional point for the three sample points it is considering, it draws the line segment between the first two (*AB* in the diagram above), drops the leftmost point (*A*), and shifts its attention one point to the right (taking *B*, *C*, and the sample point to the right of *C* as the next three points to examine). *Mathematica* proceeds in this way until it has worked its way across the entire plotting interval.

In calculating the bend angle, *Mathematica* needs to know how long one unit in the x direction is compared to one unit in the y direction. It can use the units in which the function is specified, but that isn't necessarily the right thing to do. For example, if you are plotting a physical relationship between, say, millimeters and volts, there is no particular reason to equate one millimeter to one volt for the purpose of calculating an angle. If *Mathematica* did that, it might choose a different set of sample points (and therefore would draw a different graph) if you replotted the same relationship on axes scaled in centimeters and microvolts. The designers of *Mathematica* preferred to use an algorithm that normalizes the units in x and y, so that the same curve is graphed in the same way regardless of scale. Thus, if you plot the function $\sin(x)$ over the interval $[0, 2\pi]$, and then plot $5\sin(2x)$ over the interval $[0, \pi]$, *Mathematica* chooses sample points in the same way for both plots. That is, it chooses the same number of points for both plots, and the x coordinate of the nth point in the second plot is half of the x coordinate of the nth point in the first plot, and the y coordinate of the nth point in the second plot is five times the y coordinate of the nth point in the first plot. The following somewhat cryptic code verifies this result by constructing the plots, extracting the list of sampled points from each, and testing the relationships between their x and y coordinates:

```
gr1 = Plot[ Sin[x], {x,0,2Pi}, DisplayFunction->Identity ];
gr2 = Plot[ 5 Sin[2 x], {x,0,Pi}, DisplayFunction->Identity ];
p1 = Nest[First,gr1,4];
p2 = Nest[First,gr2,4];
{x1,y1} = Transpose[p1];
{x2,y2} = Transpose[p2];
{ x1 / 2 == x2, 5 y1 == y2 }
```

```
{True, True}
```

The Scaled coordinate system runs from 0 to 1 across the plotting region in both directions, so it is independent of the original x and y units. It is suitable for measuring the bend angle, but *Mathematica* cannot use it while sampling because it isn't defined yet: The plotting region isn't determined until after the plotting algorithm has decided what points to plot. Instead, *Mathematica* performs a local rescaling for each bend angle it has to measure. For each triplet of points, *Mathematica* scales x and y, so that the smallest rectangle containing the three points becomes a square. In this diagram, the dashed rectangle on the left is rescaled into the square on the right:

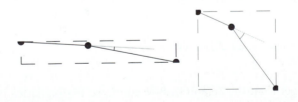

The rescaling has enlarged the bend angle; in other cases, the bend angle can be reduced.
    Notice that this algorithm tends to exaggerate the angle when the scaling factor in one direction is much larger than the scaling factor in the other direction, which

happens when the original rectangle is very tall and thin, or very short and wide. This exaggeration of the angle gives *Mathematica* a tendency to oversample when the curve it is plotting is nearly horizontal or nearly vertical. In any case, the adaptive sampling algorithm does ensure that *Mathematica* increases the number of points it samples when plotting a section of the graph that has a large curvature.

Let's look at a specific example showing how *Mathematica* chooses sample points. We will use the identity

$$\mathbf{a} \cdot \mathbf{b} = \|\mathbf{a}\| \, \|\mathbf{b}\| \cos \theta$$

in the form

$$\theta = \arccos \left(\frac{\mathbf{a} \cdot \mathbf{b}}{\|\mathbf{a}\| \, \|\mathbf{b}\|} \right)$$

to calculate bend angles. We will calculate the bend angle in degrees, rather than radians, because *Mathematica* requires the MaxBend option setting to be given in degrees. Now consider a ParametricPlot of $(\cos t, \sin t)$, which draws a circle. For t near $\pi/2$, *Mathematica* obtains three sample points: {.001, .9999995} at $t = \pi/2 - .001$, {0, 1} at $t = \pi/2$, and {-.001, .9999995} at $t = \pi/2 + .001$. For the two line segments joining these points, $\Delta x_1 = \Delta x_2 = -.001$, $\Delta y_1 = .0000005$, $\Delta y_2 = -.0000005$. The angle between the segments is only about 0.06 degrees (i.e., nearly straight) with respect to a scaling in which units in the x and y directions have equal length.

```
v1 = {-.001, .0000005}; v2 = {-.001, -.0000005};
ArcCos[v1.v2 / Sqrt[v1.v1 v2.v2]] / Degree // N
```

0.0572958

However, *Mathematica* computes the angle in a scaling in which the smallest rectangle containing the points is a square. This rectangle initially measures 0.002 by 0.0000005, so rescaling it into a square stretches the y direction by a factor of 4000 with respect to the x direction. With this scaling, the angle becomes about 127 degrees (i.e., far from straight).

```
s = {1, 4000}; {w1, w2} = {s v1, s v2}
```

{{-0.001, 0.002}, {-0.001, -0.002}}

```
ArcCos[w1.w2 / Sqrt[w1.w1 w2.w2]] / Degree // N
```

126.87

This angle is larger than the default MaxBend cutoff, so *Mathematica* computes an extra sample point.

In the graph that follows, we have drawn lines from the center to the points *Mathematica* samples along a circle. This picture was created from a result produced by ParametricPlot:

The picture shows that even when two sections of a graph have the same curvature, *Mathematica* sometimes chooses more sample points in one section than in the other. ParametricPlot computes more values than necessary to produce a reasonable image of this circle because of its tendency to oversample near horizontal or vertical tangents.

Incidentally, when you plot several functions at once by giving a list of expressions as the first argument of Plot or ParametricPlot, *Mathematica* applies the adaptive sampling algorithm to each function separately, so the functions generally are not sampled at the same values of x.

- Aliasing: One Function Impersonating Another

Like any sampling algorithm, *Mathematica*'s adaptive sampler can be fooled by oscillating curves. Remember that *Mathematica* determines the value of the plotting expression only at certain points; it *assumes* that the expression is linear between adjacent sampling points unless it has strong evidence to the contrary. If the sampled y values at three consecutive sampled values of x lie nearly on a straight line, *Mathematica* assumes that the curve is flat and doesn't investigate that region further. In fact, the curve might vary a great deal over that interval. If *Mathematica* samples a plot too infrequently, the plot may show the wrong function — an "aliased" version of the desired one. One curve impersonates another. Consider this graph:

```
Plot[x + Sin[2Pi x], {x, 0, 26} ];
```

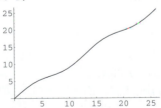

To see the curve *Mathematica* draws by default, together with the actual curve and the points where it samples, we instruct *Mathematica* to generate three graphics. We don't want to see these three plots separately, so we suppress the printing of the graphics individually by temporarily setting the variable $DisplayFunction to Identity:

```
Block[ { $DisplayFunction = Identity },
    aliasPlot = Plot[x + Sin[2Pi x], {x, 0, 26} ];
    trueCurve = Plot[x + Sin[2Pi x], {x, 0, 26},
                        PlotPoints->50, PlotStyle->Dashing[{0.01} ] ];
    samples = Join @@ Cases[ aliasPlot, {{_,_}..}, Infinity ];
    samplePts = ListPlot[ samples, PlotStyle->PointSize[.02] ];
]
```

The variable aliasPlot now contains the Graphics object that represents the aliased plot we saw above. The variable trueCurve contains a Graphics object obtained by sampling the expression at a much larger number of points, giving a more faithful representation of the curve. We used the Cases function to extract from aliasPlot the list of points sampled in the aliased plot; we then used ListPlot to make a plot of these points, which we stored in the variable samplePts. Now we use the Show function to display the three plots overlaid:

```
Show[ aliasPlot, trueCurve, samplePts ];
```

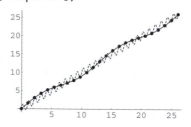

The dots represent the values sampled. The uniform spacing between the dots shows that the adaptive sampling algorithm never subdivided an interval. *Mathematica* draws straight lines between the points and misrepresents this curve. To see an even more extreme example of aliasing, repeat this experiment with the upper limit as 24 instead of 26—the aliased plot in this case is a straight line. Do you see why?

```
Block[ { $DisplayFunction = Identity },
    aliasPlot = Plot[x + Sin[2Pi x], {x, 0, 24} ];
    trueCurve = Plot[x + Sin[2Pi x], {x, 0, 24}, PlotPoints->50, PlotStyle->Dashing[{0.01} ] ];
    samples = Join @@ Cases[ aliasPlot, {{_,_}..}, Infinity ];
    samplePts = ListPlot[ samples, PlotStyle->PointSize[.02] ];
];
Show[ aliasPlot, trueCurve, samplePts ];
```

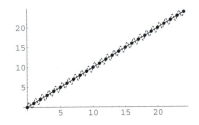

The function $\sin(2\pi x)$ has period 1. The default setting `PlotPoints->25` subdivides the interval $[0, 24]$ into 24 subintervals of length 1, so *Mathematica* samples at the values $0, 1, 2, \ldots, 24$. The term $\sin(2\pi x)$ is 0 at each of these points, so *Mathematica* sees the curve $y = x + \sin(2\pi x)$ as identical to the curve $y = x$.

We stress that aliasing behavior is *not* a problem with *Mathematica* graphics per se. Any sampling algorithm, no matter how clever, is susceptible to aliasing because of undersampling; there will always be some function that that algorithm mistakes for another function. You must be aware of this situation so that you can take steps to circumvent it if you know that the function you are working with is likely to fool the sampling algorithm. *Mathematica* can't detect aliasing for you, but at least by understanding *Mathematica*'s algorithm you have a reasonable chance of detecting it yourself.

- **Why Is the Right Half Sometimes Better Than the Left Half?**

Why is the right side of a graph sometimes drawn more accurately than the left side? Consider the function $x^2 + \cos(22x)$, which is symmetric about the y axis:

```
Plot[ x^2 + Cos[22x], {x, -4, 4} ];
```

Mathematica starts by looking at three points on the left side of the curve. The first three points sampled lie along a nearly straight line, so *Mathematica* draws straight lines connecting the first two points sampled. When it investigates the line segments containing the third sample point, *Mathematica* subdivides the interval between the third and fourth points. This graph shows where *Mathematica* samples the function:

```
samples = Plot[ x^2 + Cos[22x], {x,-4,4}, DisplayFunction->Identity ];
samplePts = Join @@ Cases[ samples, {{_,_}..}, Infinity ];
ListPlot[ samplePts, PlotStyle->PointSize[.01] ];
```

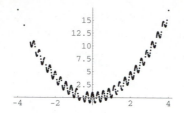

Remember that *Mathematica* draws a curve from left to right, and it never turns back to check whether it should subdivide a segment to the left of the points that it is currently investigating. That is why right sides of graphs tend to be more accurate than left sides.

Here is another example that shows the same behavior, but is a bit easier to understand:

```
Plot[ Sin[x], {x,0,48Pi}, Frame->True, Axes->None ];
```

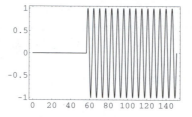

In plotting $\sin x$ in the interval $[0, 48\pi]$, *Mathematica* doesn't recognize that the expression oscillates in the interval $[0, 56]$. This is the same problem we saw in the example on page 94. The interval $[0, 48\pi]$ is divided into 24 subintervals, each of length 2π. Since 2π is the period of the sine function, *Mathematica* sees the same value at every plotting point and concludes that the function is a straight line. The only mystery is that the graph is not flat all the way across. Because of roundoff error, the increment in x from one sample point to the next is not *exactly* 2π, and after about 9 increments, the accumulated error moves the sample point far enough away from being an exact multiple of 2π to produce a y value noticeably different from 0. Thus, the bend angle between adjacent segments on the graph is large enough to trigger subdivision of the plotting interval, and as soon as any other point is sampled, *Mathematica* discovers that the function is not flat and starts sampling over enough points to give an accurate graph. The important point, however, is that *Mathematica* cannot go back to the beginning of the interval and resample; indeed, for all *Mathematica* knows, you were actually plotting the function defined as

```
f[x_] := If[ x<56, 0, Sin[x] ]
```

and for this function, the graph it produced is correct. Changing the setting of the PlotPoints option causes *Mathematica* to look at a different initial set of sample points, and almost any other choice you could make would produce a more accurate plot of $\sin x$. It is not necessary to request *more* points; it is only necessary to avoid the fortuitous coincidence of sample points with the period of the curve.

```
Plot[ Sin[x], {x,0,48Pi}, Frame->True, Axes->None, PlotPoints->15 ];
```

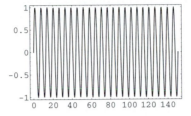

Here is one more example:

```
singraph[n_] := Plot[ Sin[x],{x,0,n}, DisplayFunction->Identity ];
Show[GraphicsArray[ singraph /@ {300,305,310,315} ]];
```

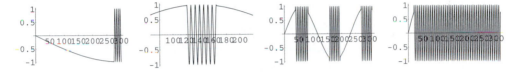

Even though the plotting intervals are nearly the same in all four plots, *Mathematica* produces very different results.

Mathematica's adaptive sampling algorithm generally produces a reasonable depiction of an expression by taking a minimum number of sample points. Be aware, however, that it can be fooled.

4.1.4 No Plot

There is more to producing a plot that just sampling an expression. This section discusses some of the steps that *Mathematica* takes in producing a plot and shows a couple of examples where no graph is rendered unless you change the order in which Plot or ParametricPlot evaluates its arguments.

▪ The Order of Evaluation

Notice that the Plot command has the attribute HoldAll:

```
Attributes[Plot]
```

```
{HoldAll, Protected}
```

This attribute specifies that *Mathematica* defer, or "hold," the evaluation of the arguments to the Plot command. Instead of evaluating its arguments immediately upon receiving them, Plot waits until it needs the value of an argument and evaluates it then. Consider the command Plot[D[x Cos[x], x], {x, 0, 2Pi}]. To evaluate this expression, *Mathematica* first sets x equal to 0, the left endpoint of the plotting interval. Then it attempts to evaluate the expression D[x Cos[x], x] within a context in which x has the value 0. This causes *Mathematica* to try to evaluate D[0 Cos[0], 0]. As you can see, this expression does not evaluate to a number:

```
D[0 Cos[0], 0]
```

General::ivar: 0 is not a valid variable.

```
D[0, 0]
```

Look at what happens when we ask *Mathematica* to plot the derivative of $x \cos(x)$ with respect to x. Notice that *Mathematica* prints the same warning message as the one above. (We omitted all but a few of *Mathematica's* warning messages.)

```
Plot[ D[x Cos[x], x], {x, 0, 10} ];
```

General::ivar: 0. is not a valid variable.

Plot::plnr: CompiledFunction[{x}, D[x Cos[x], x], -CompiledCode-][x]
       is not a machine-size real number at x = 0..

General::ivar: 0.416667 is not a valid variable.

Plot::plnr: CompiledFunction[{x}, D[x Cos[x], x], -CompiledCode-][x]
       is not a machine-size real number at x = 0.416667.

Since plotting the derivative of $x \cos(x)$ is a perfectly reasonable thing to do, we have two questions to ask: Why does *Mathematica* behave this way, and how can we work around it?

Mathematica assigns values to the plotting variable before evaluating the argument of Plot because some expressions produce unexpected results, or don't make sense, when given symbolic arguments (such as the variable x); they return a meaningful result only when applied to an explicit numerical value (as defined on page 81). Consider the function defined as

```
f[x_] := -1 /; x<0
f[x_] := 1
```

This code defines a function that returns −1 for negative arguments and 1 for non-negative arguments, but it doesn't necessarily do what you want, as these examples show:

```
{ f[-2], f[2], f[x] }
```

```
{-1, 1, 1}
```

We get the expected results when f is applied to −2 and 2. However, f[x] evaluates to 1 as well, because the criterion x<0 does not evaluate to True. In fact, the inequality can't be evaluated meaningfully until a numerical value is assigned to the symbol x. Since the pattern matcher treats any condition that is not explicitly True as being equivalent to False, evaluating the expression f[x] before x has received a numerical value causes the first rule for f to fail, and the pattern matcher uses the second rule, producing the value 1. If the Plot command didn't defer evaluation of the plotting expression, this behavior would cause Plot to plot f[x] as if it were the constant function 1. Since Plot does defer evaluation of its plotting expression, it is able to plot f[x] correctly, as we see here:

```
Plot[ f[x], {x,-2,2} ];
```

The function f is plotted correctly because the expression f[x] is evaluated separately for each numerical value that Plot assigns to x. The only way that Plot can correctly plot functions like f[x], whose definitions involve conditionals, pattern tests, and other control structures, is to put off evaluating the plotting expression until after it chooses values for the plotting variable. Since *Mathematica* users often wish to define such functions, WRI decided to make Plot handle its plotting expression in this way.

Now we know why *Mathematica* does what it does, but we still need to know how to get around it so that we can plot the derivative of $x \cos(x)$. In those cases where the plotting expression needs to be evaluated before its variable is assigned a value, you can wrap Evaluate (or Release in Version 1.2 and earlier versions of *Mathematica*) around the expression. Doing so forces *Mathematica* to evaluate the expression before choosing values for the plotting variable.

```
Plot[ Evaluate[ D[x Cos[x], x] ], {x, 0, 10} ];
```

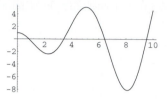

▪ Single versus Multiple Expressions

When you are dealing with a long, complicated expression, or you expect to refer to an expression frequently, it is convenient to assign a name to the expression, as we have done here:

```
a = Exp[-x] Sin[10/x];
```

Let's plot the expression a:

```
Plot[ a, {x, -2.5, -.1} ];
```

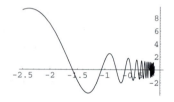

This plot works fine and looks nice. Now suppose that we want to show the asymptotic curves on the same plot. We define a new expression:

```
b = { Exp[-x], Exp[-x] Sin[10/x], -Exp[-x] };
```

But look at what happens when we try to plot b:

```
Plot[b, {x, -2.5, -.1} ];

Plot::plnr: CompiledFunction[{x}, b, -CompiledCode-][x]
     is not a machine-size real number at x = -2.5.

Plot::plnr: CompiledFunction[{x}, b, -CompiledCode-][x]
     is not a machine-size real number at x = -2.4.

Plot::plnr: CompiledFunction[{x}, b, -CompiledCode-][x]
     is not a machine-size real number at x = -2.3.

General::stop: Further output of Plot::plnr
     will be suppressed during this calculation.
```

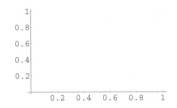

Why doesn't *Mathematica* produce a graph of the three expressions in the definition of b? The reason has to do with what Plot thinks it is plotting. Before plotting, Plot looks at its first argument. When the first argument is not a list, Plot assumes that it is graphing a single expression; when the first argument is a list, Plot assumes that it is graphing the expressions in the list. However, because Plot has the HoldAll attribute, it looks at the argument before any evaluation takes place. In the case of the expression b, Plot sees the head Symbol rather than List, because the symbol b is not replaced by a list of expressions until it is evaluated, and evaluation hasn't happened yet. So Plot doesn't realize that b represents a list of expressions, and it assumes that it is plotting a single expression.

Why does the error message refer to CompiledFunction? Plot calls *Mathematica*'s expression compiler for each expression it expects to plot, because compiled expressions can be evaluated much more quickly than interpreted ones can. The compiler compiles the expression b just fine. The problem arises because the compiled expression b returns a list of three real numbers each time it is evaluated, but Plot has already decided that it is supposed to be plotting a single expression rather than a list of expressions, so it isn't expecting a list of values. Hence the complaint.

Plot calls the compiler only once, when it needs to call it three times — once for each expression in the definition of b. The way to make Plot understand this is to force Plot to evaluate b right away instead of deferring the evaluation. Using Evaluate makes Plot do this.

```
Plot[ Evaluate[b], {x, -2.5, -.1} ];
```

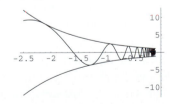

If you understand how the *Mathematica* graphics functions work, you can use them more effectively and you will understand the error messages when something doesn't work as you expect.

4.2 Three-Dimensional Function Plotting

There are four basic *Mathematica* commands for constructing plots of functions in three dimensions: Plot3D, ParametricPlot3D, ContourPlot, and DensityPlot. Plot3D constructs SurfaceGraphics objects, ParametricPlot3D constructs Graphics3D objects, ContourPlot constructs ContourGraphics, and DensityPlot constructs DensityGraphics. You usually don't need to know what type of graphics object is constructed unless you intend to manipulate or combine graphs.

4.2.1 Plot3D

Plot3D allows you to plot a surface in three dimensions specified as a function $z = f(x, y)$. You must call Plot3D with at least three arguments: an expression representing the function to be plotted, and intervals for the two independent variables specifying the region over which the function is to be plotted. The template is

Plot3D[*expression*, *interval1*, *interval2*, *options*]

By default, *Mathematica* encloses the plot in a box and puts tick marks along the three most visible edges:

Plot3D[Sin[x^2 - y^2], {x,-1,3}, {y,-2,2}];

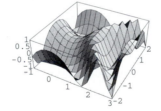

The result of Plot3D is a SurfaceGraphics object, which Plot3D constructs and implicitly calls Show to display. The object can be stored in a variable to be redisplayed with Show, or converted to Graphics3D or Graphics form, as discussed in Chapter 2.

Like Plot, Plot3D accepts optional arguments specified in the form of replacement rules. Option settings must follow the required arguments. Here is the same function as in the previous example, but with the PlotPoints option used to specify sampling over a finer grid. The BoxRatios option changes the scaling of the plot by specifying a different shape for the bounding box; in this case, we scale the surface into a cube.

```
Plot3D[ Sin[x^2 - y^2], {x,-1,3}, {y,-2,2}, PlotPoints->25, BoxRatios->{1,1,1} ];
```

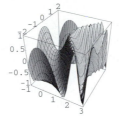

Other options accepted by `Plot3D` are listed in the section following this one.

You can also specify a pair of expressions as the first argument to `Plot3D`. The first expression is taken as the function to be plotted, and the second expression specifies the shading of the surface. In this case, the basic template is

```
Plot3D[ {expression, shading},   {var1, v1min, v1max}, {var2, v2min, v2max} ]
```

The expression that specifies shading should be a function of the plotting variables that returns a color directive (i.e., a `GrayLevel`, `RGBColor`, `CMYKColor`, or `Hue` specification). Here is an example of a surface shaded by a function:

```
Plot3D[ { Sin[x^2 - y^2], Hue[ Mod[ Sqrt[x^2+y^2]/2, 1 ] ] }, {x,-1,3}, {y,-2,2},
         PlotPoints->25 ];
```

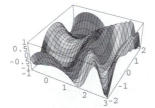

In the function `Hue[Mod[Sqrt[x^2+y^2]/2,1]]`, the inner expression `Sqrt[x^2+y^2]/2` is half of the distance of a point (x, y) from the origin; this is the value that determines the color. The function `Mod[#,1]&` is applied to this value to obtain the fractional part, since `Hue` expects arguments in the range $[0, 1]$.

If you do not specify shading by providing an additional expression to `Plot3D`, *Mathematica* uses simulated illumination to color the surface. This coloring is controlled by the `LightSources` and `AmbientLight` options, as explained in Section 7.4.2 on page 252. However, if the option `Lighting` is set to `False` instead of its default value, `True`, simulated illumination is not used and even a coloring expression will be ignored. When `Lighting` is `False`, the surface is colored according to the function specified by the `ColorFunction` option. The default `ColorFunction` setting shades the surface according to height: The highest points are white, the lowest points are black, and the points in between are shades of gray. Here is an example of this coloring method:

```
Plot3D[ Sin[x^2 - y^2], {x,-1,3}, {y,-2,2}, Lighting->False ];
```

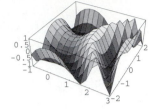

Sometimes Plot3D is unable to obtain values for an expression at certain points on the sample grid. The function may have singularities that cause it to be undefined for certain inputs; for example, $\frac{\sin xy}{xy}$ is undefined if x or y is equal to zero. In such a case, Plot3D produces a surface with holes at the points where it was unable to obtain a value.

```
Plot3D[ Sin[x y] / (x y), {x,-Pi,Pi}, {y,-Pi,Pi} ];
```

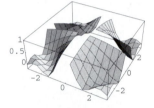

Mathematica issued 16 error messages, occupying about 50 lines of text, in the course of generating this plot; we deleted them to save space. Note that a single missing value in the sample grid generally causes four polygonal tiles on the surface to be removed, because each interior point of the grid is a corner of four tiles.

- Options Accepted by Plot3D

Here are the options accepted by Plot3D, with their default settings:

```
Options[Plot3D]
```

```
{AmbientLight -> GrayLevel[0], AspectRatio -> Automatic, Axes -> True,
  AxesEdge -> Automatic, AxesLabel -> None, AxesStyle -> Automatic,
  Background -> Automatic, Boxed -> True, BoxRatios -> {1, 1, 0.4},
  BoxStyle -> Automatic, ClipFill -> Automatic, ColorFunction -> Automatic,
  ColorOutput -> Automatic, Compiled -> True, DefaultColor -> Automatic,
  Epilog -> {}, FaceGrids -> None, HiddenSurface -> True, Lighting -> True,
  LightSources ->
   {{{1., 0., 1.}, RGBColor[1, 0, 0]}, {{1., 1., 1.}, RGBColor[0, 1, 0]},
```

```
    {{0., 1., 1.}, RGBColor[0, 0, 1]}}, Mesh -> True,
MeshStyle -> Automatic, PlotLabel -> None, PlotPoints -> 15,
PlotRange -> Automatic, PlotRegion -> Automatic,
Plot3Matrix -> Automatic, Prolog -> {}, Shading -> True,
SphericalRegion -> False, Ticks -> Automatic, ViewCenter -> Automatic,
ViewPoint -> {1.3, -2.4, 2.}, ViewVertical -> {0., 0., 1.},
DefaultFont :> $DefaultFont, DisplayFunction :> $DisplayFunction}
```

For complete explanations of these options, see Chapter 7. The rest of this section gives examples of some commonly used options as they apply to Plot3D.

Unlike Plot, Plot3D does not sample a function adaptively. Instead it samples only at points on a rectangular grid. By default, 225 samples are taken: 15 in the x direction and 15 in the y direction. We have already seen that PlotPoints allows you to specify the number of sample points used in the x and y directions. Setting PlotPoints to a number tells *Mathematica* to take that many sample points in both the x and y directions. Setting PlotPoints to a pair of numbers specifies that a different number of sample points are to be taken in the x and y directions:

```
Plot3D[ Sin[x^2 - y^2], {x,-1,3}, {y,-2,2}, PlotPoints->{20, 10} ];
```

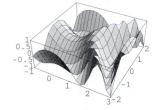

Naturally, the more sample points there are, the longer it takes to compute points and display a plot. To save time, Plot3D, by default, uses *Mathematica*'s expression compiler to convert the expression being plotted to a form that can be rapidly evaluated. In certain rare cases, however, compiling an expression may cause it not to evaluate the way you want it to. For example, if the expression requires high-precision floating-point calculations, it shouldn't be compiled, because compiled expressions always do arithmetic with machine-size numbers. In cases like these, you can use the option setting Compiled->False to instruct Plot3D not to compile the expression it is plotting.

PlotPoints and Compiled are the only options Plot3D uses that pertain to how a function is sampled. All the other options that Plot3D accepts influence how the plot is displayed, not how it is computed, so we can exhibit them by calling Plot3D once, saving the resulting SurfaceGraphics object in a variable, and then using Show to redisplay the object with different option settings.

```
Show[GraphicsArray[ Block[ {$DisplayFunction=Identity},
  {{ gr = Plot3D[ Sin[x^2 - y^2], {x,-1,3}, {y,-2,2} ],
    Show[gr,Mesh->False],
    Show[gr,Shading->False],
    Show[gr,HiddenSurface->False] },
  { Show[gr,Boxed->False],
    Show[gr,Axes->None],
    Show[gr,Boxed->False,Axes->None],
    Show[gr,ViewPoint->{0,5,0}] }} ]]];
```

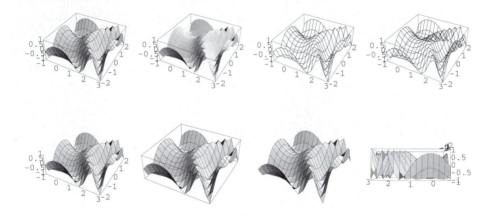

The first graphic (in the upper left corner) shows how the plot appears with the default option settings. In the other three graphics in the first row, we use the Mesh, Shading, and HiddenSurface options to turn off mesh lines, polygon shading, and hidden-surface elimination. Note that when HiddenSurface is set to False, a wireframe effect results because the polygons are not filled in. In the second row, we first use the Boxed option to suppress the bounding box, but the three edges bearing the tick marks are still drawn. To suppress the tick marks, we use the Axes option. In the third graphic, we see the surface with both axes and bounding box suppressed. In the fourth graphic, we see the surface from a different viewpoint.

4.2.2 ParametricPlot3D

The function ParametricPlot3D plots parametrized curves and surfaces. This function was defined in a package in Version 1.2 and in earlier versions of *Mathematica*. In Version 2.0, it was added to the *Mathematica* kernel, but the package continues to be included with most versions.

The command `ParametricPlot3D` produces a parametrized curve, whose values of x, y, and z are given in terms of another variable, such as t or time. The form of the command is

ParametricPlot3D[*triple of functions*, *interval*, *options*]

As usual, optional arguments must follow required arguments. Here is an example of the plotting of a parametrized curve:

```
ParametricPlot3D[ { 4Cos[-t/2] + 7Cos[t], 4Sin[-t/2] + 7Sin[t], t }, {t, 0, 8Pi} ];
```

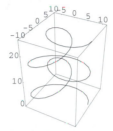

When `ParametricPlot3D` is plotting a curve, its default is to sample the parameter functions at 75 points that are equally spaced in the parameter interval. You can specify a different number of sample points with the `PlotPoints` option, but you should realize that `ParametricPlot3D`, unlike `ParametricPlot`, does *not* sample adaptively.

The command `ParametricPlot3D` can also produce a parametrized surface, whose values of x, y, and z are given in terms of two variables, such as s and t. The command is

ParametricPlot3D[*triple of functions*, *interval1*, *interval2*, *options*]

`ParametricPlot3D` bases its decision to plot a curve or a surface on the number of intervals you specify. It does not, for instance, count the number of variables in the *triple of functions* to see whether they are specified in terms of one or two parameters.

We can use `ParametricPlot3D` to model a torus, which looks a bit like a bagel or a doughnut.

```
ParametricPlot3D[ { Cos[s] (2 + Cos[t]), Sin[s] (2 + Cos[t]), Sin[t] },
                 {s, 0, 2Pi}, {t, 0, 2Pi} ];
```

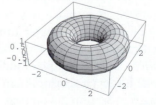

ParametricPlot3D functions similarly to Plot3D and accepts some of the same graphics option settings. In fact, you can think of

$$\text{Plot3D[} f[x,y], \{x,xmin,xmax\}, \{y,ymin,ymax\} \text{]}$$

simply as shorthand for

$$\text{ParametricPlot3D[} \{x, \ y, \ f[x, y]\}, \{x,xmin,xmax\}, \{y,ymin,ymax\} \text{]}$$

For example, you can draw the same surface with Plot3D as with ParametricPlot3D. However, the two functions are not as similar as Plot and ParametricPlot, because Plot3D produces SurfaceGraphics objects and ParametricPlot3D produces Graphics3D objects. It generally takes far longer to plot a function $z = f(x, y)$ with ParametricPlot3D than with Plot3D, as you can see from the output of Timing.

Timing[Plot3D[Sin[x y], {x, 0, 2Pi}, {y, 0, Pi}];]

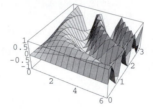

{0.516667 Second, Null}

Timing[ParametricPlot3D[{x, y, Sin[x y]}, {x, 0, 2Pi}, {y, 0, Pi}];]

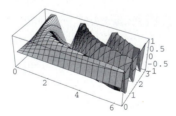

{4.26667 Second, Null}

(Note that the results from Timing include only the time for the kernel to generate the PostScript code and not the time for the PostScript interpretter to render the graphic.) There are two reasons that Plot3D takes so much less time to produce its result. One reason is that SurfaceGraphics objects have a simpler structure than Graphics3D objects have, because they were specifically designed for this kind of surface plotting. The other reason is that *Mathematica* can use a simpler hidden-feature-removal algorithm when generating PostScript code for SurfaceGraphics than it can use for Graphics3D. This difference was discussed at length in Section 2.3 on page 18.

Notice that ParametricPlot3D draws the surface somewhat differently from Plot3D. ParametricPlot3D samples at a few more values by default (although you can use the PlotPoints option with either Plot3D or ParametricPlot3D to sample on as fine a grid as you wish). Because the default setting of the BoxRatios option for ParametricPlot3D is Automatic, the parametrized plot is drawn to scale — that is, one unit in the x direction is drawn the same size as one unit in the y direction. Plot3D uses a fixed setting for BoxRatios, so its results by default always use the same shape of box (but again, you could override this by specifying BoxRatios->Automatic to Plot3D).

ParametricPlot3D is more versatile than Plot3D. Any plot that Plot3D can produce ParametricPlot3D can produce as well, but there are many surfaces (those with self-intersections, for example) that ParametricPlot3D can produce but Plot3D cannot. You will pay for extra flexibility with your time.

4.2.3 Options Shared by Plot3D and ParametricPlot3D

This section presents simple examples of a few of the options most commonly used by Plot3D and ParametricPlot3D. These options determine how graphics are displayed, not how they are computed; they have no effect on how functions are sampled.

- Viewpoint

You can change the orientation of a graph with the option ViewPoint. When you specify a viewpoint, you are telling *Mathematica* the point in space from which you are viewing the object being displayed. Changing your viewpoint is equivalent to staying in a fixed position and rotating the object. ViewPoint is specified relative to a bounding box whose longest side has length 1 and whose center is at {0,0,0}. The lengths of the other sides are determined by the BoxRatios setting (see below). The following table will help you figure out the setting of ViewPoint that corresponds to a specific orientation. See Sections 6.2.2 and 7.4.3, on pages 192 and 261 respectively, for a more detailed description of the option ViewPoint.

ViewPoint	Position
{1.3, -2.4, 2}	default setting
{0, -2, 0}	directly in front
{0, 0, 2}	directly above
{0, -2, 2}	in front and from above
{-2, -2, -2}	lower left corner
{2, -2, 2}	upper right corner

Changing ViewPoint allows you to view an object from a different perspective and thus see features that might otherwise be obscured:

```
gr = Plot3D[ Sin[x^2 - y^2], {x,-1,3}, {y,-2,2}, DisplayFunction->Identity,
             PlotLabel->(ViewPoint/.Options[Plot3D]) ];
altviewpoints = Show[gr,ViewPoint->#,PlotLabel->#]& /@
             { {0,-2,0}, {0,0,2}, {0,-2,2}, {-2,-2,-2}, {2,-2,2} };
Show[GraphicsArray[ Partition[ Prepend[altviewpoints,gr], 3 ] ]];
```

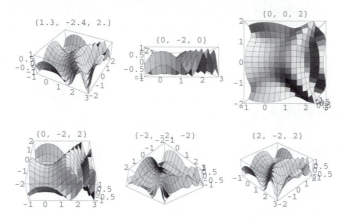

Notice that where the tick marks are displayed depends on the orientation of the graph. *Mathematica* has an algorithm to place each axis along the "most visible" edge, but you can use the AxesEdge option to specify which edge to use for each axis.

The ViewPoint option specifies not only the direction from which to view an object but also the distance at which to view it. In the following example, we construct a SurfaceGraphics object and view it from three different points that all lie along the same line. In all three plots, the line-of-sight vector is the same, but the different focal lengths lead to different degrees of perspective distortion.

```
gr = Plot3D[ Sin[x^2 - y^2], {x,-1,3}, {y,-2,2}, DisplayFunction->Identity ];
altdists = Show[gr,ViewPoint->#,PlotLabel->#]& /@
             { {.5,.5,.5}, {1,1,1}, {100,100,100} };
Show[GraphicsArray[ altdists ]];
```

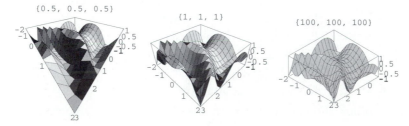

In the plot on the left, the ViewPoint is set to {.5,.5,.5}, showing us what the surface looks like if we place an eye exactly at one of the corners of the object's bounding box. Drawing the eye back along the same line of sight to the point {1,1,1} reduces the perspective distortion markedly, and by the time we have moved back to {100,100,100} the distortion is so tiny that, for all intents and purposes, we are seeing an orthogonal projection.

The ViewCenter and ViewVertical options also affect the perspective projection that *Mathematica* uses in displaying a three-dimensional object. The ViewCenter option allows you to change the point at which you are looking, and the ViewVertical option allows you to change which direction is up.

```
gr = Plot3D[ Sin[x^2 - y^2], {x,-1,3}, {y,-2,2},
             Ticks->None, DisplayFunction->Identity ];
outline = Line[{Scaled[{0.001,0.001}], Scaled[{0,1}],
             Scaled[{1,1}], Scaled[{1,0.001}], Scaled[{0.001,0.001}] }];
Show[GraphicsArray[{
    Show[ gr, ViewCenter->#, PlotLabel->SequenceForm["VC = ",#],
             Epilog -> Line[{ {0,0}, {0,1}, {1,1}, {1,0}, {0,0} }] ]& /@
        { {0,0,0}, {1,.5,0}, {1,1,1} },
    Show[ gr, ViewVertical->#, PlotLabel->SequenceForm["VV = ",#],
             Epilog -> outline ]& /@
        { {1,0,0}, {0,1,1}, {0,0,-1} }
}]];
```

VC = {0, 0, 0}   VC = {1, 0.5, 0}   VC = {1, 1, 1}

VV = {1, 0, 0}   VV = {0, 1, 1}   VV = {0, 0, -1}

▪ Bounding Box and Axes

Three options control the bounding box used in 3D graphics: Boxed, BoxStyle, and BoxRatios. Boxed controls whether or not a box is drawn, and BoxStyle controls the appearance of the box. Four additional options — Axes, AxesEdge, AxesStyle, and Ticks — control the axes along the edges of the box.

```
gr1 = Plot3D[ Sin[x^2 - y^2], {x,-1,3}, {y,-2,2}, DisplayFunction->Identity,
              PlotLabel->"Default Box" ];
gr2 = Show[ gr1, Boxed->False, PlotLabel->"No Bounding Box" ];
gr3 = Show[ gr1, BoxStyle->{Dashing[{.03,.03}],GrayLevel[.6]},
              PlotLabel->"Dashed Gray Box" ];
gr4 = Show[ gr1, Axes->False, PlotLabel->"Default Box, No Axes" ];
gr5 = Show[ gr2, Axes->False, PlotLabel->"No Box or Axes" ];
gr6 = Show[ gr3, Axes->False, PlotLabel->"Dashed Gray Box without Axes" ];
Show[GraphicsArray[ { { gr1, gr2, gr3 }, { gr4, gr5, gr6 } } ]];
```

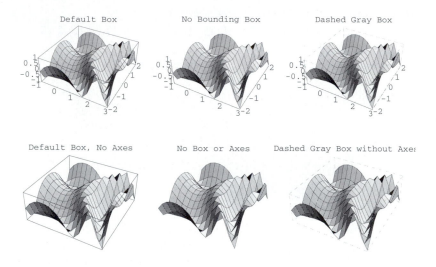

Observe that the axes are turned on and off independently of the bounding box; you can also use a setting such as this one:

$$Axes->\{False,False,True\}$$

to specify that axes should be drawn in some directions and not in others. The AxesEdge option allows you to specify along which edges of the box the axes are to be drawn, but it is usually best to allow *Mathematica* to determine this for itself, as we saw above in the ViewPoint examples. More sophisticated uses of AxesStyle and BoxStyle allow you to specify the appearance of each edge independently of the others. You can also use the Ticks option to specify where the tick marks appear along each axis, how long they are, how they are labeled, and so forth. These refinements are discussed in detail in Chapter 7; the discussion here should just give you an idea of the possibilities.

The BoxRatios option controls the shape of the box and therefore controls the way the graphics objects will be scaled. The default setting of BoxRatios for Plot3D is {1,1,.4}, which means that the surfaces plotted by Plot3D are always scaled so that the x interval and the y interval have the same length and the z interval is 40 percent as long. The setting {1,1,1} scales the surface into a cube (a box with all three edges the same length), and the special setting Automatic tells *Mathematica* to scale the edges so that one unit in the x direction, one unit in the y direction and one unit in the z direction all have the same length. Here is an example:

```
gr = Plot3D[ Sin[x^2 - y^2], {x,-1,2}, {y,-3,3}, DisplayFunction->Identity,
             PlotLabel->(BoxRatios/.Options[Plot3D]) ];
altboxratios = Show[gr,BoxRatios->#,PlotLabel->#]& /@ { {1,1,1}, Automatic };
Show[GraphicsArray[ Prepend[altboxratios,gr] ]];
```

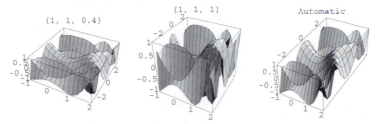

The default setting of BoxRatios for ParametricPlot3D is Automatic.

- Lighting

By default, a surface produced by Plot3D or ParametricPlot3D is colored via *Mathematica*'s simulated illumination model, which treats the surface as a flat white substance (e.g., writing paper or plaster of Paris) reflecting light from three sources: one red, one green, and one blue. You can use the AmbientLight option setting to add diffuse isotropic light to the model, and the LightSources option to change the number, color, and position of the directional light sources. You can specify SurfaceColor or FaceForm directives in the Prolog option of a ParametricPlot3D command to alter the reflecting characteristics of the surface plotted. Surfaces plotted by Plot3D are SurfaceGraphics objects, and *Mathematica* does not provide a way to alter their reflecting characteristics.

Polygon coloring and its effect on lighting were discussed in Section 3.3.5 on page 74. The coordinate systems used in specifying light sources and in computing angles of incidence and angles of reflection will be discussed in Section 6.2.3 on page 199, and the full details of simulated illumination will be given in Section 7.4.2 on page 254.

4.3 Mixed 2D and 3D Plots

4.3.1 ContourPlot

The function ContourPlot constructs a topographical map of a function, that is, a graph with contour lines representing curves of constant height along a surface. By default, the contours are equally spaced in z values. In Version 2.0 and later releases, *Mathematica* shades the regions between contours to indicate the height; by default, white indicates peaks or large values and black indicates valleys or small values.

You must call ContourPlot, like Plot3D, with at least three arguments: an expression and intervals for two variables:

ContourPlot[*expression*, *interval1*, *interval2*, *options*]

For example,

ContourPlot[Sin[x^2 - y^2], {x,-1,3}, {y,-2,2}];

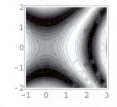

ContourPlot constructs contours numerically, by interpolation between grid points. As the example shows, this approach does not always produce perfect results. The level curves of $\sin(x^2 - y^2)$ are hyperbolas, so, for example, the white section should not have been broken or notched, because it is near the point $(1.6, -1.2)$ in the graph above. The default PlotPoints setting is 15, but with a larger value the function is sampled on a finer grid, and we get a much smoother and more accurate graph.

gr = ContourPlot[Sin[x^2 - y^2], {x,-1,3}, {y,-2,2}, PlotPoints->30];

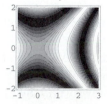

You can use other options to specify the number of contours to be drawn, whether the plot should be shaded, and other features. Here are five examples:

```
Block[ { $DisplayFunction = Identity },
    gr1 = Show[ gr, Contours->5, ContourShading-> False ];
    gr2 = Show[ gr, Contours->5, ContourLines->False ];
    gr3 = Show[ gr2, ColorFunction->(GrayLevel[1-#]&) ];
    gr4 = Show[ gr, ContourShading->False, Contours -> { 0, .2, .4, .6, .8 } ];
    gr5 = Show[ gr4, ContourStyle->({GrayLevel[#]}& /@ { 0, .2, .4, .6, .8 }) ];  ];
Show[GraphicsArray[ { gr1, gr2, gr3, gr4, gr5 } ]];
```

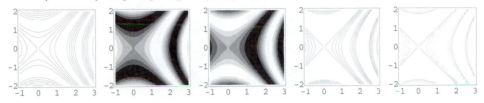

The first thing to notice about these examples is that we produced them *all* by redisplaying the same ContourGraphics object we computed above. This shows us that the calculations to locate the contour lines are not performed by ContourPlot but are repeated each time a ContourGraphics object is displayed. In the first example, we specify a different number of contour lines than the default, and we set ContourShading to False to turn off the shading of the regions between contours. We ask for five contours, but *Mathematica* draws more than that. Why? Because the Contours option specifies the number of z values for which contours are to be drawn, not the number of contour lines. In this example, we are plotting a function that oscillates, so there are several unconnected contour curves at any given value of z, and *Mathematica* draws them all. In the second example, we ask for the same number of contour levels, but we retain shading and turn off the contour lines instead. The third example is the same as the second, except that we use the ColorFunction option to specify an alternate way of shading the regions between contours; the particular shading in this example inverts the default shading so that the highest regions are black and the lowest are white. In the fourth example, we use a different form of the Contours option to specify exactly which values of z we want to see contours for; in this case, we turn off contours for negative z values and retain them for positive values. In the fifth example, we redisplay the contours chosen in the fourth example, but use the ContourStyle option to specify how we want each contour line to appear. This makes it easier to tell which contour lines represent which z values.

There is one other option affecting contour plotting that you might want to adjust occasionally: ContourSmoothing. The default setting, True, turns on a smoothing algorithm to improve the appearance of contour lines. The False setting turns smoothing off and instructs *Mathematica* to draw contours as sequences of line segments computed by linear interpolation between grid points. The effects of ContourSmoothing are almost unnoticeable if the contours are smooth to begin with, and larger settings of PlotPoints (resulting in a finer grid) also diminish the need for smoothing. If you look carefully, you will see a few differences when our example function is plotted with the default setting of PlotPoints:

```
smooth = ContourPlot[ Sin[x^2 - y^2], {x,-1,3}, {y,-2,2}, DisplayFunction->Identity ];
nosmooth = Show[ smooth, ContourSmoothing->False ];
Show[GraphicsArray[ { smooth, nosmooth } ]];
```

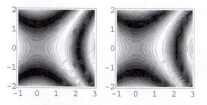

However, if the same function is plotted with PlotPoints set to 30, there is no apparent difference between the smoothed and unsmoothed plots.

The five-part example on page 114 suggests that few aspects of contour plotting are carried out by ContourPlot itself, because nearly all features of a contour plot can be changed when a ContourGraphics object is redisplayed, without ContourPlot needing to be reinvoked. This conclusion is supported by the following results:

```
Complement[ First /@ Options[ContourPlot], First /@ Options[ContourGraphics] ]
```
```
{Compiled, PlotPoints}
```

```
Complement[ First /@ Options[ContourGraphics], First /@ Options[ContourPlot] ]
```
```
{MeshRange}
```

The first result shows us the options that are accepted by ContourPlot but not accepted by ContourGraphics; the only such options relate to how the function is sampled. The second result shows us that the only option accepted by ContourGraphics but not ContourPlot is MeshRange, which used to record the x and y intervals that were specified when ContourPlot constructed a ContourGraphics object. You don't ordinarily specify the MeshRange option yourself, unless you are constructing a ContourGraphics object directly without going through ContourPlot. One further result is informative:

```
Complement[ First /@ Options[ContourGraphics], First /@ Options[Graphics] ]
```
```
{ColorFunction, ContourLines, Contours, ContourShading, ContourSmoothing,
  ContourStyle, MeshRange}
```

This shows us the options used by ContourGraphics, over and above the basic options (such as AspectRatio and PlotRange), that are used by all 2D graphics. They are the options that specifically control the appearance of contour plots. Finally, here is a list of all the options accepted by ContourPlot, with their default settings:

`Options[ContourPlot]`

```
{AspectRatio -> 1, Axes -> False, AxesLabel -> None, AxesOrigin -> Automatic,
  AxesStyle -> Automatic, Background -> Automatic, ColorFunction -> Automatic,
  ColorOutput -> Automatic, Compiled -> True, ContourLines -> True, Contours -> 10,
  ContourShading -> True, ContourSmoothing -> True, ContourStyle -> Automatic,
  DefaultColor -> Automatic, Epilog -> {}, Frame -> True, FrameLabel -> None,
  FrameStyle -> Automatic, FrameTicks -> Automatic, PlotLabel -> None, PlotPoints -> 15,
  PlotRange -> Automatic, PlotRegion -> Automatic, Prolog -> {}, RotateLabel -> True,
  Ticks -> Automatic, DefaultFont :> $DefaultFont, DisplayFunction :> $DisplayFunction}
```

These options are documented fully in Chapter 7. Options that are specific to contour plots are discussed in Section 7.5.4, which begins on page 274.

In The *Mathematica* Book, Stephen Wolfram points out that contour plots and surface plots behave in a somewhat complementary fashion: When a function varies a great deal over a small region, a surface plot is very uneven and hard to read but a contour plot has neat contours aligned closely. On the other hand, when a function varies only slightly over a wide region, a surface plot is smooth, whereas a contour plot may be uneven. These are general principles and not absolutes, however, as the following examples show:

```
surfaceplot = Plot3D[ 2*x^2 + 3*y^2, {x,-4,4}, {y,-4,4}, DisplayFunction->Identity ];
contourplot = ContourGraphics[ surfaceplot ];
Show[GraphicsArray[ { surfaceplot, contourplot } ]];
```

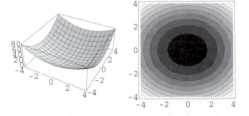

```
surfaceplot = Plot3D[ Arg[ x+ I y], {x,-4,4}, {y,-4,4}, DisplayFunction->Identity ];
contourplot = ContourGraphics[ surfaceplot ];
Show[GraphicsArray[ { surfaceplot, contourplot } ]];
```

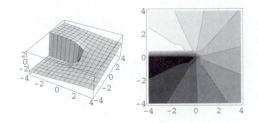

In the first example, the surface is quite smooth, but the contour plot reveals the structure better. In the second example, the abrupt variation at the branch cut of Arg is shown quite clearly in the surface plot, but extreme change confuses the contour-finding algorithm. The conclusion seems to be that surface plots and contour plots emphasize different features, and both are valuable.

We present one more example to show the usefulness of contour plots. Consider the functions $z = e^x y$ and $z = (y^2/2) - x$. It is easy to verify that the gradients of these functions are always orthogonal, indicating that the level curves of the two functions are families of orthogonal trajectories.

```
grad[f_] := { D[f,x], D[f,y] }
grad[ y Exp[x] ] . grad[ y^2/2 - x ]
```

```
0
```

It is nice to be able to see these families overlaid on the same graph. We use contour plots with ContourShading turned off and with different ContourStyle settings so that we can distinguish the two families.

```
gr1 = ContourPlot[ y Exp[x], {x,0,4}, {y,-2,2}, DisplayFunction->Identity,
        ContourStyle->GrayLevel[.6], ContourShading->False ];
gr2 = ContourPlot[ y^2/2 - x, {x,0,4}, {y,-2,2}, DisplayFunction->Identity,
        ContourStyle->Dashing[{.02,.02}], ContourShading->False ];
Show[ gr1, gr2, DisplayFunction->$DisplayFunction ];
```

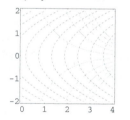

4.3.2 DensityPlot

The DensityPlot command makes a plot of the values of a function at a regular array of points. DensityPlot generates a grid and shades it according to the values of the function; in the default shading, black is used for small values, white for large values. The template for DensityPlot is:

$$\text{DensityPlot[} expression, \ interval1, \ interval2, \ options \text{]}$$

Here is an example of DensityPlot:

```
DensityPlot[ Sin[x^2 - y^2], {x,-1,3}, {y,-2,2} ];
```

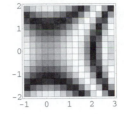

Like `Plot3D` and `ContourPlot`, `DensityPlot` accepts the `PlotPoints` option to specify how fine a grid should be used in sampling the function being plotted.

```
Block[ { $DisplayFunction = Identity },
    gr1 = DensityPlot[ Sin[x^2 - y^2], {x,-1,3}, {y,-2,2}, PlotPoints->25 ];
    gr2 = DensityPlot[ Sin[x^2 - y^2], {x,-1,3}, {y,-2,2}, PlotPoints->{25,50} ];  ];
Show[GraphicsArray[ { gr1, gr2 } ]];
```

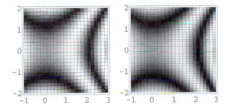

A density plot is similar to the graph produced by `Plot3D` with `Lighting` set to `False` and `ViewPoint` set to a point directly above the center of the surface. However, in `Plot3D` a 15-by-15 grid produces a 14-by-14 array of polygons, with the color of each polygon determined by the average of the function values at the corners. In a `DensityPlot`, the grid points determine shading directly, so a 15-by-15 array of sample points produces a 15-by-15 grid. The shading in a density plot is also similar to the shading between contours in a contour plot, but no attempt is made to shape the shaded regions to match the level curves of the function being plotted. Finally, a density plot is also similar to a `Raster` object, in that it is an array of cells with which values are associated, with the values interpreted as colors. The difference between the two is that the values of the cells in a `Raster` object are given directly by the entries in an array (which may be arbitrary numbers, produced by a process such as scanning a photograph) whereas the values in a density plot are computed by a function.

A graph produced by `DensityPlot` has two essential components: the mesh of lines that separate the cells and the shading function that interprets the cell values as colors. Therefore only a few options are needed to control the appearance of a density plot: `Mesh` can be set to `True` or `False` to turn the mesh lines on or off, `MeshStyle` can be set to a list of style attributes to specify the appearance of the mesh lines, and `ColorFunction` can be set to a function that computes colors from cell values. Here are some examples:

```
Block[ { $DisplayFunction = Identity },
    gr1 = DensityPlot[ Sin[x^2 - y^2], {x,-1,3}, {y,-2,2} ];
    gr2 = Show[ gr1, Mesh -> False ];
    gr3 = Show[ gr1, MeshStyle -> {GrayLevel[.9]} ];
    gr4 = Show[ gr1, ColorFunction -> (GrayLevel[1-#]&) ];  ];
Show[GraphicsArray[ { gr1, gr2, gr3, gr4 } ]];
```

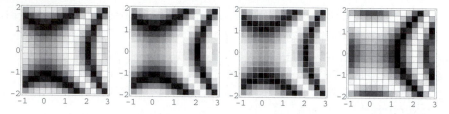

The first plot uses the default settings; the second has the mesh turned off; the third has the mesh restored but drawn in light gray instead of black; and the fourth has the normal shading reversed so that the highest points are black and the lowest are white.

There is a tradeoff between a shaded contour plot and a density plot representation of a function. If the function is smooth and the level curves are not too close together, a contour plot can show roughly the same amount of detail sampling at fewer points, but the cost of interpolation to find the contours must be considered. If the contours are irregular or too close together, sampling the function over a finer grid and using a density plot, without trying to find level curves by interpolation, is probably more reliable. A density plot can be very effective if it is computed over a fine enough grid. However, if you are using a large number of plot points (about 50 or more in either direction), you should either turn off the mesh lines or specify them to be very, very thin, because when the grid is very fine, the cells are quite small and the default thickness of the mesh lines may obscure or overwhelm the cells.

```
Block[ { $DisplayFunction = Identity },
    gr1 = DensityPlot[ Sin[x^2 - y^2], {x,-1,3}, {y,-2,2}, PlotPoints->75 ];
    gr2 = Show[ gr1, Mesh -> False ]; ];
Show[GraphicsArray[ { gr1, gr2 } ]];
```

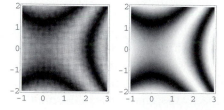

In addition to the options already mentioned that are specific to density plots, DensityPlot also accepts standard graphics options such as AspectRatio and PlotLabel. Here is a complete list of the options accepted by DensityPlot, with their defaults:

Options[DensityPlot]

```
{AspectRatio -> 1, Axes -> False, AxesLabel -> None, AxesStyle -> Automatic,
  Background -> Automatic, ColorFunction -> Automatic, ColorOutput -> Automatic,
  Compiled -> True, DefaultColor -> Automatic, Epilog -> {}, Frame -> True,
  FrameLabel -> None, FrameStyle -> Automatic, FrameTicks -> Automatic, Mesh -> True,
  MeshStyle -> Automatic, PlotLabel -> None, PlotPoints -> 15, PlotRange -> Automatic,
  PlotRegion -> Automatic, Prolog -> {}, RotateLabel -> True, Ticks -> Automatic,
  DefaultFont :> $DefaultFont, DisplayFunction :> $DisplayFunction}
```

These options are explained in detail in Chapter 7.

4.4 Plotting Data Sets: The ListPlot Functions

Functions that have the words List and Plot in their names are for plotting data. You supply data in a list (or an array), and these functions plot the values. You can generate the data within *Mathematica*, or you can use Read or ReadList to import data from a file created by another program. Common sources of data to be plotted by *Mathematica* include data acquisition software that monitors testing instruments in a laboratory, CAD/CAM software, and spreadsheets and databases.

This table lists the most important data plotting commands *Mathematica* provides:

Command	Similar to	Description
ListPlot	Plot, ParametricPlot	plots a list of data in two dimensions
ListPlot3D	Plot3D	plots a surface representing an array of heights
ListContourPlot	ContourPlot	generates a contour plot from an array of values
ListDensityPlot	DensityPlot	generates a density plot from an array of values
ListSurfacePlot3D	ParametricPlot3D	plots a surface through an array of points in space (see page 166)
ScatterPlot3D	PointParametricPlot3D	plots points in three dimensions (see page 166)

The first four commands in the table are built into *Mathematica* and are described in this chapter. The other two, ListSurfacePlot3D and ScatterPlot3D, are defined in packages distributed with *Mathematica* and are described in Chapter 5 on pages 167 and 165. This table mentions only the most basic functions; many other special-purpose data-plotting functions for producing bar charts, pie charts, labeled list plots, and other data graphics are also defined in packages.

4.4.1 ListPlot

As you saw in Chapter 3, you can plot points "from scratch" by constructing a Graphics object that contains Point primitives. There is usually no need to do so, however, because the function ListPlot is specifically designed for plotting data. The argument to ListPlot can be a list of values, in which case the x coordinates for the points are taken to be 1, 2, ...

$$\text{ListPlot}[\ \{y_1,\ y_2,\ y_3,\ \ldots\},\ options\ ]$$

The argument to ListPlot can also be a list of pairs of values, with both x and y coordinates specified explicitly.

$$\text{ListPlot}[\ \{\ \{x_1,\ f[x_1]\},\ \{x_2,\ f[x_2]\},\ \ldots\ \},\ options\ ]$$

ListPlot constructs a Graphics object to represent a list of points in exactly the same way that Plot and ParametricPlot do. The only difference is that Plot and ParametricPlot use *Mathematica*'s adaptive sampler with one or two functions to obtain a set of points to plot, whereas ListPlot simply plots the points you give it.

The following table shows the U.S. public debt in millions of dollars for the past 20 years:

Year	$ in millions
1970	370,094
1975	533,189
1980	907,701
1985	1,823,103
1990	3,233,313

Let's plot this information. The option setting Frame->True produces a framed plot with axes drawn along the edges instead of through the middle of the data.

```
ListPlot[ {370094, 533189, 907701, 1823103, 3233313},
        Frame->True, PlotLabel->"   US National Debt\nin Millions of Dollars" ];
```

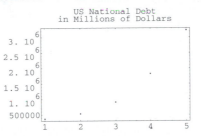

Because we did not specify the years, *Mathematica* plots the data with x values 1, 2, 3, ... If we gave pairs of values, the x axis would indicate the year in which the national debt reached a particular level. To make the points more visible, you can connect or enlarge them. With the option PlotJoined set to True, ListPlot draws straight lines connecting the points but does not draw the points; when PlotJoined is False (the default), ListPlot plots the points but does not connect them. You can use the PlotStyle option to specify the appearance of the points or lines that ListPlot plots. In the plot at the right, we use PlotStyle to draw the points 10 times larger than the default size, 0.004.

```
Block[ {$DisplayFunction = Identity},
    gr1 = ListPlot[{ {1970,370094}, {1975,533189}, {1980,907701}, {1985,1823103},
            {1990,3233313} }, PlotJoined->True, Frame->True,
            PlotLabel->"US National Debt", FrameLabel->{"Year","Millions of $"} ];
    gr2 = ListPlot[{ {1970,370094}, {1975,533189}, {1980,907701}, {1985,1823103},
            {1990,3233313} }, PlotStyle->PointSize[0.04], Frame->True,
            PlotLabel->"US National Debt", FrameLabel->{"Year","Millions of $"} ];  ];
Show[GraphicsArray[ { gr1, gr2 } ]];
```

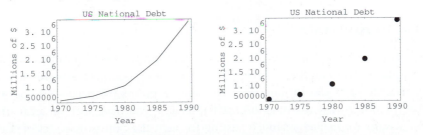

If you want to show the points *and* the lines, you can plot the data twice, first with PlotJoined set each way and then with Show to combine the plots:

Show[gr1, gr2];

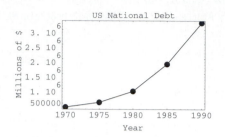

In the examples, we have concentrated on the options that are specific to the function-ality of ListPlot, namely, PlotJoined and PlotStyle. Since ListPlot constructs Graphics objects, it also accepts any options that Graphics objects accept—settings for axes, tick marks, grid lines, plot range, aspect ratio, background color, and so on. Here is a complete list of the options you can use with ListPlot, with their default values:

Options[ListPlot]

```
                        1
{AspectRatio -> -----------, Axes -> Automatic, AxesLabel -> None,
                GoldenRatio
  AxesOrigin -> Automatic, AxesStyle -> Automatic,
  Background -> Automatic, ColorOutput -> Automatic,
  DefaultColor -> Automatic, Epilog -> {}, Frame -> False,
  FrameLabel -> None, FrameStyle -> Automatic, FrameTicks -> Automatic,
  GridLines -> None, PlotJoined -> False, PlotLabel -> None,
  PlotRange -> Automatic, PlotRegion -> Automatic, PlotStyle -> Automatic,
  Prolog -> {}, RotateLabel -> True, Ticks -> Automatic,
  DefaultFont :> $DefaultFont, DisplayFunction :> $DisplayFunction}
```

See Chapter 7 for complete explanations of these options.

4.4.2   ListPlot3D

The function ListPlot3D accepts a two-dimensional array of real numbers and displays it as a surface. This is not what many *Mathematica* users expect or want. If you have a list or array of triples of numbers, representing points in space, and you want to display the points, use the function ScatterPlot3D. If you have such an array of triples and you want to display a surface passing through the points, use ListSurfacePlot3D. Both functions are defined in packages that are distributed with *Mathematica* and are described in Section 5.2.4 on page 165.

The function ListPlot3D generates a surface in three dimensions specified by an array of heights or z coordinates. The array is given as the first argument to ListPlot3D;

it must have the form of a list of lists of numerical expressions (as defined on page 81), with all the sublists having the same number of elements.

The basic form for ListPlot3D is

ListPlot3D[*array of heights, options*]

ListPlot3D generates a SurfaceGraphics object; in Version 2.0 and earlier versions, such objects required an *array of heights* of dimensions at least 4 by 4.

The values in the *array of heights* specify the heights at the vertices of the polygons that form the surface. The mesh lines that run across the surface form a rectangular grid in the xy plane; each row of the *array of heights* specifies the heights of the surface as you move along one of the horizontal lines of this grid, and each column specifies the heights along one of the vertical lines. Here is an example:

```
zvalues = {  {1,2,3,4,5},
             {3,6,4,5,3},
             {2,5,5,6,1},
             {4,7,6,7,6}  };
gr1 = ListPlot3D[ zvalues, DisplayFunction->Identity ];
gr2 = Show[gr1,PlotRegion->{{-.2,3},{-.5,1.8}}, DefaultFont->{"Courier",8},
        Epilog->{ Text["A",{.06,.35}], Text["B",{.16,.335}],
               Text["C",{.17,.505}], Text["D",{.25,.53}]} ];
Show[GraphicsArray[{gr1,gr2}]];
```

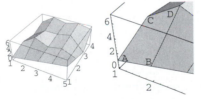

On the left, we have displayed the entire plot; on the right, we have used the PlotRegion option to zoom in on the polygons in the lower left corner of the surface. We have labeled the corners of this polygon A, B, C, and D for reference. The z coordinate of point A is the value specified by the entry in row 1, column 1 of the array zvalues, which is 1. The z coordinate of point B is given by the entry in row 1, column 2, which is 2. Likewise, the z coordinates at C and D are given by the entries in row 2, columns 1 and 2, which are 3 and 6. The other polygons in the surface are specified in similar fashion, each four adjacent values in the array zvalues specifying one polygon.

When you use ListPlot3D as just described, the surface is shaded according to simulated illumination, just as it is with Plot3D. You can also call ListPlot3D with an additional argument that explicitly specifies how the surface it plots is to be shaded. This argument should be an array of color specifications (GrayLevel, RGBColor, CMYKColor, or Hue) specifying a color for each polygonal patch on the surface. The form is

ListPlot3D[*array of heights*, *array of shades*, *options*]

Since an m-by-n array of points defines an $(m - 1)$-by-$(n - 1)$ array of quadrilaterals, the size of the *array of shades* should be one less than the size of the *array of heights* in each dimension. Here is an example:

```
c = {  { .1, .3, .5, .7 },
       { .3, .5, .7, .1 },
       { .5, .7, .1, .3}  };
ListPlot3D[ zvalues, Map[ GrayLevel, c, {2} ] ];
```

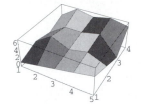

Surface shading is controlled by the Lighting option, however. When this option is set to True, the default, a surface plotted by ListPlot3D is colored by an explicit shading array if one was given, and by simulated illumination otherwise. If the Lighting option is set to False, the surface is colored according to the function specified by the ColorFunction option; if a shading array is given, it is ignored. The default ColorFunction colors the surface with gray levels by height: The shade of each polygon is determined by the average of the z values at its corners, with lower polygons shaded darker and higher ones shaded lighter.

ListPlot3D is actually a simple-minded constructor for SurfaceGraphics objects; it takes the data that define a SurfaceGraphics object as argument and wraps the head SurfaceGraphics around them. ListPlot3D accepts exactly the same options that SurfaceGraphics accepts; the only difference is that the default setting of Axes is False for SurfaceGraphics and True for ListPlot3D. Here are the options and their default settings:

Options[ListPlot3D]

```
{AmbientLight -> GrayLevel[0], AspectRatio -> Automatic, Axes -> True,
  AxesEdge -> Automatic, AxesLabel -> None, AxesStyle -> Automatic,
  Background -> Automatic, Boxed -> True, BoxRatios -> {1, 1, 0.4},
  BoxStyle -> Automatic, ClipFill -> Automatic, ColorFunction -> Automatic,
  ColorOutput -> Automatic, DefaultColor -> Automatic, Epilog -> {},
  FaceGrids -> None, HiddenSurface -> True, Lighting -> True,
```

```
LightSources ->
 {{{1., 0., 1.}, RGBColor[1, 0, 0]}, {{1., 1., 1.}, RGBColor[0, 1, 0]},
  {{0., 1., 1.}, RGBColor[0, 0, 1]}}, Mesh -> True,
 MeshRange -> Automatic, MeshStyle -> Automatic, PlotLabel -> None,
 PlotRange -> Automatic, PlotRegion -> Automatic,
 Plot3Matrix -> Automatic, Prolog -> {}, Shading -> True,
 SphericalRegion -> False, Ticks -> Automatic, ViewCenter -> Automatic,
 ViewPoint -> {1.3, -2.4, 2.}, ViewVertical -> {0., 0., 1.},
 DefaultFont :> $DefaultFont, DisplayFunction :> $DisplayFunction}
```

These options are explained in Chapter 7. Examples of the most commonly used options were given in Section 4.2.1 (page 102) on Plot3D.

4.4.3 ListContourPlot and ListDensityPlot

The command ListContourPlot takes a two-dimensional array of numerical expressions (as defined on page 81) and generates a contour plot, which, by default, is shaded so that the lighter regions represent higher values. The command ListDensityPlot accepts the same argument, but generates a density plot. As with ListContourPlot, the shade of a region is based on the height.

ListContourPlot[array, options]

ListDensityPlot[array, options]

```
array = Table[ Sin[x^2-y^2], {y,-2,2,.2}, {x,-1,3,.2} ];
gr1 = ListContourPlot[ array, DisplayFunction->Identity ];
gr2 = ListDensityPlot[ array, DisplayFunction->Identity ];
Show[GraphicsArray[ { gr1, gr2 } ]];
```

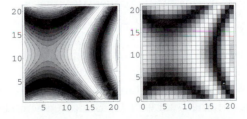

The commands ListContourPlot and ListDensityPlot construct ContourGraphics and DensityGraphics objects. They accept all the same options with the same default settings.

`Options[ListContourPlot]`

```
{AspectRatio -> 1, Axes -> False, AxesLabel -> None, AxesOrigin -> Automatic,
  AxesStyle -> Automatic, Background -> Automatic, ColorFunction -> Automatic,
  ColorOutput -> Automatic, ContourLines -> True, Contours -> 10, ContourShading -> True,
  ContourSmoothing -> True, ContourStyle -> Automatic, DefaultColor -> Automatic,
  Epilog -> {}, Frame -> True, FrameLabel -> None, FrameStyle -> Automatic,
  FrameTicks -> Automatic, MeshRange -> Automatic, PlotLabel -> None,
  PlotRange -> Automatic, PlotRegion -> Automatic, Prolog -> {}, RotateLabel -> True,
  Ticks -> Automatic, DefaultFont :> $DefaultFont, DisplayFunction :> $DisplayFunction}
```

`Options[ListDensityPlot]`

```
{AspectRatio -> 1, Axes -> False, AxesLabel -> None, AxesOrigin -> Automatic,
  AxesStyle -> Automatic, Background -> Automatic, ColorFunction -> Automatic,
  ColorOutput -> Automatic, DefaultColor -> Automatic, Epilog -> {}, Frame -> True,
  FrameLabel -> None, FrameStyle -> Automatic, FrameTicks -> Automatic, Mesh -> True,
  MeshRange -> Automatic, MeshStyle -> Automatic, PlotLabel -> None,
  PlotRange -> Automatic, PlotRegion -> Automatic, Prolog -> {}, RotateLabel -> True,
  Ticks -> Automatic, DefaultFont :> $DefaultFont, DisplayFunction :> $DisplayFunction}
```

Refer to Sections 4.3.1 (page 114) and 4.3.2 (page 118) on ContourPlot and DensityPlot, respectively, for examples of how to use these options, and to Chapter 7 and Section 7.5.4 on page 274 for detailed explanations.

4.5 Summary

Mathematica makes it easy to produce graphs of expressions representing functions, such as $f(x)$, or parametrized curves where the values of x and y are specified in terms of another variable, such as t or time. *Mathematica* makes many decisions to help you produce aesthetically pleasing, reasonably accurate pictures. There will be times, however, when you do not like the way a graph appears. This chapter has described how *Mathematica* determines what to draw and has introduced several options you can specify to change the image *Mathematica* produces.

In this chapter, we have reviewed all of the graphics-building functions that are built into *Mathematica*'s kernel. But we have come nowhere near the limits of what *Mathematica* can do, because, in addition to these functions, you can write programs to create graphics. *Mathematica*'s programming language is powerful, so simple programs can generate sophisticated graphics. In Chapter 5, we will cover the programs that WRI provides with *Mathematica* in the form of program libraries (or "packages," in *Mathematica* jargon) that can be loaded into *Mathematica* to extend its capabilities.

Chapter 5

Graphics Packages

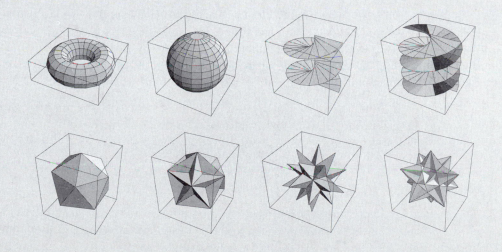

One of *Mathematica*'s virtues is its extensibility. Wolfram Research has used *Mathematica*'s own programming language to define specialized functions — such as BarChart, LabeledListPlot, MultipleListPlot, PlotVectorField3D, and RotateShape — that aren't directly supported by the built-in operations in the *Mathematica* kernel. The definitions of these functions are stored in *packages*. Each package usually contains definitions for several related functions that address a single topic, such as linear regression or combinatorics. About 130 packages are distributed with Version 2 of *Mathematica*, covering areas such as algebra, calculus, discrete mathematics, geometry, graphics, linear algebra, number theory, numerical mathematics, and statistics. For a complete list of the packages distributed with *Mathematica*, see the technical report *Guide to Standard Mathematica Packages* or the *Mathematica Quick Reference* (listed in "Suggested Readings" on page 327). This chapter describes how to load a package, explains the mechanism of contexts used in packages, and illustrates some of the functions available in the graphics packages.

5.1 Working with Packages

5.1.1 Loading a Package

Before you can use a function defined in a package, you must load the package. When you load a package, *Mathematica* reads the file containing the package and executes the code that defines that package's functions. One way to load a package is to use the command Get["*filename* "] or, equivalently, the abbreviation <<*filename*. Here the *filename* is the name of the file containing the package code. *Mathematica* looks for a file of this name in each of several directories and loads the first one it finds. If no such file is found, you get an error message:

```
<< NoFileHasThisName
```

```
Get::noopen: Can't open NoFileHasThisName.
```

```
$Failed
```

The variable $Path specifies the directories *Mathematica* is to search when you use Get to load a package. The value of $Path should be a list of directory names (stored as strings). The directories that are on the search path vary from machine to machine. Here is the value of $Path in Version 2.2 of *Mathematica* for NeXT computers:

`$Path`

```
{., ~, ~/Library/Mathematica/Packages,
  /LocalApps/Mathematica22.app/Library/Mathematica/Packages,
  /LocalLibrary/Mathematica/Packages, /LocalApps/Mathematica22.app/Install/Preload,
  /LocalApps/Mathematica22.app/StartUp}
```

A better way to load a package is to use the command `Needs["`*packagename* `"]`. The *packagename* is the name of the package in *Mathematica's* naming system, which is explained in the next section. The `Needs` command first checks if the package has already been loaded. If it has, `Needs` does nothing; otherwise, it translates *Mathematica's* name for the package into an appropriate file name, and then calls `Get` with that file name to load the package. (In recent versions of *Mathematica*, `Get` has been extended to recognize *Mathematica's* package naming system for itself; however, `Get` is still not completely equivalent to `Needs`, because `Needs` will not re-load a package that has already been loaded, and `Get` will.)

Once a package has been loaded, its functions behave as if they were built-in features of *Mathematica*. For example, the package named `Graphics`ImplicitPlot`` contains the definition of the function `ImplicitPlot`, which plots functions defined implicitly by equations. To load the package, you give the command

```
Needs["Graphics`ImplicitPlot`"]
```

Once the package is loaded, you can use `ImplicitPlot` as you would any of *Mathematica's* built-in plotting functions.

```
ImplicitPlot[ (x^2 + y^2)^2 == (x^2 - y^2), {x, -2, 2} ];
```

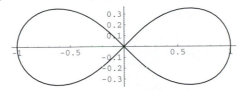

The curve defined by this equation is called a *lemniscate*.

If a particular package contains functions you expect to use frequently, you may want to have the package loaded automatically whenever you start up *Mathematica*. You can do this by adding the appropriate `<<` or `Needs` command to the file `init.m`, which is in the directory (or folder) named `StartUp` or in your home directory if you use a UNIX-based system. *Mathematica* reads this file when a new session is started.

After you have loaded a package, you might want to unload it later to free up the memory occupied by the package definitions. However, there is no practical way to do this short of restarting *Mathematica*.

5.1.2 Package Names

Because many packages are distributed with *Mathematica*, they are organized into groups by application area. All of the graphics packages, for example, have names beginning with `Graphics\``, and they are stored in a directory (or folder) called `Graphics`. The `Graphics` directory itself is stored in *Mathematica*'s main `Packages` directory.

By convention, the name of the file containing a package is the same as the name of the package, with `.m` as a suffix or extension. The package `Graphics\`Legend\`` on a UNIX computer, for example, is stored in the file `Graphics/Legend.m`. The following are names of other packages and the files in which they are contained:

Package Name	Directory and File Name
Graphics\`Graphics3D\`	Graphics/Graphics3D.m
Graphics\`Shapes\`	Graphics/Shapes.m
Geometry\`Polytopes\`	Geometry/Polytopes.m

In non-UNIX operating systems, the syntax for naming files and directories or folders is different. On Macintosh computers, for example, the file containing the package `Graphics\`Legend\`` is called `:Graphics:Legend.m`, and on MS-DOS, it is called `GRAPHICS\LEGEND.M`. Because of this variation, *Mathematica* has its own naming scheme for packages; that way, *Mathematica* code can be written the same way for all implementations (i.e., it is portable), with each version of *Mathematica* responsible for translating the machine-independent form of the name into the appropriate file name. The machine-independent form is expressed in terms of *contexts*. The function that performs this translation is `ContextToFilename`; it is used by the `Needs` command to translate package names into file names for loading by `Get`. Here is an example showing the result returned on a UNIX computer:

```
ContextToFilename["Graphics`Shapes`"]
```

```
Graphics/Shapes.m
```

5.1.3 Context

Consider the following scenario. You are at a party and a friend wants to introduce you to someone. Your friend tells his son to go get Stephen. His son returns with Stephen Jay Gould, though your friend wanted to introduce you to Stephen Wolfram. Your friend could have avoided this mishap by giving the full name of the Stephen he wanted you to meet.

Mathematica packages can use the same name to refer to different objects. Just like Messrs. Gould and Wolfram, every *Mathematica* object has a short name and a full name. You can avoid any possibility of confusion by using the full name of the object you want.

Mathematica uses the mechanism of *contexts* to avoid conflicts between names of symbols. The full name of a symbol is made up of a context and a short name. Names and contexts are separated by the grave accent or back quote (`). For example, a symbol whose short name is Faces is defined in the package Polytopes in the directory Geometry; its full name is Geometry`Polytopes`Faces, and its context is Geometry`Polytopes`. Another symbol, also named Faces, is defined in the package Graphics`Polyhedra`. Its full name is Graphics`Polyhedra`Faces.

Since the packages Geometry`Polytopes` and Graphics`Polyhedra` both contain definitions for the symbol Faces, *Mathematica* warns us about the multiple definitions when we load both packages, as shown here. (To save space, we have deleted the warning messages that *Mathematica* prints for other redefined symbols.)

```
Needs["Geometry`Polytopes`"];
Needs["Graphics`Polyhedra`"];
```

```
Faces::shdw: Warning: Symbol Faces appears in multiple contexts
    {Graphics`Polyhedra`, Geometry`Polytopes`}; definitions in context Graphics`Polyhedra`
    may shadow or be shadowed by other definitions.
```

Contexts are like rooms in a house. Related items are stored in the same room. If you are familiar with computers and file systems, you may also find it helpful to think of a context as a directory in UNIX or as a folder on a Macintosh. Like directories or folders, contexts can be nested.

After the package Graphics`Polyhedra` is loaded, the corresponding context contains definitions that create polyhedra.

```
?Graphics`Polyhedra`*
```

Cube	GreatStellatedDodecahedron	Polyhedron
Dodecahedron	Hexahedron	SmallStellatedDodecahedron
Faces	Icosahedron	Stellate
Geodesate	Octahedron	Tetrahedron
GreatDodecahedron	OpenTruncate	Truncate
GreatIcosahedron	Polyhedra	Vertices

The function Context gives the context in which a symbol resides.

```
{ Context[Octahedron], Context[ImplicitPlot] }
```

```
{Graphics`Polyhedra`, Graphics`ImplicitPlot`}
```

The context System` contains all the built-in objects.

```
{ Context[Plot], Context[Point], Context[Show] }
```

```
{System`, System`, System`}
```

▪ The Current Context and the Default Context

Mathematica has a notion of a "current" context, which is where your work is currently being performed. When you create a new symbol, *Mathematica* places it in the current context, unless you explicitly specify a different one. When you start *Mathematica*, the current context is the default context, `Global`` ``. You can always find out which context is current by examining the variable `$Context`.

The default context is analogous to the entry hall of a house or the home directory in UNIX — it is where you are when you first open the front door or log in to a system. The current context is analogous to the current directory in UNIX or to the active folder on a Macintosh, which is the directory or folder where files are created if none is explicitly specified.

The following example shows how new symbols are placed in contexts:

```
{ $Context, Context[myNewSymbol], Context[OtherContext`myOtherNewSymbol] }
```

```
{Global`, Global`, OtherContext`}
```

The value of `$Context` is `Global`` ``, indicating that `Global`` `` is our current context. We did not specify a context for the symbol `myNewSymbol`, so it was created in the default context `Global`` ``. The symbol `myOtherNewSymbol` was created in the context `OtherContext`` `` because we explicitly specified that context.

▪ Where to Look for Symbols

If you specify the full name of a symbol, including an explicit context, *Mathematica* looks for that symbol in that context, and creates it if it does not already exist. However, we usually refer to symbols by their short names, and we have seen that two different symbols can have the same short name, if they reside in different contexts. How does *Mathematica* know which one you mean, if you specify the short name only? *Mathematica* first looks for the symbol in the current context; if the symbol is not defined there, *Mathematica* searches other contexts. The variable `$ContextPath` specifies the contexts in which to search for a symbol that is not defined in the current context. *Mathematica* searches the contexts in `$ContextPath` in the order in which they are listed; if it gets to the end of the list without finding the symbol, it assumes you intended to create a new symbol, which it places in the current context (as explained earlier). `$ContextPath` is like the environment variable `$PATH` in UNIX, which specifies the directories in which to search for a file whose directory is not explicitly given.

When you start *Mathematica*, `$ContextPath` is set to include the contexts `Global`` `` and `System`` ``. When you load a package, its context is automatically added to the beginning of the context path; otherwise you would have to specify the context explicitly each time you wanted to refer to a symbol defined in the package. In this example, the contexts

Graphics`Polyhedra`, Geometry`Polytopes`, and Graphics`ImplicitPlot` were prepended to the $ContextPath when we loaded the corresponding packages.

$ContextPath

{Graphics`Polyhedra`, Geometry`Polytopes`, Graphics`ImplicitPlot`,
  Utilities`FilterOptions`, Global`, System`}

We did not load the package Utilities`FilterOptions` explicitly; it was loaded for us by one of the other packages.

As we saw earlier, the packages Graphics`Polyhedra` and Geometry`Polytopes` both define a symbol named Faces. If we request information on Faces, we obtain the usage statement specified in the package Graphics`Polyhedra`, since it is ahead of Geometry`Polytopes` in the context path.

?Faces

Faces[name] gives a list of the faces for the named solid. Each face is a list of the
  numbers of the vertices that comprise that face.

The variable $Packages keeps track of the contexts of the packages that have been loaded in the current session.

$Packages

{Graphics`Polyhedra`, Geometry`Polytopes`, Utilities`FilterOptions`,
  Graphics`ImplicitPlot`, Global`, System`}

At first glance, you might think that the variables $ContextPath and $Packages are redundant, but they are not: you can add a context to the context path without loading a package, and not every package creates its own separate context.

5.1.4 Forgetting to Load a Package

If you use a function before loading the package in which the function is defined, *Mathematica* cannot evaluate the function.

PlotVectorField[{Cos[y], Sin[x]}, {x, 0, 2 Pi}, {y, 0, 2 Pi}, PlotPoints->20]

PlotVectorField[{Cos[y], Sin[x]}, {x, 0, 2 Pi}, {y, 0, 2 Pi}, PlotPoints -> 20]

Mathematica doesn't display the vector field because we didn't load the package Graphics`PlotField`. Since *Mathematica* doesn't know about the command PlotVectorField, it creates the symbol PlotVectorField in the current context (Global`). When we ask about PlotVectorField, *Mathematica* doesn't return a usage statement, but indicates that there is a symbol named PlotVectorField in the Global` context.

```
?PlotVectorField
```

```
Global`PlotVectorField
```

If we now load the package, *Mathematica* prints a message warning us that the symbol we created when we called PlotVectorField may block us from accessing the definition in the package.

```
Needs["Graphics`PlotField`"];
```

```
PlotVectorField::shdw:
    Warning: Symbol PlotVectorField appears in multiple contexts
    {Graphics`PlotField`, Global`}; definitions in context Graphics`PlotField`
      may shadow or be shadowed by other definitions.
```

Even though we loaded the package, when we ask for information on PlotVectorField, we are not shown the usage statement specified in the package. Instead, we access the symbol PlotVectorField that was created when we first called PlotVectorField, because *Mathematica* searches for the symbol in the current context before checking the definitions in other contexts.

```
?PlotVectorField
```

```
Global`PlotVectorField
```

One way to access the function is to specify its full name.

```
?Graphics`PlotField`PlotVectorField
```

```
PlotVectorField[f, {x, x0, x1, (xu)}, {y, y0, y1, (yu)}, (options)] produces a vector
    field plot of the two-dimensional vector function f.
```

A better approach is to Remove the symbol PlotVectorField from the current context, since that symbol was created by mistake anyway.

```
Remove[PlotVectorField]
```

This Remove command removes the symbol PlotVectorField that was in the context Global`, so that symbol no longer hides the one defined by the package. Now we can see the usage statement and plot a vector field using the function PlotVectorField.

```
?PlotVectorField
```

```
PlotVectorField[f, {x, x0, x1, (xu)}, {y, y0, y1, (yu)}, (options)] produces a vector
    field plot of the two-dimensional vector function f.
```

```
PlotVectorField[{Cos[y], Sin[x]}, {x, 0, 2 Pi}, {y, 0, 2 Pi}, PlotPoints->20 ];
```

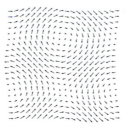

Of course, if you want to use a certain package every time you run *Mathematica*, you can have the package loaded automatically when *Mathematica* starts up, as explained in Section 5.1.1 on page 130. Then you won't have to remember to load the package yourself and the problems described in this section won't occur.

5.1.5 Master Packages

If you expect to use functions from several different packages in a directory, you may find it convenient to load a master package for that directory. This master declares all the names of all the functions in all the packages in that directory, but does not actually load any of the packages. When you use a function declared by the master package, the package containing that function is loaded if it has not been loaded already. Because *Mathematica* automatically reads in the packages as they are needed, you get both convenience and efficiency: The function names are all available as if the packages had all been loaded, yet no memory is taken up by a package until a function in the package is used.

Each directory of packages distributed with *Mathematica* contains a master package named Master`. For example, once you load the package Graphics`Master` you may use any of the functions defined in any of the Graphics packages.

```
Needs["Graphics`Master`"];
```

After this Needs statement is executed, the variable $ContextPath is updated to include all the names of the Graphics packages. However, a package is not added to the $Packages list until you call a function defined in that package—the package is not actually loaded before then.

The package Graphics`Colors` contains definitions of color names in terms of RGBColor. Once you load the master package for the graphics directory, you can use these names without having to give a separate command to read in the package Graphics`Colors`. Here we print just a few of these names; we deleted the others because the list was huge.

```
?Graphics`Colors`*
```

AliceBlue	DarkSlateBlue	Linen	SeaGreen
AlizarinCrimson	DarkSlateGray	MadderLakeDeep	SeaGreenDark
AllColors	DarkTurquoise	Magenta	SeaGreenLight
Antique	DeepOchre	ManganeseBlue	SeaGreenMedium
Aquamarine	DeepPink	Maroon	Seashell
AquamarineMedium	DimGray	MarsOrange	Sepia
AureolineYellow	DodgerBlue	MarsYellow	Sienna
Azure	Eggshell	Melon	SkyBlue
Banana	EmeraldGreen	MidnightBlue	SkyBlueDeep
Beige	EnglishRed	Mint	SkyBlueLight

These symbols are essentially aliases or shorthand notations for calls to RGBColor. If you ask for online help for one of these symbols, *Mathematica* can't give it to you because the package isn't loaded until one of its symbols is evaluated in an expression.

```
?Turquoise
```

Graphics`Colors`Turquoise

Attributes[Turquoise] = {Stub}

The Stub attribute displayed here is *Mathematica*'s way of indicating that a symbol is defined in a package that has not yet been loaded. *Mathematica* loads the package that defines a Stub symbol when the symbol is used in a way that calls for its value. (Asking for a usage message doesn't call for a value, but using the symbol in an expression does.) The package *Mathematica* loads is the one that is associated with the symbol's context. In this example, the symbol Turquoise resides in the context Graphics`Colors`, so *Mathematica* loads the package Graphics`Colors` to obtain the definition of Turquoise.

```
Turquoise
```

RGBColor[0.250999, 0.878399, 0.815699]

Now that the package containing Turquoise has been loaded, you can receive on-line help.

```
?Turquoise
```

Turquoise is a color given in the RGBColor system.

Of course, loading the package defined all the colors, not just Turquoise.

```
?Firebrick
```

Firebrick is a color given in the RGBColor system.

A master package uses DeclarePackage to tell *Mathematica* which symbols a package defines. If you look in the package Graphics`Master`, you will see a call to DeclarePackage informing *Mathematica* that the package Graphics`Colors` defines Aquamarine, Black, Blue, and other colors. Here are the first few lines of the DeclarePackage statement for Graphics`Colors` in the graphics master package:

```
DeclarePackage["Graphics`Colors`",
    {"AliceBlue", "AlizarinCrimson", "AllColors", "Antique", "Aquamarine",
     "AquamarineMedium", "AureolineYellow", "Azure", "Banana", "Beige",
     "Bisque", "Black", "BlanchedAlmond", "Blue", "BlueLight", "BlueMedium",
     "BlueViolet", "Brick", "Brown", "BrownOadder", "BrownOchre", "Burlywood",
     "BurntSienna", "BurntUmber", "Cadet", "CadmiumLemon", "CadmiumOrange",
     "CadmiumRedDeep", "CadmiumRedLight", "CadmiumYellow", "CadmiumYellowLight",
     "Carrot", "Cerulean", "Chartreuse", "Chocolate", "ChromeOxideGreen",
     "CinnabarGreen", "CMYColor", "Cobalt", "CobaltGreen", "CobaltVioletDeep",
     "ColdGray", "Coral", "CoralLight", "CornflowerBlue", "Cornsilk", "Cyan",
     "CyanWhite", "DarkOrange", "DeepOchre", "DeepPink", "DimGray", "DodgerBlue",
```

What happens when you call DeclarePackage? The context of the declared package is prepended to the context path, because the symbols in the package are stored in that context and we want them to be visible. However, DeclarePackage does not change the value of the environment variable $Packages, because the package has not yet been loaded. Look at the values of the variables $ContextPath and $Packages when we start a new session on a NeXT computer (the package FE` contains definitions used by the Notebook Front End):

$ContextPath

{Global`, System`}

$Packages

{FE`, Global`, System`}

See how these variables change after we call DeclarePackage:

```
DeclarePackage["Graphics`PlotField`",
  {"ListPlotVectorField", "MaxArrowLength", "PlotGradientField", "PlotHamiltonianField",
   "PlotPolyaField", "PlotVectorField", "ScaleFactor", "ScaleFunction"}];
```

$ContextPath

{Graphics`PlotField`, Graphics`Animation`, Global`, System`}

$Packages

{FE`, Global`, System`}

Later on, when one of the declared symbols is used, its Stub attribute tells *Mathematica* that the package defining that symbol needs to be loaded. *Mathematica* loads the package, which updates $Packages, thereby preventing the package from being loaded a second time.

▪ Making Your Own Master Packages

You can write your own master packages. For each package, create a file that declares the packages to be loaded when you call any of a specified list of symbols. In this example, we declare that the package Graphics`Spline` should be loaded when any of the following symbols are used: Bezier, CompositeBezier, Cubic, Spline, $SplineDots, SplineDots, $SplinePoints, and SplinePoints. We also declare that the package Statistics`NonlinearFit` should be loaded if any of the symbols LevenbergMarquardt, NonlinearFit, ShowProgress, and Weights are used.

```
DeclarePackage["Graphics`Spline`",
  { "Bezier", "CompositeBezier", "Cubic", "Spline", "$SplineDots", "SplineDots",
    "$SplinePoints", "SplinePoints" } ]
DeclarePackage["Statistics`NonlinearFit`",
  { "LevenbergMarquardt", "NonlinearFit", "ShowProgress", "Weights" } ]
```

Now put the file somewhere where you can load it conveniently—in one of the directories listed in the $Path environment variable, for example. Then load your package as you would any other *Mathematica* package, as explained in Section 5.1.1 on page 130.

If you use a Notebook Front End to create your master package in the form of a Notebook, make sure that any call to DeclarePackage is in an initialization cell. The contents of an initialization cell are evaluated when a Notebook is read with either << or Needs. To designate a cell as an initialization cell, select the initialization attribute from the Front End's Cell menu or Styles Inspector panel. (You should consult the manual that came with your version of *Mathematica* to learn how to do this, since it may be different in different Front Ends.)

5.2 A Sampling of Graphics Packages

Though you can draw anything you want with the graphics primitives built into *Mathematica*, you may not want to spend time figuring out how to draw a bar chart, add a legend to a plot, or draw three-dimensional vector fields. Don't worry. These functions and many more are available in packages distributed with *Mathematica*. The following table lists the packages distributed with Version 2.2 that contain functions for drawing graphics. To save space, we have listed the packages in three columns.

Directory	Packages		
DiscreteMath	Combinatorica.m	ComputationalGeometry.m	Tree.m
Examples	CellularAutomata.m	OptionUtilities.m	
Geometry	Polytopes.m	Rotations.m	
Graphics	Animation.m	Graphics.m	PlotField3D.m
	ArgColors.m	Graphics3D.m	Polyhedra.m
	Arrow.m	ImplicitPlot.m	Shapes.m
	Colors.m	Legend.m	Spline.m
	ComplexMap.m	MultipleListPlot.m	SurfaceOfRevolution.m
	ContourPlot3D.m	ParametricPlot3D.m	ThreeScript.m
	FilledPlot.m	PlotField.m	
Miscellaneous	WorldPlot.m		
ProgrammingExamples	BookPictures.m	SphericalCurve.m	
Utilities	DXF.m	FilterOptions.m	

This section presents examples of several functions listed in the table. Some of these examples may require a great deal of memory or take a long time to compute, especially those involving vector fields or three-dimensional surfaces. On some systems, you may want to restart *Mathematica* before running a large example to ensure that the maximum amount of memory is available. You will probably not be able to run all the examples in this section in a single *Mathematica* session on most computers.

Because it is easier to write a *Mathematica* package than to modify the *Mathematica* kernel, the commands defined in packages evolve much more quickly than do the parts of *Mathematica* graphics that are defined in the kernel. Wolfram Research introduces new packages and updates old ones with every release of *Mathematica*. Therefore we cannot promise that our descriptions are exhaustive; you may find packages on your system that are not discussed here. Consult the *Guide to Standard Mathematica Packages* that came with your copy of *Mathematica* for a complete list of currently available packages.

The rest of this chapter is divided into sections that organize the most commonly used graphics packages by functionality. Thus you may find functions from several different packages described in the same section, or you may find functions defined in the same package scattered across several sections. Since the *Guide to Standard Mathematica Packages* organizes functions by package, we feel it is more useful here to organize them into functional groups so you have another way to find them. For example, the package Graphics`Graphics` defines commands for drawing bar charts and pie charts, placing errors bars on data plots, combining graphics, and plotting functions or data using a log scale. We discuss these commands in different sections, but you will find them lumped together under Graphics`Graphics` in the *Guide to Standard Mathematica Packages*.

5.2.1 General Graphics Manipulations

▪ Colors

Mathematica provides several ways to specify a color. The built-in functions GrayLevel, RGBColor, CMYKColor, and Hue were discussed in Section 3.2.1 on page 40. The package Graphics`Colors` defines functions for specifying colors in other ways.

- CMYColor[c, m, y] represents a color in the CMY (cyan-magenta-yellow) system. It is basically the CMYK system without black generation; however, as implemented, it converts CMY colors to RGBColor specifications rather than to CMYKColor specifications.

- YIQColor[y, i, q] represents a color in the YIQ (NTSC video) system. This system is mathematically a linear transformation of the RGB system; that is, there is a fixed transformation matrix M such that the YIQ representation of a color can be obtained from its RGB representation by the multiplication of the RGB component vector by M, and the RGB representation can be obtained from the YIQ representation by multiplication by M^{-1}. The YIQ system is useful because it exploits the nonlinear responsiveness of the human eye. It apportions color information among the components so that the information used most by the eye, the overall light/dark value, is carried by the Y (luminance) component; the information about orange/cyan distinctions is carried by the I (in phase) component; and the remaining information is contained in the Q (quadrature) component. The Y information is all that is needed to generate a black-and-white image, and in fact, it is the only part of an NTSC video signal used by a black-and-white television. The I information distinguishes colors in the central range of human perception, and the Q information adds the rest. The NTSC standard assigns 4 MHz of bandwidth to the Y signal, about 1.5 MHz to I, and about 0.6 MHz to Q. Thus the information the eye relies on most heavily is transmitted with the greatest precision, whereas the information about color distinctions the eye cannot make well occupies the least bandwidth in the video signal. This color system might be useful if you are rendering images in *Mathematica* from data originally prepared for television broadcast. (Beware, however. The entries in the YIQ-to-RGB conversion matrix in the package Graphics`Colors` in Version 2.2 of *Mathematica* are given to only two decimal places of precision, and they do not entirely agree with the data from the reference we checked, which is listed in the "Suggested Readings" section at the end of this book. You may prefer to define your own YIQColor function if you need to be sure that the colors you see are faithful to the original data.)

- HLSColor[h,l,s] represents a color in the HLS (hue-lightness-saturation) system. This color system is used to describe colors in terms of how they are perceived by the human eye, rather than how they are generated by a computer monitor or other light source. The hue is an indication of the dominant component of the color, represented as a number between 0 and 1; it is 0 for pure red, 1/3 for pure green, and 2/3 for pure blue. The lightness is a measure of the overall brightness of the color; it is the average of the values of the color's largest and smallest RGB components. The saturation indicates the grayness of the color, measuring the relative amount by which the strongest component exceeds the weakest one. A saturation of 0 indicates that all three components are the same, which produces a shade of gray, while a saturation of 1 indicates that the color is "as different from gray as it can be"—for example, the primary colors red, green, and blue, and their complements cyan, magenta, and yellow. For the exact correspondence between the HLS and RGB systems, we refer you to a book on computer graphics (some are mentioned in the "Suggested Readings" section at the back of this book), or to the code in Graphics`Colors`.

- HSBColor[h,s,b] represents a color in the HSB (hue-saturation-brightness or hue-saturation-value) system, which is another perceptual system widely used in computer graphics. The hue component has the same meaning in the HSB and HLS systems. The formula defining saturation in the HSB system is not quite the same as that in the HLS system, but it has the same intended purpose. The brightness value measures the strongest RGB component directly, instead of averaging the strongest and weakest components as the lightness value in the HLS system does. The term "value" is sometimes used instead of "brightness," so this system is also known as the HSV color system. The function HSBColor was written into the package Graphics`Colors` before the Hue directive was added to the *Mathematica* kernel. Now it is retained for backward compatibility, but you should use Hue rather than HSBColor in any new code you write.

All of these color specification functions work the same way: They use standard formulas to convert a color specified in a system not directly supported by *Mathematica* to an equivalent representation in the RGB color system. They return RGBColor directives as their results, so they can be used anywhere an RGBColor directive can be used. Here is an example of each system:

```
Needs["Graphics`Colors`"];
{ CMYColor[.1,.3,.6],  YIQColor[.4,.3,.2], HLSColor[.2,.8,.5] }
```

```
{RGBColor[0.9, 0.7, 0.4], RGBColor[0.81, 0.188, 0.413],
  RGBColor[0.86, 0.9, 0.7]}
```

The package Graphics`Colors` also contains definitions for about 200 colors specified by name (it was about 60 colors in Version 2.1). Each color name is defined as a symbol whose value is an RGBColor directive for that color.

```
{ Red, Yellow, White, Purple, Gold, PrussianBlue, LimeGreen }
```

```
{RGBColor[1., 0., 0.], RGBColor[1., 1., 0.], RGBColor[1., 1., 1.],
  RGBColor[0.627506, 0.125507, 0.941206], RGBColor[1., 0.843104, 0.],
  RGBColor[0.18, 0.18, 0.31], RGBColor[0.196097, 0.803903, 0.196097]}
```

Once you have loaded the package Graphics`Colors`, you can specify a color by name instead of by RGB values, for example, Orange, Red, Turquoise (many of the color names were taken from the 64-color box of Crayola crayons). The variable AllColors is defined to be a list of the named colors, with the names specified as strings. (If the names were specified as symbols, the symbols would be replaced by their definitions when AllColors was evaluated.)

```
somecolors = (AllColors[[#]])& /@ Range[5,60,10];
i = 0;
f = { Text[#,{i+.45,-.1}], ToExpression[#], Rectangle[{i,0},{++i-.1,1}] }& ;
somecolors = f /@ somecolors;
Show[ Graphics[somecolors], AspectRatio->Automatic, PlotRange->All ];
```

AquamarineMedium   BlueMedium   CadmiumLemon ChromeOxideGreen   Cyan   Firebrick

If you have a color monitor, you can type in this example to see how the colors look.

Another package for using color in graphics is Graphics`ArgColors`, which defines the functions ArgColor, ArgShade, and ColorCircle for converting the argument of a complex number to a color. Here is an example using ArgShade to color a surface in a graph of a function $w = f(u)$ that maps complex numbers to complex numbers. The input variable $u = x + iy$ is represented by the x and y coordinates; the output variable $w = re^{i\theta}$ is represented by the modulus r mapped onto the z axis, with the argument angle θ used to determine the surface color. We produced the figure in the color plates by replacing ArgShade with ArgColor.

```
Needs["Graphics`ArgColors`"];
Plot3D[ {Abs[Sin[x+I y]],ArgShade[Sin[x+I y]]}, {x,-2Pi,2Pi}, {y,-2,2},
    BoxRatios->Automatic, ViewPoint->{0,-1,3} ];
```

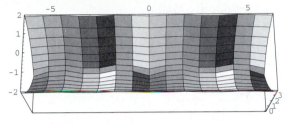

■ Combined Graphics

Using the Show command, you can combine several graphics into a single graphic. Rendering plots can be time consuming. If you don't care to see the intermediate plots, you can suppress them by setting the option DisplayFunction to Identity, as we've done in many examples throughout this book. Alternatively, in Version 2.1 or later releases of *Mathematica*, you can use DisplayTogether or DisplayTogetherArray, both of which are defined in the package Graphics`Graphics`. DisplayTogetherArray uses a GraphicsArray object to place graphics side by side:

```
Needs["Graphics`Graphics`"];
DisplayTogetherArray[{
    PieChart[{{59,Americas},{274,Europe},{656,Asia},{100,Africa}},PlotLabel->"1850"],
    PieChart[{{144,Americas},{423,Europe},{857,Asia},{141,Africa}},PlotLabel->"1900"],
    PieChart[{{330,Americas},{572,Europe},{1380,Asia},{219,Africa}},PlotLabel->"1950"],
    PieChart[{{617,Americas},{750,Europe},{2618,Asia},{472,Africa}},PlotLabel->"1980"],
    PieChart[{{736,Americas},{795,Europe},{3207,Asia},{654,Africa}},PlotLabel->"1992"] },
    PlotLabel->"Estimated World Population by Region (in Millions)" ];
```

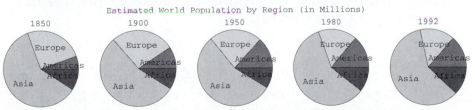

DisplayTogether combines several graphics objects into a single object so that they are superimposed. The following input draws the Golden Gate Bridge. The cables are drawn with parabolas; the bridge is drawn as a line.

```
DisplayTogether[
    (* Golden Gate Bridge *)
    Graphics[{ Line[{{-2, 0}, {2, 0}}], Line[{{-1, -0.5}, {-1, 1}}],
               Line[{{1, -0.5}, {1, 1}}] }],
    (* Cables for the Golden Gate Bridge *)
    Plot[x^2, {x, -1, 1}],
    Plot[x^2 + 4x + 4, {x, -2, -1}],
    Plot[x^2 - 4x + 4, {x, 1, 2}],
    AspectRatio -> Automatic
];
```

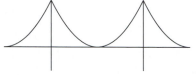

- Labeled Plots

With Plot and many of the other graphics commands, you can plot an expression or
several expressions on one graph. The first argument to Plot specifies the function or
functions to plot. When the first argument is a list, *Mathematica* plots more than one
expression on a single graph. Unfortunately, two problems can arise when you plot
several expressions together, as this example demonstrates:

```
Needs["Graphics`Legend`"];
Block[{ $DisplayFunction = Identity },
    gr1 = Plot[{E^x, x^E}, {x, 0, 5}];
     ps = { {Thickness[.02],Dashing[{.05,.03}]}, {Thickness[.01],RGBColor[1,0,1]} };
    gr2 = Plot[{E^x, x^E}, {x, 0, 5}, PlotStyle -> ps ];
    gr3 = Plot[{E^x, x^E}, {x, 0, 5}, PlotStyle -> ps, PlotLegend ->{e^x, x^e} ];  ];
Show[GraphicsArray[ { gr1, gr2, gr3 } ]];
```

In the first example, we plot e^x and x^e with the default plotting style. It is difficult to tell
whether the two curves cross or are tangent. In the second example, we use the PlotStyle
option to distinguish the curves, but it is still hard to tell which curve represents which

function if you don't already know. You have to look at the *Mathematica* input rather than at the graph itself to see which plot style corresponds to which function. In the third example, the PlotLegend option lets us indicate which is which directly on the graph. Note that we specify only the labels for the legend; the PlotLegend option associates the labels with the corresponding styles from the PlotStyle option to construct the legend box.

The code that adds the PlotLegend option to Plot is in the package Graphics`Legend`. By default, the legend is placed in the lower left corner of the graph with a drop shadow, as we saw above. There are many other options for controlling the size, color, border, spacing, label, and orientation of text, some of which we illustrate here:

```
Plot[{E^x, x^E}, {x, 0, 5}, PlotStyle -> { {Thickness[0.02], Dashing[{0.05, 0.03}]},
        {Thickness[0.01], RGBColor[1,0,1]} },
    PlotLegend ->{e^x, x^e},
    LegendPosition -> {-.6, 0},    LegendSize -> {.8, .5},
    LegendShadow -> {0, 0},        LegendOrientation -> Horizontal,
    LegendLabel -> "Functions",    LegendBackground -> GrayLevel[0.8]   ];
```

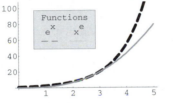

Using the option LegendPosition, we reposition the legend so that its lower left corner is at $(-.5, 0)$; this position is specified in a coordinate system in which the lower left corner of the entire graph is $(-1, -1)$ and the center of the graph is $(0, 0)$. We also change the legend's size and background color, the position of the shadow (so it is hidden), and the orientation of the text, and we add a label or title to the legend.

The PlotLegend option for Plot is actually implemented by the function ShowLegend. This function can be called directly to add a legend to any type of *Mathematica* graphics object. The graph on the left in the following illustration is constructed with the help of the MultipleListPlot function, which is defined in another package. (See Section 5.2.3 on page 164 for how this graph was constructed.) MultipleListPlot allows us to plot several data sets on a single graph, using a different plotting symbol for each, but it provides no way to indicate on the graph which symbol represents which data set. We use ShowLegend to add a key to the graph on the right, making it much more informative.

```
Block[ {$DisplayFunction=Identity},
  withlegend = ShowLegend[ dataplot, {
       { {Graphics[RegularPolygon[4,.015]],"Americas"},
         {Graphics[RegularPolygon[4,.015,{0,0}, 45Degree]],"Europe"},
         {Graphics[RegularPolygon[3,.01]],"Asia"},
         {Graphics[RegularPolygon[5,.015,{0,0},0,2]],"Africa"} },
     LegendPosition->{-.5,-.05},LegendSize -> {.6,.5}, LegendShadow -> {0, 0} } ]; ];
Show[GraphicsArray[ { dataplot, withlegend } ]];
```

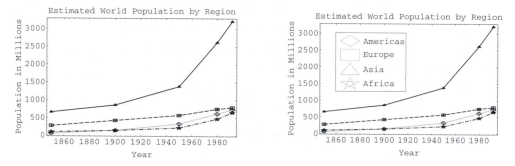

It took a bit of trial and error to find suitable settings for the size and position of the legend in this example. There are many more options that control the appearance of the legend than the examples above illustrate; refer to the documentation of Graphics`Legend` for complete details.

▪ Animations

With several versions of *Mathematica*, it is possible to make an animation or movie, that is, a plot that varies over time. Actually, *Mathematica* generates a series of plots and then displays them quickly one after another. The package Graphics`Animation` defines a collection of commands for animating graphics.

The most basic animation command defined in Graphics`Animation` is ShowAnimation, which displays an animation whose individual frames have already been computed. ShowAnimation takes one argument, a list of graphics objects to be animated. If you are making a simple animation, it is usually more convenient to use one of the higher-level animation functions that call ShowAnimation implicitly, just as it is easier to use Plot to plot a function than to sample the function yourself, build a graphics object, and display it with Show. However, if you are building a complicated animation, with different frames calculated by different algorithms, you may wish to construct the graphics objects for the frames separately and then use ShowAnimation to display them. ShowAnimation is most useful with versions of *Mathematica* that don't use a Notebook

Front End, because those versions usually require *Mathematica* to launch an external animation program to display animations. With the Notebook Front End, a sequence of graphics cells can be animated by simple point-and-click methods, which make ShowAnimation unnecessary.

In the extreme case, when you are working in a medium that does not permit any animation at all (like the pages of this book, for instance!), it is convenient to have a way to represent animations in a static form that allows the frames to be seen side-by-side. The following code defines a function animateGA that takes a sequence of frames for an animation and turns it into a GraphicsArray object. The key to animateGA is the function altPartition, which acts just like the built-in function Partition, except that it does not discard a partial sublist at the end.

```
altPartition[ l_List, k_Integer ] :=
    Module[ { m = Partition[l,k], n = Mod[Length[l],k] },
            If[ n == 0, m, Append[ m, Take[l,-n] ] ] ]
```

The function animateGA takes a list of graphics and partitions it into a GraphicsArray object, with the number of columns in the array specified by the variable $animateGAwidth. The variable $animateGAoptions may be used to specify one or more option settings for GraphicsArray that should be used with animateGA; by default, it is empty.

```
animateGA[l_List] := Show[GraphicsArray[altPartition[l,$animateGAwidth],
                          Sequence @@ Flatten[{$animateGAoptions}] ]];
$animateGAwidth = 5;
$animateGAoptions = {};
```

A convenient way to invoke animateGA is to use it as the setting of the AnimationFunction option in ShowAnimation or another animation function that calls ShowAnimation implicitly. In this example we use MoviePlot to construct an animation and use animateGA to display it. Setting $RasterFunction to Identity prevents *Mathematica* from displaying the individual frames of the animation as separate graphics.

```
Needs["Graphics`Animation`"];
Options[ShowAnimation]
```

```
{RasterFunction :> $RasterFunction, AnimationFunction :> $AnimationFunction}
```

```
Block[ { $RasterFunction = Identity, $AnimationFunction = animateGA },
    MoviePlot[ Sin[n x], {x,0,2Pi}, {n,1,9,1} ]
];
```

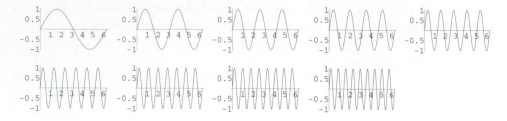

Here is another example, using MovieParametricPlot:

```
$RasterFunction = Identity;  $AnimationFunction = animateGA;
MovieParametricPlot[ {Cos[n t]Sin[t],Cos[n t]Cos[t]}, {t,0,2Pi}, {n,1,8,1},
                    AspectRatio->Automatic, Ticks->None ];
```

The function animateGA comes in handy when you are preparing a document to be used in two forms: as a Notebook, in which animations can be viewed dynamically, and as a printed document, in which animations must be displayed statically. A suitable init.m file can make the use of animateGA completely invisible, so that no changes in the source document are necessary to allow it to be viewed in different media.

Animate is a high-level, general-purpose command similar to Table. Its template is

Animate[*command*, *iterator*]

where the iterator has the form {*variable*, *min*, *max*, *inc*}. Animate executes the *command* once for each value of the *variable*, starting with the *min* value and incrementing it by *inc* until it reaches or passes the *max* value. (If you omit the increment *inc*, Animate uses the setting of the Frames option to determine how many frames to generate, and computes an increment that gives that many frames; the default setting is Frames->24.) Each invocation of the *command* should produce a graphics object; when all the objects have been created, Animate displays them as frames of an animation. Animate is careful to disable the DisplayFunction while executing the *command*, so you can safely use Animate with a command such as Plot that calls Show implicitly. If Animate were not so clever, every frame of the animation would be displayed twice, once when `Plot` created it and once as part of the animation.

The animation package also defines several commands whose names begin with `Movie`: `MoviePlot`, `MovieParametricPlot`, `MoviePlot3D`, `MovieContourPlot`, and `MovieDensityPlot`. These commands are extensions of their non-Movie counterparts, designed to make it simple to produce animations when all the frames of an animation are created by one of the built-in plotting functions. For example,

```
MoviePlot[ Sin[ n x ], { x, 0, 2Pi }, { n, 1, 5 } ];
```

is equivalent to

```
Animate[ Plot[ Sin[ n x ], { x, 0, 2Pi } ], { n, 1, 5 } ];
```

but it is a bit easier to type. The animation iterator for each `Movie` function should be placed immediately after the iterators that the non-Movie version expects, before any option settings.

The highest-level and simplest animation operator is `SpinShow`. Its template is

```
SpinShow[ 3D graphics object, option settings ]
```

The *3D graphics object* can be a `Graphics3D` or `SurfaceGraphics` object. `SpinShow` creates frames of the animation by calling `Show` repeatedly with different settings of the `ViewPoint` option. `SpinShow` calculates a sequence of viewpoints in a circle around the center of the object; when the object is displayed from these viewpoints, it appears to be spinning in space. `SpinShow` accepts options like `SpinTilt` and `SpinRange` to modify the angle and rate of spin, `SpinDistance` and `SpinOrigin` to set the viewing position for the animation, and `RotateLights` to determine whether the light sources move with the rotating object. (If they don't, the colors of the polygons in the object will change as they present different angles to the light sources.)

`SpinShow` is the oldest animation function in *Mathematica* and is, in fact, the reason that animation capabilities were added to the Notebook Front End in the first place. The first three-dimensional animations created with *Mathematica* were all of the `SpinShow` variety, and the needs of `SpinShow` influenced the development of 3D graphics in *Mathematica*. For example, versions of *Mathematica* prior to 2.0 displayed all 3D graphics using the algorithm that is now controlled by the `SphericalRegion` option setting. Without that option, the frames in a `SpinShow` animation appear to jump around, since different viewpoints allow *Mathematica* to scale a 3D graphic differently. See the discussion of the `SphericalRegion` option in Section 7.4.3 on page 264 for more details.

5.2.2 Two-Dimensional Graphics

- Logarithmic Scales

By default, plots are graphed with linear scaling. Changing the scaling—sometimes makes the difference between functions more pronounced. With the function LogPlot, we plot using logarithmic scaling—that is, we plot the logarithm of an expression as a function of x. The function LogPlot is defined in the package Graphics`Graphics`. Notice that LogPlot graphs the function e^x as a straight line:

```
Needs["Graphics`Graphics`"];
LogPlot[{E^x, x^E}, {x, 1, 5},
    PlotStyle -> {
        {Thickness[.02], RGBColor[1,0,1], Dashing[{.05,.03}]},
        {Thickness[.01]}
    }
];
```

The options and default values for LogPlot are the same as those for Plot.

```
Options[Plot] == Options[LogPlot]
```
True

In Version 2.1 and later releases of *Mathematica*, the option setting GridLines->Automatic simulates logarithmic graph paper:

```
LogPlot[{E^x, x^E}, {x, 1, 5},
    PlotStyle -> {
        {Thickness[.02], RGBColor[1,0,1], Dashing[{.05,.03}]},
        {Thickness[.01]}
    },
    GridLines -> Automatic
];
```

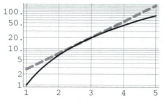

The package `Graphics`Graphics`` also defines several other functions for plotting on a logarithmic scale, as shown here:

```
?*Log*Plot
```

LinearLogListPlot	LogLinearListPlot	LogListPlot	LogLogPlot	LogPlot
LinearLogPlot	LogLinearPlot	LogLogListPlot		

Following the usual conventions, the functions with `List` in their names are for plotting data sets; the others are for plotting expressions. The function `LogLinearListPlot` generates a data plot of y versus $\log(x)$.

```
LogLinearListPlot[{{1,0},{2,1},{4,2},{8,3},{16,4}}];
```

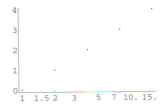

- Arrows

The package `Graphics`Arrow`` was added to *Mathematica* in Version 2.2. The function `Arrow` defined in this package combines *Mathematica* code with PostScript code to draw arrows in 2D graphics. Options are provided to specify the size and shape of the arrowhead.

```
Needs["Graphics`Arrow`"];
Options[Arrow]
```

```
{HeadScaling -> Automatic, HeadLength -> Automatic, HeadCenter -> 1,
   HeadWidth -> 0.5, HeadShape -> Automatic, ZeroShape -> Automatic}
```

Here is an example showing the use of arrows to label interesting features of a plot:

```
p[x_] := x^4 - 10x^3 + 32x^2 - 38x + 23
```

```
extrema = x /. NSolve[ p'[x] == 0, x ];
max = {maxA} = Select[ extrema, (p''[#] < 0)& ];
min = {minA,minB} = Select[ extrema, (p''[#] > 0)& ];
inflections = {infA,infB} = x /. NSolve[ p''[x] == 0, x ];
```

```
Needs["Graphics`Arrow`"];
gr1 = Plot[ p[x], {x,0,5}, DisplayFunction->Identity ];
gr2 = Show[ gr1, DefaultFont->{"Times-Roman",8},
    Epilog -> {
```

```
        Arrow[ {2,18}, {maxA,p[maxA]}+{0,1} ],
        Text["Local maximum",{2,18},{0,-2}],
        Arrow[ {1.5,4}, {infA,p[infA]}-{0,1} ],
        Arrow[ {2.6,2}, {infB,p[infB]}-{.1,0} ],
        Text["Inflection points",{2.5,2},{1,0} ],
        PointSize[.02],
        Point[{#,p[#]}]& /@ Join[extrema,inflections]
} ];
Show[GraphicsArray[ { gr1, gr2 } ]];
```

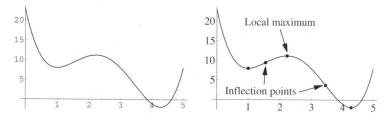

We should point out that labeling arrows is not the most appropriate use of arrows in *Mathematica* graphics because of the way *Mathematica* handles text labels. When a *Mathematica* graphic is resized, the graphical elements — including the arrows — are rescaled but the text labels are not. If the graphic on the right in this example were rescaled to be 50 percent larger, the arrows would maintain their positions relative to the axes and the curve, but their tails would drift away from the text labels, as shown:

```
Show[gr2,PlotRegion->{{-.4,1.5},{-.4,2.2}}, DisplayFunction->$DisplayFunction];
```

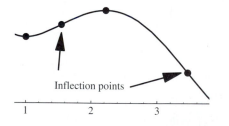

In this example, we have enlarged the graphic enormously, but have used the PlotRegion option to zoom in on the label "Inflection points." You can see that the magnification has made the points, arrowheads, tick marks, and other graphical elements much larger, but has left the text the same size. The result is that the arrow on the left no longer appears connected to its label.

▪ Splines

Instead of connecting points with line segments, as the Line primitive does, you may want to fit a smooth curve through the points. The Spline function generates such curves using a variety of algorithms. Spline's arguments are a list of points and a type of spline; depending on the type selected, Spline renders a spline through the specified points or uses them as control points.

When the second argument to Spline is Cubic, a spline is drawn through the list of points specified as the first argument. If the second argument is Bezier or CompositeBezier, the curve contains the endpoints and is controlled by the other points.

```
Needs["Graphics`Spline`"];
pts = Table[ {t-t^3,1-t^2}, {t,-1.25,1.25,.25} ];
gr1 = Graphics[{ PointSize[0.03], Point /@ pts, Spline[pts,Cubic] }];
gr2 = Graphics[{ PointSize[0.03], Point /@ pts, Spline[pts,Bezier] }];
gr3 = Graphics[{ PointSize[0.03], Point /@ pts, Spline[pts,CompositeBezier] }];
Show[GraphicsArray[{gr1,gr2,gr3}]];
```

The package Graphics`Spline` uses functions from the package NumericalMath`SplineFit` to compute the points on the spline curve. It is likely that additional spline methods will be added in future versions of this package.

▪ Filled Plots

To color or fill the area between two curves or between a curve and an axis, use the function FilledPlot in the package Graphics`FilledPlot`.

```
Needs["Graphics`FilledPlot`"];

gr1 = FilledPlot[Cos[x], {x, 0, 2Pi}, DisplayFunction->Identity ];
gr2 = FilledPlot[{Cos[x], x/10}, {x, 0, 3Pi}, DisplayFunction->Identity ];
Show[GraphicsArray[{gr1,gr2}]];
```

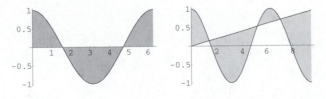

When a single function is plotted, the region between that function and the x axis is filled. When a list of functions is plotted, the regions between adjacent pairs of functions are filled in different colors. FilledPlot accepts the option Fills to specify the colors for the regions between functions, and the option Curves to specify whether the filled regions should be allowed to obscure the curves. The Curves option can be set to Back for all curves to be hidden, to Front for all curves to be drawn in front of all regions, or to None for the curves to be suppressed altogether.

You can obtain nice special effects by using cleverly defined functions with FilledPlot. For example, the following command fills the area under the curve $\sin(x)/x$ only over the interval $[-2, 2]$:

```
FilledPlot[ { Sin[x]/x, If[Abs[x]<2,0,Sin[x]/x] }, {x, -2Pi, 2Pi} ];
```

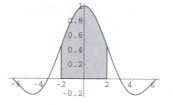

In this example, FilledPlot filled in the region between two functions, but the functions coincide everywhere except where the expression Abs[x]<2 is true, i.e., everywhere except on the interval $[-2, 2]$. Therefore the area over this interval was the only region FilledPlot filled.

The package Graphics`FilledPlot` also defines the function ListFilledPlot, which fills regions between curves defined by lists of data points.

- Complex Mappings

The functions CartesianMap and PolarMap make plots of complex-valued functions. They were developed by Roman Maeder and are described in his book *Programming in Mathematica* (Addison-Wesley, 1991) (see 'Suggested Readings" on page 327).

```
Needs["Graphics`ComplexMap`"];
DisplayTogetherArray[{ CartesianMap[Log, {-5, 5}, {-5, 5}],
                       PolarMap[Identity, {0, 1}, {0, 2Pi}] }];
```

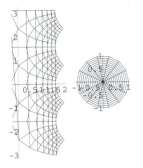

5.2.3 Data Graphics

- Bar Charts and Pie Charts

The package Graphics`Graphics` contains the function BarChart for drawing bar charts. For more flexibility, GeneralizedBarChart, StackedBarChart, and PercentileBarChart were added to this package in Version 2.1.

BarChart can be used in combination with the functions BinCounts and Frequencies defined in the package Statistics`DataManipulation`. For an example, let's generate 1000 integers in the range $[-5, 5]$ and use Frequencies to determine the number of occurrences of each integer. (Because of differences in the random number generator in different versions of *Mathematica*, you may not get the results shown here if you try this example on your system.)

```
randomUniform = Table[Random[Integer, {-5,5}], {1000}];
```

```
Needs["Statistics`DataManipulation`"]; (* defines Frequencies and BinCounts *)
uniformfreq = Frequencies[randomUniform]
```

```
{{112, -5}, {102, -4}, {74, -3}, {98, -2}, {90, -1}, {81, 0}, {96, 1},
   {85, 2}, {92, 3}, {87, 4}, {83, 5}}
```

Now we display the frequencies:

```
Needs["Graphics`Graphics`"]; (* defines BarChart *)
Block[ { $DisplayFunction = Identity },
    listplot = Show[
        ListPlot[ uniformfreq, PlotStyle->PointSize[.02] ],  (* plot the points *)
        ListPlot[ uniformfreq, PlotJoined->True ],   (* plot the line *)
        AxesOrigin->{0,0}, PlotRange->{{0,120},{-5,5}} ];
    vertbars = BarChart[ uniformfreq ];
    horizbars = BarChart[ uniformfreq, BarOrientation->Horizontal ];    ];
```

```
Show[GraphicsArray[ { vertbars, listplot, horizbars } ]];
```

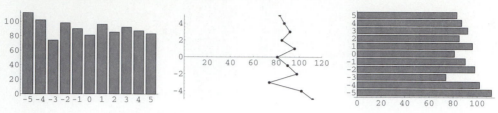

The input looks a bit formidable, but we wanted to make a point. The list uniformfreq produced by Frequencies consists of ordered pairs of counts and values. Even though the counts precede the values in the ordered pairs, BarChart places the counts on the y axis by default, which is the reverse of the ordinary convention. (Usually, the first member of an ordered pair is plotted on the x axis and the second member is plotted on the y axis.) ListPlot follows the normal convention, and therefore its plot of the same data is "transposed" from the plot produced by BarChart. You can instruct BarChart to produce a graph like ListPlot's with the option setting BarOrientation->Horizontal.

Mathematica's Random function generates numbers that are distributed uniformly (so the bars in the preceding example are all about the same height). To obtain random numbers that are normally distributed, we can use the function NormalDistribution from the package Statistics`ContinuousDistributions`. Then we can use BinCounts to count the numbers in the intervals $[0, 1], [1, 2], \ldots [9, 10]$. (This may take a while, so you might want to try it with fewer than 1000 numbers if you are using a machine that isn't particularly fast.)

```
Needs["Statistics`ContinuousDistributions`"]; (* defines NormalDistribution *)
randomNormal = Table[Random[NormalDistribution[0, 3]], {1000}];
normalfreq = BinCounts[randomNormal, {-5, 5, 1}]  (* BinCounts was loaded earlier *)
```

{33, 68, 98, 104, 141, 140, 121, 78, 64, 41}

Again, we use BarChart to display the frequency counts:

```
DisplayTogetherArray[{
    BarChart[normalfreq],
    BarChart[normalfreq,
        BarStyle -> (If[ # >= 100, RGBColor[0,0,1], RGBColor[1,0,0] ]&),
        GridLines -> Automatic,
        BarOrientation -> Horizontal ]   }];
```

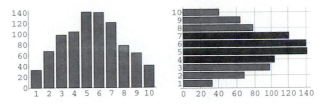

This time the bars approximate a bell-shaped curve. Note that unlike Frequencies, which produced a list of ordered pairs, BinCounts simply produced a list of counts. BarChart understands both data sets, generating the labels $1, 2, 3, \ldots$ when none are provided. The graph on the right illustrates a few of the other options accepted by BarChart. The BarStyle option is especially interesting: We use a function to pick out the counts above 100 and highlight them; in this way, we call attention to the numbers that occur more often than they would if they were selected uniformly. Here is a list of the special options BarChart accepts:

Options[BarChart]

```
{BarStyle -> Automatic, BarSpacing -> Automatic, BarGroupSpacing -> Automatic,
  BarLabels -> Automatic, BarValues -> False, BarEdges -> True,
  BarEdgeStyle -> GrayLevel[0], BarOrientation -> Vertical}
```

Note that the GridLines option we used in the previous example isn't in this list; BarChart passes along options used by Graphics so that they have their usual effects.

Here is a more elaborate example. We start with some population data for a few of the world's most densely populated countries, taken from the *Information Please Almanac* for 1993.

```
denselyPopulated = {{Bangladesh, 2255}, {Belgium, 850}, {China, 1659},
        {India, 757}, {Japan, 814}, {Netherlands, 1146}, {SouthKorea, 1138}};
popdata = Sort[ denselyPopulated, (Last[#1]<Last[#2])& ];
{popnames,popvalues} = Transpose[ popdata ];
```

The data are stored in the variable denselyPopulated in alphabetical order by country name. We sort them in order of increasing density, then separate the country names and density values into the variables popnames and popvalues. Now we can display this information on a bar chart.

```
Needs["Graphics`Graphics`"];
BarChart[ popvalues,
    PlotLabel->"World's Most Densely Populated Countries: 1991\n \n \n \n \n \n ",
    AxesLabel ->{"", "Countries          "},
    FrameLabel ->{"Persons per square mile", ""},
    FrameTicks->{Automatic,Transpose[{Range[7],popnames}]},
    BarOrientation -> Horizontal, Frame -> True];
```

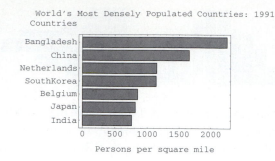

We specify the x axis label as a FrameLabel to make it appear beneath the plot, and the y axis label as an AxesLabel to make it appear above the country names instead of running vertically beside them. We pad the y label with blanks so that it is centered over the axis labels instead of over the axis itself, and we pad the plot label with blank lines to keep it from overprinting with the y label. This process may seem complicated, but it takes only a few moments of trial and error to produce an attractive graph.

Be aware that *Mathematica*'s default setting PlotRange->Automatic truncates extreme values. Truncating can produce a misleading bar chart. For example, we use the following data from the *1993 Information Please Almanac* to plot population densities. The population figures in the second column are in hundred billions, and the area figures in the third column are in millions of square miles.

```
data = { {           "Asia", 32    , 10.64 }, {           "Africa",  6.54, 11.7  },
         {"North America",  4.36,  9.36 }, {"South America",  3    ,  6.88 },
         {    "Antarctica",  0    ,  6     }, {           "Europe",  5.11,  1.9  },
         {      "Oceania",  0.28,  3.28 }, {           "USSR",  2.84,  8.65 }  };
{ name, pop, area } = Transpose[data];


Block[ { $DisplayFunction = Identity },
    gr1 = BarChart[ pop/area, BarLabels->name, PlotLabel->"Population Density",
                    BarOrientation->Horizontal, AspectRatio->.4 ];
    gr2 = Show[ gr1, PlotRange->All ];
];
Show[GraphicsArray[{ gr1, gr2 }]];
```

If you look closely at the bar chart on the left, you will notice a black line at the right edges of all the bars except the ones for Europe and Asia. These bars do not have such a line because they were cut off; as a result, the population densities of the other continents appear to be much larger, relative to those of Europe and Asia, than they actually are. To be sure that you are displaying all values to scale in a bar chart, set the option PlotRange to All, as in the graph on the right.

The function StackedBarChart draws a bar chart for several data sets at once, stacking the bars atop one another. The graph on the left gives the estimated amount of gross receipts for Macsyma, *Mathematica*, and Maple in 1986, 1987, and 1988. You can see that Macsyma lost market share, while Maple and *Mathematica* gained it. Using PercentileBarChart, you can see the receipts from each product as a percentage of total receipts.

```
DisplayTogetherArray[{
    StackedBarChart[ {5, 3, 1}, {3, 15, 31}, {0, 3, 8}, BarLabels->{1986,1987,1988}],
    PercentileBarChart[ {5, 3, 1}, {3, 15, 31}, {0, 3, 8}, BarLabels->{1986,1987,1988}] }];
```

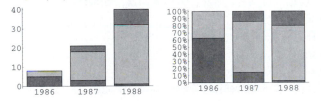

With the function GeneralizedBarChart, you specify the position, height, and width of each bar. Note that bars are drawn in the order in which they are specified, so one bar can partially or completely obscure another.

```
GeneralizedBarChart[{ {1,2,1}, {2,1.5,2}, {5,1,2.5} }, BarStyle->{ Gold,Zinc,Beige } ];
```

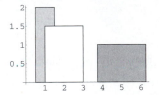

The function BarChart3D in the package Graphics`Graphics3D` makes a three-dimensional bar chart, given a rectangular array of heights. There are options to change the space between the bars in the x or y direction as well as to change the style of the edges of the bar faces.

```
Needs["Graphics`Graphics3D`"];
DisplayTogetherArray[{
    BarChart3D[ { {1,2,3}, {2,3,2} } ],
    BarChart3D[ { {1,2,3}, {2,3,2} }, XSpacing -> 0.3, YSpacing -> 0.6 ] }];
```

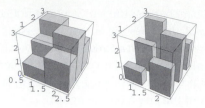

The package `Graphics`Graphics`` also contains functions for drawing pie charts. Pie charts are usually not suitable for presenting scientific data. It is much harder to judge the sizes of angles than to judge lengths or distances, making pie charts hard to read and easy to misinterpret. Even so, for small data sets with large variations in values, pie charts can be effective. Here is a pie chart of *Mathematica* users classified by field. Note that the numbers do not add up to 100; each value is drawn as a percentage of the sum of the values.

```
piedata = { {56, "   Engineering"}, {42, "Computer\nScience"}, {12,  "Business"},
            {40, "Science"}, {24, "Math"}, {26, "Other"} };
Needs["Graphics`Colors`"];
DisplayTogetherArray[{
    PieChart[ piedata ],
    PieChart[ piedata, PieExploded -> {5,6},
        PieStyle -> { AliceBlue, Green, Cyan, Orange, Yellow, Pink } ]   }];
```

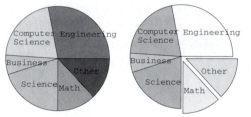

There are options to control the position and color of the wedges. Remember that the package `Graphics`Colors`` must be loaded if you want to specify colors by name rather than by the corresponding RGB values. The option `PieExploded` was added to Version 2.1 so that you can specify wedges that should be drawn a small distance from the pie.

- Labeled Data

The built-in function `ListPlot` plots a list of values consisting of *y* values or {*x*, *y*} pairs. The function `LabeledListPlot` labels each value sequentially, using its own labels or labels you specify. Here is an example that uses the population data an earlier example:

```
Needs["Graphics`Graphics`"];
Block[ { $DisplayFunction = Identity },
    gr1 = LabeledListPlot[ Transpose[{pop,area}] ];
    gr2 = LabeledListPlot[ Transpose[{pop,area,name}], AxesLabel->{"Pop.","Area"},
                PlotRange->All, AxesOrigin->{0,0}, AspectRatio->.4 ];
];
Show[GraphicsArray[{ gr1, gr2 }]];
```

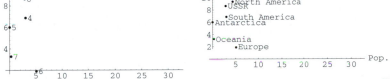

In some versions of *Mathematica*, the labels are clipped, since *Mathematica* draws the graph without considering label widths. Set the option PlotRange to All, as in the graph on the right, to display the labels completely.

The function TextListPlot uses text instead of dots to mark data points. In the left and center examples following, the points in the data set are labeled with numbers indicating the order in which they appear. In the right example, we specify the text labels.

```
l1 = {5,4,3,2,1};
l2 = {{1,5},{6,4},{4,3},{3,2},{8,1}};
l3 = {{1,5,"aa"},{6,4,"bb"},{4,3,"cc"},{3,2,"dd"},{8,1,"ee"}};
Block[ { $DisplayFunction = Identity }, gr = TextListPlot /@ {l1,l2,l3} ];
Show[GraphicsArray[gr]];
```

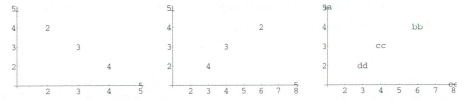

In these examples, the labels on some of the points collide with the axes; you can use a setting such as PlotRange->{{0,10},{0,6}} to prevent collisions.

- Error Bars

In addition to plotting values, the function ErrorListPlot plots error bars. The argument to ErrorListPlot is a list of pairs $\{y_i, e_i\}$ or triplets $\{x_i, y_i, e_i\}$, where each y_i value specifies a data point to be plotted, and the corresponding e_i value specifies the length of the error bar for that data point, which is drawn as a vertical line centered at the point. As usual, the values $1, 2, 3, \ldots$ are supplied if explicit x_i values are not given.

```
ErrorListPlot[ Table[{t,Sin[t],Abs[.05 Sin[23t]]},{t,0.,Pi,Pi/20}] ];
```

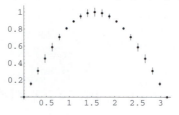

- Multiple Data Sets

The function ListPlot plots a list of values. If you want to plot several lists of data, you can combine several calls to ListPlot, but it might be difficult to tell which data set is which in the resulting plot. Alternatively, and more simply, you can use the function MultipleListPlot (written by Cameron Smith) to plot several data sets at once, using a different plotting symbol for each one.

```
Needs["Graphics`MultipleListPlot`"];
```

```
d1 = Range[10];
d2 = {0,2,4,6,8,10,12,14,16,18};
d3 = {20,18,16,14,12,10,9,8,7,6};
gr1 = MultipleListPlot[ d1, d2, d3, DisplayFunction->Identity ];
gr2 = MultipleListPlot[ d1, d2, d3, PlotJoined->True, DisplayFunction->Identity ];
Show[GraphicsArray[{gr1,gr2}]];
```

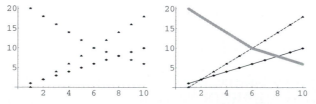

Mathematica connects the points with straight line segments when you set the option PlotJoined to True. If you connect the points, the lines are drawn in different styles. The package Graphics`MultipleListPlot` provides the function MakeSymbol to help you construct plotting symbols, and the options LineStyles and DotShapes (with default values specified by the variables $LineStyles and $DotShapes) to control the appearance of the plot. Here is a moderately complicated example of these features; the population data were taken from the 1993 edition of the *Information Please Almanac*.

```
popdata = {{59,144,330,617,736},{274,423,572,750,795},
                {656,857,1380,2618,3207},{100,141,219,472,654}};
popyears = {1850, 1900, 1950, 1980, 1992};
popareas = {Americas, Europe, Asia, Africa};

$LineStyles = { {GrayLevel[.6]}, {Dashing[{.02,.01}]}, {},
                            {Dashing[{.02,.01,.002,.01}]} };

$DotShapes = Apply[
    MakeSymbol[RegularPolygon[##]]&,
    { {4,.015}, {4,.015,{0,0}, 45 Degree}, {3,.01}, {5,.015,{0,0},0,2} },
    {1}
];

dataplot = MultipleListPlot[ Sequence @@ ( Transpose[{popyears,#}]& /@ popdata ),
    PlotJoined->True, PlotLabel->"Estimated World Population by Region",
    Frame->True, FrameLabel->{"Year","Population in Millions"}, PlotRange->All ];
```

On page 147 in Section 5.2.1 we show how to add a legend to this graphic, indicating the correspondence between plotting symbols and data sets. A graphic created with MultipleListPlot is much more useful with such a legend.

5.2.4 Three-Dimensional Graphics

■ Scatter Plots

Because ListPlot plots a list of points in two dimensions, many users incorrectly think that ListPlot3D plots a list of points in three dimensions. Instead, ListPlot3D accepts an array of height values and generates a surface from them. If you want to plot points in three-dimensional space, you need to construct a Graphics3D object containing

Point primitives and use Show to display it. This process is carried out by the function ScatterPlot3D, which is defined in the package Graphics`Graphics3D`.

```
Needs["Graphics`Graphics3D`"];
pts = Table[ {t, Cos[t]^2, Sin[2t]}, {t, 0, 5Pi, Pi/15} ];
ScatterPlot3D[pts];
```

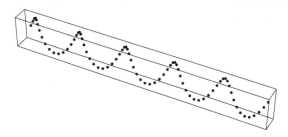

The function PointParametricPlot3D, defined in the package Graphics`ParametricPlot3D`, computes points and displays them in a single operation. PointParametricPlot3D is related to ScatterPlot3D in the same way that ListParametricPlot is related to ListPlot.

```
Needs["Graphics`ParametricPlot3D`"];
PointParametricPlot3D[ { v Cos[u], v Sin[u], v }, {u,0,2Pi,Pi/10}, {v,-2,2} ];
```

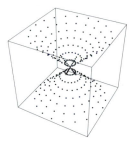

▪ Parametrized Curves and Surfaces

There are two definitions of ParametricPlot3D; one is built into the *Mathematica*'s kernel, and the other is defined in the package Graphics`ParametricPlot3D`. Which one should you use? We recommend using the built-in function, since the package function may not be supported in future releases of *Mathematica*.

The package Graphics`ParametricPlot3D` also contains the functions CylindricalPlot3D and SphericalPlot3D for making parametrized surface plots in cylindrical and spherical coordinates, as the examples here show:

```
Needs["Graphics`ParametricPlot3D`"];
gr1 = CylindricalPlot3D[ Sqrt[ 9 - (r Cos[2 theta])^2 ],
        {r,0,3}, {theta,0,2Pi,Pi/20}, PlotRange->All, DisplayFunction->Identity ];
gr2 = SphericalPlot3D[ (2 + Sin[phi])(3 + Cos[theta]),
        {theta, 0, 2Pi}, {phi, 0, Pi, Pi/18}, DisplayFunction->Identity ];
Show[GraphicsArray[{gr1,gr2}]];
```

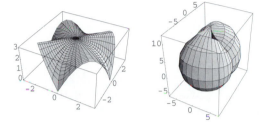

ListPlot3D plots an array of z values that are assumed to lie over a rectangular mesh in the xy plane. The function ListSurfacePlot3D, defined in the package Graphics`Graphics3D`, is more general: It takes an array of points (x, y, and z coordinates) to generate vertices in a polygonal mesh, so the distances between rows or between columns need not be constant.

```
Needs["Graphics`Graphics3D`"];
ulist = {-3,-1,-.5,.1,.4,1.3,2};
vlist = {-1.8, -.7, 0, .5,.8,1,1.4,1.7,2};
f[u_,v_] := { u + v, u - v, u v };
pts = Outer[ f, ulist, vlist ];
ListSurfacePlot3D[pts];
```

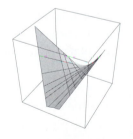

■ Surfaces of Revolution

The command SurfaceOfRevolution, in the package Graphics`SurfaceOfRevolution`, plots the surface generated by the rotation of a curve around an axis. If the first argument of SurfaceOfRevolution is a single expression, it is interpreted as a function $z = f(x)$ to be plotted, and the graph of this function in the xz plane produces the curve to be rotated. If the first argument is a list of two functions, these functions are interpreted as defining a parametrized curve in the xz plane. If the first argument is a list of three functions, these functions define a parametrized curve in space. The setting RevolutionAxis->$\{x,y,z\}$ specifies the line through the origin and the point (x,y,z) as the axis of rotation; the default setting is $\{0,0,1\}$, which specifies the z axis. Here are examples illustrating the possibilities:

```
Needs["Graphics`SurfaceOfRevolution`"];
Block[ {$DisplayFunction=Identity},
    gr1 = SurfaceOfRevolution[ x^3, {x,-1,1} ];
    gr2 = SurfaceOfRevolution[ {(t+.1)/4,Cot[t]}, {t,.5,2.9} ];
    gr3 = SurfaceOfRevolution[ {2+Cos[t],Sin[t],t}, {t,0,Pi} ];
    gr4 = SurfaceOfRevolution[ {6t,2t,t}, {t,0,1}, RevolutionAxis->{5,-1,0} ];
];
Show[GraphicsArray[{gr1,gr2,gr3,gr4}]];
```

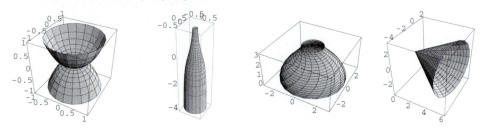

▪ Contour Surfaces

The built-in function ContourPlot plots a family of curves defined implicitly by the fixing of values of z in the equation $z = f(x, y)$. The analogous function ContourPlot3D, defined in the package Graphics`ContourPlot3D`, plots surfaces defined implicitly by the fixing of values of w in the equation $w = f(x, y, z)$. By default, ContourPlot3D plots only the surface defined by setting $w = 0$, but the option Contours can be set to a list of w values to plot several surfaces at once. Here is an example:

```
Needs["Graphics`ContourPlot3D`"];
ContourPlot3D[ x^2+y^2+z^2, {x,-3,3},{y,0,3},{z,0,3}, Contours->{1,4,9} ];
```

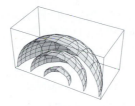

The package Graphics`ContourPlot3D` also defines the function ListContourPlot3D, which takes a three-dimensional array of real numbers representing values of a function $f(x, y, z)$ over a rectangular grid in space, and fits contour surfaces through the data points in much the same way that ContourPlot fits contour curves through an array of points in the plane.

- Mathematical Solids

With the graphics primitive Polygon, you can construct nearly any three-dimensional figure. The package Graphics`Shapes` contains definitions of some common shapes using Polygon. Six of these shapes appear in the following example. (This example requires a great deal of memory. If you have limited memory on your system, you may wish to restart *Mathematica* before running this example. Doing so will clear out old results so that all the memory on your computer will be available for this computation.)

```
Needs["Graphics`Shapes`"];
Show[ GraphicsArray[ Graphics3D /@
    { Cone[], Torus[], Cylinder[], Sphere[], Helix[], DoubleHelix[] }
]];
```

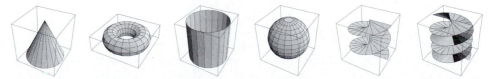

The shapes are defined as functions so that you can adjust the parameters that specify them. The Cylinder function, for example, accepts arguments that specify the radius and height. All of these functions also allow you to specify the number of polygons used to draw a shape; you can get smoother surfaces by increasing the number of polygons. Note that the functions defined in Graphics`Shapes` return lists of Polygon primitives as their results. It is necessary to place each list inside a Graphics3D object to display it.

Regular polyhedra are defined in the package Graphics`Polyhedra`. Be aware that this package was enhanced in Version 2.0. The following commands will not necessarily display polyhedra if you are using Version 1.2 or an earlier version of *Mathematica*.

(Again, if you have limited memory on your system, you may wish to restart *Mathematica* before running this example.)

```
Needs["Graphics`Polyhedra`"];
Show[ GraphicsArray[ Polyhedron /@
    { Hexahedron, Octahedron, Icosahedron, GreatDodecahedron,
        GreatStellatedDodecahedron, GreatIcosahedron } ] ];
```

Unlike the shapes in Graphics`Shapes`, each of which is defined by a separate function, the regular polyhedra are all specified by the assignment of different symbolic names to the single function Polyhedron. Also, the result of Polyhedron is a Graphics3D object, not a list of Polygon primitives, so you do not need to apply Graphics3D again. You can use the Vertices function to obtain the list of vertices of a polyhedron, as in this example:

```
Vertices[Octahedron]
```

```
{{0, 0, 1.41421}, {1.41421, 0, 0}, {0, 1.41421, 0}, {0, 0, -1.41421},
  {-1.41421, 0, 0}, {0, -1.41421, 0}}
```

If you want the faces of a polyhedron, you can use the Faces function:

```
Faces[Octahedron]
```

```
{{1, 2, 3}, {1, 3, 5}, {1, 5, 6}, {1, 6, 2}, {2, 6, 4}, {2, 4, 3}, {4, 6, 5},
  {3, 4, 5}}
```

The numbers in this result are indices into the corresponding list of vertices; for example, the triple {2,6,4} indicates that one of the triangular faces of the octahedron is obtained by the joining of the second, sixth, and fourth points in the list of vertices. If you want the explicit list of Polygon primitives, simply extract it from the Graphics3D object produced by Polyhedron, as follows:

```
Cases[ Polyhedron[Octahedron], _Polygon, Infinity ]
```

```
{Polygon[{{0., 0., 1.41421}, {1.41421, 0., 0.}, {0., 1.41421, 0.}}],
  Polygon[{{0., 0., 1.41421}, {0., 1.41421, 0.}, {-1.41421, 0., 0.}}],
  Polygon[{{0., 0., 1.41421}, {-1.41421, 0., 0.}, {0., -1.41421, 0.}}],
  Polygon[{{0., 0., 1.41421}, {0., -1.41421, 0.}, {1.41421, 0., 0.}}],
  Polygon[{{1.41421, 0., 0.}, {0., -1.41421, 0.}, {0., 0., -1.41421}}],
  Polygon[{{1.41421, 0., 0.}, {0., 0., -1.41421}, {0., 1.41421, 0.}}],
```

```
Polygon[{{0., 0., -1.41421}, {0., -1.41421, 0.}, {-1.41421, 0., 0.}}],
Polygon[{{0., 1.41421, 0.}, {0., 0., -1.41421}, {-1.41421, 0., 0.}}]}
```

This command searches for all occurrences of Polygon objects in the result of the Polyhedron function; the third argument, Infinity, tells Cases to search at all levels of the Graphics3D object (not just at the top level, which is the default).

The package Graphics`Polyhedra` also defines functions such as Stellate, Geodesate, and Truncate to manipulate polyhedra. Refer to the *Guide to Standard Mathematica Packages* for more information about these functions.

5.2.5 Mixed 2D and 3D Graphics

▪ Curves Defined Implicitly (Plots of Equations)

If you want to plot a curve, or a set of curves, in the plane given by an implicit formula, use the function ImplicitPlot.

ImplicitPlot[*eqn*, {*x*, *a*, *b*}] draws a graph of the set of points that satisfy the equation *eqn*. The variable *x* is associated with the horizontal axis and ranges from *a* to *b*. The remaining variable in the equation is associated with the vertical axis. ImplicitPlot[*eqn*, {*x*, *a*, *x1*, *x2*, ..., *b*}] allows you to specify values of *x* where special care must be exercised. ImplicitPlot[{*eqn1*, *eqn2*, ...}, {*x*, *a*, *b*}] allows more than one equation to be plotted, with PlotStyle set as in the Plot function. When ImplicitPlot is specified with two iterators—that is, ImplicitPlot[*eqn*, {*x*, *a*, *b*}, {*y*, *a*, *b*}]—it uses a contour plot method of generating the plot. This form does not allow specification of intermediate points.

```
Needs["Graphics`ImplicitPlot`"];
ImplicitPlot[{x^2 + 2 y^2 == 36, x^2 + y^2 == 9}, {x, -6, 6},
    PlotStyle -> { Dashing[{0.03}], Thickness[0.007] } ];
```

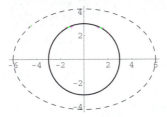

Notice that ImplicitPlot draws a figure to scale automatically. In other words, one unit in the x direction is drawn the same size as one unit in the y direction.

▪ Vector Fields

The packages Graphics`PlotField` contains functions for plotting vector, gradient, Hamiltonian, and Polya vector fields, as well as functions for plotting a list of vectors.

```
Needs["Graphics`PlotField`"];
Block[ { $DisplayFunction = Identity },
    gr1 = PlotVectorField[ {y,-x}, {x,-2,2}, {y,-2,2} ];
    gr2 = PlotGradientField[ x y, {x,-5,5}, {y,-5,5} ];
];
Show[GraphicsArray[ { gr1, gr2 } ]];
```

The functions in this package accept the options MaxArrowLength, ScaleFactor, and ScaleFunction to determine the size of the vectors plotted, and the option ColorFunction to specify how vectors are colored.

The package Graphics`PlotField3D` contains definitions for the functions PlotVectorField3D and PlotGradientField3D for plotting fields in three dimensional space. (This example is another one that requires a great deal of memory. If you have limited memory on your system, you may wish to restart *Mathematica* before running this example.)

```
Needs["Graphics`PlotField3D`"];
Block[ { $DisplayFunction = Identity },
    gr1 = PlotVectorField3D[{-y/z, (x + y)/z, 0}, {x,-1,1}, {y,-1,1}, {z,1,2},
                VectorHeads -> True ];
    gr2 = PlotGradientField3D[ x y + y z + x z, {x,-5,5}, {y,-5,5}, {z,-5,5} ];
];
Show[GraphicsArray[ { gr1, gr2 } ]];
```

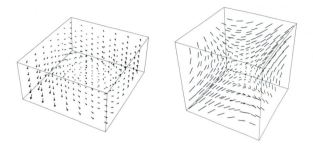

As the example shows, these two functions draw vectors without arrowheads unless the option VectorHeads is set to True.

5.2.6 Application Areas

The packages in this section are not graphics packages as such; they are packages devoted to particular application areas. We mention them here because they each include a significant graphics capability.

- Graph Theory and Combinatorics

The package on graph theory and combinatorics (DiscreteMath`Combinatorica`) includes routines for drawing directed and undirected graphs. This package was written by Steven Skiena to accompany his book *Implementing Discrete Mathematics: Combinatorics and Graph Theory with Mathematica*, to which we refer you for examples. You will find bibliographic information for Skiena's book on page 328, in the "Suggested Readings" section at the end of this book.

- Computational Geometry

The package DiscreteMath`ComputationalGeometry` on computational geometry includes commands for drawing planar graphs and Voronoi diagrams.

- Maps of the World

With the functions in the package Miscellaneous`WorldPlot`, you can draw a map of a country, several countries, or the world. Here is a map of South America with outlines around each country:

```
Needs["Miscellaneous`WorldPlot`"];
```

```
WorldPlot[ SouthAmerica ];
```

The first argument of WorldPlot indicates the countries to be plotted; it should be a single country name or a list of names. Names of countries must be specified as strings (that is, you must enter them with quotation marks). However, the names of continents or regions (such as SouthAmerica in the example above) must not be quoted because they are actually symbols defined as lists of the constituent countries.

```
InputForm[ Oceania ]
```

```
{"Indonesia", "Papua-New Guinea", "Fiji", "Australia", "New Zealand"}
```

```
WorldPlot[ {"Australia", "New Zealand"} ];
```

The package Miscellaneous`WorldNames` contains seven regions or continents, as well as the entire world.

```
?Miscellaneous`WorldNames`*
```

```
Africa       Europe      NorthAmerica SouthAmerica World
Asia         MiddleEast  Oceania
```

You can use online help to see the countries in a region.

```
??MiddleEast
```

MiddleEast contains the names of the countries of the Middle East
    defined in the WorldData database.

```
MiddleEast = {"Egypt", "Israel", "Lebanon", "Syria", "Turkey",
    "SaudiArabia", "Yemen AR", "Yemen PR", "Oman", "UAE", "Bahrain",
    "Kuwait", "Iraq", "Iran", "Jordan", "Qatar"}
```

You can also give a pair as an argument to WorldPlot. The first element in the pair is a list of countries; the second element is a shading function. If you specify RandomColors or RandomGrays, the countries will be drawn in randomly chosen colors or gray shades.

```
Block[ { $DisplayFunction = Identity },
    gr1 = WorldPlot[ {Oceania, RandomGrays},
            WorldProjection -> Mollweide, WorldToGraphics->True ];
    gr2 = WorldPlot[ {{"Australia","New Zealand"},RandomColors},
            WorldProjection->Mercator, WorldToGraphics->True ];
];
Show[GraphicsArray[ { gr1, gr2 } ]];
```

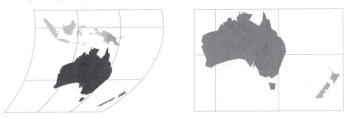

We set the option WorldToGraphics to True to force WorldPlot to produce a Graphics object; by default, it returns a WorldData object, which is a more compact representation but one that would have confused GraphicsArray. The option WorldProjection allows you to specify the projection used in drawing the map; for example, the Mollweide projection used in the graphic on the left makes the world look round instead of flat. Other projections include Albers, Equirectangular, and Sinusoidal. You can also specify your own shading function, as shown here:

```
Needs["Graphics`Colors`"]; (* make sure the color names are defined! *)
shadeFunction[country_String] :=
    Switch[country,
        "USA", Purple,  "Greenland", Green,  "Mexico", Red,
        _, Gray        (* all other countries are drawn in gray  *) ]
WorldPlot[ {NorthAmerica, shadeFunction}, WorldBackground -> SeaGreen,
    WorldGrid -> None, WorldFrame -> Thickness[0.01] ];
```

The coordinates of each country are associated with that country's name by rules attached to the symbol WorldData.

```
WorldData["Peru"]
```

```
{{{-1101, -4224}, {-850, -4577}, {-515, -4726}, {-360, -4871}, {-202, -4820},
   {-202, -4822}, {-266, -4829}, {-300, -4742}, {-6, -4517}, {-6, -4517},
   {-146, -4376}, {-158, -4206}, {-227, -4243}, {-253, -4197}, {-253, -4197},
   {-308, -4374}, {-452, -4441}, {-564, -4392}, {-566, -4231}, {-661, -4238},
   {-657, -4174}, {-657, -4174}, {-750, -4120}, {-1050, -4170}, {-1050, -4170},
   {-1101, -4224}}}
```

This example shows the coordinates for the boundary of Peru, given as latitude and longitude in minutes.

- *Mathematica* and AutoCAD

If you want to import a graphic produced by *Mathematica* into AutoCAD, you will find the package Utilities`DXF` helpful. The function WriteDXF writes a Graphics3D object to AutoCAD's DXF format.

```
Needs["Graphics`Shapes`"];
s = Show[Graphics3D[Sphere[]]];
```

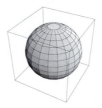

```
Needs["Utilities`DXF`"];
WriteDXF["sphere.dxf", s];
```

Graphics3D is the only data type that WriteDXF accepts. If you want to generate a .dxf file of a SurfaceGraphics object (such as the result of a Plot3D command), you must convert it to a Graphics3D object. You do this by applying the function Graphics3D to a SurfaceGraphics object. Here is an example:

```
p = Plot3D[Sin[x y], {x, 0, Pi}, {y, 0, 2Pi}];
```

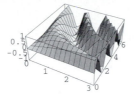

```
WriteDXF["plot3D.dxf", Graphics3D[p]];
```

Now the file named plot3D.dxf contains definitions that can be imported into AutoCAD.

5.3 Summary

If you use only the functions built into *Mathematica*, you will limit yourself or possibly spend time reinventing a function that WRI has already provided.

To use a function defined in a package, you must load the package with << or the Needs command. Alternatively, you can instruct *Mathematica* to load packages that you need when you start up the program, or you can load a Master` package and *Mathematica* will automatically load the appropriate package when you call functions declared in that package. You can also use these package-loading constructs with packages you write or obtain from MathSource, *The Mathematica Journal* electronic supplementary disk, or an electronic bulletin board or archive.

This chapter has presented an overview of the graphics-related packages that are distributed with Version 2.2 of *Mathematica*. We have provided a few examples for each package to give you an idea of its capabilities, but because the packages evolve with each new release of *Mathematica*, we have not attempted to be comprehensive. For a handy reference to the contents of packages, see Nancy Blachman's *Mathematica Quick Reference*, and for a complete description of all the standard *Mathematica* packages, consult the *Guide to Standard Mathematica Packages*, which is included in the documentation shipped with *Mathematica*. These books are listed in "Suggested Readings," beginning on page 327.

Chapter 6

Coordinate Systems

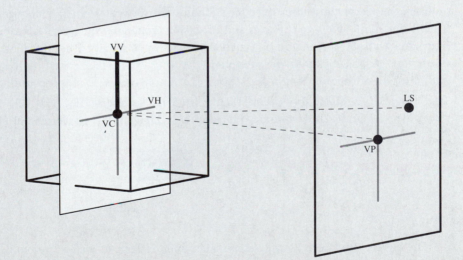

This chapter describes the coordinate systems used in *Mathematica* graphics. The multiplicity of coordinate systems used in creating an image is perhaps the worst feature of *Mathematica*. The systems each have a particular purpose and make sense for that purpose, but the relationships among them are complicated and sometimes unintuitive.

6.1 Two-Dimensional Graphics

6.1.1 The Coordinate Systems

In a 2D graphics object, several coordinate systems are active at once: the object coordinate system, the scaled coordinate system, several text coordinate systems, and the PlotRegion coordinate system. The interplay between these coordinate systems determines how a 2D graphic is mapped into a drawing area.

- Object Coordinates

The object coordinate system is the one in which you specify graphics primitives such as Point, Line, and Polygon (unless you use the Scaled modifier, described below). If you specify an explicit PlotRange, it is expressed in object coordinates; the AxesOrigin setting is also expressed in object coordinates. The frame drawn by the Frame option outlines the rectangle whose object coordinates are specified by the PlotRange. The default tick mark labels on the axes and the frame (generated by Ticks->Automatic and FrameTicks->Automatic) represent object coordinates. If you specify other tick mark positions, you use object coordinates, as you do if you use the GridLines setting to specify grid lines. All of the numbers in the following example represent object coordinates.

```
Show[Graphics[{ Circle[{5,8},4], Line[{{2,14},{16,3}}], Rectangle[{15,7},{24,12}] },
    Axes->True, AspectRatio->Automatic, PlotRange->{{1,25},{3,15}}, AxesOrigin->{0,0} ]];
```

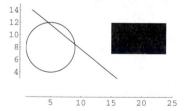

The built-in functions Plot, ParametricPlot, and ListPlot, as well as functions such as BarChart and PolarPlot defined in the standard packages, produce Graphics objects containing Point, Line, and other graphics primitives with positions expressed in object coordinates. The part of *Mathematica* that generates PostScript code for Graphics objects treats the objects generated by Plot and the other plotting functions the same as it treats Graphics objects you create "manually."

▪ Scaled Coordinates

The scaled coordinate system is used when you specify the Scaled modifier. Its relation to the object coordinate system is established by the PlotRange. If the effective PlotRange (whether specified by you or computed by the Automatic algorithm) is {{*xmin*,*xmax*},{*ymin*,*ymax*}}, then the point whose Scaled coordinates are $(0,0)$ is the point whose object coordinates are (*xmin*, *ymin*), and the point whose Scaled coordinates are $(1,1)$ is the point whose object coordinates are (*xmax*, *ymax*). In other words, the origin of the scaled coordinates is at the lower left corner of the plot range rectangle, and the scaled point $(1,1)$ is at the upper right corner. Note that the corners of the plot range rectangle are generally *not* the corners of the drawing area; in general, the plot range is mapped into a subrectangle of the drawing area to leave room for tick marks and other features.

In this example, we create a Graphics object using Scaled coordinates to draw two points and two lines, and redisplay the object with different option settings.

```
gr1 = Graphics[{ PointSize[.1], Thickness[.02], GrayLevel[0],
        Point[Scaled[{0,0}]], Point[Scaled[{1,1}]],
        Line[ { Scaled[{.03,.5}], Scaled[{.97,.5}] } ],
        Line[ { Scaled[{.5,.03}], Scaled[{.5,.97}] } ]
}, Frame->True, Background->GrayLevel[2/3], DisplayFunction->Identity ];
gr2 = Show[ gr1, PlotRange->{{0,10},{0,5}} ];
gr3 = Show[ gr1, PlotRange->All ];
gr4 = Show[ gr1, PlotLabel->"Example of\nScaled Coordinates" ];
gr5 = Show[ gr1, PlotRegion->{{.1,.9},{.1,.9}} ];
gr6 = Show[ gr1, PlotRange->{{1,4},{1,5}}, Axes->True, AxesOrigin->{0,0} ];
Show[GraphicsArray[{ {gr1,gr2,gr3}, {gr4,gr5,gr6} }]];
```

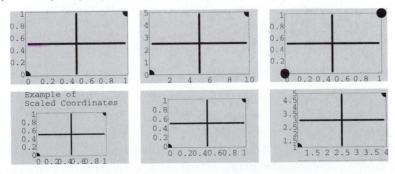

In each graphic, the gray background fills the drawing area, allowing us to see how the object coordinate system (outlined by the frame) fits into the drawing area. The PlotRange setting specifies the scale of the object coordinates, but regardless of the object scale we use, the points and lines specified with Scaled coordinates have the same positions relative to the frame. Options such as PlotLabel, PlotRegion, and AxesOrigin may affect how the frame outlining the PlotRange fits into the drawing area, but the point is that the Scaled coordinates remain attached to the frame, not to the drawing area as a whole.

Scaled coordinates are not restricted to values between 0 and 1, but values outside that range represent points that lie outside the PlotRange rectangle. In the horizontal direction, coordinates less than 0 or greater than 1 represent points to the left or right of the PlotRange; in the vertical direction, they represent points below or above it. However, since graphics primitives are ordinarily clipped to the plotting rectangle, you won't be able to see features positioned outside the rectangle unless you use the setting PlotRange->All.

Scaled coordinates are useful when the PlotRange option is set to Automatic (the default) or All. For example, if you explicitly specify {{0,2},{1,4}} as the PlotRange, you can calculate that the point whose scaled coordinates are (.3, .8) has object coordinates (.6, 3.4). But it is usually easier to let *Mathematica* calculate the PlotRange (especially when you are using Plot to graph a function); in this case, Scaled coordinates give you a convenient way to place a text label in the upper right corner of a graph without knowing the object coordinates:

```
label = Text[ "Density Function of a\nNormal Distribution", Scaled[{1,1}], {1,1} ];
Plot[ Evaluate[ D[Erf[x],x] ], {x,-2,2}, AspectRatio->Automatic, Epilog->label ];
```

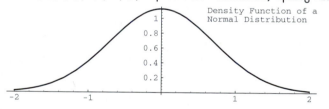

You can also use a hybrid form of scaled and object coordinates. An expression of the form

$$\texttt{Scaled[} \{dx,dy\}, \{x,y\} \texttt{]}$$

represents the point whose position is obtained if you start at the point (x, y) in object coordinates and move away from it by the offset (dx, dy) in scaled coordinates. For example, the specification Scaled[{.5,.2},{1,3}] denotes the point obtained if you start at the point whose object coordinates are $(1, 3)$ and move to the right by half the width of the plot range and then up by 20 percent of the height of the plot range. The package Graphics`MultipleListPlot` distributed with *Mathematica* uses this hybrid form of Scaled coordinates to draw plotting symbols around data points. For example, if the plotting symbol is a square, the function

```
Line[ { Scaled[{-.01,-.01},#], Scaled[{.01,-.01},#], Scaled[{.01,.01},#],
        Scaled[{-.01,.01},#], Scaled[{-.01,-.01},#] } ]&
```

is constructed; this function takes the object coordinates of a data point as its argument and returns a specification for a Line object that draws a square centered around the data point whose width and height are equal to 2 percent of the width of the plot range.

- Text Coordinates

Each piece of text in a graphic establishes a coordinate system of its own. Its scale is determined by the bounding rectangle of the text: The origin of the text coordinates is at the center of this rectangle, and the scale is chosen so that the lower left corner of the text rectangle is at $(-1, -1)$ and the upper right corner is at $(1, 1)$. However, the edges of this "bounding rectangle" are parallel to the axes in *object* coordinates. When text is rotated, the text bounding rectangle encloses a much larger area than the text itself occupies. In the following diagram, for example, the light gray rectangle represents a piece of unrotated text, the dark gray rectangle represents the same text rotated about its center through an angle of 35 degrees, and the black outline represents the bounding rectangle of the rotated text.

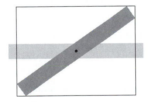

Text coordinates are related to object coordinates in this way: If the specification of the text primitive is

$$\text{Text}[\ string, \ \{x,y\}, \ \{dx,dy\}, \ \{mx,my\} \ ]$$

then the point whose coordinates are (dx, dy) in text coordinates is "attached" to the point whose coordinates are (x, y) in object coordinates. It isn't possible to specify the relationship between the scales of the two coordinate systems, however, because the object coordinate system can change scale if the graphic is enlarged or reduced, whereas the text is always rendered at the point size specified. Here is an example:

```
gr1 = Graphics[{ Point[{6,2}], Point[{0,0}], PointSize[.04], Point[{4,1}],
        Text[ FontForm["SOME TEXT",{"Courier",12}], {4,1} ] }, PlotRange->All,
        Frame->True, FrameTicks->None, Background->GrayLevel[2/3] ];
gr2 = Show[ gr1, PlotRange->{{0,6},{0,2}}, DisplayFunction->Identity ];
ga = GraphicsArray[{ gr1, gr2 }, GraphicsSpacing->.2 ];
Show[ga]; Show[ga]; Show[ga];
```

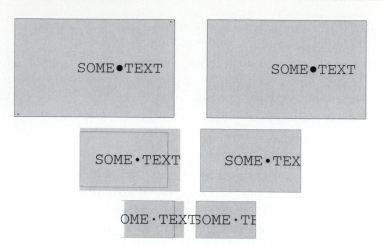

The same two graphics objects are displayed at three sizes. (Remember that resizing *Mathematica* graphics is not a function of the *Mathematica* kernel, but a function of the program that is displaying the graphics: a Notebook Front End, for example, or the psfix utility.) The only difference between these graphics is that the one on the left in each row has a PlotRange setting of All and the one on the right has an explicit PlotRange setting of {{0,6},{0,2}}. In each graphic, the gray background fills the entire drawing area allowing us to see how the frame surrounding the PlotRange is mapped into the drawing area and how this mapping is influenced by the text. In all six graphics, the string "SOME TEXT" is centered on the point whose coordinates are {4,1} in object coordinates. In the first row, the drawing area is large enough for the text to fit entirely inside the frame, so both graphics look the same. In the second row, the drawing area has been reduced, and so the graphical elements scale down but the text remains the same size. In both graphics in this row, the requirement to keep the center of the text attached to the point {4,1} has caused the text to extend outside the frame.

In the graphic with PlotRange set to All, the text is not permitted to be clipped; the only way to meet this additional requirement and still keep the center of the text at {4,1} is to shrink the frame surrounding the PlotRange so that it no longer occupies the entire drawing area. In the graphic with an explicit PlotRange setting, the text is clipped at the frame and the frame still fills the drawing area, but even so, the part of the text that was not clipped occupies a much larger percentage of the area of the graphic than it did before because reducing the drawing area did not reduce the text. In the third row, the drawing area is so small that the string is simply too wide to fit at the given point size, but even though the string now spills entirely out of the drawing area, the relationship between text coordinates and object coordinates is maintained: The center of the string is always at the point whose object coordinates are {4,1}.

- PlotRegion

The PlotRegion option uses a coordinate system that runs from 0 to 1 across the width and height of the drawing area. This system is similar to the scaled coordinate system described earlier, but the rectangle defining scaled coordinates is the one into which the PlotRange is mapped, which, as we saw, is usually not the entire drawing area. The PlotRegion specifies a rectangle inside the drawing area into which all features of a graphic are scaled. No other aspect of *Mathematica* graphics uses the PlotRegion coordinates, because all other graphics features are mapped into the rectangle defined by the PlotRegion. This example shows how the rectangle in graphics coordinates specified by the PlotRange is mapped into the part of the display area specified by the PlotRegion:

```
gr1 = Graphics[{ Circle[{5,8},4], Line[{{2,14},{16,3}}], Rectangle[{15,7},{24,12}] },
        AspectRatio->Automatic, PlotRange->{{0,30},{0,15}},
        Frame->True, FrameTicks->None, Background->GrayLevel[2/3] ];
gr2 = Append[ gr1, PlotRegion->{{0,.5},{.5,1}} ];
gr3 = Append[ gr1, PlotRegion->{{.2,.8},{.2,.8}} ];
Show[GraphicsArray[{ gr1, gr2, gr3 }]];
```

In each graphic, the entire drawing area is filled with gray, but the PlotRange rectangle is mapped only into the part of the drawing area specified by the PlotRegion setting. In the example on the left, the default PlotRegion setting causes the PlotRange rectangle to fill the entire drawing area. In the center example, the setting {{0,.5},{.5,1}} instructs *Mathematica* to map the PlotRange rectangle into a rectangle whose coordinates in the PlotRegion coordinate system satisfy the inequalities $0 \leq x \leq .5$ and $.5 \leq y \leq 1$. In the example on the right, the setting {{.2,.8},{.2,.8}} instructs *Mathematica* to map the PlotRange rectangle into a rectangle whose coordinates satisfy the inequalities $.2 \leq x \leq .8$ and $.2 \leq y \leq 8$.

6.1.2 An Extended Example

In this section, we display a single graphics object again and again, each time with a different option setting, to give you a feel for how the different graphics coordinate systems interact. We encourage you to experiment with still more settings until you are sure you understand the concepts.

Our example graphic contains four points, a line, and a rectangle specified in object coordinates, and four more points specified in scaled coordinates. The elements specified in object coordinates are drawn in black and white, and the points in scaled coordinates are drawn in light gray, so that we can distinguish between the two coordinate systems. The entire drawing area is filled with a dark gray background, and the Frame option is used to draw an outline around the rectangle specified by the PlotRange. The frame is drawn as a thin white line. Here is the code:

```
gr = Graphics[{
        (* graphical elements specified in object coordinates *)
        GrayLevel[0], PointSize[.1],
        Point /@ { {0,0}, {0,1}, {1,1}, {1,0} },
        GrayLevel[1], Rectangle[{0,0},{1,1}],
        GrayLevel[0], Line[{ {0,0}, {0,1}, {1,1}, {1,0}, {0,0} }],
        (* elements specified in Scaled coordinates *)
        GrayLevel[2/3], PointSize[.05],
        Point[Scaled[#]]& /@ { {0,0}, {0,1}, {1,1}, {1,0} }
}, Background->GrayLevel[1/3],
    Frame->True, FrameStyle->GrayLevel[1], FrameTicks->None
];
```

And here is its default appearance:

```
Show[gr];
```

The frame fills the edges of the drawing area; the graphics elements fall just inside the frame because of the way the Automatic algorithm computes the PlotRange. If you look closely, you will see that the light gray points (specified in scaled coordinates) are centered on the corners of the frame and the black points (specified in object coordinates) are centered on the corners of the rectangle. These points are easier to see in the next picture because the setting PlotRange->All prevents the dots representing the points from being clipped.

```
Show[gr,PlotRange->All];
```

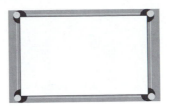

If we override *Mathematica*'s choice of plot range with an explicit PlotRange setting, it becomes even clearer that the Scaled points are attached to the frame and the other points are not.

```
Show[gr,PlotRange->{{-1,2},{-1/4,3/2}}];
```

When we add tick marks to the frame, the frame is forced into a smaller region of the drawing area so that there will be room for the tick labels.

```
Show[gr,PlotRange->{{-1,2},{-1/4,3/2}},FrameTicks->Automatic];
```

If the text is larger, the frame must get smaller.

```
Show[gr,PlotRange->{{-1,2},{-1/4,3/2}},FrameTicks->Automatic,
        DefaultFont->{"Courier",12}];
```

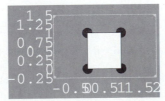

Adding a label across the top of a plot also forces the frame to shrink, to leave room for the label.

```
Show[gr,PlotRange->{{-1,2},{-1/4,3/2}},FrameTicks->Automatic,PlotLabel->"My Picture" ];
```

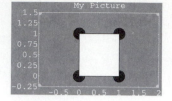

Changing the AspectRatio setting changes the shape of the drawing area and the PlotRange rectangle.

```
Show[gr,PlotRange->{{-1,2},{-1/4,3/2}}, AspectRatio->1,
            FrameTicks->{{0,1,2},{0,{.5,"one-half"},1}} ];
```

Adjusting the PlotRegion to {{.5,1},{0,.5}} confines everything but the background color to the lower right quarter of the drawing area.

```
Show[gr,PlotRange->All,FrameTicks->Automatic,PlotRegion->{{.5,1},{0.,.5}}];
```

6.1.3 Display of 2D Graphics

These are the five steps performed when *Mathematica* displays a graphics object:

1. The AspectRatio setting is inspected to determine the shape of the drawing area.

2. The entire drawing area is filled with the Background color, if one was specified.

3. The PlotRegion setting is inspected to determine what subrectangle of the drawing area the graphic is permitted to occupy. (By default, this is the whole drawing area.) After this step, we know the region of the drawing area into which the graphic is to be mapped.

4. If the `PlotRange` setting is `Automatic`, a plot range is computed by an internal algorithm (described in our discussion of the `PlotRange` option in Section 7.1.1 on page 212); if an explicit plot range is specified, it is used. If the `PlotRange` setting is `All`, the plot range is the smallest rectangle in object coordinates large enough to enclose all of the graphical elements (points, lines, polygons, etc.), taking into account the thicknesses of the lines and the radii of the dots representing the points. In any case, we know after this step what rectangle in the object coordinate space is to be displayed. This rectangle also defines scaled coordinates; its lower left corner is `Scaled[{0,0}]` and its upper right corner is `Scaled[{1,1}]`.

5. The bounding rectangles for text that result from tick labels, axis labels, and plot labels are attached to the plot range rectangle determined in the step 4. If the setting `PlotRange->All` is given, text specified by `Text` primitives within the `Prolog`, `Epilog`, and main graphics list is also considered at this stage. Each piece of text specifies a point in its own coordinate system and a point in the object coordinate system that are to be mapped to the same point in the display area (as explained in the discussion of text coordinates in Section 6.1.1 on page 183). You can visualize the situation as a collection of little metal rectangles pinned to a large rubber sheet with a rectangle drawn on it: The rectangles represent the pieces of text, which don't change size; the rubber sheet represents the plane of the object coordinates; and the rectangle represents the plot range rectangle. As the rubber sheet is stretched, the metal rectangles pinned to it are carried along; the problem is to stretch the rubber sheet to the largest possible size so that (1) the rectangle has the shape specified by the `AspectRatio` setting, and (2) the rectangle and all the little metal rectangles fit inside the `PlotRegion` rectangle.

Some of the steps outlined above are performed by the *Mathematica* kernel when it generates PostScript code for a graphic; others are actually carried out by PostScript code at the time the graphic is rendered by a PostScript interpreter. The problem remaining after step 5 is a linear programming problem, and it *must* be solved within the PostScript code for two reasons: The sizes of the bounding rectangles of the text are not accessible at any higher level, and the graphic may be resized (in a graphics cell in a Notebook, for example) after the *Mathematica* kernel has generated the PostScript code. Changing the size of the display area will often change the solution to the linear programming problem. The PostScript procedure that solves this problem is called `Mlp`, for "*Mathematica* linear program." The program may have no solution (for example, one of the pieces of text may be too large to fit inside the display area); in this case, the algorithm returns a compromise. In any event, the scaling parameters returned by the `Mlp` procedure map the `PlotRange` rectangle and all the text into the `PlotRegion` rectangle.

6.2 Three-Dimensional Graphics

More coordinate systems are needed in 3D graphics than in 2D graphics. Moreover, the computations involved in projecting 3D graphics into a plane and scaling that flat image into a display area are more complicated than the scaling computations in 2D graphics. Still, many of the concepts involved in displaying 3D graphics are generalizations of their two-dimensional counterparts.

6.2.1 Coordinate Systems for Specifying Objects

▪ Object Coordinates

As with 2D graphics, the object coordinate system in Graphics3D objects is the one in which the positions of graphics primitives are specified (unless the Scaled modifier is used, as described below). In SurfaceGraphics objects, the object coordinate system is the one whose z coordinate specifies the array of z values and whose x and y coordinates are specified by the MeshRange setting. The object coordinate system also specifies the PlotRange and the positions of tick marks (in the Ticks setting) and grid lines (in the FaceGrids setting).

In 2D graphics, the PlotRange setting specifies a rectangle in the two-dimensional object coordinate space that is to be mapped into the display area. In 3D graphics, the PlotRange setting specifies a cuboidal region in the three-dimensional object coordinate space that is to be mapped into the display area, but before this volume can be displayed in three dimensions, it must be projected into a two-dimensional plane, as explained in Section 6.2.2, on perspective projection (page 192).

▪ Scaled Coordinates

As in 2D graphics, there is a scaled coordinate system in 3D graphics whose coordinates run from 0 to 1 along each dimension of the PlotRange. Scaled coordinates in 3D graphics require three coordinates instead of two; other than that, they function exactly like their two-dimensional counterparts.

The hybrid form of Scaled that combines object and scaled coordinates is also available in 3D graphics, but the form is

$$\text{Scaled}[\ \{x, y, z\},\ \{dx, dy, dz\}\ ]$$

This form means that the object coordinates of a point are given first, followed by an offset in scaled coordinates. Note that this order is the reverse of the order used for Scaled coordinates in 2D graphics. Neither the online usage message for Scaled nor the description of scaled coordinates in The *Mathematica* Book indicates that this surprising reversal is intentional. The fact that it has not been corrected in the five years that *Mathematica* has been on the market suggests that *Mathematica* users seldom use Scaled coordinates in 3D graphics. The reversed order may be fixed in a future release, however, so be careful if you decide to use this feature. Meanwhile, you can study the following graphics to convince yourself that the reversal is real (it took us quite a while to convince ourselves).

```
gr1 = Graphics[{
    PointSize[.04], Point[{.5,0}], Point[{2.5,0}],
    GrayLevel[.7], Thickness[.02], Line[{ Scaled[{0,1}], Scaled[{.5,0},{0,0}] }],
    GrayLevel[.3], Thickness[.02], Line[{ Scaled[{0,1}], Scaled[{0,0},{.5,0}] }]
}, Frame->True, AspectRatio->Automatic, PlotRange->{{-2,3},{-2,3}} ];
gr2 = Graphics3D[{
    PointSize[.04], Point[{.5,0,0}], Point[{2.5,0,0}],
    GrayLevel[.7], Thickness[.02], Line[{ Scaled[{0,1,0}], Scaled[{.5,0,0},{0,0,0}] }],
    GrayLevel[.3], Thickness[.02], Line[{ Scaled[{0,1,0}], Scaled[{0,0,0},{.5,0,0}] }]
}, BoxRatios->Automatic, PlotRange->{{-2,3},{-2,3},{0,1}}, Axes->{True,True,False},
    ViewPoint->{0,0,1} ];
Show[GraphicsArray[{gr1,gr2},GraphicsSpacing->.3]];
```

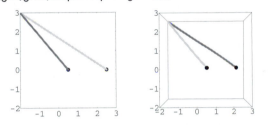

The code for the 3D graphic is identical to the code for the 2D graphic except that a z coordinate of 0 has been added to the specifications of all the points. Notice that the dark gray and light gray lines have switched positions. If you think about it, you will see that this switch proves that the coordinate systems in the hybrid form of Scaled have been reversed as just described. This was the simplest example we could construct that illustrated the point clearly and convincingly.

■ Text Coordinates

The Text primitive allows pieces of text to be attached to 3D graphics. As in 2D graphics, each piece of text has its own coordinate system, in which offsets and rotations are specified. A text coordinate system is attached to a point in object coordinates, and the text is placed in the display area relative to the projected image of the point of attachment.

```
Show[Graphics3D[{
    Cuboid[{0,0,0},{1,1,1}],
    Text[FontForm["CUBE",{"Courier-Bold",20}],
        {.1,.9,.75}, {-1,1}, {Cos[Pi/4],Sin[Pi/4]} ]
} ],PlotRange->All ];
```

Note that the setting PlotRange->All does not cause 3D graphics to be scaled to leave room for text; in the example, the text is clipped (the lower right corner of the E) even though PlotRange->All was specified.

6.2.2 Coordinate Systems for Perspective Projection

You will need the information in this section only if you are manipulating the perspective and lighting settings in 3D graphics. The discussion here is at a slightly higher level of mathematical sophistication than most of the other material in this book. This level of detail is necessary for a precise description of how *Mathematica* handles perspective and illumination, but, a precise description may be more than you need, so feel free to skim or skip this material if you are content with the default settings *Mathematica* uses to display and illuminate three-dimensional scenes.

▪ The Theory of Perspective Projection

Mathematica displays 3D graphics scenes (given as Graphics3D objects or SurfaceGraphics objects) by perspective projection. Perspective projection mimics the way our eyes see real objects (except that it is monocular; stereo vision effects are not taken into account). A perspective projection is determined by three parameters: a viewpoint, a view center, and a vertical vector. The viewpoint is the point where the your eye is located, the view center is the point where the your gaze is directed (i.e., what you are looking at), and the line of sight is the line joining these two points. The viewpoint and view center specify the projection up to rotation around the line of sight; the last degree of freedom is removed by the specification that the view vertical vector (which can point in any direction except parallel to the line of sight) must appear vertical in the projected two-dimensional image.

Here is a picture illustrating these notions:

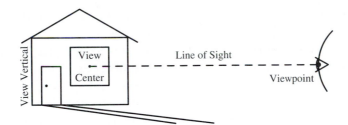

A viewer is standing in the road looking into the window of a house; the line of sight joins the viewer's eye to some object inside the house. The view vertical direction is what distinguishes a viewer standing erect from a viewer lying down in the road: If the viewer is standing up, the wall of the house appears vertical, but if the viewer is lying down, the wall appears horizontal and the floor appears vertical.

Now that you know the physical situation that *Mathematica*'s viewing model is intended to simulate, we will use this diagram to specify the process more precisely:

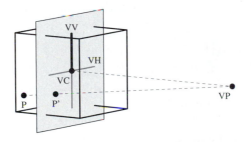

The data you specify to *Mathematica* are the viewpoint, labeled VP; the view center, labeled VC; and the view vertical vector, labeled VV. The two-dimensional projected image ultimately displayed is formed in the unique plane containing VC and perpendicular to the line of sight (the line joining VC to VP); this plane is shaded in the diagram. Points in the three-dimensional scene are projected into this plane as follows. The image of a point P is the point P' in which the line joining P to VP intersects the image plane. The sample point P in the picture lies on the far side of the image plane from the viewpoint, but this is not necessary; as long as the line joining P to VP is not parallel to the image plane, the intersection point P' will exist. The first stage of the perspective projection is the projection of all the points in the three-dimensional scene into the image plane in this way. Naturally, a line segment in space is mapped to the line segment in the image plane joining the images of the original segment's endpoints; likewise, a polygon in space is mapped to the polygon in the image plane defined by the images of the original polygon's vertices.

To keep the diagram simple, we choose a special configuration in which the line of sight is perpendicular to one of the faces of the bounding box. However, the viewpoint and view center need not be positioned in this way. Indeed, *Mathematica*'s default settings for viewpoint and view center determine a line of sight that is not perpendicular to any face of the box. The image plane is still the plane containing the view center and perpendicular to the line of sight.

There is also no reason to expect that the view vertical vector as specified lies in the image plane, so it has to be projected along with all the other elements of the three-dimensional scene. Its image will be a vector lying in the image plane; this vector will be nonzero provided that the vertical vector is not perpendicular to the image plane (equivalently, provided that it is not parallel to the line of sight). The vector labeled VV in the diagram is actually the projected image of the view vertical vector. Consider this example:

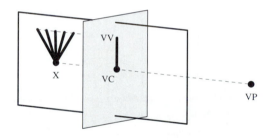

The plane containing the point X is perpendicular to the image plane and contains the line of sight; in fact, X lies on the line of sight. The several vectors shown emanating from X all have the same vector VV as their projection in the image plane, so specifying any one of these vectors as the view vertical vector leads to the same displayed image.

One point bears special mention. If you imagine the viewpoint VP receding to infinity along the line of sight, you will see that in the limit, the rays joining the viewpoint to points on the image plane become parallel lines. Thus the limiting case as the focal length becomes infinite is orthogonal projection. The greater the distance between viewpoint and view center, the less distortion in the images of objects in the three-dimensional scene. This is evident in the following example, in which the bounding box looks more "box-like" (i.e., more like an orthogonal image of a box) as the magnitude of the ViewPoint setting increases.

```
Needs["Graphics`Polyhedra`"];
stellicos = Stellate[Icosahedron[]];
Show[GraphicsArray[
    Graphics3D[stellicos,ViewPoint->(#{1,-2,1.5})]& /@ {.5,.75,1,1.25,2,5}
]];
```

Once all the objects in the three-dimensional scene have been projected into the image plane, the projected image is mapped into the display area. The view center point is positioned at the center of the display, and the image is oriented so that the image VV of the view vertical vector lies along the y axis of the display. The line that becomes the x axis is the line labeled VH (for "view horizontal") in the diagram on page 193; it is the unique line perpendicular to both the line of sight and the image of the view vertical vector.

■ Perspective Projection Coordinates

As we have explained, the data required to specify a perspective projection are a viewpoint, a view center, and a vertical vector. To specify this information to *Mathematica* and thereby determine how it will display a three-dimensional scene, you use the ViewPoint, ViewCenter, and ViewVertical options. The setting for each of these options should be a list of three real numbers, representing a point for ViewPoint and ViewCenter and a vector for ViewVertical. Surprisingly, however, these option settings are not all specified in the same coordinate system.

ViewCenter and ViewVertical are given in scaled coordinates, which run from 0 to 1 along each edge of the bounding box, as explained earlier. ViewPoint, however, is given in a coordinate system that is scaled according to the proportions of the bounding box, as specified by the setting of the BoxRatios option. The origin of the ViewPoint coordinate system is at the center of the box, and the length of the longest edge of the box is taken as the unit length in all three directions. The coordinate along the longest edge runs from -0.5 to 0.5, and the coordinates along the other two edges run from $-a$ to a and $-b$ to b, where a and b are chosen so that the proportions $a : b : 0.5$ agree with the proportions specified by the BoxRatios setting.

For example, if the BoxRatios setting is $\{1,2,1/2\}$, the longest edge is the y axis; the x axis is half as long as the y axis and the z axis is one-fourth as long. Therefore the coordinates in the ViewPoint system for this box shape run from -0.25 to 0.25 in x, from

-0.5 to 0.5 in y, and from -0.125 to 0.125 in z. In general, if br is the BoxRatios setting, the computation br/(2.0 Max[br]) yields the maximum coordinate value in the ViewPoint system for points in the bounding box (i.e., it produces the coordinates of the front upper right corner), and the negative of this result yields the minimum value for each coordinate (i.e., the coordinates of the back lower left corner). Here is a *Mathematica* function, vprange, that takes a BoxRatios setting as its argument and returns the ranges of ViewPoint coordinates for the bounding box:

```
vprange[br_] := ({-1,1} #)& /@ ( br / (2.0 Max[br]) )
Print["For box ratios ",N[#]," the viewpoint range is ",vprange[#]]& /@
        { {1,1,.4}, {1,1,1}, {1,2,1/2} };
For box ratios {1., 1., 0.4} the viewpoint range is
   {{-0.5, 0.5}, {-0.5, 0.5}, {-0.2, 0.2}}
For box ratios {1., 1., 1.} the viewpoint range is
   {{-0.5, 0.5}, {-0.5, 0.5}, {-0.5, 0.5}}
For box ratios {1., 2., 0.5} the viewpoint range is
   {{-0.25, 0.25}, {-0.5, 0.5}, {-0.125, 0.125}}
```

The result returned by vprange is the counterpart of the PlotRange setting in ViewPoint coordinates instead of object coordinates.

The unfortunate thing about the ViewPoint coordinate system is that its interpretation changes according to the object being displayed. A ViewPoint setting of {1.3,-2.4,2.0} (the default) designates a different point in space relative to an object with BoxRatios set to {1.0,1.0,0.4} (the default for SurfaceGraphics) than it does relative to an object whose bounding box has any other shape. This means that when you are preparing multiple images for side-by-side comparison, you can't assume that a common ViewPoint setting for all of the objects you display will guarantee that the same perspective projection is used to create all the images. If, for example, you are preparing an animation showing the evolution of some three-dimensional object, you must make sure to control the BoxRatios setting, either by setting fixed BoxRatios or by setting BoxRatios to Automatic and setting a fixed PlotRange; otherwise, consecutive frames of the animation will be shown from different viewpoints and thus might give a confusing or misleading impression. Here is an example:

```
sg = Plot3D[ Sin[x]Cos[y], {x,0,2Pi}, {y,0,2Pi}, DisplayFunction->Identity,
        Axes->False, ViewCenter->{.5,.5,.5}, ViewPoint->{2,.5,0},
        Epilog->{ Line[{{0,0},{0,1},{1,1},{1,0},{0,0}}],
            PointSize[.04],GrayLevel[1],Point[{.5,.5}],
            PointSize[.02],GrayLevel[0],Point[{.5,.5}] } ];
ga = Show[sg,BoxRatios->{1,#,.4},PlotLabel->#]& /@ Range[.6,1.3,.1];
Show[GraphicsArray[ Partition[ga,4] ]];
```

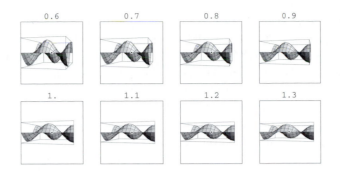

All the graphics in this example have the same ViewPoint setting, {2, .5, 0}. They depict the same SurfaceGraphics object with only the BoxRatios setting changing; the x and z components are fixed, but the y component gradually increases from 0.6 to 1.3. In the graphics in the top row, the BoxRatios setting makes the y axis edges of the box shorter than the x axis edges, so the y coordinate of 0.5 in the ViewPoint setting specifies a viewpoint beyond the box in the y direction. However, as the y edges grow longer the ViewPoint is less distant beyond the box in the y direction. In the graphic in the lower left corner, the x and y edges are the same length, and in the remaining graphics in the lower row, the y edges are longest. Changing which edge of the box is longest changes the interpretation of the ViewPoint coordinates; the result is that the y coordinate of 0.5 now always specifies a viewpoint in the plane of one face of the bounding box. Furthermore, the x coordinate of 2 in the ViewPoint setting starts to mean different distances in the x direction once the x axis edges are no longer determining the scale of the ViewPoint coordinates. If you are working with a version of *Mathematica* that can animate graphics, you might prefer to view the frames as an animation so that you can more easily discern how the changing BoxRatios setting affects the viewpoint.

One other quirk deserves mention. The origin of the ViewPoint coordinate system is always at the center of the bounding box, whose coordinates in the scaled coordinate system are $(.5, .5, .5)$. Since this point is also the default choice of view center, it follows that if you take an object whose ViewPoint is at (x, y, z) in ViewPoint coordinates and change its ViewPoint to (kx, ky, kz), you have moved the viewpoint radially outward from the view center by a factor of k along the line of sight. This reduces the degree of perspective distortion, but otherwise gives the same view of the three-dimensional object. However, if the view center is at some other point than the center of the bounding box, the line of sight does not emanate from the origin of the ViewPoint coordinates, so changing the viewpoint from (x, y, z) to (kx, ky, kz) moves it along a line that is not the line of sight. This causes a rotation of the displayed image around the view center. *Mathematica* is doing correctly what it was asked to do, so this is not a bug (unless you count it as a bug in the design of the system); still, you should be wary of this effect if you are using a view center other than the center of the bounding box. For example,

```
sg = Plot3D[ Sin[x]Cos[y], {x,0,2Pi}, {y,0,2Pi}, DisplayFunction->Identity,
        Axes->False, Epilog->{ Line[{{0,0},{0,1},{1,1},{1,0},{0,0}}],
            PointSize[.04],GrayLevel[1],Point[{.5,.5}],
            PointSize[.02],GrayLevel[0],Point[{.5,.5}] } ];
ga1 = Show[sg,ViewCenter->{.5,.5,.5},ViewPoint->(#{1.3,-2.4,2})]& /@ {.6,.8,1,2};
ga2 = Show[sg,ViewCenter->{1,1,1},ViewPoint->(#{1.3,-2.4,2})]& /@ {.6,.8,1,2};
Show[GraphicsArray[ {ga1,ga2} ]];
```

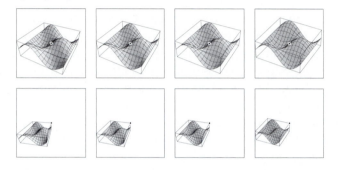

The same object is displayed in all graphics, but in the top row, the ViewCenter setting is {.5,.5,.5}—the center of the box, whereas in the bottom row, it is {1,1,1}—the upper right back corner. This is another effect that is easier to see in an animation than in a sequence of still frames.

Why did WRI decide to use this coordinate system for specifying the ViewPoint, especially since it is not used by any other feature of 3D graphics? We can't answer that question with certainty, but we can provide some historical perspective. The original version of *Mathematica* didn't provide the ViewCenter and ViewVertical options, and animation was added in the late beta testing stages. The original design therefore took into account only individual images in which the line of sight was always directed toward the center of the bounding box. It probably seemed reasonable and useful to specify the viewpoint in a system that adapted itself to the shape of the bounding box when transitions from one image to another were not being considered. When animation was first introduced, it was used primarily to show the same object from different viewpoints (with the function SpinShow defined in the package Graphics`Animation`, for example), not to show objects with different box ratios from the same viewpoint, so the potential difficulties were not evident. When ViewCenter and ViewVertical were introduced (in Version 2.0), they were thought of as being confined to the bounding box, so the scaled coordinate system seemed most appropriate for those options. However, it was deemed impossible at that point to redefine the ViewPoint option, since that would have broken a great deal of code already written. Had all the present functionality been envisioned at the outset, different choices might have been made, but it is too late to change things now.

6.2.3 Coordinate Systems for Simulated Illumination

So far, we have explained how objects are projected from three dimensions to two, but we have not explained how polygons are colored by the simulated illumination model. The details of this process are explained elsewhere in this book (Sections 3.3.5 and 7.4.2 on pages 74 and 254, respectively), in the discussions of the `LightSources` and `AmbientLight` options and the `SurfaceColor` and `FaceForm` directives. However, these discussions refer to the angles formed between a polygon's normal vector and the lines joining a point on the polygon to the light source and the viewpoint. To understand how these angles are measured, it is necessary to know the coordinate system in which lighting calculations are performed. It is *neither* the object coordinate system *nor* the scaled coordinate system.

To explain lighting coordinates, we return to the diagram we used in Section 6.2.2 on page 192 to analyze perspective projection. Using the labels from that diagram, we can define the lighting coordinates as a coordinate system whose unit y vector is the vector VV and whose unit x vector is the vector lying on line VH, with length equal to that of VV and forming a righthanded coordinate system with VV and the vector from VC to VP. The vector from VC to VP is the unit z vector—that is, the image plane is the plane whose equation is $z = 0$—and the plane $z = 1$ is the plane parallel to the image plane and containing the viewpoint.

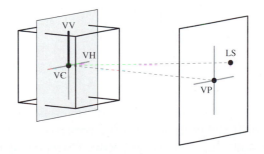

The point labeled LS is a light source; we have shown only one for simplicity, but you can specify as many as you like. The position of a light source is given as a triple (x, y, z), but *Mathematica* effectively normalizes this to $(\frac{x}{z}, \frac{y}{z}, 1)$. (Of course, this implies that z should not be 0; in fact, light sources with z coordinates of 0 or less cast no light in *Mathematica*. You could think of light sources with negative z coordinates as illuminating the polygon faces that are facing away from you.) Each light source specifies not a conical bundle of light rays, as a spherical wave front emanating from a point source would specify, but a bundle of rays along lines parallel to the line joining the light source to the view center. Loosely speaking, you can think of the light source in the diagram as a point source that has receded to infinity along the line joining VC to LS; the rays emanating from an infinitely distant point source are parallel lines.

For lighting calculations, the effect is as if a change of coordinates were made so that all the vertices of all the polygons in the scene were specified in the lighting coordinate system. Each polygon's surface normal is computed in this coordinate system, and the angles between this vector and the lines joining a point on the polygon to the viewpoint and to each light source are the ones that determine how the polygon is colored when the scene is displayed. Unfortunately, this scheme causes a problem in the lighting model: Color distinctions disappear as the distance from viewpoint to view center increases. The reason is not hard to see. If the distance from viewpoint to view center is taken as the unit length in z, and the length of the image of the view vertical vector remains the unit length in x and y, then moving the viewpoint further out along the line of sight amounts to a rescaling that foreshortens the three-dimensional scene in the z direction, essentially squashing the scene orthogonally toward the image plane. This diagram illustrates that effect:

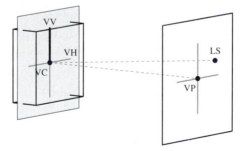

Since points near the image plane are projected more faithfully (in the sense that distances between such points are more nearly preserved) than points farther away, it follows that this squashing reduces perspective distortion, as we explained earlier. However, it also changes the directions of the normals of all the polygons in the scene. To see this, consider that in the limiting case of the scene being squashed flat, all the polygons end up lying in the image plane, so they all have exactly the same normal vector—the line of sight. Since all polygons now present the same angles to the viewpoint and to all the light sources, it follows that (except for differences due to surface reflectance properties specified by the SurfaceColor directive) they must all have the same color. This conclusion is borne out by the following example:

```
gr = Plot3D[ Sin[x^2-y^2], {x,-1,3}, {y,-2,2},
            Axes->False, DisplayFunction->Identity ];
ga = Show[gr,ViewPoint->(# {1.3,-2.4,2})]& /@ {.5,1,2,5,10};
Show[GraphicsArray[ga]];
```

The line of sight in each graphic is the same; we specified all viewpoints along a single line, with the focal length increasing from left to right. As the length increases, the distortion in the shape of the bounding box becomes smaller, but the polygons that make up the surface take on a uniform gray appearance. Unfortunately, there is no way to overcome this effect; it is a consequence of the way *Mathematica* does its lighting calculations. (If you are using *Mathematica* on a computer that has a color monitor, you may want to type in and execute the code for this example, since the effect is even more noticeable in color than in black and white.)

6.2.4 Converting Coordinates From Three to Two Dimensions

After reading Section 6.2.1, you might wonder why WRI chose a method of lighting computations that leads to this unfortunate graying effect. The answer may lie in the fact that the lighting coordinate system we have described is especially convenient in displaying a 3D graphic as a two-dimensional image, because the x and y coordinates of the lighting system lie in the projection plane. A conversion from three dimensions to two dimensions has to be performed at some point in the creation of a two-dimensional image of a three-dimensional object; by using this lighting system, *Mathematica* can simply throw away the z coordinates after the lighting calculations are complete, and the remaining x and y coordinates will give a correct planar perspective projection of the three-dimensional scene into two dimensions. This saves a step in calculations.

In fact, the development proceeded in the reverse direction: The computations to project three-dimensional polygons to two dimensions were coded into *Mathematica*'s kernel *before* the current lighting model was developed. The method of performing lighting calculations in a coordinate system that used the x and y coordinates of the final image was hotly debated within WRI, and was ultimately selected both because it saved steps in creating 3D graphics (by using x and y coordinates that were already being computed) and because it allowed the light sources to be specified relative to the viewer's position. An earlier lighting model (used in versions of *Mathematica* prior to 1.2) treated light sources as being specified in the same coordinate system as that of the the graphics primitives; this meant that when you moved an object, the light sources moved with it. The WRI designers felt that it was more intuitive for the light sources to remain attached to the viewing plane (i.e., to the plane of the computer monitor), so that they are attached to the viewer's position rather than to the objects being illuminated.

Here is a summary of the steps in specifying and displaying 3D graphics in *Mathematica*:

1. You specify the objects to be displayed. If you are displaying a Graphics3D object, you use the object or scaled coordinate systems to specify the positions of points, lines, and polygons. If you are displaying a SurfaceGraphics object, the z coordinates of the corners of the polygons that make up the surface are specified by the array of z values in the SurfaceGraphics object, and the x and y coordinates are taken from the object's MeshRange option setting. The SurfaceGraphics object's polygons are then treated as if they were specified in a Graphics3D object.

2. *Mathematica* unifies the object and scaled coordinate systems. It is at this stage that the PlotRange setting takes effect. If you specify the PlotRange explicitly, your setting is used; if you give the setting Automatic, *Mathematica* computes ranges for the x, y, and z coordinates (as described in the section on the PlotRange option in Section 7.1.1 on page 212). The plot range determines the relationship between object and scaled coordinates, enabling *Mathematica* to convert all coordinates into the scaled coordinate system.

3. The ViewCenter, ViewVertical, and ViewPoint convert scaled coordinates into lighting coordinates. The ViewCenter and ViewVertical are specified in scaled coordinates, but the ViewPoint is given in its own coordinate system. The relationship of this system to the scaled system is given by the BoxRatios setting, as explained in Section 6.2.2 on page 192 on perspective projection. The ViewPoint, ViewCenter, and ViewVertical are used to calculate the x and y coordinates of the lighting system by perspective projection, while the z coordinate is calculated by scaling so that the distance from the ViewCenter to the ViewPoint is 1, as described in Section 6.2.3 on page 199 on simulated illumination.

4. *Mathematica* performs computations for simulated illumination and hidden-feature elimination by deleting points, lines, and polygons that should be hidden in the final image and assigning colors to those that remain.

5. *Mathematica* discards the z coordinates of all objects. The remaining x and y coordinates form a two-dimensional system in which the three-dimensional objects have been correctly projected into two dimensions. At this point, the graphics elements are treated as if they had been specified in a 2D `Graphics` object. This is the step in which the two-dimensional option settings, such as `AspectRatio`, `PlotRegion`, `Prolog`, and `Epilog`, come into play.

6. Text primitives specified in a `Graphics3D` object are handled at this stage: *Mathematica* converts the three-dimensional point to which a text primitive is attached into two-dimensional coordinates along with all the other three-dimensional points, and the text is then treated as if it had been specified in two dimensions. For example, the hidden feature elimination algorithm never causes text to be hidden by polygons, nor does changing the `ViewVertical` cause the baseline of the text to be tilted.

6.3 Summary

In this chapter, we have described in detail how *Mathematica* displays 2D and 3D graphics. *Mathematica* does a good job of insulating users from the details of this process. Just as you don't need to understand how an internal combustion engine works to drive a car, you don't need to know the details of simulated illumination or aspect ratio scaling to produce a plot with *Mathematica*. But if you want to use options like `PlotRegion` or `BoxRatios` to get under *Mathematica*'s hood and fine-tune its performance, it helps to know the information we have given you here.

Our description of *Mathematica*'s graphics calculations is not guaranteed to correspond to the way *Mathematica* performs these calculations internally. For example, our model of *Mathematica*'s perspective projection and simulated illumination accounts for *Mathematica*'s observed behavior and agrees with the statements made in The *Mathematica* Book about how these steps are performed, but there are other ways of carrying out the calculations that may be more computationally robust or more efficient, even though they are equivalent in an ideal mathematical sense. Also, our description is based on empirical evidence combined with our knowledge of the mathematics of perspective. WRI has yet to provide lucid and detailed descriptions of how *Mathematica* handles perspective and lighting, and there may be special cases unknown to us that do not fit the model described above. The information in this chapter represents our best attempt to explain the behavior we have observed in light of the generalizations recorded in The *Mathematica* Book.

Chapter 7

Options

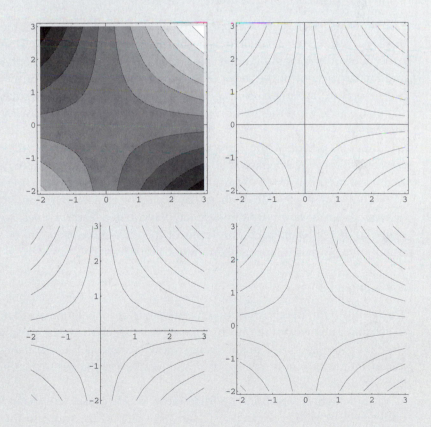

This chapter describes the options that can be supplied to the graphics data types (described in Chapter 2) and graphics-building commands (described in Chapter 4). These options fall naturally into groups related by functionality, and they are presented that way here. At the end of the book are three tables of graphics symbols and options. One shows, for each graphics function, all the options that it accepts; the other shows, for each option, all the functions that accept it.

7.1 Options Used by All Graphics Functions

The graphics options listed in this section are accepted by every graphics data type and every graphics-building command. However, some of them have different interpretations for 2D and 3D graphics.

7.1.1 Options for Scaling Graphics

To understand the first few options, consider that every 2D or 3D graphic *Mathematica* displays, is ultimately rendered as a flat image in a rectangular region, whether on paper, a computer monitor, or on some other output medium. The options AspectRatio and PlotRegion control the shape of that region and the position of the image within it. The option PlotRange controls how the elements of a graphic are scaled to fit within the image area. Thus these three options affect all graphics at the lowest, final level of rendering.

We have described the AspectRatio and PlotRegion options as they apply to 2D Graphics objects. In 3D graphics, these settings take effect after three-dimensional objects have been converted to two dimensions by perspective projection. For example, after a polygon in a Graphics3D object has been projected into the drawing plane, it can be treated as if it were a two-dimensional polygon in a Graphics object so that it can be scaled to fit the AspectRatio. For details of the three-dimensional-to-two-dimensional perspective projection, consult Section 6.2.4 on page 201.

▪ AspectRatio

The setting of the AspectRatio option specifies the ratio of height to width for a graphic — the shape, if you will, of the "picture frame" into which the graphical image is painted. Note that the size of the picture is not specified, since all *Mathematica* graphics are assumed to be arbitrarily rescalable. Only the shape of the rectangular plotting field is given by AspectRatio.

The default is AspectRatio->1/GoldenRatio, which causes the shape of the picture frame to be a "golden rectangle." That is, the ratio of the width to the height of the completed plot is the golden ratio:

$$\frac{1 + \sqrt{5}}{2} \approx 1.6180339887498948482\ldots$$

This choice may seem arbitrary, since it is completely independent of the particular graphic being displayed, but it was carefully considered. A fixed value is used to ensure that when you plot a function whose range you don't know in advance, you will not get a graph so tall and thin or so short and wide as to be illegible. (The particular value 1/GoldenRatio was chosen because it is considered aesthetically pleasing—rectangles of this shape occur frequently in ancient Greek architecture and in early Renaissance painting.) An example helps to show why this shape is reasonable. The range of the function $\frac{1}{x}$ on the interval $[-1, 1]$ is $(-\infty, \infty)$; compare the plot produced with *Mathematica's* default setting of AspectRatio to the one that the "true" aspect ratio produces:

```
gr1 = Plot[ 1/x, {x,-1,1}, DisplayFunction->Identity ];
gr2 = Show[ gr1, AspectRatio->Automatic ];
Show[GraphicsArray[ {gr1, gr2} ]];
```

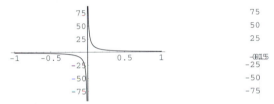

The special setting AspectRatio->Automatic tells *Mathematica* to select an aspect ratio that permits graphics to be drawn in their "natural shape"—that is, a shape determined by the range of coordinates in the graphics objects being drawn. In two-dimensional graphics, this causes the unit length in the x direction to be the same as the unit length in the y direction. While the default AspectRatio->1/GoldenRatio makes sense for the plotting functions Plot, ParametricPlot, and ListPlot, the Automatic setting is probably a more appropriate default setting for Graphics because when you assemble a Graphics object directly, it is often to represent a geometric figure in which the relationship of the unit lengths in x and y is meaningful (as in the examples below). For this reason, you might want to place the command

```
SetOptions[ Graphics, AspectRatio->Automatic ];
```

in the initialization file init.m, which is read when you start *Mathematica*, so the default will be reset each time you start a new *Mathematica* session. Doing so will not affect the scaling of function plots constructed by Plot or ParametricPlot or ListPlot because those commands have their own option settings, but it will make it a little easier to construct circles that look like circles and squares that look like squares.

Here is an example illustrating the effect of the AspectRatio option. In all three cases, *Mathematica* is drawing two circles side by side. In the first graphic, the default setting causes the circles to be compressed into a golden rectangle. In the second, the AspectRatio setting of 1 causes the circles to be compressed even further, to fit into a square. (In other words, a setting of 1 means a ratio of 1 : 1 in the drawing space, not in the object space.) Only in the third example, which uses an AspectRatio setting of Automatic, do the circles appear circular.

```
twocircles = Graphics[ { Circle[{0,0},1], Circle[{2,0},1] },
                                    Frame->True, FrameTicks->None ];
Show[GraphicsArray[{ twocircles, Append[twocircles,AspectRatio->1],
                     Append[twocircles,AspectRatio->Automatic] }]];
```

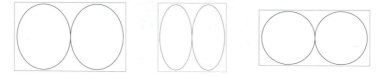

The AspectRatio is actually used *twice* in the display of 2D graphics. The preceding example does not make this clear because it contains no text, but the next example uses frame axes to illustrate this effect. In this example, note that the width of the tick labels on the y axis is greater than the depth of the tick labels on the x axis. *Mathematica* reduces the width of the frame enclosing the PlotRange to allow the y axis labels to fit within the drawing area. It also reduces the frame's height, not only by the amount necessary to accommodate the x axis labels but by more, so that the frame as well as the display area has the shape specified by the AspectRatio. In this case, the AspectRatio is 1, specifying a square, and you can see that the frame and the drawing region are both squares, even though this means that there is unoccupied space within the drawing area above and below the frame.

```
gr = Graphics[{ GrayLevel[0], PointSize[.1],
        Point /@ { {0,0}, {0,1}, {1,1}, {1,0} },
        GrayLevel[1], Rectangle[{0,0},{1,1}],
        GrayLevel[0], Line[{ {0,0}, {0,1}, {1,1}, {1,0}, {0,0} }]
}, Background->GrayLevel[1/3],PlotRange->{{-1,2},{-1/4,3/2}},
    Frame->True, FrameStyle->GrayLevel[1], AspectRatio->1,
    FrameTicks->{{0,1,2},{-1,-.5,0,{.5,"one-half"},1}}
];
Show[gr];
```

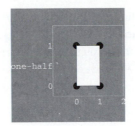

Actually, this dual use of the AspectRatio is controlled by the Mnodistort flag in the Post-Script code *Mathematica* generates. This flag is normally set, causing the PlotRange rectangle as well as the drawing area to have the shape specified by AspectRatio. You can unset the flag, as we have done in this illustration:

Show[gr];

When the Mnodistort flag is unset, the AspectRatio setting controls the shape of the drawing area but *not* the shape of the PlotRange rectangle. In this case, the graphics elements are scaled independently in x and y, so the drawing area is filled in both directions. As the name Mnodistort suggests, this filling may cause distortion in the final displayed image.

There is no graphics option setting to control the state of the Mnodistort flag, because the setting of this flag is not part of the PostScript code generated by the *Mathematica* kernel. Instead, it is supplied as part of the *Mathematica* PostScript prolog that is attached to a graphic when it is displayed on a monitor or printer. Most Notebook Front Ends allow you to set options for rendering a graphic; the option that corresponds to the Mnodistort flag should be a check box or other true/false switch with a name like "Preserve aspect ratio." (On the NeXT computer, this switch is found under "Graphics Attributes" in the Style Inspector panel.) If you use *Mathematica* through a command-line interface rather than a Notebook Front End, the *Mathematica* kernel invokes a separate graphics-rendering utility to display graphics as they are generated; you can probably control the Mnodistort flag by setting an appropriate option flag when this utility is invoked, but you will have to check the machine-specific documentation that came with your version of *Mathematica* to find out what option to use. If you use the psfix utility to prepare *Mathematica* graphics for printing on a PostScript printer, you can use the -stretch command-line option to control the setting of the Mnodistort flag.

The Mnodistort flag also interacts with the PlotRegion option setting, so be sure to read the next section if you want complete information about Mnodistort.

- PlotRegion

The PlotRegion option specifies what region of the final display area a graphic should occupy. It allows you to leave a border or margin around the edges of the picture frame whose shape is given by AspectRatio. The setting for PlotRegion must be a pair of intervals; these intervals define the rectangle into which the graphical image is scaled. For example, the setting {{.2,.8},{.1,.7}} specifies that the image should be scaled into the rectangle whose left and right edges are positioned 20 percent and 80 percent of the way from left to right across the full display area and whose bottom and top edges are 10 percent and 70 percent of the way up the full height of the display area. The PostScript clipping path is set to the rectangle specified by the PlotRegion setting, so that elements of the graphic (such as points, lines, polygons, axes, and text) that might otherwise be mapped outside this rectangle are instead clipped off and do not appear. The only exception is that the PlotRegion setting does not affect the application of the color selected by the Background option; the background color applies to the entire drawing area, including the border around the graphic.

If you specify a PlotRegion whose shape is not the same as the shape of the overall drawing area, the graphic may or may not fill the entire PlotRegion, depending on whether the flag Mnodistort has been set within the PostScript code to prevent distortion. By default, the flag is true. You can control it from a Notebook Front End by selecting a graphics cell and toggling the "Preserve aspect ratio" setting, which may be in a Style Inspector panel or in a Graphics menu. The psfix program accepts the option setting -stretch to control the Mnodistort flag; the flag is true if -stretch is not specified and false if it is. When the flag is true, the graphic is scaled within the PlotRegion to occupy a subrectangle whose aspect ratio is the aspect ratio of the drawing area. Here is an example:

```
gr = Plot[Sin[x],{x,0,2Pi}, Frame->True, FrameTicks->None,
    Background->GrayLevel[2/3], AspectRatio->1/2, PlotRegion->{{0,.5},{0,1}} ];
```

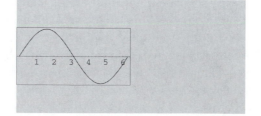

The `AspectRatio` specifies a drawing area whose height is half its width, but the `PlotRegion` restricts the graphic to the left half of the drawing area. The `Background` color fills the entire drawing area, allowing us to see how the graph has been scaled. Its width is half the width of the drawing area, but its height was chosen so that the aspect ratio of the graph matches the aspect ratio of the drawing area. In general, when the `Mnodistort` flag is true, the graphic is scaled to fill the largest subrectangle of the `PlotRegion` whose aspect ratio matches the aspect ratio of the drawing area. Here is the same graphic, rendered with the `Mnodistort` flag set to false:

```
Show[gr];
```

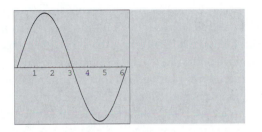

This time the graph is allowed to stretch to fill the entire `PlotRegion`, even though this means that the final aspect ratio is not the one specified by the `AspectRatio` setting.

The default setting for `PlotRegion` is `Automatic`, which instructs *Mathematica* to set the clipping path to the borders of the picture frame, allowing graphics objects to be imaged into any part of the drawing area. This is effectively the same as a setting of {{0,1},{0,1}}; the only difference is that no PostScript code for adjusting the `PlotRegion` is generated when `PlotRegion` is `Automatic`, whereas an explicit setting of {{0,1},{0,1}} generates code that sets up a new clipping path identical to the one already in effect.

The lower left corner of the `PlotRegion` need *not* be (indeed, usually isn't) the point whose scaled coordinates are Scaled[{0,0}]; nor will Scaled[{1,1}] in general give the upper right corner of the `PlotRegion`. This is because certain text elements (such as tick mark labels on axes) are scaled into the `PlotRegion` and they usually extend outside the region of scaled coordinates. See Chapter 6 for an explanation of how *Mathematica*'s various coordinate systems are related to one another.

Here is a situation in which `PlotRegion` can be useful:

```
Needs["Graphics`Shapes`"];
s = Sphere[1];
gr1 = Graphics3D[ s ];
gr2 = Graphics3D[ s, Boxed->False];
gr3 = Graphics3D[ s, Boxed->False, PlotRegion -> {{-.25,1.2},{-.25,1.2}} ];
gr4 = Graphics3D[ s, PlotRegion -> {{-.25,1.2},{-.25,1.2}} ];
Show[GraphicsArray[{ gr1, gr2, gr3, gr4 }, GraphicsSpacing->.3 ]];
```

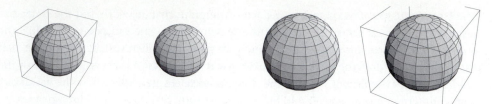

In the first graphic, the sphere is drawn enclosed in a bounding box as usual. The sphere and box together fill the image area. In the second graphic, the setting Boxed->False prevents the box from being drawn, but since *Mathematica* still leaves room for the invisible box when scaling the graphic into the image area, the sphere does not fill the area well. In the third graphic, we use the PlotRegion option to instruct *Mathematica* to scale the graphic for a region slightly larger than the true image area. Scaling allows the sphere to fill the image better. In the fourth graphic, we restore the box to make it clearer how the PlotRegion setting has affected the scaling; the box now spills outside the image area of the graphic and is clipped. Here is another example in which we use PlotRegion to zoom in on a corner of a SurfaceGraphics object for closer inspection:

```
gr1 = ListPlot3D[{{1,2,3,4,5},{3,6,4,5,3},{2,5,5,6,1},{4,7,6,7,6}},
                   DisplayFunction->Identity ];
gr2 = Show[gr1,PlotRegion->{{-.2,3},{-.5,1.8}}];
Show[GraphicsArray[{gr1,gr2}]];
```

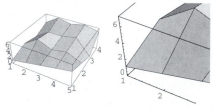

- PlotRange

The PlotRange option sets up a clipping region and thereby specifies *indirectly* how a graphic is scaled into the display region defined by PlotRegion. In 2D graphics, the setting of PlotRange specifies a clipping region in the plane and the sizes of axes are determined from this region. The axes and tick marks in turn affect the scaling from graphics coordinates to display coordinates that maps the graphic into the PlotRegion. In 3D graphics, the PlotRange option governs the clipping of graphical elements to the three-dimensional bounding box, thereby establishing the conversion from graphics coordinates to box coordinates. Other options, whose explanations follow (such as SphericalRegion), then control the mapping of the three-dimensional box coordinate system into the two-dimensional display coordinate system.

The most general setting for the PlotRange option is a list of pairs, two for 2D graphics and three for 3D graphics. Each pair $\{a,b\}$ specifies that the interval from a to b on the corresponding axis is to be drawn and that graphics primitives that lie outside that interval are to be clipped. Any pair may be replaced by either of the special keywords All and Automatic. All means that *Mathematica* should select an interval for that coordinate that will permit all graphics primitives to be shown without clipping; Automatic means that *Mathematica* should select an interval that may clip outlying features in order to give a better picture of the elements at the center of the graphic. Automatic may also be used for the maximum endpoint of an interval with the minimum specified explicitly; this tells *Mathematica* to choose the maximum according to the distribution of the data. (Curiously, *Mathematica* does not accept Automatic for the minimum with an explicit maximum, even though the problem seems to be symmetric.) Some examples of valid PlotRange settings for 3D graphics are

```
{ {1,10}, {-5,5}, {2,3} }
{ {-2,Automatic}, {-1,1}, All }
{ All, All, Automatic }
```

Here is an illustration:

```
gr1 = Plot3D[ Sin[x^2 - y^2], {x,-1,3}, {y,-2,2}, DisplayFunction->Identity ];
gr2 = Show[ gr1, PlotRange->{Automatic,Automatic,{-.4,.4}}, BoxRatios->Automatic ];
gr3 = Show[ gr2, ClipFill->GrayLevel[0] ];
Show[GraphicsArray[ { gr1, gr2, gr3 } ]];
```

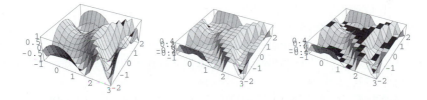

If you use PlotRange to override the default z range in a SurfaceGraphics object, you may also want to use ClipFill to call attention to values that have been clipped.

Note that for the purposes of PlotRange, the mixed two-dimensional/three-dimensional types ContourGraphics and DensityGraphics count as three-dimensional objects. The z component of the PlotRange specification for these types tells *Mathematica* whether to "clip" values of the function being plotted, just as it does with SurfaceGraphics objects.

Some abbreviations are permitted. You may simply say All to mean {All,All} in 2D graphics or {All,All,All} in 3D graphics. Similarly, you may say Automatic to mean

{Automatic,Automatic} or {Automatic,Automatic,Automatic}. You may also give a single pair of numbers {*a*, *b*} to mean that the last coordinate (which corresponds to the dependent variable in plots of functions) is to use the specified range and that the ranges of independent variables are to be Automatic.

PlotRange settings of the form {*min*,Automatic} have not always functioned properly in all versions of *Mathematica*. This feature didn't work at all in some older versions, and an attempt to use it produced an error message like this one:

```
PlotRange::prng:
    Value of option PlotRange -> {{0, 1}, {10, Automatic}}
    is not All, Automatic, or an appropriate list of range specifications.
```

In the version current at this writing, the feature is stable, but it doesn't always return what you expect:

```
gr = Plot3D[ Sin[x]Cos[y], {x,0,2Pi},{y,0,2Pi}, PlotRange->{3,Automatic} ];
```

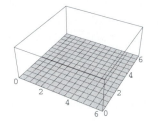

```
FullOptions[ gr, PlotRange ]
```

```
{{0., 6.28319}, {0., 6.28319}, {3., 1.02367}}
```

Note the third pair of numbers, which specifies the interval to be plotted along the *z* axis. It is surprising that *Mathematica* selects an interval whose "maximum" value is smaller than the specified minimum, but considering that the function under consideration produces only values between -1 and 1, it is not clear what else *Mathematica* should or could have done.

The computation of the plot range when you use an Automatic setting is somewhat complicated. *Mathematica* computes the plotting range by analyzing each coordinate separately from the others. For each coordinate, *Mathematica* starts by determining the minimum and maximum values specified in all the graphical elements that make up the picture. Then it does a statistical analysis in order to detect "outliers"—isolated points far away from the main body of the graphic. Such points occur, for example, when a function like $1/x^2$ is sampled near a singularity. If they were permitted to determine the plotting range, the scaling necessary to accommodate them would cause all the other features of the graph to be compressed into a small indistinguishable mass. To avoid this, *Mathematica* discards outliers when determining the plotting range in each coordinate. Here is a graph that *Mathematica* truncates in this way, shown once with the PlotRange that *Mathematica* selects and once with all sampled values included:

```
gr1 = Plot[ Sec[x] Sin[9x], {x, -Pi/2, Pi/2}, Frame->True, DisplayFunction->Identity ];
gr2 = Show[ gr1, PlotRange-> All ];
Show[GraphicsArray[ {gr1, gr2} ]];
```

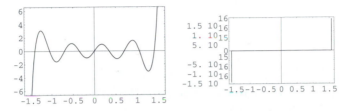

The frame axes allow us to see that *Mathematica* has truncated the graph on the left. Noting where the graph meets the top and bottom edges of the frame, we can see that even though we asked for a plot extending from $-\frac{\pi}{2}$ to $\frac{\pi}{2}$, *Mathematica*'s default is to display the graph over a slightly smaller interval. The setting PlotRange->All in the graph on the right causes interesting features in the middle to be dwarfed by the values at the edge of the range. Relatively uninteresting asymptotic behavior is overemphasized, and the graph appears flat between the endpoints. (Incidentally, the graph on the right occupies a slightly smaller area because *Mathematica* had to scale it down in order to make room for the tick mark labels.)

After discarding outliers, the Automatic algorithm extends the PlotRange in two ways. First it extends the interval along each axis to include the zero point, if doing so doesn't require extending the plotting interval by more than roughly 20 percent. After the zero-point expansion, if any, has been performed, let a and b be the interval endpoints along one of the axes; then *Mathematica* sets the final range along that axis to be

$$\{1.025a - .025b, 1.025b - .025a\}$$

The length of this interval is $1.05(b - a)$; in effect, *Mathematica* expands the range by 5 percent around its center, providing a border around the graphical elements so that they do not touch the edges of the bounding structure. It is important to be aware of these expansion effects if you are preparing an illustration for publication and are trying to size a graphic to exact specifications. You have probably designed your own border into your layout and don't want the additional white space that the expansion efforts create. If so, remember that they are part of the Automatic algorithm and you can always turn them off by specifying an explicit PlotRange setting.

The plot range expansions are most easily explained by example:

```
w = {{0, 8}, {2, 8}, {3, 3}, {4, 8}, {6, 8}, {7, 3}, {8, 8},
      {10, 8}, {8, 1}, {6, 1}, {5, 6}, {4, 1}, {2, 1}};
w3 = { w, 2+w, 50+w };
```

First we define w, a list of points specifying the outline of a polygon. Then we make three copies of w: one in the original position, one translated by two units in x and y, and one translated by 50 units. The next calculation shows us the intervals in x and y occupied by each copy of w.

```
range[m_] := {Min[#],Max[#]}& /@ Transpose[m]
range /@ w3
```

```
{{{0, 10}, {1, 8}}, {{2, 12}, {3, 10}}, {{50, 60}, {51, 58}}}
```

The original w extends from 0 to 10 in x and from 1 to 8 in y. The copy translated by 2 units runs from 2 to 12 and 3 to 10, and the third copy runs from 50 to 60 and 51 to 58. The shape of each copy is the same, however; all three copies of w are 10 units wide and 7 units high. Here is how *Mathematica*'s automatic plot range algorithm scales them:

```
makepicture = Graphics[Polygon[#],Frame->True,FrameTicks->None]&;
Show[GraphicsArray[{ makepicture /@ w3 }]];
```

We used the Frame option to outline the three graphics to make the interval expansion obvious. Compare the PlotRange that *Mathematica* computed for each graphic to the actual ranges of coordinates we computed earlier:

```
PlotRange /@ (makepicture /@ w3)
```

```
{{{-0.25, 10.25}, {-0.2, 8.2}}, {{-0.3, 12.3}, {2.825, 10.175}},
  {{49.75, 60.25}, {50.825, 58.175}}}
```

In the first graphic, the x interval already included the zero point on the x axis, so no extension in x was needed; however, *Mathematica* extended the y interval downward to include 0. In the second graphic, the automatic PlotRange algorithm decided to extend the x interval $[2, 12]$ to $[0, 12]$, but not to extend the y interval $[3, 10]$ to $[0, 10]$. In the third graphic, *Mathematica* decided that the intervals $[50, 60]$ and $[51, 58]$ were much too far from 0 to be worth extending, so neither axis' zero point was included. The zero-point expansion accounts for the large gaps at the bottom of the first graphic and at the left of the second graphic. Finally, the 5 percent expansion in all directions explains why none of the three "W" shapes quite touches its surrounding frame.

Although it is a refinement that you will probably never need to worry about, for the sake of completeness we present one more example to show how sophisticated the automatic PlotRange algorithm is. Consider the function rect:

```
rect[m_] := Block[ {a,b,c,d}, {{a,b},{c,d}}=range[m]; {{a,c},{a,d},{b,d},{b,c}} ];
Show[Graphics[{Polygon[rect[50+w]],GrayLevel[.7],Polygon[50+w]}]];
```

Applying rect to a list of points returns a new list of points defining the corners of the smallest rectangle (with sides parallel to the axes) that encloses the points. In other words, rect converts a polygon into a rectangle that occupies the same interval on the x and y axes. The range function defined earlier verifies that rect does the right thing when applied to the polygons in w3.

```
r3 = rect /@ w3;
range /@ r3 == range /@ w3
```

True

Now we plot the resulting rectangles:

```
Show[GraphicsArray[{ makepicture /@ r3 }]];
```

Even though the ranges of coordinates in the rectangles are the same as the ranges of coordinates in the "W" shapes, the plotting intervals are not extended to include the origin. (They do undergo the 5 percent expansion, however.) This demonstrates that it is not merely the endpoints of the plotting interval but also the distribution of points within the interval that affects whether the interval is extended to include the origin. Refer to the definition of includepoint on page 239 for more on the subject of extending a plot range to include the origin.

If you give the setting All for any coordinate, *Mathematica* proceeds as in the Automatic case, except that it does not discard outliers. The expansion by 5 percent is still performed.

Another point about PlotRange->All is that it takes text primitives into account, which the Automatic setting does not. The following example shows the difference in scaling and clipping for a graphics object that contains text.

```
gr1 = Graphics[{
    Line[{ {0,0}, {2,0}, {2,4}, {0,4}, {0,0} }], PointSize[.02],
    Point[{1,1}], Text[FontForm["centered",{"Times-Bold",12}],{1,1}],
    Point[{1,2}], Text[FontForm["lower left",{"Helvetica",10}],{1,2},{-1,-1}],
    Point[{1,3}], Text[FontForm["upper right",{"Courier-Oblique",15}],{1,3},{1,1}]
}];
gr2 = Append[gr1,PlotRange->All];
Show[GraphicsArray[{gr1,gr2}]];
```

The default setting that all graphics text use for the PlotRange option is Automatic. The Automatic algorithm for determining the plot range was designed with function plotting in mind, particularly the step of discarding outlying points. This step doesn't make as much sense when Graphics objects are used to represent geometric figures rather than graphs of functions. For example, if you specify a collection of circles, rectangles, and triangles to be displayed, you probably don't want *Mathematica* to discard one of your triangles because it is too far away from the rest of the figures and is therefore uninteresting. It seems more reasonable for the default PlotRange to be Automatic for Plot and ParametricPlot, but to be All for Graphics; that way, function plots are still handled the way they are now, but geometric figures are not truncated. Among other things, this corrects the problem with the BarChart function described on page 160. You can reset the default PlotRange setting for Graphics by executing the command

```
SetOptions[Graphics,PlotRange->All];
```

If you want this command to be carried out automatically every time you start *Mathematica*, you can add it to the initialization file init.m for your copy of *Mathematica*.

PlotRange can also be used as a function; refer to Section 7.9.1 on page 293 for an explanation of this usage.

7.1.2 Options for Overlays and Underlays

If you think of the AspectRatio option as specifying the shape of the "picture frame" into which *Mathematica* paints a picture, then you can think of these option settings as preparing the "canvas" before and after the picture is painted.

▪ Background

When a *Mathematica* graphic is displayed, the entire picture frame (*not* just the part specified by the PlotRegion setting) is filled with the color specified by the Background option. This happens before any of the graphic's other code is executed. The setting for the Background option must be either an explicit color specification (in terms of RGBColor, Hue, CMYKColor, or GrayLevel) or the word Automatic (the default). If Automatic is specified, *Mathematica* actually generates no PostScript code to fill the background, leaving it white. This example shows the effect of various Background settings:

```
gr1 = Plot3D[ Sin[x]Cos[y], {x,0,2Pi}, {y,0,2Pi}, DisplayFunction->Identity ];
gr2 = Show[ gr1, Background->GrayLevel[.7] ];
gr3 = Show[ gr1, Background->GrayLevel[.2] ];
Show[GraphicsArray[{ gr1, gr2, gr3 }]];
```

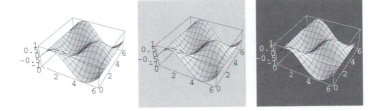

The first graphic has the default Background setting Automatic, so no background is drawn. The second graphic uses a gray level of 0.7 as background, and the third uses a gray level of 0.2. Note that certain features specified with Automatic settings, such as AxesStyle, BoxStyle, and DefaultColor, change color from black to white to improve contrast when the Background is dark. The cutoff for this change is a Background setting with a gray level of less than 0.5.

▪ Prolog

The Prolog option allows you to specify a graphics primitive or, more typically, a list of graphics primitives, to be rendered before the body of a graphics object is rendered. The Prolog setting paints a "backdrop" over which a graphics object is drawn. In both 2D and 3D graphics objects, the Prolog should consist of two-dimensional objects. In 2D graphics, the Prolog objects use the same coordinate system the rest of the graphic does; in 3D graphics, they use two-dimensional Scaled coordinates, in which the image area is scaled from 0 to 1 in both directions.

The graphics elements specified in the Prolog setting are drawn in the same "graphics context" as are the main elements of a graphic. In particular, they are *not* scoped, which means that directives that modify the appearance of graphics elements can "leak" out of the prolog and into the body of a graphic. Here is an example that illustrates this effect:

```
gr1 = Graphics[ Line[{ {0,0}, {1,1} }] ];
gr2 = Graphics[ Line[{ {0,0}, {1,1} }],
        Prolog -> { GrayLevel[.8], Thickness[.08], Circle[{.2,.6},.3] } ];
gr3 = Graphics[ Line[{ {0,0}, {1,1} }],
        Prolog -> { { GrayLevel[.8], Thickness[.1], Circle[{.2,.6},.3] } } ];
Show[GraphicsArray[{gr1,gr2,gr3}]];
```

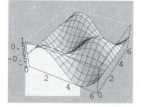

All three graphics objects have a single Line as the only element in the body of the graphic. In the first image, there is no Prolog and the line is colored with the default color, which is black. In the second image, the GrayLevel and Thickness directives affect not only the Circle object in the prolog but also the line in the body. In the third image, the Prolog setting is specified with an extra level of nesting, which restricts the scope of the directives in the prolog so that they cannot affect the body of the image. It is a matter of opinion whether this treatment of the prolog should be regarded as a bug in *Mathematica*; in any case, it is easy to work around once you know about it. (Note that the Circle in our example is clipped to the plot region defined by the body of the graphic.)

The *Mathematica* Book states that the prolog graphics elements are drawn before the main body but after axes, boxes, frames, tick marks, and labels. This statement is true for 2D graphics but not for 3D graphics, as this example shows:

```
Plot3D[ Sin[x]Cos[y], {x,0,2Pi},{y,0,2Pi}, Background -> GrayLevel[.6],
    Prolog -> { GrayLevel[.9], Rectangle[{0,0},{.5,.5}] } ];
```

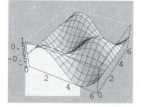

Part of the bounding box is drawn in light gray. This is the effect of "leakage" from the GrayLevel setting in the prolog—which demonstrates that the bounding box is drawn *after* the prolog, not before, as claimed in The *Mathematica* Book. Moreover, the edges of the faces containing the axes are drawn in black and are not obscured by the Rectangle in the prolog, proving that they too were drawn after and not before the prolog. In fact, *Mathematica* is tricky in how it draws axes in 3D graphics: It draws the axes, then the prolog, then the bounding box, then the body of the graphic; and then it redraws the faces containing axes because they might have been obscured by part of the body. The color *Mathematica* uses in redrawing the axes is the color it thinks they were drawn in originally, without taking into account modifications made by the prolog.

Note also that even though the lower left corner of the rectangle was specified as {0,0}, it doesn't coincide with the lower left corner of the image. This is to be expected because the axis labels have caused the image area to be enlarged a bit; in fact, it is generally impossible to know the scaled coordinates of the actual image area in a *Mathematica* graphic unless you know what labels are being used and the size and font in which they are set. The *Mathematica* Book's assertions that certain features are specified in "a 0, 1 coordinate system running across the width and height of the graphic" is thus a little white lie: Usually it is something like a $-.02, 1.1$ coordinate system in x and another nearly-but-not-quite 0, 1 system in y.

- Epilog

The Epilog option is similar to the Prolog option, except that graphics elements specified in the Epilog are rendered last rather than first. There is thus no concern about leakage out of the Epilog into other parts of the graphic. Settings generally do not leak into the epilog, as the following example illustrates:

```
gr1 = Graphics[ Line[{ {0,0}, {1,1} }], Epilog -> { Circle[{.2,.6},.3] } ];
gr2 = Graphics[ { GrayLevel[1/2], Line[{ {0,0}, {1,1} }] },
        Epilog -> { Circle[{.2,.6},.3] } ];
gr3 = Graphics[ GrayLevel[1/2], Epilog -> { Circle[{.2,.6},.3] } ];
Show[GraphicsArray[{gr1,gr2,gr3}]];
```

If you think carefully about this example, you will find it confusing. Why is the circle gray in the third image but not in the second? The answer is simple but unexpected: the list that encloses the GrayLevel and Line in the second example has the side effect of setting up a local graphics context, which terminates when the body does and thus cannot affect the Circle in the epilog. In the third example, there was no need to enclose the body in a list, since it contained only the single item GrayLevel[1/2]. Without the list, the scope of this directive was not restricted, so it affected the circle. This is an unusual example, of course—how often do you want to draw a graphic whose body contains no visible elements?

Here is a more useful example of what you can do with Epilog:

```
Plot[ { x, Sqrt[x] }, {x, 0, 4}, AspectRatio->Automatic,
    PlotRange->{{0,4},{0,2.5}},
    Epilog -> {  Text[ "y = x", {2,2}, {1.3,-1} ],
                 Text[ "y = Sqrt[x]", {2,Sqrt[2]}, {-1,1.4} ],
                 Dashing[ {0.03} ], Line[ {{0,1}, {1,1}} ],
                 Dashing[ {0.03} ], Line[ {{1,1}, {1,0}} ]  }];
```

As usual, in constructing this example, we had to fiddle a bit with the specifications of the Text primitives to get them to appear in the right positions relative to the other elements of the graphic. This is sometimes the most time consuming and least productive part of illustration making.

- PlotLabel

The PlotLabel option specifies an object (often, but not necessarily, a string) to be positioned over a graphic as a label or title. The OutputForm of the object is used unless another form, such as InputForm, is explicitly requested. The object may be wrapped with FontForm to specify the font to be used; otherwise, the setting of the DefaultFont option determines the font. If necessary, the PlotRange rectangle is reduced within the drawing area to leave room to display the PlotLabel object. Here is an example:

```
gr0 = Plot[ Cos[x^2/4], {x,0,2Pi}, DisplayFunction->Identity ];
gr1 = Show[ gr0, PlotLabel->Cos[x^2/4] ];
gr2 = Show[ gr0, PlotLabel->InputForm[Cos[x^2/4]] ];
gr3 = Show[ gr0, PlotLabel->FontForm[InputForm[Cos[x^2/4]],{"Helvetica",10}] ];
Show[GraphicsArray[{gr1,gr2, gr3}]];
```

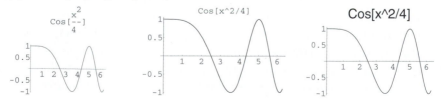

In all three plots, the expression Cos[x^2/4] is the PlotLabel. In the plot on the left, this expression is represented in OutputForm, which uses multiple lines for fractions and exponents, and the graph of the function has to be scaled down to leave room for the PlotLabel. In the other two plots, the PlotLabel is represented in the linear InputForm, leaving more room for the graph. In the first two plots, the default font is used for the PlotLabel, but in the third plot, we have specified the 10-point Helvetica font.

If you use *Mathematica* on a system that displays each graphic in a separate window, you may find it difficult to keep track of which graphic was produced by which command when you have several graphics windows open at once. Some systems place the line number of the command that produced a graphic in the title bar of the graphic's display window; others do not. You may find it helpful to use PlotLabel to label each graphic with the line number or the text of the command that produced it.

7.1.3 Options for Axes

Any graphics object in *Mathematica* may be drawn with or without coordinate axes. The options in this section control whether axes are drawn and how they appear. These options are accepted for all forms of graphics, but 2D graphics support additional options for controlling axes that 3D graphics do not, so be sure to read Section 7.2 on page 237 for the rest of the information about two-dimensional axes. In particular, the "standard" axis options presented here do not always function as expected when combined with frame axes.

- Axes

The option Axes can be specified in any graphics object or graphics-building function to specify which coordinate axes (if any) should be drawn. In general, the setting for Axes is a list with one entry for each coordinate (i.e., two entries for 2D graphics and three for 3D graphics); each entry is either True or False to specify whether the corresponding axis should be drawn. The settings Axes->True and Axes->False are permitted as abbreviations to turn on or off all axes simultaneously.

In both 2D and 3D graphics, Axes->False means that no axis lines are drawn, but this may not be apparent in 3D graphics unless the bounding box is also suppressed because axes in 3D graphics are drawn along the edges of the bounding box.

The Axes option "controls" the other options in this group, in the sense that if an axis is turned off by a False setting in the Axes specification, then it and its associated attributes (ticks and axis label) will not be drawn, regardless of how they may be specified.

The default setting for the Axes option is different for different graphics functions.

The data types Graphics, GraphicsArray, Graphics3D, SurfaceGraphics, ContourGraphics, and DensityGraphics all have Axes->False as the default, as do the mixed two-dimensional and three-dimensional plotting functions ContourPlot, DensityPlot, ListContourPlot, and ListDensityPlot. The three-dimensional plotting functions ListPlot3D, ParametricPlot3D, and Plot3D all have Axes->True as the default. Note that axes are drawn for ContourGraphics and DensityGraphics even though the Axes setting is False; this confuses many *Mathematica* users, but the reason is simple: The axes on those graphics are frame axes rather than interior axes (see Section 7.2 on page 237 for more information).

The functions ListPlot, ParametricPlot, and Plot have Automatic as their default setting for the Axes option. This default is a holdover from the days before Version 2.0, when the Axes option had a different interpretation (see Section 7.8, page 287, on obsolete graphics options, for a discussion of this). In Version 2.0 and later versions, Axes->Automatic means the same thing as Axes->True. Graphics functions also accept None as a valid setting of the Axes option, which means the same thing as Axes->False.

- AxesLabel

The AxesLabel option is used to specify text labels to be drawn on coordinate axes. Valid settings include None to specify no labels (which is the default), a single expression, to specify a label for the dependent axis (the y axis in 2D graphics and the z axis in 3D graphics), and a list of two expressions for 2D graphics, or three expressions for 3D graphics, specifying a label for each axis. In 2D graphics, axis labels are centered at the positive ends of the axes. In 3D graphics, each axis label is placed near the center of the same edge of the bounding box that carries tick marks for that axis.

Like the PlotLabel, axis labels are represented in OutputForm unless another form is specified, and FontForm can be used to specify a font other than the default font. Regrettably, there is no convenient way to specify a color other than the default color for axis labels.

Here is an example showing the use of axis labels in 2D and 3D graphics:

```
Block[ { $DisplayFunction = Identity },
    gr1 = Plot[ 100/P, {P,20,200}, AxesLabel->{"Pressure","Volume"} ];
    gr2 = Plot3D[ 2000 / (P T), {P,20,200}, {T,10,40}, AxesLabel->{"P","T","V"} ];
];
Show[GraphicsArray[{ gr1, gr2 }]];
```

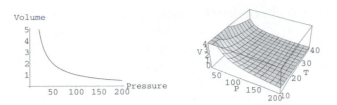

In the two-dimensional plot, the x axis label is placed horizontally at the end of the axis. *Mathematica* is forced to scale down the plot in order to leave room for the label within the drawing area; the longer the label, the more the label and plot are reduced. For that reason, the AxesLabel option in 2D graphics is most suitable for short labels such as "X" and "Y". If you need a long label on an axis, you can use the Epilog option to position a Text primitive to serve as a label, or you can use frame axes, whose labels run along the axes instead of being positioned at the ends of the axes. See the example on page 243 for an illustration.

- AxesStyle

The AxesStyle option specifies the appearance of the lines that represent the coordinate axes. The general setting of the AxesStyle option is a list of style specifications, one for each coordinate axis (i.e., two for 2D graphics and three for 3D graphics). Each style specification is itself a list, containing graphics directives that govern the Thickness, Dashing, and color specifications of lines. As a special case, if all axes are to be drawn in the same style, only a single style specification list is needed. Thus the setting

$$\text{AxesStyle -> \{ Thickness[.01], Dashing[\{.1,.05\}] \}}$$

is equivalent to

```
AxesStyle -> { {Thickness[.01], Dashing[{.1,.05}]}, {Thickness[.01], Dashing[{.1,.05}]} }
```

and not equivalent to

$$\text{AxesStyle -> \{ \{Thickness[.01]\}, \{Dashing[\{.1,.05\}]\} \}}$$

It is easy to forget about the sublists and assume that the first form will make the x axis thick and the y axis dashed, when actually it causes both axes to be both thick and dashed.

```
Plot[ Sin[x], {x,0,2Pi}, AxesStyle->{Thickness[.01],Dashing[{.1,.05}]} ];
```

▪ Ticks

The Ticks option for graphics functions specifies the location, appearance, and labeling of tick marks on the coordinate axes.

The general setting of the Ticks option is a list of two elements for 2D graphics or three elements for 3D graphics, specifying tick marks for each axis. The simplest specifications for each axis are None, which means to place no ticks on that axis, and Automatic, which tells *Mathematica* to use an internal algorithm to decide how to place tick marks. The abbreviation Ticks->None tells *Mathematica* to use a setting of None for each axis — that is, to place no tick marks at all; Ticks->Automatic means to place ticks automatically on each axis. For each axis, you may also specify a list of explicit tick mark settings; each entry in this list should have one of the following forms:

$$loc$$
$$\{loc, lbl\}$$
$$\{loc, lbl, len\}$$
$$\{loc, lbl, len, style\}$$

where *loc* is a number specifying the location of the tick mark along the axis, *lbl* is an expression whose OutputForm is to be used as the label at that location, *style* is an attribute or list of attributes specifying the style (color, thickness, and dashing) for the tick mark, and *len* is either a number specifying the length of the tick mark or a list $\{pos, neg\}$ specifying the lengths in the positive and negative directions. The length specifications are interpreted as fractions of the total width of the graphic. This scheme is rather tricky, so here is an example:

```
xticks = { -1, 1/2, {1,"one"}, {-1/2,"-.5",.02}, {1/4,1/4,.05,RGBColor[1,0,0]},
    {3/4,"3/4",{.03,.01},{GrayLevel[.6],Thickness[.01]}} };
Plot[ x, {x,-1,1}, Ticks->{xticks,Automatic} ];
```

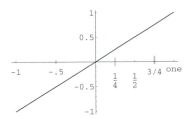

The example specifies six ticks for the x axis, but uses the Automatic setting to instruct *Mathematica* to compute y axis ticks for itself. Observe that the ticks need not be specified in any particular order. Only the location of the first two ticks is specified; they are drawn with the default style and length settings, and the OutputForm of the location values is used as a label. Note in particular that the label at $\frac{1}{2}$ is drawn as a vertical fraction; we used an explicit label string at $\frac{3}{4}$ to get the appearance of a horizontal fraction instead. We specified the total lengths of the ticks at $-\frac{1}{2}$ and $\frac{1}{4}$, so *Mathematica* centered ticks of those lengths on the axis, but for the tick at $\frac{3}{4}$ we specified positive and negative lengths separately.

This is a somewhat more useful example:

```
Block[ { $DisplayFunction = Identity, sym },
    gr1 = Plot[ Sin[x], {x,0,2Pi}, DefaultFont->{"Symbol",8},
            Ticks->{ {0,{Pi/2,"p/2"},{Pi,"p"},{3Pi/2,"3p/2"},{2Pi,"2p"}},
                {-1,-.5,0,.5,1} } ];
    gr2 = Plot[ Sin[x], {x,0,2Pi}, DefaultFont->{"Symbol",8},
            Ticks->{ {0,{Pi/2,"p/2"},{Pi,"p"},{3Pi/2,"3p/2"},{2Pi,"2p"}},
                {-1,-.5,0,.5,1} }, PlotLabel->"y=sin(x)" ];
    gr3 = Plot[ Sin[x], {x,0,2Pi}, DefaultFont->{"Symbol",8},
            PlotLabel->FontForm["y=sin(x)",{"Times-Roman",8}],
            Ticks->{ {0,{Pi/2,"p/2"},{Pi,"p"},{3Pi/2,"3p/2"},{2Pi,"2p"}},
                {-1,-.5,0,.5,1} } ];
];
Show[GraphicsArray[{ gr1, gr2, gr3 }]];
```

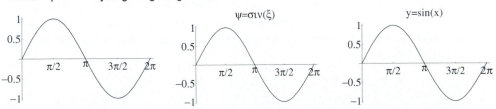

The tick labels on the x axis are printed in the PostScript "Symbol" font to allow us to use the Greek letter "π." In all three graphics, we use the DefaultFont option to avoid having to give a separate FontForm expression for each tick label. This approach works fine for the graphic on the left, but since the DefaultFont option sets the default font for all text in a graphic, the PlotLabel in the center graphic becomes illegible. We fix this in the graphic on the right by using an explicit FontForm for the PlotLabel.

One further generalization is permitted: You may specify for each axis a function that computes the tick mark setting to use for that axis. This function will be called with two arguments, the minimum and maximum values along the axis, and should return a valid tick mark specification (which may be None to suppress ticks or Automatic to fall back on *Mathematica*'s built-in algorithm) to be used for that axis. The setting Ticks->*func* means the function *func* will be used for each axis. With care, you could, for example, devise an algorithm that positions major and minor ticks along a logarithmic axis and use it in semilog and log-log plots in lieu of *Mathematica*'s default algorithm. Note that the minimum and maximum values supplied to the tick function will be the values *after* the 5 percent expansion described in the discussion of the PlotRange option in Section 7.1.1, which can be found on page 212.

Unfortunately, a piece of bad judgment in the code-generation routines for tick mark labels introduced a bug that affects how certain labels are displayed: Tick mark labels on the horizontal axis in 2D graphics are *always* represented in the PostScript code that *Mathematica* generates as if they had been specified by a call of the form

$$\text{Text}[\ label,\ \{tickpoint,0\},\ \{0,2\}\ ]$$

where *label* is the text of the tick mark label and *tickpoint* is the x coordinate at which the tick mark is supposed to appear. Recall that the third argument to the Text primitive specifies an offset in text coordinates. The offset of 2 in the vertical direction was intended to ensure that tick mark labels appear some distance below the axis rather than centered on it (where the default displacement of 0 would have placed it) or abutting it (where a displacement of 1 would have placed it). But also recall that the scale of the text coordinates depends on the size of the bounding box of the text, so the deeper the text, the more distance a unit in the text system represents in the graphics system. This means that the more lines of text you put in tick mark labels on the x axis, the farther the labels move from the axis. (Actually, it is even more complicated because lines aren't all the same height, either.) Here is an example that shows this behavior:

```
Plot[ Sin[x], {x,0,2Pi}, Ticks -> { {Pi/4,Pi/2,Pi,(3Pi/2)^(51/50),2Pi}, Automatic } ];
```

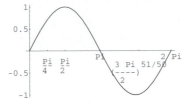

The tick mark labels have neither a common baseline, a common horizontal axis, nor a common sinkage below the x axis—they are a mess. And this mess cannot be remedied by the insertion of blank lines into the labels because *Mathematica* cleverly ignores blank lines in computing the area occupied by a piece of text. For ordinary lab work, the labels may be acceptable, but if you are preparing high-quality illustrations for publication, you should not rely on *Mathematica* to produce axis labels. Create a graphic without labels instead, and export it to a graphic design application such as Adobe Illustrator to add text.

7.1.4 Options for Generating PostScript Code

The options in this group directly affect the way that *Mathematica*'s graphics objects are converted into PostScript code.

- ColorOutput

The ColorOutput option provides a primitive form of color separation capability by allowing you to specify how colors are rendered when a graphic is displayed. The value specified for this option is a function that tells *Mathematica* how to transform colors when it generates PostScript code for a graphic. This function is applied to all the color settings in the graphic after all other color effects (such as plotting styles or simulated lighting) have been calculated.

The default setting for ColorOutput is Automatic, which means that colors are left essentially unchanged: RGBColor specifications are converted to invocations of the Post-Script setrgbcolor operator; GrayLevel specifications invoke setgray; and CMYKColor specifications invoke setcmykcolor. You may also set ColorOutput to RGBColor, CMYKColor, or GrayLevel to specify that *Mathematica* should convert all colors to RGB form, CMYK form, or gray levels internally before it generates PostScript code. Finally, you may specify a function of your own to be applied to each color setting to determine how it should be rendered. The best way to understand this is by example.

```
invert[GrayLevel[x_]] := GrayLevel[1-x]
invert[RGBColor[r_,g_,b_]] := RGBColor[1-r,1-g,1-b]
```

```
gr = Plot3D[ Sin[x]Cos[y], {x,0,2Pi}, {y,0,2Pi}, Background->GrayLevel[.8] ];
```

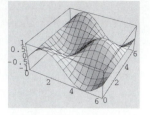

```
Show[ gr, ColorOutput->invert ];
```

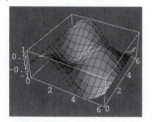

The ColorOutput option is ignored for graphics nested inside a Rectangle primitive or a GraphicsArray object. The feature simply is not implemented in the code that handles nested graphics (as of Version 2.2). This is an unfortunate oversight, and we know of no workaround.

Finally, to illustrate the color separation applications of ColorOutput, we consider a function that allows us to break up a graphic into layers of cyan, magenta, yellow, and black to prepare plates for four-color printing. The function should convert colors into gray levels four different ways, once for each ink color. To make printing plates for a graphic, the graphic should be rendered four times, with ColorOutput set to use each of the four color-to-grayscale conversions. This produces four different grayscale images, each of which should then be halftoned as black and white. The black dots of the cyan layer should be printed with cyan ink, the black dots of the magenta layer with magenta ink, and similarly for the yellow and black layers, to produce the composite image. Here is a simple version of such a function:

```
sep[   cyan,CMYKColor[c_,m_,y_,k_]] := GrayLevel[1-c]
sep[magenta,CMYKColor[c_,m_,y_,k_]] := GrayLevel[1-m]
sep[ yellow,CMYKColor[c_,m_,y_,k_]] := GrayLevel[1-y]
sep[  black,CMYKColor[c_,m_,y_,k_]] := GrayLevel[1-k]

sep[(cyan|magenta|yellow),GrayLevel[k_]] := GrayLevel[1]
sep[                black,GrayLevel[k_]] := GrayLevel[k]

sep[x_,y_RGBColor] := sep[x,RGBtoCMYK[y]]
```

This definition is in three parts to handle the three kinds of color specification that *Mathematica* understands. The first part says that you should convert an explicit CMYKColor to cyan, magenta, yellow, or black simply by extracting the appropriate component and inverting it (because a setting of 1 represents the darkest possible value in a CMYKColor specification but the lightest value in a GrayLevel). The second part says that a GrayLevel specification should affect only the black layer of the separation. The third part says that to handle an RGBColor, you should first convert the RGBColor to an equivalent CMYKColor and then deal with that with the rules already given. A simple (and not very accurate) way of converting an RGB specification to a CMYK specification is the following:

```
RGBtoCMYK[RGBColor[r_,g_,b_]] :=
    Block[ { v=1-{r,g,b}, k }, k=Min[v]; CMYKColor @@ (Append[v-k,k]) ]
```

This definition attempts to do some basic undercolor removal, but it assumes that the printing inks mix perfectly and are perfect subtractive complements to the positive colors (i.e., that cyan ink absorbs all and only red light, that magenta ink absorbs all and only green light, and likewise for yellow ink and blue light). These assumptions are unrealistic, of course, which is the first reason that this approach to color separation is unreliable. (The built-in *Mathematica* function ToColor does a better job.) For convenience, we can define

```
sep[x_] := sep[x,#]&
```

so that the value of, say, sep[cyan] is the function that, when applied to a color, produces the cyan component of that color. Then if gr is a variable containing a graphics object for which we want to produce color separations, we should be able to say

```
Show[ gr, ColorOutput -> sep[cyan]    ];
Show[ gr, ColorOutput -> sep[magenta] ];
Show[ gr, ColorOutput -> sep[yellow]  ];
Show[ gr, ColorOutput -> sep[black]   ];
```

to produce four grayscale images from which to prepare printing plates. These input statements do indeed produce four images, but, unfortunately, they aren't useful for printing for two reasons, in addition to the RGB-to-CMYK conversion problem mentioned previously. One reason is that *Mathematica* does not handle ColorOutput properly; bugs in the code (present up through Version 2.2, at least) cause background colors, mesh lines on surfaces, and other features to be converted incorrectly. The other and more fundamental reason, which would remain even if the bugs were fixed, is that this method of separation assumes that the four printing passes (to lay down the four colors of ink on the page) are in perfect register—a completely unreasonable assumption. No provision is made for enlarging the inked areas to "trap" holes in the printed image inks that occur when a failure of alignment causes two regions inked in different colors to be separated by white space instead of meeting along a common edge. Since no printing process can guarantee perfect alignment in large volume printing, this method of color separation is not useful.

- DefaultColor

The DefaultColor option specifies the color to be used for text labels and for lines, points, and other features whose color is not specified by any other means. The default setting, DefaultColor->Automatic, tells *Mathematica* to select a default color that contrasts with the Background color. The choice is somewhat arbitrary, as this example indicates:

```
gr0 = Plot3D[ Sin[x]Cos[y], {x,0,2Pi},{y,0,2Pi}, DisplayFunction->Identity ];
gr1 = Show[ gr0, Background->GrayLevel[.495] ];
gr2 = Show[ gr0, Background->GrayLevel[.505] ];
Show[GraphicsArray[{gr1,gr2}]];
```

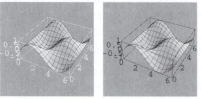

The only difference between the two graphics is a 1 percent difference in the darkness of the background, but since the threshold value of 0.5 was crossed, one graphic uses white as the default color and the other uses black.

Note that the default color setting does not affect the color of otherwise uncolored objects in 3D graphics, even though it does affect such objects in 2D graphics.

```
gr1 = Graphics[{ Polygon[{ {0,0}, {1,0}, {0,1} }],
        Thickness[.03], Line[{{0,0},{1,1}}] }, DefaultColor->GrayLevel[1/2] ];
gr2 = Graphics3D[{ Polygon[{ {0,0,0}, {1,0,0}, {0,1,1} }],
        Thickness[.03], Line[{{0,0,1},{1,1,0}}] },
        DefaultColor->GrayLevel[1/2], Lighting->False ];
Show[GraphicsArray[{gr1,gr2}]];
```

In this example, the Polygon and the Line are colored gray in the Graphics object but not in the Graphics3D object — even though the bounding box in the Graphics3D object is affected by the DefaultColor setting. We have no idea why *Mathematica* uses DefaultColor this way.

▪ DefaultFont

The DefaultFont option specifies the font to be used for any text that doesn't have a font specified. This includes plot titles specified by the PlotLabel option, axis labels, tick marks, and text specified with the Text primitive. Settings for this option should have the form {*font*, *size*}, as used with FontForm. The default setting of this option is DefaultFont :> $DefaultFont, which means that each time a graphic is rendered, the current value of the global variable $DefaultFont is used as the graphic's default font. This arrangement is convenient because it allows us to respecify the default simultaneously for graphics of all types. The initial value of $DefaultFont is usually {"Courier",10}, which means that the Courier 10-point font is used. This choice is suitable for graphics displayed on a computer monitor, which are usually sized to fill a large area of the screen. The low resolution of most monitors also makes it desirable to use a large font so that the text will be legible. Nevertheless, in print publications, graphics are usually printed at a smaller size, and the default font size can cause text labels to overwhelm an image. Most of the graphics in this book were generated with a $DefaultFont setting of {"Courier",6.5}, and the images themselves were scaled down to between 25 percent and 50 percent of their original area.

Here is an example of the use of the option DefaultFont:

```
gr1 = Graphics[{Text["Text in Courier",{1,1}]}];
gr2 = Graphics[{Text["Text in Times",{1,1}]},DefaultFont->{"Times-Roman",12}];
gr3 = Graphics[{Text["S p a b g",{1,1}]},DefaultFont->{"Symbol",12}];
Show[GraphicsArray[{ gr1, gr2, gr3 }]];
```

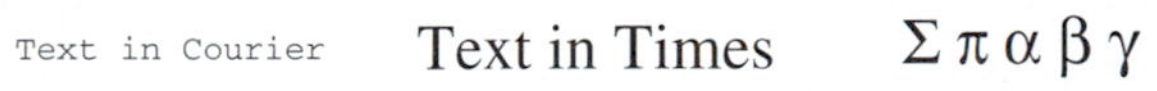

Text in Courier   Text in Times   Σ π α β γ

▪ DisplayFunction

The DisplayFunction option specifies the function to apply to both graphics and sound objects in order to display them. The setting of DisplayFunction should be a function (that is, either a "pure function" object or the name of a function). When *Mathematica* is asked to display a graphics object (either explicitly by a call to Show, or implicitly by one of the plotting functions), it responds by extracting the object's `DisplayFunction` function and applying it to the object. This usually causes a representation of the object to be displayed on the computer monitor. When `Show` is used, the value returned by the display function becomes the result of the `Show` operation.

The default setting of `DisplayFunction` for all graphics functions and graphics objects is `DisplayFunction :> $DisplayFunction`. This means that when *Mathematica* displays an object, it fetches the current value of the variable `$DisplayFunction` and applies it to the object. The default value of `$DisplayFunction` is the pure function `(Display[$Display,#1])&`. When this function is applied to a graphics object, the function `Display` is invoked with the variable `$Display` as its first argument and the graphics object as its second argument. `Display` is the *Mathematica* function that actually performs the conversion from *Mathematica*'s representation of graphics and sound objects to PostScript code. `Display` expects its first argument to be an output stream, or list of streams, and it writes the PostScript form of its second argument as text to the specified stream(s).

The variables `$Display` and `$DisplayFunction` are used to make it convenient to change globally the way graphics are displayed. The setting of `$Display` specifies the default destination for PostScript code generated from graphics objects; assigning a new value to `$Display` doesn't change what PostScript code is generated for an object, but specifies a new output stream to which that code is sent. Since the value of `$Display` is fetched each time a graphic is displayed, changing `$Display` immediately causes all graphics to be sent to the new destination, even if you are redisplaying a graphics object that was created before you changed `$Display`. (Of course, this doesn't apply to graphics objects that have an explicit setting of the `DisplayFunction` option that is different from the default.) If you want *Mathematica* to convert graphics into some other form than PostScript code, you can redefine `$DisplayFunction` to invoke some other function than `Display`. For example, if you want 3D graphics to be rendered by an external ray-tracing program, you can define a function that converts `Polygon` objects into a form that the program can understand, and set up `$DisplayFunction` to call this conversion function and feed its output to the ray-tracer.

On *Mathematica* systems that use a Notebook Front End, the default setting of `$Display` is usually the string `"stdout"`, and it is the responsibility of the Front End to detect the PostScript code in the stream it receives from the kernel and place each graphic in a Notebook cell of its own. On UNIX systems, where the *Mathematica* kernel is run in a terminal window under a windowing system such as X Windows or Open Look, the value of `$Display` is usually a string that represents a pipe to a PostScript interpreter that opens a separate window for each graphic.

The following example shows how to use `$Display` to send *Mathematica* graphics to files:

```
$FileDisplay::vector="Graphics being written to file \"`1`\"."
$FileDisplay := ( $GrFile = StringJoin[ $GrPrefix, ToString[++$GrCount], ".ps" ];
                    Message[ $FileDisplay::vector, $GrFile ];
                    $GrFile );
$GrPrefix = "mgr";
$GrCount = 0;
$Display := $FileDisplay
```

Because the assignment $Display := $FileDisplay is delayed (because the operator :=
rather than = is used), $FileDisplay is reevaluated each time *Mathematica* needs the value
of $Display. The definition of $FileDisplay also uses a delayed assignment, which means
that every time *Mathematica* wants to display a graphic, the code in the definition of
$FileDisplay is re-evaluated. This code increments the counter $GrCount, concatenates
the string $GrPrefix with the string form of $GrCount and the suffix ".ps", and saves the
resulting string in $GrFile. Then it issues the message $FileDisplay::vector, substituting
the value of $GrFile in the message, and finally returns the value of $GrFile. Thus each
time we ask *Mathematica* to display a graphic, the variable $Display generates a new
file name, displays a message, and returns the generated name as the file to which
PostScript code should be written. So the first graphic we display is written to the file
mgr1.ps, the second to mgr2.ps, and so on.

In most respects, *Mathematica* treats sounds in the same way it treats graphics.
In particular, the same function Display that converts graphics objects to PostScript
code can also convert sounds to PostScript (but this won't be useful unless your Post-
Script interpreter understands the commands *Mathematica* uses to play sounds). The
only difference in how graphics and sounds are displayed is that the default setting
of the DisplayFunction option for sound objects and sound-generating functions is
DisplayFunction :> $SoundDisplayFunction, and the default value of $SoundDisplayFunction
is (Display[$SoundDisplay,#1])&. This dual use of DisplayFunction makes it convenient
to vector sounds to a different process than graphics, which might be necessary on a
system that uses different programs to play sounds and render graphics.

▪ StringConversion

StringConversion is an option to specify conversions to be performed on strings as they
are written to an output stream. *Mathematica* is capable of working with strings that
contain 16-bit characters, but many other programs are not. Even those that are capable
may use different conventions from those *Mathematica* uses for how such strings are
stored. When strings are written to a file to be read by other programs, it is usually
desirable to filter out special characters or to convert them to a form that is acceptable
to the programs that read the file.

Display (and other functions that open output streams, such as OpenWrite) use the StringConversion option to specify a string conversion function, which should be given either as the name of a function or as a pure function object. This function is applied to every string that is written to the opened stream. It should accept a string as an argument and return a string that can be written to the output stream. Two special values may also be used: None, to specify no string conversion (bytes of a string are written to the file, and it is up to the receiving program to know where special characters appear), and Automatic, which tells *Mathematica* to convert 16-bit characters and control characters such as *newline* and *tab* to "escaped" forms represented by the backslash character (\). Here is a mildly silly example of a user-defined string conversion function:

```
alphabet = Characters["abcdefghijklmnopqrstuvwxyz"];
Alphabet = Characters["ABCDEFGHIJKLMNOPQRSTUVWXYZ"];
convrules = Thread[alphabet->Reverse[alphabet]] ~Join~ Thread[Alphabet->Reverse[Alphabet]];
strconv[s_] := StringReplace[s,convrules];
```

```
gr = Plot[ Sin[x],{x,0,2Pi}, PlotLabel->"A Silly Example", DisplayFunction->Identity ];
Display[ $Display, gr, StringConversion->strconv ];
```

Note, however, that the following example may work differently than you might expect, although the input is similar to the previous example:

```
gr = Plot[ Sin[x],{x,0,2Pi}, PlotLabel->"Another Example", DisplayFunction->Identity ];
Display[ $Display, gr, StringConversion->StringReverse ];
```

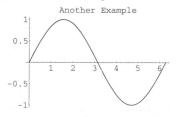

Why are the plot label and the tick labels not reversed? It appears that the function specified by StringConversion is applied separately to each character of each string, not to the string as a whole. The reverse of a one-character string is the same string, so the

StringReverse function doesn't change the strings at all. This reinforces the idea that the StringConversion option is intended for character set conversion and not for general text manipulation.

Note that StringConversion is an option for Display, *not* for the graphics object being displayed; Display is the only graphics-related function that accepts this option. In particular, you should not include a StringConversion setting directly in the list of options of a graphics object, either when you assemble the object or when you display it with Show. If you want to use a special StringConversion with a particular graphic, specify the graphics object's DisplayFunction option to be a call to Display that incorporates the desired StringConversion setting. The following example shows what does and doesn't work. (The Block statement allows us to suppress display by temporarily redefining $DisplayFunction without having to change the object's default setting of the DisplayFunction option.)

```
Block[{ $DisplayFunction=Identity },
    gr = Plot[Sin[x],{x,0,2Pi},PlotLabel->"Another Example"];
];
Show[ gr, StringConversion->strconv ];
```

Graphics::optx: Unknown option StringConversion in -Graphics-.

```
Show[ gr, DisplayFunction->(Display[ $Display, #, StringConversion->strconv ]&) ];
```

7.2 Additional Axis Options for 2D Graphics

Mathematica's 2D graphics objects (those with head Graphics) and 2D/3D graphics objects (with head ContourGraphics or DensityGraphics) accept several options in addition to the basic axis-control options supported by all *Mathematica* graphics.

- AxesOrigin

The AxesOrigin option specifies where axes drawn by the Axes option should cross. The default setting is Automatic, which means that *Mathematica* uses an internal algorithm to position the axes. In Graphics objects, this algorithm usually chooses the origin {0,0} if it would be within the region of the xy plane defined by the PlotRange setting.

The AxesOrigin option can conflict with the PlotRange option, as the following example shows:

```
gr1 = Plot[ x^3 - x, {x,-2,2}, DisplayFunction->Identity ];
gr2 = Show[ gr1, AxesOrigin->{-2,0} ];
gr3 = Show[ gr1, PlotRange->{{-1,2},{0,2}} ];
gr4 = Show[ gr1, AxesOrigin->{-2,0}, PlotRange->{{-1,2},{0,2}} ];
Show[GraphicsArray[{{gr1,gr2},{gr3,gr4}}]];
```

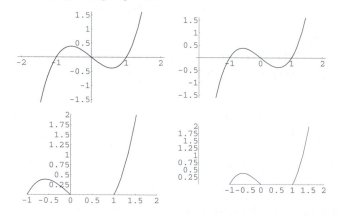

The plot in the upper left corner is rendered with default settings of PlotRange and AxesOrigin. The two plots in the top row leave the PlotRange unspecified, while the two plots in the bottom row specify the PlotRange as {{-1,2},{0,2}}. The two plots on the left leave the AxesOrigin unspecified, while the two on the right specify the AxesOrigin as {-2,0}. Now consider the plot on the lower right: We have explicitly selected a PlotRange that does not include the AxesOrigin we selected. *Mathematica* does its best to comply with both requests: It draws the axes so that, if extended, they will cross at the specified origin point, but it labels the axes only within the range specified by PlotRange. (In fact, this can happen even when you use the Automatic setting of PlotRange, if you specify an AxesOrigin outside the range that *Mathematica* selects.) If you want axes that actually meet at their origin, you must choose an origin that lies within the plotting range (or, equivalently, choose a plotting range that contains the origin). The algorithm *Mathematica* uses with the setting AxesOrigin->Automatic always chooses an origin within the plotting range.

Suppose you are plotting a function whose range of values you don't know in advance, but you want to be certain that the axes meet at a point you have chosen. In that case, you may have to plot the function in two steps: First have *Mathematica* determine a plot range and then enlarge the range to include your desired origin. Here is some code to help you do that:

```
includepoint[x_,{a_,b_}] := {Min[##],Max[##]}& @@ {x,a,b} /; Head[x] =!= List
includepoint[pt_List,range:{{_,_}...}] :=
    Apply[includepoint,Transpose[{pt,range}],{1}] /; Length[pt] == Length[range]
```

The first rule for includepoint extends an interval, if necessary, so that it includes a specified value. The second rule takes a point (which is a list of coordinates) and a plot range (which is a list of intervals, one for each coordinate) and uses the first rule to extend the intervals that make up the plot range so that they include the coordinates of the point. This example shows how to use includepoint:

```
gr = Plot[ 30 - 25x + 10x^2 - x^3, {x,1,5}, DisplayFunction->Identity ];
Show[ gr, PlotRange->includepoint[{3,5},PlotRange[gr]],
                    AxesOrigin -> {3,5}, DisplayFunction->$DisplayFunction ];
```

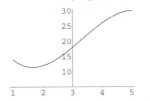

First, we plot the function, allowing *Mathematica* to select a suitable plot range. We don't know whether the range *Mathematica* selects will include our desired origin point, so we skip the step of generating PostScript code and displaying the graphic. Next, we use Show to display the graphic with the PlotRange set explicitly (via includepoint) to be the smallest region that is guaranteed to include both the original plot range and the desired origin point. This might seem like extra work, but the cost in computing time is negligible because the two steps have almost no overlap in functionality: All of the sampling of the function and the construction of the graphics object is done in the first step, and all of the PostScript generation and display work is done in the second step.

The next example illustrates the behavior of AxesOrigin with ContourGraphics objects:

```
cp1 = ContourPlot[ x y, {x,-2,3}, {y,-2,3}, DisplayFunction->Identity,
                    Axes->True, AxesOrigin->{0,0} ];
cp2 = Show[ cp1, ContourShading->False ];
cp3 = Show[ cp2, Frame->False ];
cp4 = Show[ cp3, AxesOrigin->Automatic ];
Show[GraphicsArray[{cp1,cp2,cp3,cp4}]];
```

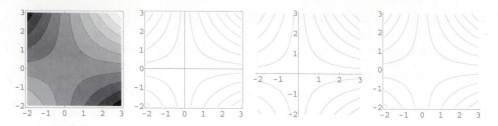

The first graphic, cp1, is specified to have interior axes that intersect at {0,0}; however, the axes are invisible because of the contour shading. In the second graphic, cp2, the shading is turned off and the axes become visible. They don't have tick marks, however, because the frame axes are still turned on. In the third graphic, cp3, the frame axes are turned off and the tick marks appear on the interior axes. Finally, in the fourth graphic, cp4, *Mathematica* is instructed to locate the axes and puts them at the edges of the contour plot.

DensityGraphics objects accept the AxesOrigin option, but this option is virtually useless. The shading of the density plot draws over the axes and obscures them, just as with ContourGraphics when contour shading is enabled. A contour plot can still be useful with the shading turned off because of the contour lines, but a density plot without shading is simply be a rectangular grid that conveys no information about the function being plotted. (In fact, *Mathematica* doesn't even provide a way to turn off the shading in a DensityGraphics object.) Only by tinkering with the PlotRange can you even see that the axes are drawn.

```
dp0 = DensityPlot[ x y, {x,-2,3}, {y,-2,3}, DisplayFunction->Identity ];
dp1 = Show[ dp0, Axes->True, AxesOrigin->{0,0} ];
dp2 = Show[ dp1, PlotRange->{{-3,4},{-3,4},Automatic} ];
Show[GraphicsArray[{dp1,dp2}]];
```

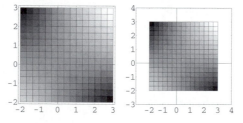

Drawing axes seems to be of questionable value, and it is interesting that the DensityPlot function doesn't even accept the AxesOrigin option, even though (as the example shows) the DensityGraphics objects created bu DensityPlot do accept it.

▪ Frame, FrameStyle, FrameTicks, FrameLabel and RotateLabel

The options Frame, FrameLabel, FrameStyle, and FrameTicks are analogous to Axes, AxesLabel, AxesStyle, and Ticks, but they specify a set of axes drawn around the edges of a 2D graphic rather than across it. Although for most purposes, it is sufficient to think of a graphic as having "a frame", the four edges that make up the frame can actually be treated as four independent axes. Therefore each of the frame options can take a list of four elements, specifying the attributes for the four edges individually. The edges are specified in the order bottom, left, top, right.

The Frame option specifies whether a frame should be drawn around a graphic. Setting Frame to True or False turns on or off all four edges simultaneously. The most general setting is a list of four elements, each of which is either True or False, indicating that one of the edges of the frame should or should not be drawn. A list of only two elements is also accepted; the first element controls the top and bottom edges (the x axes), and the second element controls the left and right edges (the y axes). The Frame option enables or disables the other frame-related options; for example, a FrameLabel won't be drawn along an edge for which Frame is set to False. (If you want to label an edge but don't want to draw it, you can set FrameStyle to match the background color so that the edge is "invisible," and set FrameTicks for that edge to None.) The default setting of Frame is False for Graphics and True for ContourGraphics and DensityGraphics.

The FrameStyle option specifies the attributes (color, thickness, and dashing) with which the edges of a frame should be rendered. It functions similarly to the AxesStyle option. If you want to set a single attribute (such as a color) and have it apply to all four edges, you can set FrameStyle to that attribute. If you want to specify several attributes and have them all apply to all edges, you can set FrameStyle to a list of those attributes. If you want to specify different attributes for different edges, you must set FrameStyle to a list of sublists of attributes. If you use a list of two sublists, the top and bottom edges are drawn with the attributes from the first sublist and the left and right edges are drawn with the attributes from the second sublist. If you use a list of four sublists, you can specify attributes for all four edges independently. Here are some examples:

FrameStyle->RGBColor[1,0,0]	make all frame edges red
FrameStyle->Thickness[.02]	make all edges thick
FrameStyle->{RGBColor[1,0,0],Thickness[.02]}	make all edges both red and thick
FrameStyle->{{RGBColor[1,0,0]},{Thickness[.02]}}	make top and bottom red and left and right thick
FrameStyle->{{RGBColor[1,0,0]},{Thickness[.02]}, {GrayLevel[.8]},{Dashing[{.05,.05}]}}	make bottom edge red, left edge thick, top edge light gray, and right edge dashed

To keep the examples short, we have used only one attribute in each sublist, but this is not necessary: You can specify a thickness *and* a color *and* a dashing style for an edge. You can also use Automatic as the setting for any edge or all edges; Automatic draws frame edges in the default thickness, without dashing, in the color specified by the DefaultColor option. The default setting of FrameStyle is Automatic.

The FrameTicks option specifies tick marks for the edges of a frame. The simplest settings are None, which tells *Mathematica* not to draw tick marks on frame axes, and Automatic, which tells *Mathematica* to use its own algorithm to position tick marks. You can also give a list of two or four tick specifications; if you give two, the first one is for the horizontal edges and the second is for the vertical edges, and if you give four, they specify the tick marks for each edge separately. The tick specifications are the same as those used by the Ticks option to place ticks on interior axes: None, Automatic, or a list of tick descriptions, each of which specifies one tick mark's position, label, length, and style. See the discussion of the Ticks option in Section 7.1.3 on page 226 for an example. The default setting of FrameTicks is Automatic.

The FrameLabel option specifies labels to be placed on the edges of the frame. The labels are handled in a manner similar to handling of the PlotLabel and AxesLabel options: They needn't be strings, they are printed in OutputForm unless another form is specified, and they are printed in the default font unless FontForm is used. The setting should be one of the following: None, to suppress frame labels; a single object, to label the left edge; a list of two objects to label the bottom and left edges; and a list of four objects, to label all four edges. In a list of two or four objects, you can use None for an individual edge that you do not want labeled. The default setting for FrameLabel is None.

Here is an example that uses the frame options together:

```
sym[s_String] := FontForm[s,{"Symbol",8}];
Plot[ Cos[th]^2, {th,0,Pi/2}, Frame->True,
        FrameStyle -> GrayLevel[.7],
        GridLines -> Map[ {#,{GrayLevel[.7]}}&,
                            { Range[0,Pi/2,Pi/16],  Range[0,1,.2] }, {2} ],
        FrameTicks -> {{0,{Pi/8,sym["p/8"]},{Pi/4,sym["p/4"]},
                        {3Pi/8,sym["3p/8"]},{Pi/2,sym["p/2"]}},
                        {#,ToString[100#]}& /@ Range[0,1,.1] },
        FrameLabel -> {"Angle of Incidence","% Reflectance"},
        PlotLabel ->
        "    Intensity of Reflected Light\nas a Function of Angle of Incidence" ];
```

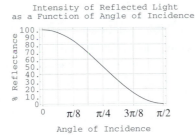

By the way, the function plotted in this example shows how the intensity of diffuse reflected light falls off as the angle between the light rays and the surface normal increases. See the discussion of *Mathematica*'s simulated illumination options, Sections 3.3.5 and 7.4.2 on pages 74 and 254, for an application of this information.

The RotateLabel option specifies whether labels on vertical frame axes should be rotated to become vertical. The setting of this option must be either True (the default) or False. If the setting is True, labels on vertical frame axes are rotated to run along the axes. This option is not very flexible because there is no way to specify that one label should be rotated and the other not, and there is no way to specify whether a vertical label should run bottom to top or top to bottom (they always run bottom to top). The following example shows why rotated labels are desirable.

```
gr1 = Plot[ 100/P, {P,10,200}, AxesLabel->{"Pressure","Volume"},
                    Background->GrayLevel[3/4], DisplayFunction->Identity ];
gr2 = Show[ gr1, Frame->{True,True,False,False}, FrameLabel->{"Pressure","Volume"} ];
gr3 = Show[ gr2, RotateLabel->False ];
Show[GraphicsArray[{ gr1, gr2, gr3 }]];
```

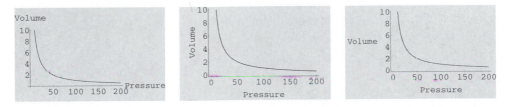

All three graphics are drawn into rectangles of the same height and width. In all three, we use a light gray background so we can see how well each plot fills the available drawing area. In the graphic on the left, we use interior axes and axes labels; in the center graphic, we use frame axes and a rotated y axis label; and in the graphic on the right, we use frame axes and an unrotated y axis label. You can see that the plot itself—presumably the object of interest in these graphics—has had to be shrunk in the graphic on the left to leave room for the x axis label and in the graphic on the right to leave room for the y axis label. The use of frame axes with rotated labels on the vertical axis creates a graphic that fills its available area, with the least wasted space and with the most area used for the actual plot.

An important point is that frame axes suppress ticks on interior axes. That is, if Axes->True and Frame->True are both specified, the axes will be drawn but ticks will never be placed on them, even if explicit tick marks are specified with the Ticks option. (The *Mathematica* Book says only that suppression happens when the Ticks setting is Automatic, so it may be a bug that will be fixed in a future release.)

7.3 Other 2D Graphics Options

▪ GridLines

The GridLines option allows you to tell *Mathematica* where and how to draw grid lines, which are similar to the rules on graph paper. GridLines->None (the default) specifies that no grid lines be drawn. GridLines->Automatic instructs *Mathematica* to use an internal algorithm to decide where to draw grid lines. The general form of the GridLines setting is a list of two elements specifying grid lines for the x and y axis separately. For each axis, you may specify None, Automatic, or a list of explicit grid line positions; each entry in this list should be either a number, indicating the position of a grid line or a pair {*pos*, *style*}, in which *pos* is a number and *style* is a list of attributes specifying the style (color, thickness, and dashing) for the grid line. Here is an example:

```
gr1 = Plot[ Sin[x], {x,0,2Pi}, GridLines->Automatic, DisplayFunction->Identity ];
gr2 = Show[ gr1, GridLines->{ Range[2,6,2], Range[-1,1,.2] } ];
major = {1,1/2,-1/2,-1};
minor = {#,{GrayLevel[.7]}}& /@ Complement[ Range[-1,1,1/10], major, {0} ];
gr3 = Show[ gr1, GridLines->{ Automatic, Join[major,minor] } ];
Show[GraphicsArray[{ gr1, gr2, gr3 }]];
```

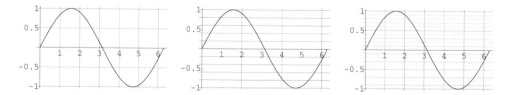

In the first plot, we ask *Mathematica* to position grid lines where it thinks they look best. In the second plot, we explicitly specify lists of grid line positions in x and y. In the third plot, we ask *Mathematica* to position grid lines automatically in x, but for grid lines across the y axis, we specify a list of positions and styles. The variable major contains a list of the positions of major grid lines. We construct the variable minor by starting with a list of positions for minor grid lines, then using Complement to strike out 0 (because that is the position of the x axis) and the major grid line positions. We map across the resulting list a function that pairs each minor grid position with the specification {GrayLevel[.7]}, so that minor grid lines are drawn in light gray instead of the default black.

Note that the *style* specification for a grid line must be a list. Unlike some other options, GridLines does *not* accept a single style attribute as equivalent to a list of attributes. For example, if you want to place a light gray grid line at position 1, you must say {1,{GrayLevel[.8]}} and not merely {1,GrayLevel[.8]}. If you use the latter form, no error message is generated, but the GrayLevel setting is ignored.

The GridLines option accepts one other kind of setting: a function to be called with two arguments specifying the left and right endpoints of a plotting interval. The function is called twice, once for the x axis and once for the y axis, and it is expected to return a valid specification for grid line positions. This allows you to replace *Mathematica*'s automatic grid line positioning algorithm with one of your own. Note that the endpoints supplied to your function are the ones obtained *after* the 5 percent expansion described in Section 7.1.1 on page 212 has been applied, so you may want to compensate for that in your function. Here is an example grid positioning function that inserts 10 equally spaced grid lines between the maximum and minimum positions, after undoing the 5 percent expansion:

```
gridpos[min_,max_] := Block[{lo,hi,ctr},
                        {lo,hi} = {min,max};
                        ctr = (lo+hi)/2;
                        {lo,hi} = ctr + ({lo,hi}-ctr)/1.05;
                        Range[ lo, hi, (hi-lo)/9 ]
                      ];
Plot[ Sin[x], {x,0,2Pi}, GridLines->gridpos ];
```

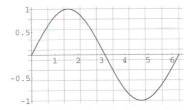

Mathematica's internal algorithm for positioning grid lines is much more sophisticated than the example indicates; it attempts to position grid lines at "nice" values. The function LogPlot defined in the package Graphics`Graphics` intercepts the GridLines option and uses its own algorithm in place of *Mathematica*'s internal algorithm to position grid lines when the Automatic setting is specified. Thus it can place grid lines along a logarithmic scale instead of the linear scale that *Mathematica* otherwise uses. If you are trying to write a grid line positioning algorithm of your own, you might want to look at the code for LogPlot to see one way of doing this.

- GraphicsSpacing

The GraphicsSpacing option is used by GraphicsArray to specify how much space to leave between adjacent graphics within the array. The setting should be either a number greater than 0 or a pair of such numbers to specify the horizontal and vertical spacing separately. The number is interpreted as a fraction of the width or height of a graphic in the array. For example, the setting {.1,.2} means that the space between adjacent graphics in a row should be 10 percent of the width of a graphic, and the space between rows (i.e., the space between graphics in a column) should be 20 percent of the height of a graphic. The default setting is 0.1; a setting of 0 eliminates the spacing altogether and causes the graphics to abut. Here is an example showing that:

```
opts = Sequence[ Axes->True, Ticks->Automatic, Frame->True, FrameTicks->None,
                 DisplayFunction->Identity ];
gr = Plot[#[x],{x,-Pi,Pi},Evaluate[opts]]& /@ {Sin,Cos,Tan,Sec,Cot,Csc};
gr = Partition[gr,3];
Show[GraphicsArray[ gr, GraphicsSpacing->0 ]];
```

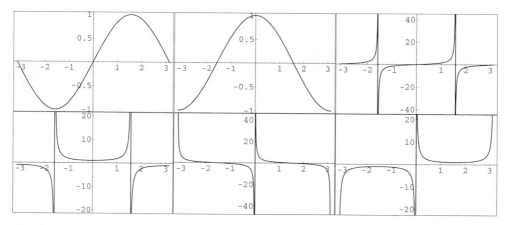

Here is the same array with spacing specified separately in the horizontal and vertical directions:

```
Show[GraphicsArray[ gr, GraphicsSpacing->{.2,.3} ]];
```

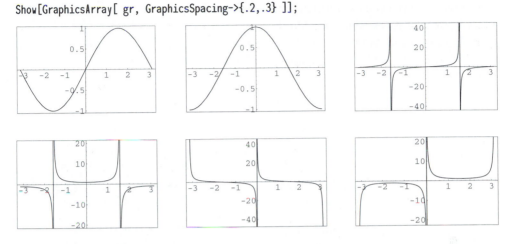

7.4 Options Used by All 3D Graphics

7.4.1 The Bounding Box

- AxesEdge

The Axes option controls whether or not axes are drawn, and the Ticks option controls where along the axes the tick marks are placed. However, there are four edges on which each axis could be drawn, so the AxesEdge option specifies which edges to use. The default setting is Automatic, which means that *Mathematica* uses an internal algorithm to decide where to place the axes. The general form is a list of three specifications (one for each axis), and each specification is either Automatic or a list of two elements, each of which is either 1 or −1, indicating that the axis should be positioned at the maximum or minimum end of one of the other two axes. For example, of the four edges along which the x axis could be drawn, two are along the face that touches the minimum end of the y axis and two are along the face that touches the maximum end; paired the other way, two edges lie on the face that touches the minimum end of the z axis and two lie on the face that touches the maximum end. Specifying {-1,1} as the first element of the AxesEdge list tells *Mathematica* to draw the x axis on the edge where the minimum y face meets the maximum z face.

Mathematica's internal algorithm attempts to place each axis along the "most visible" edge. In general, it selects an edge whose projection lies on the convex hull of the projected bounding box in preference to one that does not; of two edges on the hull, it selects the longer one. This algorithm is very effective; there is seldom any reason to overrule it by an explicit AxesEdge setting. Here are a few examples:

```
gr1 = Graphics3D[{ Point[{0,0,0}] }, Axes->Automatic ];
gr2 = Append[ gr1, ViewPoint->{0,-2,0} ];
gr3 = Append[ gr1, ViewPoint->{1,1,1} ];
gr4 = Append[ gr3, AxesEdge->{{-1,1},{1,-1},{1,1}} ];
Show[GraphicsArray[{ gr1, gr2, gr3, gr4 }]];
```

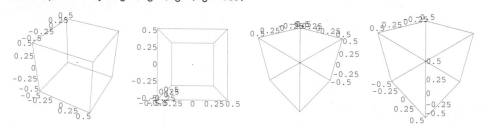

The leftmost graphic uses the default ViewPoint and the default setting AxesEdge->Automatic. Here, *Mathematica* makes reasonable choices for the axes edges. In the second graphic, the ViewPoint has been chosen so that none of the four possible edges for the y axis is on the convex hull of the projected bounding box, and all four edges are the same length. *Mathematica* makes a seemingly arbitrary choice of which edge to use, but it is not clear that any of the other three possibilities would have been better. In the third graphic, the ViewPoint has been moved again, and the automatic algorithm has chosen once again to place each axis on the longer edge on the border of the projected bounding box, but the collision of the tick mark labels at the corners makes it arguable that this was not the best choice. In the graphic on the right, we prefer to use the AxesEdge option to override *Mathematica*'s choices and place the axes so that the labels do not collide, even though this requires us to label one of the interior edges.

▪ Boxed

The Boxed option specifies whether to draw the edges of the bounding box in a 3D graphic. The possible settings are True (the default) and False. This is an all-or-nothing option; there is no provision to draw some edges and not others.

```
gr1 = ParametricPlot3D[ {r Cos[th], r Sin[th], th}, {r,0,1}, {th,0,2Pi},
                        BoxRatios->{1,1,2}, DisplayFunction-> Identity ];
gr2 = Show[ gr1, Boxed->False ];
gr3 = Show[ gr1, Boxed->False, Axes->False ];
Show[GraphicsArray[{ gr1, gr2, gr3 }]];
```

Note that axes are drawn separately from the bounding box. Even when Boxed->False is used to suppress the bounding box, the edges bearing the axes are drawn unless the setting Axes->False is also specified.

- BoxRatios

The BoxRatios option specifies the shape of the bounding box into which a 3D graphic is scaled. The setting should be either Automatic or a list of three positive real numbers $\{rx, ry, rz\}$. If the latter is used, the box is shaped so that its edges are in those proportions; for example, the setting $\{1,2,4\}$ shapes the box so that the y axis is twice as long as the x axis and half as long as the z axis (before the perspective projection). The Automatic setting instructs *Mathematica* to use the "natural lengths" of the edges, as determined by the PlotRange. For example, if a particular graphics object has a PlotRange of $\{\{-1,1\},\{0,3\},\{2,10\}\}$ (whether this was set explicitly or computed automatically by *Mathematica*), setting its BoxRatios to Automatic causes *Mathematica* to make a box whose proportions are $2:3:8$. In a sense, BoxRatios is the three-dimensional analog of AspectRatio.

The default setting of BoxRatios used for Graphics objects (including objects produced by ParametricPlot3D) is Automatic; the default for SurfaceGraphics objects (which usually are produced by Plot3D) is $\{1,1,.4\}$.

In the following example, the same surface is displayed three times: once with the default box ratios, once with the setting $\{1,1,1\}$ so that the bounding box is forced to become a cube, and once with the "natural" box ratios.

```
gr1 = Plot3D[ x y, {x,-2,2}, {y,-3,3}, DisplayFunction->Identity ];
gr2 = Show[ gr1, BoxRatios->{1,1,1} ];
gr3 = Show[ gr1, BoxRatios->Automatic ];
Show[GraphicsArray[{ gr1, gr2, gr3 }]];
```

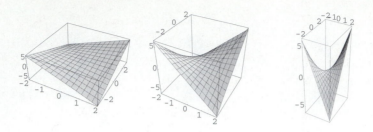

- BoxStyle

The BoxStyle option specifies how the bounding box should be rendered. The default setting is Automatic, which draws the box in thin unbroken lines in a color chosen to contrast with the Background setting. BoxStyle can also be set to a list of attribute directives that includes Dashing, Thickness, and color specifications. Naturally, the BoxStyle setting is irrelevant if Boxed->False has been used to suppress the bounding box altogether.

Since axes are drawn independently of the bounding box, you can specify a different appearance for the edges that do and do not bear axes by using BoxStyle and AxesStyle in combination, as shown here:

```
gr0 = Plot3D[ Sin[x]Cos[y], {x,0,2Pi},{y,0,2Pi}, DisplayFunction->Identity ];
gr1 = Show[ gr0, BoxStyle->{Dashing[{.03,.03}],GrayLevel[.7]},
                AxesStyle->{Thickness[.01],GrayLevel[.2]} ];
gr2 = Show[ gr0, BoxStyle-> {GrayLevel[.9],Thickness[.02]},
                AxesStyle->{GrayLevel[.2], Dashing[{.05,.02}]} ];
Show[GraphicsArray[{ gr1, gr2 }]];
```

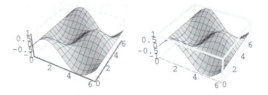

The graphic on the right shows that the axes edges are sometimes drawn before and sometimes after the bounding box edges, even within the same graphic! This fact severely limits the usefulness of BoxStyle and AxesStyle. We can only hope that the interaction of axes and the bounding box will be made more predictable in a future version of *Mathematica*.

■ FaceGrids

The FaceGrids option specifies whether and where to draw grid lines on the faces of the bounding box. The default setting is None, which indicates that no face grids are to be drawn. The setting All instructs *Mathematica* to draw grids on all faces of the box, with grid lines positioned by an internal algorithm. The most general setting for FaceGrids is a list of elements, each of which is either a face designator *face* or a pair {*face*, *grid*}. A face designator is a list containing two 0s and either a 1 or a −1, in any order; for example, the designator {0,0,1} specifies the face at the upper end of the *z* axis, and the designator {0,-1,0} specifies the face at the lower end of the *y* axis. A *grid* designator is a pair of lists, each of which specifies grid lines in one direction across a face. Each entry in a grid line list is either a number, indicating the position of a grid line, or a pair containing a number and a list of attribute directives telling how to draw the grid line at that position.

FaceGrids is one of the least used and most complicated graphics options. The following example builds up a face grid specification step by step and bears careful study:

```
xyticks = Range[0,2Pi,Pi/2];
xymajor = xyticks;
xyminor = Complement[ Range[0,2Pi,Pi/8], xymajor ];
zmajor = Range[-1,1,1/2];
zminor = Complement[ Range[-1,1,1/4], zmajor ];
majorstyle = {GrayLevel[.5],Thickness[.006]};
minorstyle = {GrayLevel[.7],Dashing[{.03,.01}]};
xymajor = {#,majorstyle}& /@ xymajor;
xyminor = {#,minorstyle}& /@ xyminor;
zmajor = {#,majorstyle}& /@ zmajor;
zminor = {#,minorstyle}& /@ zminor;
xygrids = Join[xymajor,xyminor];
zgrids = Join[zmajor,zminor];
facegrids = {
                { {-1,0,0}, { xygrids, zgrids } },
                { {0,1,0}, { xygrids, zgrids } },
                { {0,0,-1}, { xygrids, xygrids } }
};
gr1 = Plot3D[ Sin[x]Cos[y], {x,0,2Pi}, {y,0,2Pi}, PlotPoints->17,
           FaceGrids->facegrids, ViewPoint->{1.3,-1.8,.6},
           Ticks-> {xyticks,xyticks,Automatic}, DisplayFunction->Identity ];
gr2 = Show[ gr1, HiddenSurface->False, MeshStyle->Thickness[.008] ];
```

```
Show[GraphicsArray[{gr1,gr2}],GraphicsSpacing->.2,AspectRatio->.28];
```

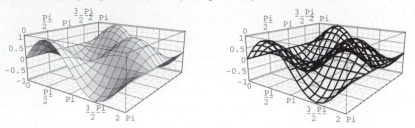

The variable xymajor contains specifications for the major grid lines in the x and y directions; the variable xyminor contains specifications for the minor x and y grid lines. Likewise, the variables zmajor and zminor contain specifications for major and minor grid lines in z, and the variables majorstyle and minorstyle specify the attributes for the major and minor grid lines. Face grids are placed on the faces of the box that are behind or beneath the surface being plotted, and the HiddenSurface option is used to remove the polygons making up the surface so that only the mesh lines are drawn. The PlotPoints option is used to make the sample grid divisions coincide with the face grid positions so that the mesh lines will line up with the face grid lines. The Ticks option is used to make the tick marks in x and y agree with the major face grid divisions.

7.4.2 Polygon Shading

The options discussed in this section control how polygons in 3D graphics are shaded.

▪ Shading and Lighting

The Shading option specifies whether polygons in Graphics3D and SurfaceGraphics objects are to be shaded. The Lighting option specifies whether simulated illumination is to be used in the shading. Each of these options should be set to True or False; the default for both is True. Taken together, these options determine the coloring method used for shading polygons. They interact differently for Graphics3D and SurfaceGraphics objects.

In Graphics3D objects, if Shading is False, all polygons are colored white. If Shading is True, the method of polygon shading is controlled by the Lighting option: If Lighting is True, polygons are colored by simulated illumination; if False, polygons are colored by explicit color directives. Here is an example showing the effects of the combinations:

```
Needs["Graphics`Shapes`"];
s = Sphere[];
Show[GraphicsArray[{
    Graphics3D[ {GrayLevel[.4],s}, Shading->True,  Lighting->True  ],
    Graphics3D[ {GrayLevel[.4],s}, Shading->True,  Lighting->False ],
```

```
  Graphics3D[ {GrayLevel[.4],s}, Shading->False, Lighting->True  ],
  Graphics3D[ {GrayLevel[.4],s}, Shading->False, Lighting->False ]
}]];
```

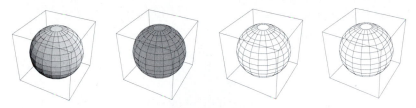

As you can see, the Shading option takes precedence over the Lighting option for Graphics3D objects.

For SurfaceGraphics objects, the situation is reversed; the Lighting option takes precedence over the Shading option. If Lighting is False, the surface is colored according to the function specified by ColorFunction option; the default setting ColorFunction->Automatic shades the surface according to height. If Lighting is True but Shading is False, the surface is colored white. If Lighting and Shading are both True, the surface is colored by a ColorFunction if one is specified or (if ColorFunction is Automatic) by a coloring array if one is present or by simulated illumination otherwise.

The fact that the Lighting option takes precedence over the Shading option for SurfaceGraphics objects seems to be inconsistent with the description of Shading in The *Mathematica* Book, and it is definitely inconsistent with the behavior of these options for Graphics3D. Therefore it seems quite possible that this interaction will be changed in a future version of *Mathematica*. Nevertheless, the Shading and Lighting options were designed with different purposes in mind, and either one alone behaves reasonably when the other is left at its default setting. We present them together here because they share the general purpose of controlling how polygons are shaded; in all probability, the designers of *Mathematica*'s graphics never intended for them to be used in combination.

When the setting Shading->False takes effect, all polygons are colored white, regardless of the settings of the Background and DefaultColor options.

```
gr1 = Graphics3D[ s, Shading->False, Background->GrayLevel[0.7] ];
gr2 = Graphics3D[ s, Shading->False, DefaultColor->GrayLevel[0.4] ];
Show[GraphicsArray[{ gr1, gr2 }]];
```

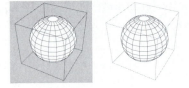

You can, however, use the ColorOutput function to change the colors of the polygons (along with everything else in the graphic).

```
invert[GrayLevel[x_]] := GrayLevel[1-x];
Show[Graphics3D[ s, Shading->False,
                 Background->GrayLevel[0.7], ColorOutput->invert ]];
```

- AmbientLight and LightSources

When simulated illumination is used to shade polygons in a 3D graphic (as determined by the Shading and Lighting options), the color of a polygon is determined by the color and intensity of the light it reflects to the viewer from the light incident upon it. The incident light is of two kinds: directed light rays, whose direction, color, and intensity are specified by the LightSources option setting; and isotropic ambient light, specified by the AmbientLight option setting. The way the polygon reflects light is determined by its diffuse and specular albedoes, as specified by the SurfaceColor directive. We discussed SurfaceColor on page 74 in Section 3.3.5, but our discussion of simulated illumination here is more complete. By the way, there is no way to specify a SurfaceColor for the polygons in a SurfaceGraphics object; they always behave as diffuse white reflectors — the equivalent of specifying

SurfaceColor[GrayLevel[1], GrayLevel[0]]

for the polygons in a Graphics3D object. If you want to display specular highlights on a surface plotted by Plot3D, convert the SurfaceGraphics option to Graphics3D form and insert an appropriate SurfaceColor directive. Here is an example showing how to do that:

```
sg = Plot3D[ Cos[x]Sin[y], {x,0,2Pi}, {y,0,2Pi}, DisplayFunction->Identity ];
g3Da = Graphics3D[sg];
g3Db = Insert[ g3Da, SurfaceColor[GrayLevel[.1],GrayLevel[.8],6], {1,1} ];
Show[GraphicsArray[{ sg, g3Da, g3Db }]];
```

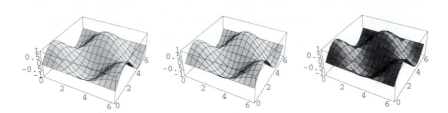

The first graphic shows the SurfaceGraphics object as Plot3D created it; the second shows the surface after it is converted to Graphics3D form, which does not change its appearance, only its internal representation; and the third shows the Graphics3D object with a SurfaceColor directive inserted to decrease the surface's diffuse reflection and add some specular reflection.

We would like to point out that simulated illumination is one of the most sophisticated aspects of *Mathematica*'s 3D graphics. For most purposes, the default lighting characteristics are adequate, and when they are not, it is often easier to color a surface with an explicit coloring function (if it was generated by Plot3D) or by setting Lighting->False and using a ColorFunction (for SurfaceGraphics objects) or explicit color directives (for polygons in a Graphics3D object). The rest of this section is quite technical, and you may want to explore other alternatives for coloring a graphic before spending time tinkering with the AmbientLight and LightSources options. We both have had the frustrating experience of working on a graphics project with a definite goal in mind and spending hour after hour displaying the same graphic with different lighting specifications, trying to discover by trial and error how to achieve the desired effect.

The setting for the AmbientLight option must be a color directive (GrayLevel, Hue, RGBColor, or CMYKColor) specifying the color and intensity of the light. The default setting is GrayLevel[0], meaning that there is no ambient illumination. A polygon reflects ambient light equally in all directions according to its diffuse reflection albedo (as specified by a SurfaceColor directive); for example, a polygon with albedo specified as GrayLevel[.5] reflecting ambient light specified as GrayLevel[.8] is displayed with shading GrayLevel[.4] (if there are no other light sources in the scene). *Mathematica* does not perform specular reflection of ambient light; if, say, a polygon's reflectance is specified as SurfaceColor[GrayLevel[0],GrayLevel[1]], and the only light is ambient light, the polygon appears black.

To illustrate how *Mathematica* treats ambient light, we will conduct a simple experiment. We will assemble a scene containing many polygons with different reflectance properties and illuminate the scene only with ambient light. Since specular reflection depends on the observer's line of sight, we will display the scene from several different viewpoints so that we can see what effect (if any) the specular component of each polygon's reflectance has on the light reflected to the viewer. The specular reflection should have no effect from any viewpoint, so that polygons with different specular albedoes but the same diffuse albedo will always have the same color. Only the diffuse albedo will determine how much of the ambient light is reflected, and, since this is diffuse reflection, the light reflected from a given polygon will be the same no matter what viewpoint we use. We start by creating the array of polygons:

```
quad[p_,q_,r_] := Polygon[{p,q,q+r-p,r}]
rect[p_] := quad[ p, p+{1,0,0}, p+{0,1,1} ]
p = Table[ { SurfaceColor[GrayLevel[i/4],GrayLevel[j/4]], rect[ {i,j,j} ] },
                {i,0,4}, {j,0,4} ];
```

This code assigns to p a 5×5 array of squares with various surface characteristics. The polygons in the same row all have the same diffuse reflectance albedo, and the polygons in the same column all have the same specular reflectance albedo. The polygon in the lower left corner reflects no light at all, and the polygon in the upper right has perfect reflectance (diffuse and specular albedo both specified as GrayLevel[1]). Next, we define a function that takes a viewpoint as its argument and displays the array of polygons as seen from this viewpoint.

```
pic[vp_] := Graphics3D[ p,
                Lighting->True, AmbientLight->GrayLevel[.8], LightSources->{},
                Axes->True, AxesEdge->{{-1,-1},{-1,-1},{-1,-1}},
                AxesStyle->{Thickness[.05],GrayLevel[.9]}, ViewPoint->vp ]
```

The function pic displays the polygons in the list p with ambient light of GrayLevel[.8] and no other light sources. We force *Mathematica* to always place the axes on the same edges of the bounding box so that we can use them as a frame of reference when we view the polygons from different viewpoints. Now we generate a list of viewpoints:

```
vwpts = { {1,3,1}, {-3,4,1}, {-1,-3,2}, {0,0,2} };
vwpts = Prepend[ vwpts, ViewPoint /. Options[Graphics3D] ];
```

The first viewpoint in the list vwpts is the default viewpoint, and the others are chosen so that we see the polygons from many different angles. Finally we display the polygons as seen from these viewpoints.

```
Show[GraphicsArray[ pic /@ vwpts ]];
```

As we expected, specular reflection has no effect: In each column, all the polygons are colored the same from every viewpoint, and all the polygons with diffuse albedo GrayLevel[0] are colored black. This proves that ambient light is not reflected specularly. The fact that polygons increase in brightness across the rows confirms that the diffuse albedo does determine the reflection of ambient light.

The setting for the LightSources option must be a list of directional light specifications. Each such specification must have the form

$$\{ \textit{direction, color} \}$$

where *direction* is a vector specifying the direction of the light, and *color* is a directive specifying its color (GrayLevel, RGBColor, Hue, or CMYKColor). Each element of the LightSources list may be thought of as specifying a point light source located infinitely far away in the given direction, so the light rays falling from it onto the polygons are all parallel to one another. The light reflected from a polygon is the sum of the diffuse and specular reflections from each light source, plus the reflected ambient light.

To understand specular and diffuse reflection of directional light, it helps to look at another example. We will use a sphere as our test surface, and show the effect of different light sources and different reflection properties on the polygons in the sphere. Actually, since only half of the sphere is visible from any viewpoint, we will use a hemisphere to avoid wasting time computing the appearances of polygons we can't see. Here is code to create a hemisphere that uses the Sphere function from the package Graphics`Shapes` as a starting point:

```
Needs["Graphics`Shapes`"];
sphere = Sphere[1,30,20];
Within[ {{a_,b_},{c_,d_},{e_,f_}}, {{g_,h_},{i_,j_},{k_,l_}} ] :=
    N[ (a >= g) && (b <= h) && (c >= i) && (d <= j) && (e >= k) && (f <= l) ]
BoundingBox[ p_Polygon ] := Map[ {Min[#],Max[#]}&, Transpose[ p[[1]] ] ]
vol = {{-2,2}, {-2,0}, {-2,2}};
hemisphere = Select[ sphere, Within[ BoundingBox[#],vol ]& ];
```

Now we define a function to display the sphere with selected lighting characteristics:

```
pic2[diff_,spec_,exp_,amb_,lsdir_,lslev_] :=
Graphics3D[ {SurfaceColor[GrayLevel[diff],GrayLevel[spec],exp],hemisphere},
            Background->GrayLevel[1/3], Boxed->False,
            Lighting->True, AmbientLight->GrayLevel[amb],
            LightSources->{ { lsdir, GrayLevel[lslev] } },
            ViewPoint->{0,-2,0}, PlotRegion->{{-.1,1.1},{-.1,1.1}} ]
```

The function pic2 takes six arguments. The first argument specifies the diffuse reflection albedo of the polygons in the hemisphere, and the second specifies the specular reflection albedo. We can eliminate either kind of reflection by setting the corresponding parameter to 0. The third argument specifies the specular exponent, which we will explain shortly. The fourth argument specifies the level of ambient illumination; we can eliminate ambient light by setting this argument to 0. The fifth and sixth arguments specify the direction and intensity of light from the only directional light source in the scene. By varying a few of these parameters at a time we can gain an understanding of the different kinds of reflection in *Mathematica*'s lighting model.

We have already seen how diffuse reflection of ambient light works. Diffuse reflection of directional light works this way: Light striking a point on a surface is reflected equally in all directions at an intensity of $d\cos\alpha$, where d is the diffuse reflection albedo and α is the angle between the direction of the light and the surface normal at the point of reflection. (This is known as Lambert's law of reflection.) There is no reflection if α is greater than 90 degrees. The intensity of light reflected to the viewer's eye is a function of the angle the surface presents to the light, but *not* of the angle from which the viewer observes the surface. These five views of the hemisphere show the effects of diffuse reflection:

```
Show[GraphicsArray[{ pic2[1,0,1,0,#,1]& /@ Table[ {i/4,.6,1}, {i,-6,6,3} ] }]];
```

In all five views, the surface has the same reflectance characteristics: perfect diffuse reflectance (albedo 1) and no specular reflectance. There is no ambient light, and the directional light has intensity 1. Only the angle at which the light strikes the surface changes from image to image. In the leftmost image, the light strikes the hemisphere from the upper left; in the center image, it swings around to front center; and in the rightmost image, it comes from the upper right. In the left and right images, you can see that polygons more than 90 degrees away from the light source remain black. Reducing either the intensity of the incident light or the albedo of the surface would linearly scale down the intensity of the reflected light.

Specular reflection is more complicated. *Mathematica* uses a variant of the Phong shading model, computing specular reflection as follows. Suppose a ray of light with direction vector **v** strikes a point on a polygon that has surface normal vector **n** and specular albedo s. The *primary* reflection ray is the "mirror image" ray, which is the ray in the plane of **v** and **n** emanating from the point of incidence at the same angle to **n** that **v** makes, but on the opposite side. The intensity of this ray is s times the intensity of the incident light. Let θ be the angle between the viewer's line of sight and this primary ray; then the intensity of the light ray reflected to the viewer is $s \cos^n \theta$, where n is the "specular exponent" of the surface. To visualize this, think of a cone with its vertex at the point of incidence and its axis on the primary reflection ray; all the rays on this cone have equal intensity, and the intensity falls off as the cone opens out into a plane. When the angle θ exceeds 90 degrees, no light is reflected from that source. Here is a diagram to help you see what is going on:

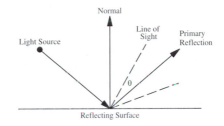

The following graphs show the effect of the specular exponent on the intensity of the reflected light as the angle between the mirror image ray and the line of sight increases. Note that at exponent 6, essentially no light is reflected at angles greater than 50 degrees, and at exponent 200, the critical angle is about 10 degrees.

```
Show[GraphicsArray[{
    Plot[ Cos[x Degree]^#, {x,0,90}, PlotRange->All, DisplayFunction->Identity,
    PlotLabel->StringJoin["Specular Exp ",ToString[#]] ]& /@ {1,2,6,200}
}]];
```

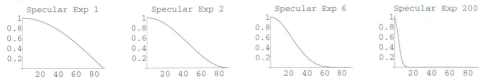

This example gives you a visual impression of how localized specular reflection is at exponent 6:

```
Show[GraphicsArray[{ pic2[0,1,6,0,#,1]& /@ Table[ {i/4,.6,1}, {i,-6,6,3} ] }]];
```

In the diffuse reflection model, the brightest polygon in the illuminated patch is the one that is "full-face" to the incident light, but since light is reflected equally in all directions, that brightest spot is of equal brightness regardless of the angle between the light and the viewer's line of sight. In the specular model, the brightest polygon the viewer sees is *not* the one that is perpendicular to the light; instead, it is the one whose surface normal bisects the angle between the direction of the incident light and the viewer's line of sight, because that is the polygon that reflects the incident light directly to the viewer.

The next example shows the combination of specular reflection, diffuse reflection of directional light, and diffuse reflection of ambient light:

```
Show[GraphicsArray[{
    pic2[  0, 1,6,  0, {2,-1,1},1 ],  (* no diffuse, specular, no ambient, direct *)
    pic2[ .8, 0,6,  0, {2,-1,1},1 ],  (* diffuse, no specular, no ambient, direct *)
    pic2[ .8, 0,6, .3, {2,-1,1},0 ],  (* diffuse, no specular, ambient, no direct *)
    pic2[ .8, 1,6, .3, {2,-1,1},1 ]   (* all of the above *)
}]];
```

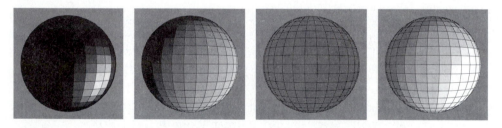

In the first three graphics we see the separate effects of (respectively) specular reflection of direct illumination, diffuse reflection of direct illumination, and diffuse reflection of ambient illumination. In the fourth graphic we see how the effects of these three different reflection models combine to give a realistic picture of an sphere.

Because the light reflected from a polygon is the sum of the light reflected from each source, you can get the effect of more intense illumination by placing several light sources at the same point. The setting

```
LightSources -> { {{1,2,1},RGBColor[0,1,0]}, {{1,2,1},RGBColor[0,1,0]} }
```

produces greens that are twice as saturated as they would have been if a single green light source had been used. This is a useful trick to remember since *Mathematica*'s default light sources tend to produce diluted, pastel colors. We are indebted to Peter Altenberg, art director for *The Mathematica Journal*, for pointing out this trick, which he frequently uses to prepare strong colors for *Journal* covers.

```
p = { SurfaceColor[GrayLevel[1]], Polygon[{{0,0,0},{1,0,0},{1,1,1},{0,1,1}}] };
ls = {{1,2,1},RGBColor[0,1,0]};
Show[GraphicsArray[{
    Graphics3D[ p, Lighting->True, LightSources->{ls} ],
    Graphics3D[ p, Lighting->True, LightSources->{ls,ls} ],
    Graphics3D[ p, Lighting->True, LightSources->{ls,ls,ls} ],
    Graphics3D[ p, Lighting->True, LightSources->{ls,ls,ls,ls} ]
}]];
```

7.4.3 Perspective Projection

Before you read this section, we recommend that you review Section 6.2.2 on page 192, in which we explain the theory of perspective projection and how it is implemented in *Mathematica*. The information in this section focuses on how to use the options governing perspective projection, but it assumes that you already have a mental model of what they are for.

We give examples of how to use the ViewPoint, ViewCenter, and ViewVertical options in Section 4.2.3 on page 109.

- ViewPoint

The ViewPoint option specifies the point in space from which to view the three-dimensional scene represented by a Graphics3D or SurfaceGraphics object. Changing the ViewPoint setting moves the viewer with respect to the object, which is equivalent to moving the object with respect to the viewer. That is, viewing an object from a sequence of points on a circle around the center of the object is equivalent to standing still and rotating the object around its center. Here we present seven views of the same surface, as seen from seven viewpoints arranged in a quarter-circle lying in a plane parallel to the xy plane and slightly above the top of the bounding box:

```
gr = Plot3D[ Sin[x]Cos[y], {x,0,2Pi}, {y,0,2Pi},
                Axes->None, DisplayFunction->Identity ];
vplist = Table[ { 3Cos[t], 3Sin[t], .3 }, {t,0,90 Degree,15 Degree} ];
grlist = Show[ gr, ViewPoint -> # ]& /@ vplist;
Show[GraphicsArray[ grlist ]];
```

The function SpinShow, defined in the package Graphics`Animation`, produces animations of rotating objects by varying the ViewPoint in precisely this manner.

The setting for the ViewPoint option should be a list of three numbers specifying the coordinates of the viewpoint in the viewpoint coordinate system. This system, which is not used by any other feature of *Mathematica* graphics, is scaled according to the proportions of the bounding box, as specified by the setting of the BoxRatios option. The origin of the ViewPoint coordinate system is at the center of the box, and the length of the longest edge of the box is taken as the unit length in all three directions. The coordinate along the longest edge runs from -0.5 to 0.5, and the coordinates along the other two edges run from $-a$ to a and $-b$ to b, where a and b are chosen so that the proportions $a : b : 0.5$ agree with the proportions specified by the BoxRatios setting. This means that the interpretation of the ViewPoint setting is different for objects whose BoxRatios are different.

To see how the interpretation of the ViewPoint setting depends on the BoxRatios setting, consider this example:

```
grlist = Show[ Graphics3D[{ Polygon[{{0,0,0},{0,1,0},{1,1,0},{1,0,0}}],
                            Polygon[{{0,0,1},{0,1,1},{1,1,1},{1,0,1}}] }],
          ViewPoint->{1.5,1.5,.3}, DisplayFunction->Identity,
          BoxRatios->{1,1,#} ]& /@ {.1, .2, .3, .6, 1, 1.5, 2 };
Show[GraphicsArray[ grlist ]];
```

All seven graphics use the same ViewPoint setting, {1.5,1.5,.3}. In the first three graphics, the z coordinate of .3 positions the viewer above the top of the bounding box. In the middle graphic, where the BoxRatios setting is {1,1,.6}, the viewpoint lies in the plane of the top of the box; in the remaining three pictures, the viewpoint is below the top of the box.

The default setting for ViewPoint is {1.3,-2.4,2.}, which always specifies a viewpoint that is to the right of, in front of, and above the center of the bounding box (but how far to the right, in front, and above depends on the BoxRatios setting).

For additional examples of how to use the ViewPoint option, see Section 4.2.3 on page 109. For a detailed explanation of how the viewpoint is used in computing perspective projections, refer to Section 6.2.2, which starts on page 192.

- ViewVertical

The `ViewVertical` option determines the orientation of the displayed image of a `Graphics3D` or `SurfaceGraphics` object. The setting of the `ViewVertical` option should be a list of three real numbers, specifying the coordinates of a vector in space. The setting is given in scaled coordinates, which run from 0 to 1 along each edge of the bounding box. When you ask *Mathematica* to display a 3D graphics object, it must construct a perspective projection mapping. *Mathematica* chooses a mapping that makes the image of the object's `ViewVertical` vector vertical (and, more specifically, pointing up rather than down) in the displayed image. This is always possible unless the `ViewVertical` vector is specified to be parallel to the line of sight (i.e., the line joining the viewpoint to the view center). Specifying a `ViewVertical` parallel to the line of sight produces an error message.

The default setting of `ViewVertical` is {0,0,1}, which means that 3D graphics by default are drawn so that the z axis is vertical with its positive end at the top of the image.

Again, for examples of how to use the `ViewVertical` option, see Section 4.2.3 on page 109 and for a detailed explanation of how *Mathematica* computes perspective projections, refer to Section 6.2.2, which starts on page 192.

- ViewCenter

The `ViewCenter` option specifies the point to use as the center of the perspective projection when displaying a 3D graphics object. Like `ViewVertical`, `ViewCenter` should be given in scaled coordinates. The `ViewCenter` setting is used in two ways. First, the `ViewCenter` is used in conjunction with the `ViewPoint` to define the part of the perspective projection that flattens three-dimensional objects into a plane *P* in space. The plane *P* is chosen to be the unique plane that contains the `ViewCenter` point and is perpendicular to the line joining the `ViewPoint` to the `ViewCenter`. Second, the `ViewCenter` is used in conjunction with the `ViewVertical` vector to establish a correspondence between the plane *P* and the image plane (the surface of your computer monitor or a piece of paper in your laser printer, for example). *Mathematica* maps the plane *P* onto the image plane so that the image of the `ViewCenter` point is at the center of the plotting rectangle, and rotates the image around this point so that the image of the `ViewVertical` vector points up.

Note that the plotting rectangle normally does not fill the entire drawing area; it is usually scaled into a subrectangle of the drawing area to leave room for text such as plot labels, axis labels, and tick labels. Its position may also be affected by the `PlotRegion` option setting. Therefore the `ViewCenter` point will not end up at the exact center of the drawing area unless labels are turned off and `PlotRegion` is left at its default setting

Automatic (which includes the entire drawing area).

The default setting of ViewCenter is {.5,.5,.5}, which places it at the center of the bounding box. Examples showing the effect of the ViewCenter option are given in Section 4.2.3 on page 109; a detailed explanation of how *Mathematica* computes perspective projections, appears in Section 6.2.2 on page 192. Pay special attention to the discussion on the interaction of the ViewPoint and ViewCenter when you use a ViewCenter that is not at the center of the bounding box on page 197.

- SphericalRegion

The SphericalRegion option specifies whether *Mathematica* should scale a 3D graphic to leave room in the plotting rectangle for a sphere enclosing the bounding box. This option is useful when you want to prepare an animation of a three-dimensional object rotating around its center. To understand this, consider the analogous two-dimensional situation. First we define the function rotrect:

```
Norm[ v_ ] := Sqrt[ v.v ];
rotrect[{a_,b_},{c_,d_},theta_,circ_] :=
    Module[ { cc = N[Cos[theta]], ss = N[Sin[theta]], m, ctr, u, v },
        m = {{cc,-ss},{ss,cc}};
        ctr = ({c,d}+{a,b})/2;
        {u,v} = ({c,d}-{a,b})/2;
        { Polygon[ (ctr + (m.#))& /@ { {u,v}, {u,-v}, {-u,-v}, {-u,v} } ],
            If[ circ===True, Circle[ ctr, Norm[{u,v}] ], Sequence@@{} ]
        }
    ]
```

The function rotrect takes arguments specifying the lower left and upper right corners of a rectangle, just as the Rectangle primitive does. However, it also takes an argument specifying an angle, theta, through which the rectangle should be rotated about its center. When theta is 0, the rectangle is drawn with its edges parallel to the x and y axes. The fourth argument of rotrect specifies whether to draw a circle enclosing the rotated rectangle. Here are ten graphics objects showing various uses of rotrect:

```
Show[GraphicsArray[{
    Graphics[ rotrect[ {1,2}, {4,4}, # Degree, False ], AspectRatio->Automatic,
        Frame->True, FrameTicks->None ]& /@ { 0, 15, 45, 60, 85 },
    Graphics[ rotrect[ {1,2}, {4,4}, # Degree, True ], AspectRatio->Automatic,
        Frame->True, FrameTicks->None ]& /@ { 0, 15, 45, 60, 85 }
}]];
```

In each row of this display, we show the same rectangle, first without tilt, then with tilts of 10, 45, 60, and 85 degrees. In the top row, the rectangle enclosing the plotting region has a different shape for each tilt angle, and the image of the rectangle occupies less and then more of the plotting rectangle as the tilt increases. In the bottom row, the circle present in all five graphics forces their plotting regions to be scaled to the same size, so the tilted rectangles are all drawn to the same scale and have the same area. If you imagine a sequence of graphics animating the tilting of the rectangle from left to right across each row, you see that, without the circle, the rectangle appears to shrink and grow as it rotates, while the rotating rectangle in the bottom row always stays the same size.

The same thing happens when you try to fit images of a rotating cuboid in space into a rectangular picture frame. When the edges of the cuboid are nearly parallel to the edges of the frame, the cuboid can be scaled to a larger size than when a diagonal of the cuboid is parallel to the edges of the frame. If you are animating a sequence of images of a rotating cuboid (such as the bounding box of a 3D graphic), you see the cuboid (and the objects contained within it) appear to shrink and grow, or advance and recede, as the viewing angle changes. This can make it difficult to interpret the frames of the animation as being different views of the same object. The SphericalRegion option stabilizes this effect by instructing *Mathematica* to leave enough room to draw a sphere surrounding the bounding box, regardless of the viewing angle. The sphere is not actually drawn, but leaving space for it forces all views of the object from whatever viewpoint, to be scaled to the same size, just as the circle in the two-dimensional example forced all the tilted rectangles to be drawn to the same scale. Here is an example showing the effect of SpehricalRegion:

```
sincos = Plot3D[ Sin[x]Cos[y], {x,0,2Pi}, {y,0,2Pi}, ViewPoint->{1,1,1},
         Ticks->None, Background->GrayLevel[2/3], PlotPoints->{12,10} ];
```

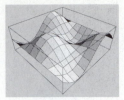

```
Show[ sincos, ViewPoint->{4,8,0} ];
```

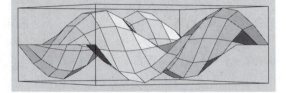

```
Show[ sincos, ViewPoint->{4,8,0}, SphericalRegion->True ];
```

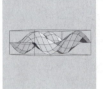

All three graphics are drawn with exactly the same height. In the first two graphics, the SphericalRegion option has its default setting of False, so the shape of the plotting rectangle is chosen to enclose the image of the bounding box. In the first graphic, the edges of the bounding box are not parallel to the edges of the plotting rectangle, so a great deal of space within the plotting rectangle is unoccupied. In the second graphic, the edges of the bounding box are parallel to the edges of the plotting rectangle, so the shape of the plotting rectangle is filled by the image of the three-dimensional object, leaving almost no wasted space. Also, that three-dimensional object is scaled to a larger width at the given height and therefore occupies more area on the page and causes the object to appear to have grown or moved closer to the viewer. The third graphic is drawn from the same viewpoint as the second, but this time we have set SphericalRegion to True, so *Mathematica* leaves enough room in the plotting region to draw a sphere surrounding the bounding box. This makes the object appear smaller than necessary for this particular viewpoint, but it ensures consistent scaling when the same object is shown from many different viewpoints.

When the SphericalRegion option is set to True, the ViewCenter and ViewVertical options are disregarded; *Mathematica* uses the center of the bounding box as the view center and orients the image so that the positive z axis is up.

The earliest (prerelease, beta-test) versions of *Mathematica* did not have the functionality of SphericalRegion. When animation capabilities were added to the Notebook Front End on the Macintosh, the first animations showed spinning objects, and the developers observed how the scaling changed from frame to frame, making the animations jumpy. To eliminate the jumpiness, they added spherical-region calculations to the code that displayed 3D graphics, but provided no way to turn these calculations off. All released versions of *Mathematica* prior to Version 2.0 worked this way. This strategy fixed the animations, but caused many graphics (those in which the edges of the bounding box were parallel to the edges of the plotting rectangle) to be drawn with excessive white space, even when they were not being animated. In Version 2.0, the SphericalRegion option was added to give control of this feature to the users.

7.5 Special 3D Graphics Options

7.5.1 Options for Graphics3D Objects

Graphics3D objects accept two special options that control the handling of polygons that intersect with or are obscured by other polygons.

Rather than using an algorithm that actually *removes* hidden features, *Mathematica* ordinarily displays a three-dimensional object simply by drawing it in back-to-front order, so that the parts most distant from the viewing point are drawn before the parts that are closer. (In computer graphics this is known as the *painter's algorithm*.) In this way, features that should be hidden are obscured when other features are painted over them. For this scheme to work, *Mathematica* has to be able to sort the parts of a 3D graphic into strict back-to-front order. This is not possible if there are polygons in the scene that pierce one another, so *Mathematica* has to break up polygons in a three-dimensional scene to avoid piercing. This task is trivial for SurfaceGraphics objects because of the restricted nature of the surfaces they can represent; thus SurfaceGraphics can be displayed quickly with little computational effort. (This is why the SurfaceGraphics data type was introduced into *Mathematica*.) For general Graphics3D objects, the computations are more difficult and time consuming. *Mathematica* always does these computations whenever a Graphics3D object is displayed; the options PolygonIntersections and RenderAll simply specify what to do with the dissected polygons after they are computed.

▪ PolygonIntersections

The PolygonIntersections option specifies whether intersecting polygons should be left unchanged. Its default setting is True. If a Graphics3D object is passed through Show with PolygonIntersections set to False, the result is a new Graphics3D object in which all polygons have been broken down into nonintersecting triangles. For example,

```
triangles = { Polygon[{ {0,0,0}, {0,2,0}, {2,1,2} }],
                Polygon[{ {2,0,0}, {2,2,0}, {0,1,2} }] };
gr1 = Graphics3D[triangles];
gr2 = Show[ gr1, PolygonIntersections->False];
Show[GraphicsArray[{gr1,gr2}]];
```

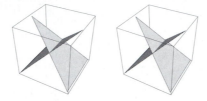

The two images look the same, but if we examine their component polygons, we see a difference. The object gr1 still contains the original triangles with which it was specified, but gr2 does not.

```
Cases[gr1,_Polygon,Infinity] === triangles
```

True

```
newpolys = Chop[Cases[gr2,_Polygon,Infinity]]
```

```
{Polygon[{{2., 0, 0}, {2., 2., 0}, {1., 1.5, 1.}}],
 Polygon[{{0, 0, 0}, {0, 2., 0}, {1., 1.5, 1.}}],
 Polygon[{{0, 0, 0}, {1., 1.5, 1.}, {1., 0.5, 1.}}],
 Polygon[{{1., 0.5, 1.}, {1., 1.5, 1.}, {0, 1., 2.}}],
 Polygon[{{2., 0, 0}, {1., 1.5, 1.}, {1., 0.5, 1.}}],
 Polygon[{{1., 0.5, 1.}, {1., 1.5, 1.}, {2., 1., 2.}}]}
```

(We applied Chop because the zeroes would otherwise have been rendered as minuscule floating-point numbers.) Note that the scene has been decomposed not merely into nonintersecting *polygons* but into nonintersecting *triangles*. This is easy to see if we redisplay the new polygon list:

```
Show[Graphics3D[{GrayLevel[.8],newpolys}],Lighting->False,ViewPoint->{0,-2,2}];
```

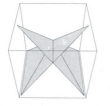

- RenderAll

The RenderAll option specifies whether PostScript code should be generated for all polygons. Its default is True, which means that all polygons are rendered, but they are painted in back-to-front order so that features that are supposed to be hidden will be obscured by other features painting over them. When RenderAll is set to False, however, the PostScript code for hidden polygons is never generated. It takes much more time and effort for *Mathematica* to generate PostScript code in this case, but the resulting code is only a fraction as large as it would be with RenderAll set to True. Ordinarily, it is more advantageous to have quick execution at the cost of large code size, but if you are generating huge graphics involving hundreds or thousands of polygons, you may wish to make the tradeoff in the other direction. This is especially true if you are planning to export a graphic produced by *Mathematica* to another program, such as a desktop publishing application.

7.5.2 Options for Special 3D Graphics Types

- ColorFunction

The ColorFunction option specifies how surfaces are to be colored. It is accepted by SurfaceGraphics, ContourGraphics, and DensityGraphics objects, and by the functions that create them. (In the case of SurfaceGraphics, the ColorFunction setting is ignored in favor of simulated lighting unless the Lighting option is set to False; for ContourGraphics, the ColorFunction is used only if ContourShading is True.) All three of these graphics data types accept an array of z values representing points on a surface sampled over a rectangular grid, and they depict the surface as shaded polygonal regions in two or three dimensions. The ColorFunction setting specifies how each region is to be shaded. It should be a function mapping real numbers in the interval [0, 1] to color specifications (RGBColor, GrayLevel, or other colors). The default ColorFunction, which may be specified explicitly with the setting ColorFunction->Automatic, simply wraps GrayLevel around its argument, converting numbers between 0 and 1 to gray intensities from black to white.

The situation is especially simple for DensityGraphics objects: Each element of the array of z values corresponds to one rectangular region in the density plot. The z values are first clipped to the PlotRange interval if necessary; then the clipped values are scaled from that interval to the interval [0, 1], and the scaled values are fed to the coloring function. The resulting colors are used to color the density plot.

The situation for SurfaceGraphics is only slightly more complicated. An $m \times n$ dimensional array of z values defines an array of $(m-1) \times (n-1)$ rectangular patches, each having four neighboring points from the z array as corners. The z value of each patch is taken to be the average of the z values at the corners *after* the z values have been clipped to lie in the `PlotRange` interval. These averaged values are then mapped into the interval [0, 1] and fed to the coloring function to determine the colors of the patches.

The situation for `ContourGraphics` is substantially more complicated because the regions bounded by the contours in a contour plot may have essentially any shapes. However, the principle is the same: A z value is associated with each region; these values are mapped from the `PlotRange` interval into the interval [0, 1]; and the resulting values are fed to the coloring function to determine how each region will be shaded.

Here are some examples of the use of `ColorFunction`:

```
mycf[x_] :=    If[ x>.5, GrayLevel[1], GrayLevel[0] ];
Block[ { $DisplayFunction = Identity },
    gr1 = DensityPlot[ Sin[x^2 - y^2], {x,-1,3}, {y,-2,2},
            Mesh->False, PlotPoints->30, ColorFunction-> Hue ];
    gr2 = ContourPlot[ Sin[x^2 - y^2], {x,-1,3}, {y,-2,2},
            PlotPoints->30, ColorFunction-> Hue ];
    gr3 = DensityPlot[ Sin[x^2 - y^2], {x,-1,3}, {y,-2,2}, PlotPoints->30,
            MeshStyle->{GrayLevel[.7],Thickness[.001]}, ColorFunction-> mycf ];
];
Show[GraphicsArray[{ gr1, gr2, gr3 }]];
```

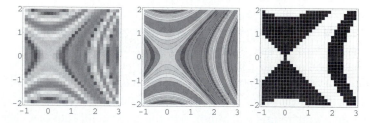

In the first two graphics, we have used `Hue` as the color function in order to shade the plots with colors instead of gray levels. In the third plot, we have used the function `mycf` to draw a sharp distinction between the values above and below the average value of the function: `mycf` colors values above the half way mark white and those below black.

The `ColorFunction` option is used by the `Raster` 2D graphics primitive in much the same way it is used in `DensityGraphics`: Entries in the raster array are clipped to a "plot range" (which is the interval [0, 1] by default, but another interval may be specified), mapped from that range to [0, 1], and converted to colors by the `ColorFunction` setting.

Finally, don't confuse the `ColorFunction` option with the `ColorOutput` option. The colors specified by the `ColorFunction` setting are modified by the `ColorOutput` function when a graphics object is converted to PostScript code, just like any other color specifications in a *Mathematica* graphic. To demonstrate this, we redisplay the graphics object gr3 we created above, this time with its colors filtered through a `ColorOutput` function that exchanges black and white:

```
invert[GrayLevel[x_]] := GrayLevel[1-x]
invert[RGBColor[r_,g_,b_]] := RGBColor[1-r,1-g,1-b]

Show[gr3,ColorOutput->invert,
      Background->GrayLevel[.9], Mesh->False,
      DisplayFunction->$DisplayFunction];
```

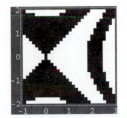

As you can see, `ColorFunction` did its job of separating the regions into above-average and below-average, and then `ColorOutput` exchanged the colors. (We added the background to the plot to make the axis labels visible, because the `ColorOutput` function turned them white.)

- MeshRange

The `MeshRange` option is used in `SurfaceGraphics`, `ContourGraphics`, and `DensityGraphics` objects to record the intervals on the x and y axes over which a function is sampled to produce the array of z values being plotted. The setting of `MeshRange` should be a pair of intervals, one for x and one for y. The plotting functions `Plot3D`, `ContourPlot`, and `DensityPlot`, which assemble graphics objects by sampling a function over a rectangular grid, incorporate an appropriate setting for the `MeshRange` option into the objects they construct. These functions do not accept the `MeshRange` option; however, the functions `ListPlot3D`, `ListContourPlot`, and `ListDensityPlot`, which accept an array of z values as argument, allow you to specify a `MeshRange` setting to record the x and y values corresponding to this array. (Compare this to the function `ListSurfacePlot3D`, defined in the package `Graphics`Graphics3D``, which takes an array of x, y, z triples as argument instead of an array of z values; this function has no need of a `MeshRange` option because it receives the x and y coordinates along with the z coordinates.) The intervals specified in the `MeshRange` setting are used to determine tick marks on axes. The special setting `Automatic` is equivalent to `{{1,m},{1,n}}`, where the dimensions of the array of z values are $m \times n$.

Here are some examples of the `MeshRange` option:

```
gr1 = Plot3D[ Sin[x]Cos[y], {x,0,2Pi}, {y,0,2Pi}, DisplayFunction->Identity ];
gr2 = Show[ gr1, MeshRange->{{-10,10},{1,5}} ];
gr3 = Show[ gr1, MeshRange->Automatic ];
gr4 = ListPlot3D[ Table[Sin[i]Cos[j],{j,0,2Pi,Pi/7},{i,0,2Pi,Pi/7}],
            MeshRange->{{0,2Pi},{0,2Pi}}, DisplayFunction->Identity ];
Show[GraphicsArray[{ gr1, gr2, gr3, gr4 }, AspectRatio->.2 ]];
```

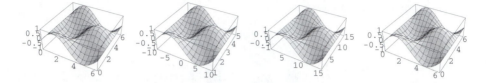

The first graphic, on the far left, was produced with Plot3D in the usual way. In the second graphic, we overrode the MeshRange setting automatically provided by Plot3D; doing this is of questionable value in real applications, but it allows us to see that the axis labels do depend on the MeshRange setting. In the third graphic, we specified the setting Automatic, which in this case is equivalent to a setting of {{1,15},{1,15}} (because the default setting of PlotPoints in Plot3D is 15, so the surface was sampled over a 15×15 grid). The fourth graphic was constructed with ListPlot3D; we used a Table command to construct the array of z values and the MeshRange option to record the x and y intervals so that the axes would be labeled properly. In effect, we re-created manually the same steps that Plot3D performs for us automatically.

Incidentally, the MeshRange option was present in early versions of *Mathematica*. It was not needed because those versions did not support labeled axes in three-dimensional plots, so there was no need to remember what range of x and y values had been used to produce an array of z values. Once three-dimensional axes were added, the *Mathematica* developers realized that there would have to be some way to record this information, so the MeshRange function was invented.

7.5.3 Mesh Options for Surface and Density Graphics

Graphical objects of type SurfaceGraphics and DensityGraphics are drawn with a mesh of lines running in the x and y directions. In a SurfaceGraphics object, the intersections of these mesh lines are the points whose heights are specified in the data array of the object; the polygons that make up the surface have these points as their corners. In a DensityGraphics object, the cells themselves represent the data values and the mesh lines are simply dividers separating the cells. In both forms of graphics, the options Mesh and MeshStyle govern the appearance of the mesh.

The Mesh option specifies whether mesh lines should be drawn. The setting True (the default) causes lines to be drawn, and the setting False suppresses them. The option MeshStyle specifies the appearance of mesh lines. Its setting should be Automatic or a list of graphics directives consisting of colors or Thickness and Dashing specifications. For example,

```
ms = {Thickness[.02],GrayLevel[.7]};
Block[ { $DisplayFunction = Identity },
    gr1 = DensityPlot[ x y, {x,-1,1}, {y,-1,1}, MeshStyle -> ms ];
    gr2 = Plot3D[ x y, {x,-1,1}, {y,-1,1}, MeshStyle -> ms, ViewPoint->{0,0,2} ]; ];
Show[GraphicsArray[ { gr1, gr2 } ]];
```

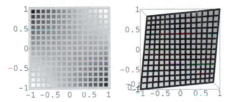

In the density plot on the left, the MeshStyle setting is obeyed, but in the surface plot on the right, the Thickness specification is obeyed whereas the GrayLevel specification is not. Why does this happen? Sadly, this is the result of not one but two bugs in the design of the PostScript code used to draw mesh lines in SurfaceGraphics. The commands that set colors for drawing the interiors of the polygons that make up the surface are not scoped within a gsave/grestore pair, so they would contaminate the mesh lines. But this bug is masked by a 0 setgray command that is hardcoded into the definition of the Metetra procedure that draws the polygons and their edges. The effect is that colors specified in a MeshStyle setting don't have any effect on SurfaceGraphics. We expect that this problem will be rectified in a future release of *Mathematica*; meanwhile, you have the same choice for mesh lines in surface plots that Henry Ford is said to have offered to purchasers of the Model T: "Any color you like, so long as it's black." Incidentally, density plots aren't subject to this problem because DensityGraphics objects are drawn with the Mimage procedure rather than Metetra.

Surfaces represented by polygons in a Graphics3D object, such as those created by ParametricPlot3D, do not respond to the Mesh and MeshStyle options. This is because the lines that appear on these surfaces are not "mesh lines" but rather are the highlighted edges of the component polygons in the surface. When *Mathematica* displays a Graphics3D object, it has no way of knowing that that object was produced by ParametricPlot3D, so it has no basis for treating the polygon edges specially. The way to suppress the seeming mesh lines or modify their appearance is to use the EdgeForm[] declaration, which instructs *Mathematica* not to highlight polygon edges.

7.5.4 Options for Contour Plots

The options in this section are used only by ContourGraphics objects and by the functions ContourPlot and ListContourPlot, which produce ContourGraphics objects as their results. Contour plots use contour lines of a function in lieu of the x, y mesh used in the surface and density plots produced by SurfaceGraphics and DensityGraphics objects. The options described here control the appearance of contour plots, specifying how many contours are drawn and where they are located, the appearance of the contour lines, and whether the regions between contours are shaded. In addition to the examples below, you might also want to look at those on page 114 in Section 4.3.1, which discusses the ContourPlot function.

▪ ContourLines

The ContourLines option specifies whether to draw contour lines. Possible settings are True and False, and the default is True. This example shows why you might sometimes want to turn off the contour lines.

```
gr1 = ContourPlot[ Sin[x^2 - y^2], {x,-1,3}, {y,-2,2}, ContourLines->False,
          Contours->30, DisplayFunction-> Identity ];
gr2 = Show[ gr1, ContourLines->True ];
gr3 = ContourPlot[ Sin[x^2 - y^2], {x,-1,3}, {y,-2,2}, PlotPoints->60,
          Contours->30, DisplayFunction-> Identity ];
gr4 = ContourPlot[ Sin[x y], {x,1,7}, {y,1,7}, ContourLines->False,
          Contours->40, DisplayFunction-> Identity ];
Show[GraphicsArray[ { gr1, gr2, gr3, gr4 } ]];
```

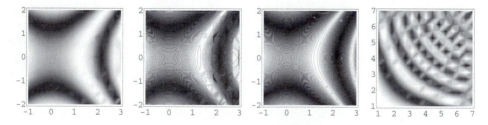

Contours are determined in a contour plot by interpolation between grid points in the array of values in a ContourGraphics object. The algorithm that finds contour lines is susceptible to aliasing, which can cause misleading breaks or turns in the lines. The shading is more robust, perhaps because the eye smooths out some of the blemishes. Even though there are a few uneven gray spots in the first graph, the graph gives a fairly faithful picture of the behavior of the function. The contours in the second graph, however, are so jagged and misleading as to make the graph useless. In fairness to *Mathematica*, we have to say that it is unwise to ask for 30 contours to be drawn from a 15-by-15 grid; requesting 30 contours with the PlotPoints option set to 60 produces the third plot, which is much more acceptable. The fourth plot depicts a different function; we included it because it reveals nicely the effect of the underlying grid on the contour shading. When *Mathematica* attempts to interpolate 40 contours through a 15-by-15 grid, the aliasing is so severe that the features of the grid show clearly through the shading algorithm. The picture is awful as a graph of the function $\sin(xy)$, but it is instructive as an illustration of how *Mathematica* shades contour plots.

- Contours

The Contours option specifies the values of z at which contours are to be plotted. The simplest setting is a positive integer n; the default setting is 10. A setting of n indicates that n contours should be drawn. In this case, *Mathematica* subdivides the z range specified by the PlotRange option into $(n + 1)$ subintervals, so that there are n interior division points between subintervals, and then draws contours through those n values of z. For contour plots, the default z range simply runs from the minimum to the maximum value in the array of z values, but setting PlotRange to something other than the default changes *Mathematica*'s choice of which contours to plot, as the following example shows:

```
gr1 = ContourPlot[ y, {x,0,1}, {y,0,1}, Contours->4, DisplayFunction-> Identity ];
gr2 = Show[gr1, PlotRange->{1/4,3/4} ];
gr3 = Show[gr1, PlotRange->{-3,3} ];
Show[GraphicsArray[ { gr1, gr2, gr3 } ]];
```

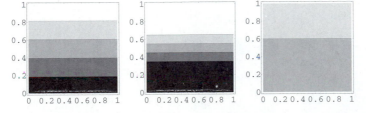

In the first plot, the function values range from 0 to 1, and requesting four contours causes *Mathematica* to divide this range into five parts, at the values $\frac{1}{5}$, $\frac{2}{5}$, $\frac{3}{5}$, and $\frac{4}{5}$. In the second case, the z range is specified to run from $\frac{1}{4}$ to $\frac{3}{4}$, so all four contours lie within that range. In the third case, the z range runs from -3 to 3, so the contour at $z = \frac{3}{5}$ is the only one that actually passes through the region over which the function is being plotted.

The other setting permitted for the Contours option is a list of z values. In this case, *Mathematica* attempts to draw contours through the specified values, using the same interpolation algorithm as before. The only difference is that *Mathematica* skips the step of selecting values through which to plot contours, because the user has already selected them.

- ContourShading

The ContourShading option specifies whether the regions between contour lines should be shaded. Permitted settings are True (the default) to enable shading and False to disable it. When shading is enabled, the ColorFunction option controls how shading is performed. The default ColorFunction setting causes the regions with the highest z value to be shaded white and the regions with the lowest z value to be shaded black, with regions in between shaded in gradations of gray. For further details, refer to our discussion of the ColorFunction option in Section 7.5.2 on page 269.

In the preceding section on ContourLines, we saw an example showing why you might want to turn off the display of contour lines in a contour plot and use only the contour shading. In the orthogonal trajectory example on page 118 in Section 4.3.1, we saw a complementary example in which we turned off shading and showed only the contour lines so that we could overlay two contour plots with the Show command. If we hadn't suppressed the shading, the second contour plot would have painted over the first one and obscured it. Incidentally, if you set both ContourLines and ContourShading to False, *Mathematica* will produce an empty square as a contour plot.

```
gr1 = ContourPlot[ Sin[x^2 - y^2], {x,-1,3}, {y,-2,2}, DisplayFunction->Identity ];
gr2 = Show[ gr1, ContourLines -> False];
gr3 = Show[ gr2, ContourShading -> False ];
gr4 = Show[ gr1, ContourShading -> False ];
Show[GraphicsArray[ { gr1, gr2, gr3, gr4 } ]];
```

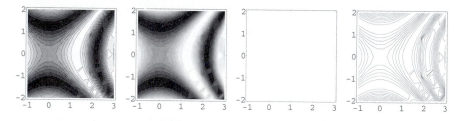

- ContourSmoothing

The ContourSmoothing option specifies how contour lines should be smoothed. This setting is quite mysterious. The Reference Guide entry in The *Mathematica* Book says that the permitted settings are Automatic, None, and positive integers. However, the online help in Version 2.2 says this:

?ContourSmoothing

ContourSmoothing is an option for contour plots. With ContourSmoothing ->
  False, contour lines are computed using linear interpolation. With
  ContourSmoothing -> True, cubic interpolation is used.

The default setting is True in Version 2.2. The following example shows that the settings True and False do have some effect in some cases, but it is not clear what "cubic interpolation" process is being performed to produce this effect.

```
smooth = ContourPlot[ Sin[x^2 - y^2], {x,-1,3}, {y,-2,2}, DisplayFunction->Identity ];
nosmooth = Show[ smooth, ContourSmoothing->False ];
Show[GraphicsArray[ { smooth, nosmooth } ]];
```

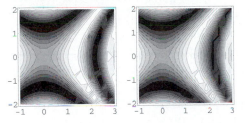

Experiments show that Automatic, None, and positive integers are all accepted as settings for ContourSmoothing, but since we observed no difference in the effects of these settings, we conclude that the contour smoothing feature is only partially implemented and still under development.

- ContourStyle

The ContourStyle option specifies the styles to use in drawing contour lines. It is the counterpart for contour plotting of the PlotStyle option used by Plot, ListPlot and ParametricPlot, and the MeshStyle option used by Plot3D and DensityPlot. The most general setting is

$$\{ \{directives_1\}, \{directives_2\}, \ldots \{directives_1\} \}$$

where each $directives_i$ represents one or more graphics directives affecting the appearance of lines, or the special setting Automatic. Directives affecting lines are colors (GrayLevel, RGBColor, CMYKColor, and Hue) and Thickness and Dashing specifications. The Automatic setting specifies that the default style should be used. You can also specify a single directive or a single list of directives, which causes all contour lines to be drawn in the same style.

In the following example, we plot a boring function so that we can easily tell which contour line corresponds to which z value. In the plot on the left, ContourStyle is specified as a list of directives, so all the directives in the list are applied to each contour. In the plot on the right, one of the entries in the ContourStyle list is itself a list, so *Mathematica* applies styles to the contours separately.

```
gr1 = ContourPlot[ y, {x,0,1}, {y,0,1}, DisplayFunction->Identity,
         Contours->{.2, .8, .4, .6 }, ContourShading->False,
         ContourStyle->{ RGBColor[1,0,0], Dashing[{.14,.02,.02,.02}],
                 Thickness[.02] } ];
gr2 = ContourPlot[ y, {x,0,1}, {y,0,1}, DisplayFunction->Identity,
         Contours->{.2, .8, .4, .6 }, ContourShading->False,
         ContourStyle->{ Automatic, {RGBColor[1,0,0]},
                 Dashing[{.14,.02,.02,.02}], Thickness[.02] } ];
Show[GraphicsArray[ { gr1, gr2 } ]];
```

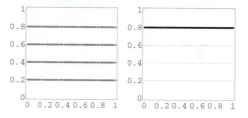

Specifying a list of styles makes it easier to tell which contour corresponds to which z value, especially in a plot in which contour shading has been turned off. Note that the styles are applied to the contours in sorted order, which need not be the order in which the contours were specified. In the plot on the right, the value 0.8 is not the last value in the Contours list, but it is the largest, so the last entry in the ContourStyle list is used for the $z = 0.8$ contour.

7.5.5 Options for SurfaceGraphics

- HiddenSurface

The HiddenSurface option specifies whether hidden surfaces in SurfaceGraphics are to be eliminated. More correctly, it specifies whether polygons representing the surface are to be drawn. If they are drawn, folds in the surface may cause parts of the surface at the back to be hidden by parts in front. If they are not drawn, then the surface is represented only by the mesh lines and features in back are visible through the mesh. The setting for HiddenSurface must be True or False; the default is True. Obviously, options that control artificial lighting (Lighting, LightSources, and AmbientLight) have no effect if HiddenSurface is set to False (since there are then no polygons to be illuminated).

Here is a surface plot shown with and without polygons:

```
gr1 = Plot3D[ Sin[x]Cos[y], {x,0,2Pi}, {y,0,2Pi},
                ViewPoint->{1.3,-1.5,.6}, DisplayFunction->Identity ];
gr2 = Show[ gr1, HiddenSurface->False, MeshStyle->{Thickness[.01]} ];
gr3 = Show[ gr2, Mesh->False ];
Show[GraphicsArray[{ gr1, gr2, gr3 }, AspectRatio->.2 ]];
```

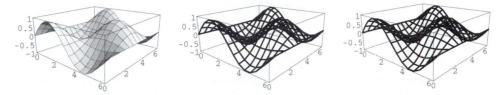

Incidentally, you might think that if you set both of the HiddenSurface and Mesh options to False you would get an empty plot. Since such a result would not be very useful, *Mathematica* doesn't do this. If you set HiddenSurface to False, a mesh is drawn regardless of the setting of the Mesh option, as the third graphic demonstrates.

- ClipFill

If an explicit PlotRange setting is used in a SurfaceGraphics object, the z coordinates of the surface may fall outside the range. In that case, the surface is "clipped": Values greater than the maximum are replaced by the maximum value, and values less than the minimum are replaced by the minimum value. Clipping creates plateaus at the top and bottom faces of the bounding box, which, by default are drawn the same way as any other parts of the surface, concealing the clipping effect. This may produce a misleading plot. The ClipFill option allows you to specify an alternate treatment of the clipped regions. The setting ClipFill->None causes the clipped regions not to be drawn; the surface has holes in it where clipping occurs. The setting ClipFill->{a,b}, where a and b are color specifications, causes regions clipped at the minimum to be colored with color a and regions clipped at the maximum to be colored with color b. The setting ClipFill->a is equivalent to ClipFill->{a,a}. The default behavior is specified with ClipFill->Automatic. Here is an example:

```
Plot3D[ Sin[x]Cos[y], {x,0,2Pi},{y,0,2Pi}, PlotRange->{-.5,.5}, ClipFill->None ];
```

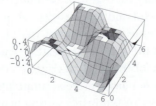

```
Plot3D[ Sin[x]Cos[y], {x,0,2Pi},{y,0,2Pi}, PlotRange->{-.5,.5},
    ClipFill->{GrayLevel[1],GrayLevel[0]} ];
```

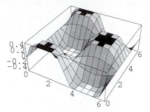

Specifying colors for clipped regions has no effect if either HiddenSurface or Shading has been set to False, but ClipFill->None still suppresses the polygons and mesh lines in the clipped regions.

7.6 Options for Plotting Functions

Mathematica has six commands for making graphs of functions: Plot, ParametricPlot, Plot3D, ParametricPlot3D, ContourPlot, and DensityPlot. All six create a graph or plot of a function by sampling the function at various points and then drawing a graphical representation based on the sampled values. The options described in this section control the way sampling is performed or the appearance of the resulting plot.

There is an important difference between the graphics options described in this section and the ones described in earlier sections. The latter were all "intrinsic" to one or more of the graphics data types. For example, the aspect ratio of a graphic is a property of the graphics object and can be changed with a command such as

Show[object, AspectRatio->1]

to give a different appearance when the graphics object is displayed. The plotting operators allow such options to be specified, but the operators themselves don't use this information — they simply pass it along to the graphics objects they construct, to be acted on when the object is displayed. The options in this section, however, are not properties of the graphics objects themselves but of the process by which the graphics objects are produced. Therefore they cannot be altered by Show. If, for example, you have created a plot of a function and you wish to "zoom in" on a certain interesting feature, you can use Show to alter the setting of the PlotRange option to enlarge the plot in the neighborhood of the interesting feature and clip off the rest. However, doing so only effects a scaling of the original graphic: The same information is being presented at a larger size. If you need a more accurate plot, with more points plotted, you cannot use Show to increase the PlotPoints setting because the graphics object itself *has* no PlotPoints setting. You must use the Plot command to generate a new graphics object in which more points have been sampled.

7.6.1 Options Used by All Sampling Plot Functions

All of the graphics operators that sample functions use these two options.

▪ Compiled

The Compiled option is used by all plotting functions (and some other *Mathematica* functions that have nothing to do with graphics) to specify whether the expressions they work with should be compiled. A plotting function typically samples the function it is plotting at dozens or hundreds of points; this process can be sped up enormously if the function being sampled is compiled before the plotting begins. For this reason, Compiled->True is the default for all plotting functions. However, compiled functions in *Mathematica* use machine-size arithmetic only, so if the function you are plotting requires high-precision floating-point arithmetic or extremely large integers in order to be computed accurately, then you should use the setting Compiled->False.

Another thing to be aware of is that the compiler does not (and should not) evaluate the expressions it is given to compile; it simply compiles them. This means that a command such as this one causes the function Exp[-x^2] Sin[x] to be compiled:

Plot[Exp[-x^2] Sin[x], {x,0,10}]

But if you give the two commands

f[x_] := Exp[-x^2] Sin[x]
Plot[f[x], {x,0,10}]

Mathematica compiles only the reference to f[x]; when that compiled expression is evaluated, it causes f[x] to be computed in the ordinary way, which means the benefits of compiling are lost. In this case, the command

Plot[Evaluate[f[x]], {x,0,10}]

would work as desired, because evaluation of the function f[x] at the symbolic argument x would simply produce the symbolic expression Exp[-x^2] Sin[x], which Plot would then compile. A function computed by an algorithm that expects numerical arguments and doesn't respond properly to symbolic ones wouldn't be an apt candidate for this treatment, however.

For more information about *Mathematica's* expression compiler, refer to the technical report *The Mathematica Compiler*, published by WRI.

▪ PlotPoints

In 3D graphics, the PlotPoints option specifies how many sample points to use in plotting a function of the form $f(x, y)$. The setting PlotPoints->{a, b} causes the x interval to be subdivided into $a - 1$ subintervals by the choice of a equally spaced points; similarly, the y interval is subdivided into $b - 1$ subintervals. The function is sampled at the $a \times b$ corner points of the resulting grid (and only at those points, since three-dimensional plotting in *Mathematica* is not adaptive). The setting PlotPoints->a is an abbreviation for PlotPoints->{a, a}.

In 2D graphics, the setting PlotPoints->a causes the plotting interval to be subdivided in the same way, but since two-dimensional plotting in *Mathematica* is adaptive, this is only an initial step. More sample points are usually chosen, according to the adaptive sampling algorithm described in Section 4.1.3 on page 89.

The default setting for PlotPoints in 2D graphics is 25 for Plot and ParametricPlot. The default setting for PlotPoints in 3D graphics is 15 (implying {15,15}) for Plot3D, ContourPlot, and DensityPlot, and Automatic (for ParametricPlot3D). The Automatic setting is a special case for ParametricPlot3D, necessitated by its dual role as a curve-plotter and a surface plotter. The *Mathematica* Book tells us that this setting causes ParametricPlot3D to use 75 points when plotting curves and a 15-by-15 grid when plotting surfaces. In fact, experimentation indicates that, in some versions at least, ParametricPlot3D uses a 20-by-20 grid when plotting surfaces with PlotPoints->Automatic, as the following example shows:

```
gr = ParametricPlot3D[ {x,y,x+y}, {x,0,2Pi}, {y,0,Pi}, DisplayFunction->Identity ];
Length[ Cases[gr,_Polygon,Infinity] ]
```

361

There are 361 polygons in the result because $361 = 19^2$. *Mathematica* has used a 20-by-20 array of points to construct a 19-by-19 array of polygons.

7.6.2 Options Controlling Two-Dimensional Adaptive Sampling

The functions Plot and ParametricPlot use the same adaptive sampling algorithm to determine what points to plot in order to get an accurate graph of a function. No other plotting functions use an adaptive algorithm.

▪ MaxBend

The MaxBend option specifies the maximum acceptable bend angle between successive line segments on a curve. To see what that means, suppose that *A*, *B*, and *C* are three points already sampled on the curve, as shown in this diagram:

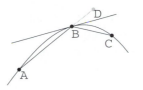

The "bend angle" that *Mathematica* works with is the angle by which the secant line *BC* bends away from the direction of the secant *AB*. In the diagram, this is the angle *CBD* formed by *BC* with the produced segment *BD* obtained by extending *AB* through *B*. If this bend angle exceeds the MaxBend specification, the adaptive sampling algorithm bisects the interval on the x axis corresponding to the longer of *AB* and *BC*, and computes an additional sample point at the midpoint. This process of subdivision is repeated recursively until either the bend angles of all adjacent pairs of segments are less than the MaxBend tolerance or the limit on the number of subdivisions has been reached. For a more complete description of how the MaxBend setting is used in adaptive sampling, refer to the discussion in Section 4.1.3 that starts on page 89.

Note that the setting for MaxBend is given in degrees. The default setting used by both Plot and ParametricPlot is MaxBend->10, specifying a tolerance of 10 degrees. If you wish to specify a tolerance in radians, you can divide by *Mathematica*'s built-in constant Degree to convert radians to degrees. For example, the setting MaxBend -> (Pi/20 / Degree) tells *Mathematica* to use a bend angle tolerance of 9 degrees, since π radians is 180 degrees.

- PlotDivision

The PlotDivision option specifies the maximum number of recursive subdivisions that Plot and ParametricPlot may use in attempting to generate a smooth curve; the default setting is 20 for both commands. If *Mathematica* has subdivided an interval as many times as specified by PlotDivision, it makes no further subdivisions, but simply plots the curve with the points it has already computed, no matter how great the bend angle between segments. Without this limit, *Mathematica* could go into an infinite descent if asked to plot a function that was not continuously differentiable over the plotting interval. For example, the plot

```
Plot[Tan[x],{x,0,3Pi}];
```

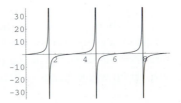

would produce this problem, since the tangent function is discontinuous at odd integer multiples of $\frac{\pi}{2}$. In fact, this points up an interesting confusion that is common among new or naïve users of *Mathematica*, who tend to assume that the vertical segments in that plot are *Mathematica*'s means of indicating vertical asymptotes at the points of discontinuity. Quite the contrary: These segments are undesirable artifacts of the sampling algorithm and reflect *Mathematica*'s decision to give up trying to make the plot smooth at those points. Note that if *Mathematica* had actually encountered one of the discontinuity values in sampling the function, it would have reacted quite differently: It would have reported an error in evaluating the function and presented the plot as two separate curves, one to the left and one to the right of the discontinuity.

Complete details of the adaptive sampling algorithm are given in Section 4.1.3 that starts on page 89.

7.6.3 A Line Style Option for Two-Dimensional Plotters

The PlotStyle option is used by Plot, ParametricPlot, and ListPlot to specify the style of lines or points to be plotted. The setting for PlotStyle should be a list of lists of graphics directives, with one sublist for each curve. Here is an example:

```
Plot[ {Exp[-x],Exp[-x]Sin[10/x],-Exp[-x]}, {x, -2.5, -.1},
    PlotStyle->{{GrayLevel[.8],Dashing[{.02,.02}]},
        {},{GrayLevel[.8],Dashing[{.02,.02}]}} ];
```

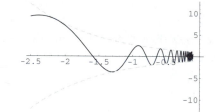

In this graph, we specified dashed gray lines for two of the three curves being plotted. We used an empty list as a placeholder for one of the curves, indicating that we wanted it to be drawn in the default style.

If you specify more drawing styles than the number of curves being plotted, the extra styles are ignored. If you specify fewer styles than curves, *Mathematica* reuses the styles from the beginning of the list when it runs out of them.

It is strange that ParametricPlot3D does not accept the PlotStyle option. Of course, this option would not make sense for the surface-plotting function of ParametricPlot3D, but it would be appropriate and useful when ParametricPlot3D is used to plot curves in space.

7.6.4 A Special Option for ListPlot

The PlotJoined option is used only by ListPlot; it specifies whether the points plotted should be joined by a line. With the setting PlotJoined->False, the points are drawn as Point objects and no connecting line is drawn. With the setting PlotJoined->True, the list of points is used to specify a Line object, which connects them, and no points are drawn. If you want the points *and* the line, you can use ListPlot twice and then use Show to combine the resulting plots, or you can use another plotting function such as MultipleListPlot. This function, written by Cameron Smith, is defined in the package Graphics`MultipleListPlot` distributed with *Mathematica*.

7.7 Default Values for Graphics Options

Several global variables are used to control the display of graphics objects. The default settings of graphics options are arranged so that changing one of these variables affects the way all graphics are subsequently displayed. This is accomplished by means of a standard *Mathematica* idiom: If SomeOption, is the name of an option for a function, then the option setting

$$\text{SomeOption} :> \text{\$SomeOption}$$

tells *Mathematica* that each time it needs to know the setting of the option SomeOption, it should use the current value of the variable $SomeOption. If a setting like this is incorporated into a graphics object, and the object is displayed several times, changing the value of the variable $SomeOption between displays will change the way the object is displayed. This arrangement works because the option is specified as a delayed-evaluation rule (:> as opposed to ->); if the option were specified as an immediate-evaluation rule, the variable $SomeOption would be consulted only once, when the graphics object was first assembled. There is nothing special about the dollar sign ($) in the variable name, except that it is conventional in *Mathematica* programming to use names beginning with dollar signs for global "environment variables," and to associate such names with the options they control. It is the use of RuleDelayed (:>) rather than Rule (->), not the similarity of names, that makes this mechanism work.

▪ DefaultFont

$DefaultFont gives the default font to use for text in graphics; it is the default setting for the DefaultFont option. The usual setting of $DefaultFont is {"Courier", 10.}, which gives 10-point type in the Courier typeface. This setting is appropriate for displaying graphics on a typical computer monitor, but most of the graphics in this book were prepared with a $DefaultFont setting of {"Courier", 6.5} instead, so that tick labels and other text would not overwhelm the graphics.

- Display and DisplayFunction

$DisplayFunction gives the default setting for the option DisplayFunction in graphics functions. Its default value is

$$\text{\$DisplayFunction = Display[\$Display, \#1] \&}$$

$Display gives a list of files to be used with the default $DisplayFunction. Its default value depends on the way *Mathematica* is configured on the computer you are using. Usually the string "stdout" on systems that use a Notebook Front End; on UNIX systems, it is often a string that denotes a pipe to an external PostScript interpreter.

- SoundDisplay and SoundDisplayFunction

$SoundDisplayFunction gives the default setting for the option DisplayFunction in sound functions. Its default value is

$$\text{\$SoundDisplayFunction = Display[\$SoundDisplay, \#1] \&}$$

$SoundDisplay gives a list of files and pipes to be used with the default $SoundDisplayFunction. Its default value depends on the way *Mathematica* is configured on the computer you are using.

- StringConversion

$StringConversion is *supposed* to give the default setting for the option StringConversion in Display (and other commands that open output streams, such as OpenWrite). The default value of $StringConversion is

$$\text{\$StringConversion = None}$$

Unfortunately, setting $StringConversion has no effect on graphics display (in Version 2.2, at least) because of an oversight in setting the defaults for the Display command.

Options[Display]

{StringConversion -> None}

The default setting of the StringConversion option for Display is None, not $StringConversion. For comparison, the setting is correct in OpenWrite.

```
Options[OpenWrite,StringConversion]
```

{StringConversion :> $StringConversion}

The default StringConverstion setting for Display will probably be corrected in a future version of *Mathematica*. For now, if you frequently need to use a nonstandard StringConversion function, you may wish to add the command

```
SetOptions[ Display, StringConversion :> $StringConversion ];
```

to your init.m file so that setting the $StringConversion variable will have the appropriate effect on strings displayed in graphics (such as labels on plots, axes, and tick marks, and text produced by Text primitives).

7.8 Obsolete Graphics Options

Version 1 of *Mathematica* provided some graphics options that are no longer needed because their functions have been subsumed by more powerful features that were introduced with Version 2. If you have libraries of old *Mathematica* code, you may still encounter these options from time to time. When you use an obsolete option, *Mathematica* gives you a message telling you that the option is obsolete and suggesting another option. This section briefly discusses the obsolete graphics options and the new options that have replaced them.

The Axes option has changed its meaning and been supplemented by other options, notably AxesOrigin. In Version 1, you could say Axes->None to suppress axes, Axes->Automatic to have them drawn and positioned by *Mathematica*, and Axes->{x, y} to have them drawn to intersect at {x, y}. In Version 2, the Axes option specifies only whether the axes should or should not be drawn, and the AxesOrigin option specifies where they should intersect.

The ContourLevels and ContourSpacing options have been superseded by Contours. In Version 1, you could set the ContourLevels option to specify how many contours you wanted drawn in a contour plot, and the ContourSpacing option to specify how far apart (in the z variable) you wanted the contours to be. In Version 2, you can set Contours to a positive integer to specify that you want that number of contours equally spaced in z between the minimum and maximum function values, or you can specify an explicit list of z values (which need not be equally spaced) at which to draw contours.

The Framed option has been superseded by Frame. In Version 1, a frame around a graphic was a simple rectangle that was or was not present, so the option Framed could be set to True or False. There were no FrameTicks, FrameStyle, or FrameLabel options, however.

The Plot3Matrix option has been superseded by ViewCenter and ViewVertical. In Version 1, you could use the Plot3Matrix option to directly specify a projection matrix to be used in mapping three-dimensional objects into the picture plane. This was the only way to achieve a mapping that had the center of the bounding box anywhere other than at the center of the graphic, or that had any other vector than {0,0,1} as the "up" direction. Unfortunately, this option was never properly documented and was not even correctly implemented in some versions of *Mathematica* (in fact, setting Plot3Matrix to certain values could cause *Mathematica* to crash). The options ViewPoint, ViewCenter, and ViewVertical allow you to specify any persepective projection, and they are more convenient and intuitive than Plot3Matrix.

The PlotColor option has been superseded by ColorOutput. In Version 1, the PlotColor option could be set to True or False to indicate whether *Mathematica* should use color specifications in the PostScript code it generated. If PlotColor was True, colors specified with RGBColor were translated into the PostScript setrgbcolor operator; if PlotColor was False, *Mathematica* converted colors to gray levels internally and used the setgray operator in its PostScript output. CMYKColor did not exist in Version 1, so *Mathematica* never used the setcmykcolor operator. The effect of PlotColor->True can now be achieved with ColorOutput->Automatic (the default), and PlotColor->False can be translated as ColorOutput->GrayLevel.

7.9 Option Manipulation

In this section, we briefly summarize the commands *Mathematica* provides for working with option settings. We have divided them into three groups: commands for reading option settings, commands for setting options, and commands for filtering options inside a *Mathematica* program.

We have included option manipulation commands in this book because *Mathematica*'s graphics commands rely so heavily on options to control how graphics are created and displayed. Be aware, however, that *Mathematica*'s option manipulation commands are not solely for use with graphics; many other types of *Mathematica* operations also use option settings. For example, you can specify options to the NIntegrate command to specify what algorithm should be used in evaluating an integral—here are the available options with their defaults:

Options[NIntegrate]

```
{AccuracyGoal -> Infinity, Compiled -> True, GaussPoints -> Automatic, MaxRecursion -> 6,
  Method -> Automatic, MinRecursion -> 0, PrecisionGoal -> Automatic,
  SingularityDepth -> 4, WorkingPrecision -> 16}
```

You can also read the option settings associated with an output stream to find out how expressions written to that stream will be formatted:

```
Options["stdout"]
```

```
{FormatType -> OutputForm, PageWidth -> 90, PageHeight -> 22, TotalWidth -> Infinity,
  TotalHeight -> Infinity, StringConversion :> $StringConversion}
```

In our descriptions of the option manipulation commands, however, we have focused on their use with graphics.

7.9.1 Commands for Reading Option Settings

You can use the commands in this group to find out what option settings *Mathematica* uses in displaying a graphic. You may want to know what default setting a graphics command uses, or you may have forgotten what setting you specified for a graphic you produced and want to read the setting from the graphics object.

▪ Options

The Options function has two main uses: To find out what options a command accepts (and their default settings) and to find out what option settings have been specified in an expression. For example, to find out what option settings the DensityGraphics data type accepts, you can say Options[DensityGraphics] and *Mathematica* responds with the list of default option settings:

```
Options[DensityGraphics]
```

```
{AspectRatio -> 1, Axes -> False, AxesLabel -> None, AxesOrigin -> Automatic,
  AxesStyle -> Automatic, Background -> Automatic, ColorFunction -> Automatic,
  ColorOutput -> Automatic, DefaultColor -> Automatic, Epilog -> {}, Frame -> True,
  FrameLabel -> None, FrameStyle -> Automatic, FrameTicks -> Automatic, Mesh -> True,
  MeshRange -> Automatic, MeshStyle -> Automatic, PlotLabel -> None,
  PlotRange -> Automatic, PlotRegion -> Automatic, Prolog -> {}, RotateLabel -> True,
  Ticks -> Automatic, DefaultFont :> $DefaultFont, DisplayFunction :> $DisplayFunction}
```

Note that this is a list of replacement rules, specifying the option names and their default values. If you don't care about the default values, but only want to know the option names, you can map the function First across the result of Options.

```
First /@ Options[DensityGraphics]
```

```
{AspectRatio, Axes, AxesLabel, AxesOrigin, AxesStyle, Background, ColorFunction,
  ColorOutput, DefaultColor, Epilog, Frame, FrameLabel, FrameStyle, FrameTicks, Mesh,
  MeshRange, MeshStyle, PlotLabel, PlotRange, PlotRegion, Prolog, RotateLabel, Ticks,
  DefaultFont, DisplayFunction}
```

To get an idea of the other use of `Options`, suppose we have used `DensityPlot` to plot a function, creating a `DensityGraphics` object. We can use `Options` to find out what option settings are specified for that object.

```
dg = DensityPlot[ Sin[x]Cos[y], {x,0,2Pi}, {y,0,2Pi}, DisplayFunction->Identity ];
Options[dg]
```

```
{PlotRange -> Automatic, DisplayFunction :> Identity, ColorOutput -> Automatic,
  Axes -> False, PlotLabel -> None, AxesLabel -> None, Ticks -> Automatic,
  Frame -> True, FrameStyle -> Automatic, FrameTicks -> Automatic, FrameLabel -> None,
  Prolog -> {}, Epilog -> {}, AxesStyle -> Automatic, Background -> Automatic,
  DefaultColor -> Automatic, DefaultFont :> $DefaultFont, RotateLabel -> True,
  Mesh -> True, MeshStyle -> Automatic, AspectRatio -> 1, PlotRegion -> Automatic,
  ColorFunction -> Automatic, MeshRange -> {{0., 6.28319}, {0., 6.28319}}}
```

If you compare this result to the first one, you will see that the setting for `MeshRange` is different. The default setting of `MeshRange` for `DensityGraphics` is `Automatic`—the setting used if a `DensityGraphics` object is created without an explicit `MeshRange` setting. But when `DensityPlot` creates a `DensityGraphics` object, it inserts an appropriate setting for `MeshRange` into the object. Applying `Options` to that object returns the `MeshRange` setting present in that object, not the default setting that you get by applying `Options` to the symbol `DensityGraphics`.

The `Options` function accepts an optional second argument specifying the names of the options whose settings you want to know. The second argument can be a single option name, indicating that you want to know the setting for that option only:

```
Options[Plot,AspectRatio]
```

```
                      1
{AspectRatio -> -----------}
              GoldenRatio
```

or it can be a list of option names, indicating that you want to know the settings for those options but no others.

```
Options[ ContourPlot, {Contours, ContourShading, ContourStyle} ]
```

```
{Contours -> 10, ContourShading -> True, ContourStyle -> Automatic}
```

As with the one-argument form, the two-argument form of `Options` returns the default settings associated with a symbol if applied to that symbol, and returns the settings actually present in an expression if applied to that expression.

```
Options[ dg, {MeshRange, Axes, Frame} ]
```

```
{Axes -> False, Frame -> True, MeshRange -> {{0., 6.28319}, {0., 6.28319}}}
```

The result of `Options` is a list of option settings, which *Mathematica* represents as a list of replacement rules. Sometimes this form is not what you want. For example, if you want to know how many plotting points the `Plot3D` function uses by default, you can say

```
Options[Plot3D,PlotPoints]
```

```
{PlotPoints -> 15}
```

but you might need the value of the `PlotPoints` setting rather than the rule that specifies this value. In such cases, you can use the result of `Options` as an argument to the `ReplaceAll` operator.

```
PlotPoints /. Options[Plot3D]
```

```
15
```

The construction

$$\textit{option name} \; /. \; \texttt{Options[} \textit{command or expression } \texttt{]}$$

is a standard idiom of *Mathematica* programming for obtaining the value to which an option is set by a command or in an expression.

The `?` operator (or the `Information` command) will not display the option settings for a symbol that has the `ReadProtected` attribute. You can retrieve these setting with the `Options` function.

- FullOptions and FullGraphics

The `FullOptions` function is similar to the `Options` function, except when an option setting has the value `Automatic`, indicating that *Mathematica* should use an internal algorithm to compute an appropriate setting. The symbol `Automatic` is the default setting for `PlotRange` and many other graphics options. `FullOptions` performs the calculations to determine what settings would actually be used in displaying a graphic, and substitutes those values for the `Automatic` settings. To illustrate `FullOptions`, we begin by constructing a sample graphics object `gr`:

```
gr = Plot[ Sin[x], {x,0,2Pi}, AspectRatio->Automatic, DisplayFunction->Identity ];
```

Now compare the results of `Options[gr]` and `FullOptions[gr]`:

```
Options[gr] // Sort
```

```
{AspectRatio -> Automatic, Axes -> Automatic, AxesLabel -> None,
  AxesOrigin -> Automatic, AxesStyle -> Automatic, Background -> Automatic,
  ColorOutput -> Automatic, DefaultColor -> Automatic, Epilog -> {}, Frame -> False,
  FrameLabel -> None, FrameStyle -> Automatic, FrameTicks -> Automatic,
  GridLines -> None, PlotLabel -> None, PlotRange -> Automatic,
  PlotRegion -> Automatic, Prolog -> {}, RotateLabel -> True, Ticks -> Automatic,
  DefaultFont :> $DefaultFont, DisplayFunction :> Identity}
```

```
Short /@ FullOptions[gr] // Sort
```

```
{AspectRatio -> 0.31831, Axes -> {True, True}, AxesLabel -> {None, None},
  AxesOrigin -> {0., 0.}, AxesStyle ->
   {{GrayLevel[0.], Thickness[0.002]}, {GrayLevel[0.], <<1>>}},
  Background -> Automatic, ColorOutput -> Automatic, DefaultColor -> Automatic,
  DefaultFont -> {Courier, 6.5}, DisplayFunction -> Identity, Epilog -> {},
  Frame -> {False, False, False, False}, FrameLabel -> {None, None, None, None},
  FrameStyle -> {None, None, None, None}, FrameTicks -> {None, None},
  GridLines -> {None, None}, PlotLabel -> None,
  PlotRange -> {{-0.15708, 6.44026}, {-1.05, 1.05}}, PlotRegion -> Automatic,
  Prolog -> {}, RotateLabel -> True, Ticks -> {<<2>>}}
```

We used the Short function primarily to suppress the display of the Ticks setting, since it is quite lengthy — for each tick mark, a line segment of a given size and color is specified. Note that most Automatic settings returned by Options, such as the settings for AspectRatio, PlotRange, and AxesOrigin, have been replaced by explicit values. The delayed-evaluation rules specifying settings for DefaultFont and DisplayFunction have also been converted to explicit, evaluated forms. A few options are not handled by FullOptions, however: Background, ColorOutput, DefaultColor, and PlotRegion. It is not clear why FullOptions does not convert these settings to explicit forms; this may be an unintended feature that will be corrected in a future version of *Mathematica*.

The next example shows an inconsistency between FullOptions and Options:

```
Options[ gr, {PlotRange, PlotRegion, FrameTicks} ]
```

```
{PlotRange -> Automatic, FrameTicks -> Automatic, PlotRegion -> Automatic}
```

```
FullOptions[ gr, {PlotRange, PlotRegion, FrameTicks} ]
```

```
{{{-0.15708, 6.44026}, {-1.05, 1.05}}, Automatic, {None, None}}
```

In the two-argument form of Options, the result is a list of replacement rules — in effect, a list of option settings. In the two-argument form of FullOptions, however, the result is a list of the values to which options have been set rather than a list of option settings.

The purpose of the function FullGraphics is similar to that of FullOptions: It replaces option settings of Automatic with explicit values. The difference between FullGraphics and FullOptions is that FullOptions returns only the list of expanded option settings, whereas FullGraphics returns a complete graphics object in which the option settings have been expanded. The result of FullGraphics is therefore suitable for input to Show.

One situation in which you might want to use FullGraphics is when saving a graphics object to a file for later reloading. This line of code writes the InputForm of a graphics object gr to the file grfile:

```
ff = OpenWrite["grfile",FormatType->InputForm]; Write[ff,gr]; Close[ff];
```

Later you could execute the command Get["grfile"] to reload the graphics object, but you can't be sure that the object will display in exactly the same way as before. For example, the default setting of the DefaultFont option is DefaultFont:>$DefaultFont. If the value of the variable $DefaultFont is different than it was when the file was written, then the reloaded object will use a different default font for plot labels, tick labels, and other text. But if you wrote the object with the command Write[ff,FullGraphics[gr]] instead of Write[ff,gr], these dependencies would be expanded when the file was written, and you could be certain that the reloaded object would display exactly as it did when it was saved. The Save command performs a similar but not identical function. If you saved the graphics object with the command

```
Save[ "grfile", gr ];
```

the Save command would detect the dependence of gr on the variable $DefaultFont and would save the current definition of $DefaultFont as well as gr to the file grfile. Reading the file with Get would restore the value of $DefaultFont as well as gr, ensuring that gr would display as it did before, but it would also reset the $DefaultFont for any other graphics you displayed thereafter, which might not be desirable.

The functions FullOptions and FullGraphics can also expand the special setting PlotRange->All:

```
gr = Plot[ Tan[x], {x,0,2Pi}, PlotRange->All, DisplayFunction->Identity ];
FullOptions[ gr, PlotRange ]
```

$$\{\{-0.15708,\ 6.44026\},\ \{-4.08294\ 10^{14},\ 1.67401\ 10^{16}\}\}$$

▪ PlotRange as a Function

The PlotRange option can also be used as a function. When called with a graphics object as its argument, PlotRange returns the plot range that *Mathematica* uses in displaying that object. If the object's option list contains an explicit setting for PlotRange, this value is returned, but if the PlotRange setting in the object is All or Automatic, PlotRange calculates the plot range that *Mathematica* will actually use and returns that. Here is an example:

```
gr = Plot[ Sin[x], {x,0,2Pi}, DisplayFunction->Identity ];
PlotRange[gr]
```

```
{{-0.15708, 6.44026}, {-1.05, 1.05}}
```

```
Options[gr,PlotRange]
```

```
{PlotRange -> Automatic}
```

```
FullOptions[gr,PlotRange]
```

```
{{-0.15708, 6.44026}, {-1.05, 1.05}}
```

As you can see, PlotRange acts like FullOptions rather than Options.

7.9.2 Commands for Setting Options

The commands in this group allow you to specify options for a symbol or expression. With these commands, you can redisplay a graphics object with different option settings, or reset the default settings for a command so that all graphics subsequently created will use the new settings.

▪ SetOptions

The function SetOptions allows you to change the default settings associated with a symbol, such as a graphics command or a data type. The template for SetOptions is

SetOptions[*symbol*, *option setting(s)*]

The *option setting(s)* should be one or more replacement rules specifying default settings for options associated with the *symbol*.

You should use SetOptions when you want to make a permanent change to the options a command uses. For example, *Mathematica*'s default setting for the PlotPoints option of Plot3D is 15. If you want to make a single plot using 25 plotting points, you could give the setting PlotPoints->25 as an optional argument when you call Plot3D to make that plot. But if you think that 15 points is almost never enough, and you want *all* the three-dimensional plots you create to use 25 points, you will find it more convenient to say

```
SetOptions[ Plot3D, PlotPoints->25 ];
```

than to keep specifying the PlotPoints setting for each plot.

Once you have used SetOptions to reset a default, the new default remains in effect for the rest of that *Mathematica* session (or until you use SetOptions to change it again). If you want to reset a default for every *Mathematica* session you run, you can put a SetOptions command in your init.m file. You should remember, however, that customizing your copy of *Mathematica* in this way will make it slightly incompatible with other people's copies. Since default settings operate behind the scenes, as it were, it is easy to forget you have made such a change, so you may some day be baffled to find that your copy of *Mathematica* is producing different results from those produced by a colleague's copy with the same input.

The SetOptions function returns as its result a list of the (new) default option settings for the symbol whose defaults are being reset. The list contains the current defaults for all options associated with the symbol, not only the options whose defaults were just reset.

The SetOptions function can be used only to set defaults for options that a symbol already recognizes; it cannot add option settings for new options that were not formerly associated with the symbol. If you try to specify a default setting for the Contours option of the symbol DensityPlot, for example, you get an error message.

```
SetOptions[ DensityPlot, Contours->10 ];
```

```
SetOptions::optnf: Contours is not a known option for DensityPlot.
```

This is a safety measure to keep you from attaching inappropriate options to a symbol.

Although you cannot associate new definitions or rewriting rules with a symbol that has the Protected attribute, you can use SetOptions to change its default option settings. You cannot change the option settings associated with a Locked symbol, however.

- Show

You can use SetOptions when you want to change the default options associated with a command or data type, but you cannot use it to modify the options recorded in a graphics object after the object has been created. If you want to redisplay a graphics object with different option settings (as opposed to creating a new graphics object from scratch using the new settings), you can use the Show command. Show is discussed at length in Section 2.6.1, which starts on page 25.

- Options

The function Options can be used to read the option settings for a symbol or expression, but it can also be used on the left side of an assignment statement to set default options for a symbol. You use Options this way when you are programming a function of your own, to specify what options the function will accept and what the inital defaults for those options will be. Here is a trivial example to show you how it is done:

```
Options[f] = { a->b, c->d, x:>y };
```

You cannot use the command SetOptions for this purpose because SetOptions can only reset defaults for options that have already been associated with a symbol. On the other hand, you can use SetOptions to reset the defaults associated with a Protected symbol, whereas you are not permitted to assign a value to Options[s] if the symbol s has the Protected attribute. So SetOptions and Options do not fully duplicate each other's capabilities.

If you want to remove all option settings from the symbol sym, without affecting rewriting rules, messages, attributes, or other information associated with the symbol, use the command

Options[sym] = {}

Using Unset or Clear would not remove the options, and using ClearAll or Remove would remove other information as well.

- ClearAll and Remove

Mathematica provides several ways to remove information that has been associated with a symbol. They are, in order of increasing strength, Unset, Clear, ClearAll, and Remove. The Unset operation removes a value that has been assigned to a symbol, and the Clear operation removes rewriting rules associated with the symbol. However, neither removes option settings that have been associated with the symbol. The ClearAll command removes values, rewriting rules, attributes, defaults, messages, and options, leaving only the symbol itself. The Remove command goes one step further and removes the symbol entirely. If you are programming a *Mathematica* function of your own and you want to erase what hou have done and start from scratch, be sure to use ClearAll or Remove, or you may find leftover options or other information interfering with your work when you reuse the symbol.

7.9.3 Commands for Filtering Options

If you try to invoke a built-in command with an inappropriate option setting, you will get an error message. For example, BoxRatios is an option for 3D graphics only, so we get an error when we specify a BoxRatios setting to a two-dimensional plotting command such as ParametricPlot.

ParametricPlot[{Cos[t],Sin[t]}, {t,0,2Pi}, BoxRatios->{1,1,.4}];

ParametricPlot::optx:
    Unknown option BoxRatios in ParametricPlot[{Cos[t], Sin[t]}, {t, 0, 2 Pi},
      BoxRatios -> {1, 1, 0.4}].

If this error comes from a ParametricPlot command entered in an interactive *Mathematica* session, the error message provides feedback that helps the user correct the mistake and continue working. Sometimes, though, you want to program a function of your own that calls ParametricPlot or other built-in functions. In such a case, you don't usually want error messages from an "inner" function call to be returned to the user of your function. To avoid this, it is good programming practice to filter out inappropriate option settings in your own code before you invoke a built-in function.

A typical example of a function that filters options is LogPlot, defined in the package Graphics`Graphics`. (We described LogPlot in Section 5.2.2 on page 152.) LogPlot enhances *Mathematica's* repertoire of plotting functions by providing the ability to plot on a logarithmic scale. LogPlot itself does not construct a logarithmic plot; instead, it takes arguments provided by the caller, reassembles them into a suitable form, constructs a list of tick marks appropriate for a logarithmic axis, and calls ParametricPlot to construct the actual plot. LogPlot accepts all the same options as ParametricPlot, but LogPlot itself uses only the Ticks, FrameTicks, and GridLines options, passing on to ParametricPlot other option settings that are not particularly concerned with logarithmic plotting, such as Background and PlotLabel. LogPlot must be careful about which options it passes on, because a user who mistakenly specifies the BoxRatios option in a call to LogPlot will be confused by an error message with the tag ParametricPlot. The code for LogPlot detects such errors and filters out inappropriate options before they reach ParametricPlot.

Mathematica provides various commands for checking the validity of option settings. The built-in function OptionsQ returns True if its argument has a valid form for option settings (i.e., if the argument is a replacement rule or a list of replacement rules) and False otherwise. The package Utilities`FilterOptions` defines the function FilterOptions, which takes a symbol and one or more option settings and returns a sequence containing only those options that are accepted by that symbol. The package Examples`OptionUtilities` defines the functions OptionList, OptionExtract, and OptionSelect for extracting a list of options from a graphics object and filtering out the ones that are inappropriate. The package ProgrammingExamples`OptionUse` does not define any functions that you would want to call, but it is a prototype showing how to define a function that accepts option settings. Finally, the functions defined in the package Graphics`Graphics`, such as LogPlot, provide good examples of how to define functions that accept option settings from the user, filter out certain options for processing, eliminate inappropriate settings, and pass on the rest for handling by another function.

7.10 Summary

This chapter has shown you all of the options accepted by the built-in graphics functions of *Mathematica*. You will probably find that you use a few of these options frequently and the rest only in special circumstances (or not at all). Tables summarizing the graphics options in functional groups may be found beginning on page 317.

When you write graphics functions of your own, if you want your code to be reusable and generally useful, you should ensure that your functions accept all of the relevant options and handle them in a way that is consistent with their use in the built-in functions (usually this means just accumulating them and passing them as additional arguments to Show). That way your code will fit in seamlessly as an extension of *Mathematica*. The graphics packages distributed with *Mathematica*, described in Chapter 5, provide excellent examples of how this can be accomplished.

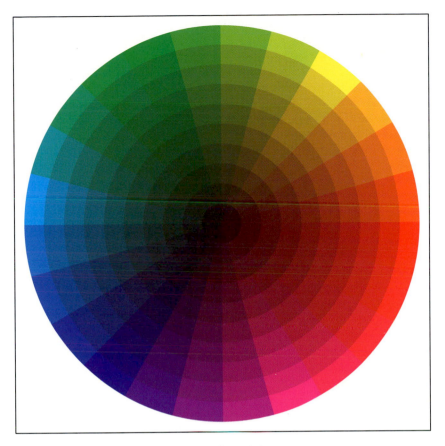

SECTION 3.2.1
A color wheel.

SECTION 3.2.1
The RGB color cube.

SECTION 5.2.1
The HLS double hexcone
color model.

SECTION 5.2.1
The HSV hexcone color model.

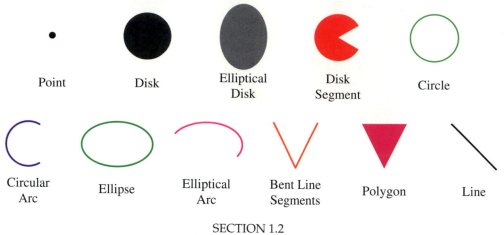

SECTION 1.2
The 2D graphics primitives.

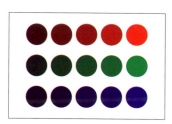

SECTION 3.2.1
An array of colored points
specified with `RGBColor`.

SECTION 3.2.1
An array of colored points specified
with `CMYKColor`.

SECTION 3.2.1
An array of colored points specified with `HUE`.

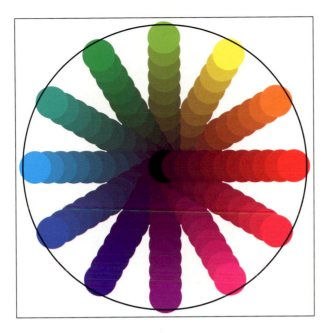

SECTION 3.2.1
This graph shows the
different colors that
can be generated with
the command Hue.

SECTION 3.2.4
An array of colors produced by using Raster together with the option ColorFunction
set to Hue(RGBColor[#,0,#]&), and (RGBColor[1-#,0,1-#]&).

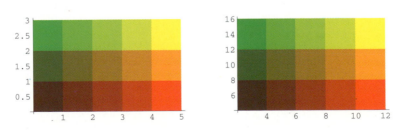

SECTION 3.2.4
An array of colors produced by using RasterArray.

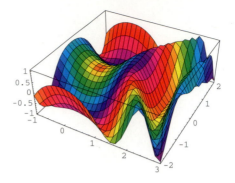

SECTION 4.2.1
A surface shaded by specifying a
pair of expressions as the first
argument to `Plot3D`. Here we
use the shading function `Hue` to
produce a rainbow-like effect.

| AquamarineMedium | BlueMedium | CadmiumLemon | ChromeOxideGreen | Cyan | Firebrick |

SECTION 5.2.1
Once you have loaded the package `Graphics`Colors``, you can specify a color by name
instead of RGB values.

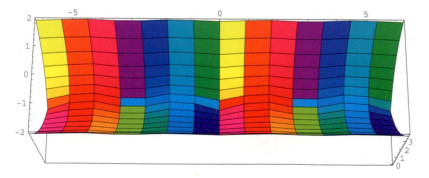

SECTION 5.2
A surface shaded using `Plot3D` together with the directive `ArgColor` from the package
`Graphics`ArgColors``.

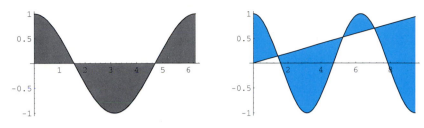

SECTION 5.2.1

The function `FilledPlot` in the package `Graphics`FilledPlot`` colors or fills the area between the curve and an axis or between two curves.

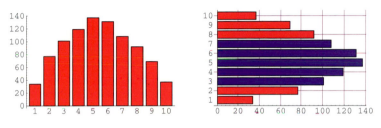

SECTION 5.2.3

The package `Graphics`Graphics`` contains the function `BarChart` for drawing bar charts.

SECTION 5.2.3
By default, the bars produced by `Stacked BarChart` and `PercentileBarChart` are drawn in different colors.

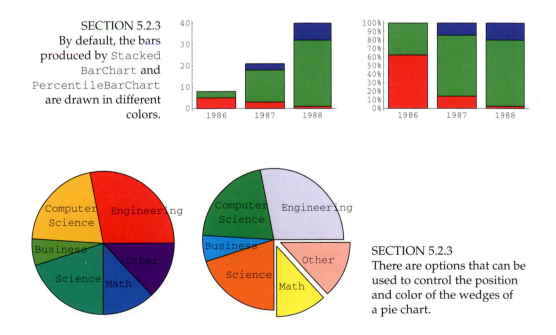

SECTION 5.2.3

There are options that can be used to control the position and color of the wedges of a pie chart.

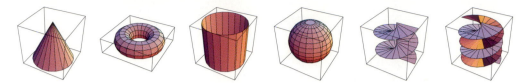

SECTION 5.2.4

The package `Graphics`Shapes`` contains definitions of some mathematical solids including a cone, a torus, a cylinder, a sphere, a helix, and a double helix.

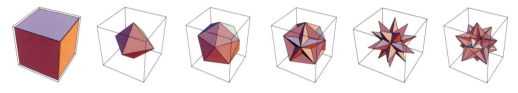

SECTION 5.2.4

Regular polyhedra are defined in the package `Graphics`Polyhedra``.

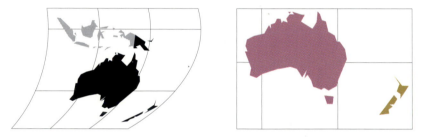

SECTION 5.2.6

With the functions in the package `Miscellaneous`WorldPlot``, you can draw a map of a country, several countries, or a region of the world. Here we color the countries in shades of gray and different colors.

SECTION 5.2.6

Here is a map of the world with bodies of water shaded in `SeaGreen`, Greenland in `Green`, Mexico in `Red`, the United States in `Purple`, and all the other countries in `Gray`.

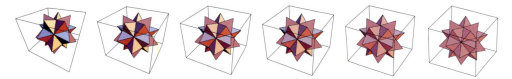

SECTION 6.2.2
Notice how the surface shading depends on the setting of the `ViewPoint`.

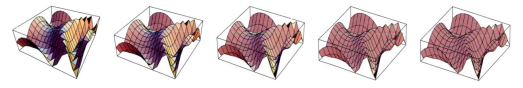

SECTION 6.2.3
In these graphics, the `ViewPoint` setting is increased from left to right. The closer
the `ViewPoint` is to the surface, the more vibrant the colors.

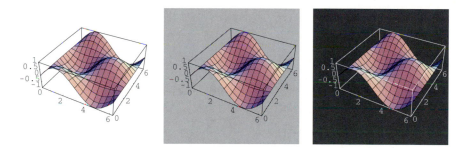

SECTION 7.1.2
When a *Mathematica* graphic is displayed, the entire picture frame is filled with the color
specified by the `BackGround` option.

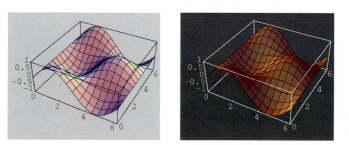

SECTION 7.1.4
By setting the `ColorOutput`
option, we can invert the
colors in a graphic.

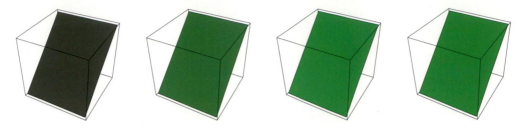

SECTION 7.4.2
We obtain different intensities of green by placing one, two, three,
and four green light sources at the same point.

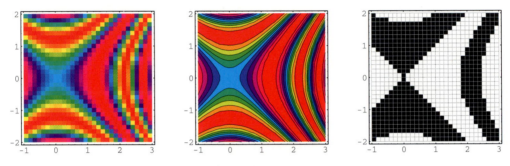

SECTION 7.5.2
Here we use the `ColorFunction` option to specify how to shade
a contour plot (middle) and two density plots.

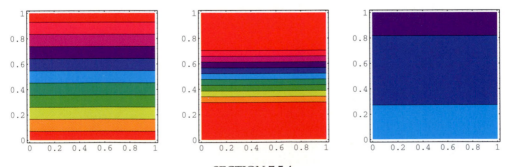

SECTION 7.5.4
Setting `ColorFunction` to `Hue` and `Contours` to 10 makes
the example colorful.

Appendix:
Code to Produce the Figures

Nearly all of the illustrations in this book were prepared exclusively with *Mathematica*. Most are examples showing how to use *Mathematica*'s graphics commands, so the code to produce the illustrations is given in the text. In these cases, the emphasis was on writing *Mathematica* code, so we placed primary importance on making the code easy to read and understand. The content of the graphics themselves was secondary—for example, in illustrating the `Plot3D` command, we were free to plot any function we liked, as long as we showed the syntax of `Plot3D`.

However, most books are not how-to books about graphics programming, and their illustrations have points to make that have nothing to do with how the code to produce the illustrations was written. A few of the figures in this book are of that kind, and it would have been distracting to provide the code for them in the text. But we didn't want to omit that code from the book, so we collected it in this appendix. The graphics presented here are in fact some of our best examples of *Mathematica*'s use as an illustration tool because they are the ones in which the idea being communicated by a graphic was more important than the way in which the graphic was coded. The code for these figures is more involved that the code for most of the how-to examples in the rest of the book, but it is more representative of the kind of programming you will do if you will be using *Mathematica* to prepare illustrations for a lab report, a textbook, a journal article, or other technical document.

A.1 Graphics Primitives and Directives

Here we show many of the two-dimensional graphics primitives. The figure appears in Section 1.2 on page 6.

```
Show[GraphicsArray[{
    {Graphics[{
        PointSize[0.02], Point[ {0,.5} ], Text[ "Point", {0,0} ],
        { GrayLevel[0.2], Disk[ {1,.5},.25 ] }, Text[ "Disk", {1,0} ],
        { GrayLevel[0.5], Disk[ {2,.5},{.25,.35} ] },
                                            Text[ "Elliptical\n   Disk", {2,0} ],
        { RGBColor[1,0,0], Disk[ {3,.5},.25,{Pi/6,11Pi/6} ] },
                                            Text[ "   Disk\nSegment", {3,0} ],
        { RGBColor[0,1,0], Circle[ {4,.5},.25 ] }, Text[ "Circle", {4,0} ]
    },
        PlotRange->All, AspectRatio->Automatic, DefaultFont->{"Times-Roman",8}
    ]},
    {Graphics[{
        { RGBColor[0,0,1], Circle[ {5,.5},.25,{Pi/3, 5Pi/3} ] },
                                            Text[ "Circular\n   Arc",{5,0} ],
        { RGBColor[0,1,.1], Circle[ {6,.5},{.4,.25} ] }, Text[ "Ellipse", {6,0} ],
        { RGBColor[1,0,1], Circle[{7,.5},{.4,.25},{-Pi/6, 5Pi/6}] },
            Text[ "Elliptical\n   Arc", {7,0} ],
        { RGBColor[1,.2,0], Line[ {{7.75,.75},{8,.25},{8.25,.75}} ] },
            Text[ "Bent Line\nSegments", {8,0} ],
        { RGBColor[.9,0,.7], Polygon[ {{8.75,.75},{9,.25},{9.25,.75}} ] },
            Text[ "Polygon", {9,0} ],
        { GrayLevel[0], Line[{{9.75,.75},{10.25,.25}}] }, Text[ "Line", {10,0} ]
    },
        PlotRange->All, AspectRatio->Automatic, DefaultFont->{"Times-Roman",8}
    ]}
}]];
```

Point   Disk   Elliptical   Disk   Circle
                 Disk   Segment

Circular   Ellipse   Elliptical   Bent Line   Polygon   Line
Arc   Arc   Segments

The next graph shows the three-dimensional graphics primitives in *Mathematica*. It was easier to use the AxesLabel to label the features than to invoke the Text primitive several times. We positioned the ViewPoint so that the box would run parallel to the label.

```
Show[Graphics3D[{
    Cuboid[{0,0,0},{1,1,1}],
    PointSize[.02], Point[{2,.5,.5}],
    Line[{ {2.5,1,1}, {3,0,0}, {3.5,.5,1} }],
    Polygon[{ {4,1,1}, {4.5,0,0}, {5,.5,.5} }]
},
    PlotRange->{{-.5,5.5},{-.1,1.1},{-.1,1.1}}, BoxRatios->Automatic,
    ViewPoint->{0.293, -2.824, 0.767}, Ticks->None, Axes->{True,False,False},
    DefaultFont->{"Times-Roman",8},
    AxesLabel->
    {"    Cuboid          Point        Line            Polygon",None,None}
]];
```

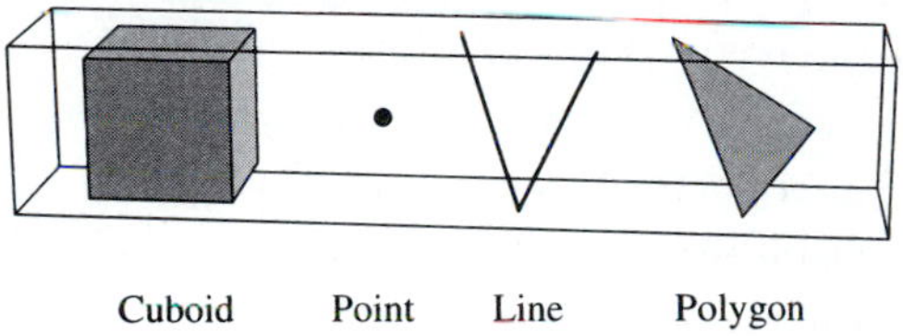

Cuboid   Point   Line   Polygon

This figure also appears in Section 1.2 on page 6.

A.2 The Loop

We needed a simple example of a configuration that could not possibly arise in the graph of a surface $z = f(x, y)$ to illustrate a discussion of hidden feature removal. The figure in Section 2.3 on page 18 depicts a self-intersecting surface. We conceived the figure as an extrusion of a self-intersecting parametrized curve in the plane:

```
ParametricPlot[{(t-1)t(t+1),1-t^2}, {t,-1.15,1.15},
        PlotRange->All, AspectRatio->Automatic, Ticks->None ];
```

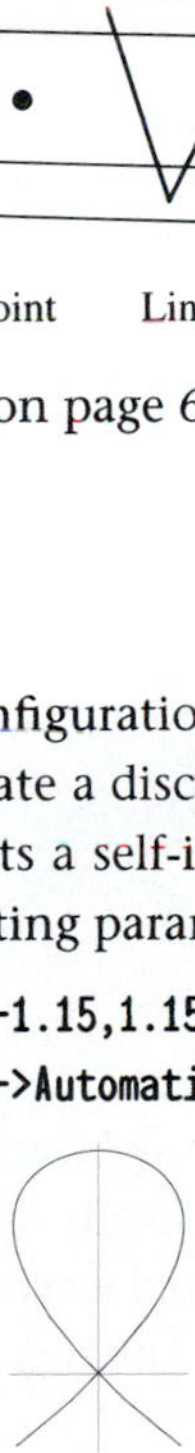

We played with the parameter functions and the plot range until we got a pleasing shape. Once we had the curve down, we resampled it so as to have a manageable set of points to work with.

```
l = Table[{(t-1)t(t+1),1-t^2}, {t,-1.2,1.2,.1}];
```

This gave us a list of 25 points on the curve. We regarded these as y and z coordinates and made two copies of the curve in the planes $x = 0$ and $x = 1$ to get a 2-by-25 array of points in space.

```
m = { Insert[#,0,1]& /@ l, Insert[#,1,1]& /@ l };
Dimensions[m]
```

```
{2, 25, 3}
```

Next we used the MakeQuads function to turn a 2-by-25 array of points into a 1-by-24 array of polygons, and displayed the polygons.

```
MakeQuads[ vl_List ] := MakeQuads[vl,{1,1},Polygon] /; (TensorRank[vl]>=2)
```

```
MakeQuads[vl_List?((TensorRank[#]>=2)&), cc:{_Integer,_Integer}, fn_:Polygon] :=
Block[{ l = vl, ll, mesh, c1, c2 },
    ll = RotateLeft /@ l;
    {c1,c2} = cc;
    mesh = {l, ll, RotateLeft[ll], RotateLeft[l]};
    If[c1 == 1, mesh = Map[Drop[#, -1]&, mesh, {1}] ];
    If[c2 == 1, mesh = Map[Drop[#, -1]&, mesh, {2}] ];
    Map[ fn, Transpose[ mesh, {3,1,2} ], {2} ]
]
```

```
p = MakeQuads[m];  Show[Graphics3D[p], PlotRange->All];
```

The ribbon looked much too thick, so we recomputed m with various values of the x coordinates until we got something we liked. A value of 0.5 looked about right. We also experimented with the three-dimensional viewpoint selector in the *Mathematica* Front End to select a perspective from which the picture would be most easily understood.

```
m = { Insert[#,0,1]& /@ l, Insert[#,.5,1]& /@ l };  p = MakeQuads[m];
pic = Show[Graphics3D[p],PlotRange->All,ViewPoint->{1.5,-.6,1.3}];
```

The last step was to use Show[pic,Boxed->False] to remove the bounding box. This figure appears in Section 2.3 on page 18.

A.3 The *Mathematica* Ribbon

This figure appears on page 38, the first page of Chapter 3. It doesn't have any particular meaning; we simply thought it was an interesting way to exhibit some of *Mathematica*'s 2D and 3D graphics primitives.

```
t = N[ Table[ i Degree, {i,0, 350, 10} ] ];
p1 = {Cos[#],Sin[#]}& /@ t;
p2 = {.9Cos[#],.9Sin[#]}& /@ (t + N[5 Degree]);
q = Flatten[ Transpose[ {p1,p2} ], 1 ];

Needs["Graphics`Shapes`"];
s = Sphere[1,40,30];

gs = Show[Graphics[Graphics3D[{EdgeForm[],s}]],
    AspectRatio->Automatic, DisplayFunction->Identity ];

rotmatrix[ d_ ] := Block[ {t=N[d Degree],c,s},
    {c,s} = {Cos[t],Sin[t]}; {{c,-s},{s,c}} ]

ribbonpts = { {1,-3.25}, {12,-4}, {9,0}, {12,4}, {1,3.25} };
ClearAll[ribbon]
ribbon[p_,d_,f_] := Block[ { m = f rotmatrix[d],l },
    l = (p + (m.#))& /@ ribbonpts;
    {Polygon[l], {GrayLevel[0],Line[l]}} ]

gr = Show[Graphics[{
    {GrayLevel[1/3], ribbon[{0,-.2},-70,.15]},
    {GrayLevel[1/5], ribbon[{0,0-.25},-100,.15]},
    {Thickness[.015],GrayLevel[.75],Line[q]},
```

```
        Polygon[q],
        {GrayLevel[1],Disk[{0,0},.88]},
        {GrayLevel[2/3],Disk[{0,0},.7]},
        {Thickness[.015],Circle[{0,0},.7]},
        Rectangle[{-.73,-.73},{.73,.73},gs],
        Text[FontForm["Mathematica",{"Times-Italic",10}],{0,.1}]
}], AspectRatio->Automatic ];
```

One point to note is that, since text in a *Mathematica* graphic does not resize itself when you resize the graphic, we were forced to use a different point size in this example than we used in the real chapter opener figure. In that copy of the illustration we used 24-point type instead of the small type used here.

A.4 The Rotated Text Picture

In displaying text, *Mathematica* computes a rectangle that bounds the text. In this diagram, we use Polygon to draw rectangles to represent text and rotated text. To obtain the rectangle for the rotated text, we multiplied the coordinates of the rectangle representing unrotated text by the matrix returned by the function rotmatrix. In this diagram, the light gray rectangle shows the bounding rectangle of horizontal text, the dark gray rectangle represents the same text rotated about its center through an angle of 35 degrees, and the black outline shows the bounding rectangle of the rotated text.

```
rotmatrix[th_] := Block[ {t = N[th Degree], c, s },
                        {c,s} = {Cos[t],Sin[t]};  {{c,s},{-s,c}} ]
rotatearound[p_,q_,th_] := p + ( (q-p) . rotmatrix[th] )
rect[ { {xmin_,xmax_}, {ymin_,ymax_} } ] :=
```

```
      { {xmin,ymin}, {xmax,ymin}, {xmax,ymax}, {xmin,ymax} }
bounds[ pts_List ] := {Min[#],Max[#]}& /@ Transpose[pts]
ClosedLine[pts_] := Line[ Append[pts,First[pts]] ]
r = rect[ { {1,10}, {1,2} } ];
ctr = (Plus @@ r) / Length[r];
rr = rotatearound[ ctr, #, 35 ]& /@ r;
b = rect[ bounds[rr] ];
Show[Graphics[{
    GrayLevel[2/3], Polygon[r],
    GrayLevel[1/3], Polygon[rr],
    GrayLevel[0], ClosedLine[b], PointSize[.02], Point[ctr]
}], PlotRange->All, AspectRatio->Automatic];
```

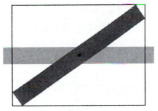

This figure appears in Section 3.2.5 on page 62 and also in Section 6.1.1 on page 183.

A.5 Adaptive Sampling Pictures

A.5.1 Sampled Points

To depict the points that *Mathematica* samples along a curve, we drew vertical lines from the x axis to the end points of each line segment plotted when *Mathematica* draws the curve. This figure can be found in Section 4.1.3 on page 89.

```
plot = Plot[ (x - 1)(x - 3)(x - 4), {x, .5, 4.5}, DisplayFunction->Identity ];
curves = Cases[ plot, _Line, Infinity ];
points = Join @@ (First /@ curves);
lines = {Line[{{#[[1]],0},#}],Point[#]}& /@ points;
samplepic = Graphics[{ Thickness[0.001], PointSize[.015], lines }, Axes->Automatic ];
Show[GraphicsArray[{ samplepic, plot }]];
```

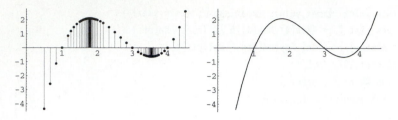

In the next figure, we drew lines from the origin to the end points of the line segments that *Mathematica* plots when drawing a circle.

```
plot = ParametricPlot[ {Sin[x], Cos[x]}, {x, 0, 2Pi}, DisplayFunction->Identity ];
curves = Cases[ plot, _Line, Infinity ];
points = Join @@ (First /@ curves);
lines = {Line[{{0,0},#}],Point[#]}& /@ points;
Show[Graphics[{ Thickness[0.001], PointSize[.015], lines },
        Axes->None, AspectRatio->Automatic, PlotRange->All ];
```

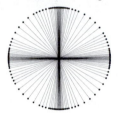

This figure appears in Section 4.1.3 on page 92.

A.5.2 Subdividing the Sampling Interval

To illustrate how MaxBend works, we drew the curve $x - x^3$, together with three points along the curve and line segments connecting the first and second points and the second and third points. We extended the first line segment to a point not along the curve and drew this extension with a gray line. We also labeled the points and drew the tangent at the middle point, as you can see here:

```
Block[ {f,p,tan,DotLine,interpolate,A,B,C,D,t},
    f[x_] := x - x^3;
    p[x_] := {x,f[x]};
    tan[a_] := Block[ {y,m},
        Function[{t},{t,y+m(t-a)}] /. {y->f[a],m->f'[a]} ];
    DotLine[l_] := Prepend[ Point/@l, Line[l] ];
    interpolate[x_,y_,n_] := x + n(y-x);
    Show[Plot[ Evaluate[f[x]], {x,.25,.77}, Axes->None,
```

```
            DisplayFunction->Identity ],
    t = tan[.53];
    A = p[.3];
    B = p[.53];
    C = p[.7];
    D = interpolate[A,B,1.4];
    Graphics[{
        Line[{t[.27],t[.72]}],
        PointSize[.03],
        {GrayLevel[.6],DotLine[{B,D}]},
        DotLine[{A,B,C}],
        Text["A",A,{-1.2,1.5}], Text["B",B,{-1,2}],
        Text["C",C,{1,2}], Text["D",D,{-1.2,1.2}]
    }],
    DisplayFunction -> $DisplayFunction ] ];
```

This figure appears in Section 4.1.3 on page 89.

A.5.3 Scaling for MaxBend

We constructed several functions to show how *Mathematica* scales each set of three sample points. The function newpic takes three points as its argument. It draws the bounding box of the three points with dashed lines; then it draws a line connecting the first point to the second, and a line connecting the second point to the third, and plots the points and indicates the angle between the two line segments. The function scalepic calls newpic twice, once with the three points and once with three points scaled so that they lie within a square.

```
ClearAll[Norm,scale,dirangle,scalepts];

Norm[v_] := Sqrt[v.v]
scale[ x_, {a_,b_}, {c_,d_} ] := c + (d-c)(x-a)/(b-a)
dirangle[v_] := N[ Arg[ v . {1,I} ] ]
scalepts[pts_] := Block[ {rr}, rr = Transpose[ {Min[#],Max[#]}& /@ Transpose[pts] ];
                          scale[#,rr,{{-1,-1},{1,1}}]& /@ pts ]
```

```
ClearAll[boxlines];
boxlines[ {a_,b_}, {c_,d_} ] := boxlines[ { {a,b}, {c,d} } ]
boxlines[ { {a_,b_}, {c_,d_} } ] := Line[ { {a,c}, {b,c}, {b,d}, {a,d}, {a,c} } ]

ClearAll[newpic]
newpic[ p_, q_, r_ ] := newpic[{p,q,r}];
newpic[ {p_, q_, r_} ] :=
    Block[ { pp, rr, ss, u = q-p, v = r-q, nu, nv },
        { nu, nv } = Norm /@ {u,v};
        pp = scale[ 1 + Min[1,nv/nu], {0,1}, {p,q} ];
        rr = 0.4 Min[ nu, nv ];
        ss = {Min[#],Max[#]}& /@ Transpose[{p,q,r}];
        Show[Graphics[{
                {
                    AbsoluteDashing[{10,10}],
                    boxlines[ss]
                },
                {
                    GrayLevel[.6],
                    Line[{q,pp}]
                },
                Line[{p,q,r}],
                AbsolutePointSize[5],
                Point /@ {p,q,r},
                Circle[ q, rr, Sort[{dirangle[v], dirangle[u]}] ]
            }],
            AspectRatio->Automatic
        ]
    ]

ClearAll[scalepic]
scalepic[pts_] :=
Show[
    Block[{ $DisplayFunction=Identity, gr1,gr2, ar1,ar2 },
        gr1 = newpic[pts];
        gr2 = newpic[scalepts[pts]];
        ar1 = FullOptions[gr1,AspectRatio];
        ar2 = FullOptions[gr2,AspectRatio];
        Graphics[{
            Rectangle[ {0,-ar1/2},{1,ar1/2}, gr1 ],
```

```
        Rectangle[ {1.1,-ar2/4},{1.6,ar2/4}, gr2 ]
    },
        AspectRatio->Automatic
    ]
  ]
];
scalepic[ { {0,1}, {3,.8}, {7,0} } ];
```

This figure appears in Section 4.1.3 on page 91.

A.6 Perspective Projection Pictures

Don't let the length of this example scare you off. Drawing even a simple house requires
a fair amount of code.

```
wirebox[{{xl_,xh_},{yl_,yh_},{zl_,zh_}}] :=
    Block[ {pts = Outer[List,{xl,xh},{yl,yh},{zl,zh}]},
        Flatten[{
            Map[Line,Transpose[pts,{1,3,2}],{2}],
            Map[Line,Transpose[pts,{3,1,2}],{2}],
            Map[Line,pts,{2}]
        }]
    ]
Cross[{a_,b_,c_},{d_,e_,f_}] := { b f - c e, c d - a f, a e - b d }
Norm[v_] := Sqrt[v.v]
Unit[v_] := v / Norm[v]
ClosedLine[ l_ ] := Line[ Append[l,First[l]] ]
plane[ p_, n_, v_ ] :=
    Block[ { uu = N[v], vv = Unit[N[n]] },
        uu = Cross[uu,vv];
        vv = Cross[vv,uu];
        ClosedLine[ { p + uu + vv, p + uu - vv, p - uu - vv, p - uu + vv } ]
    ]
```

```
solidplane[ p_, n_, v_ ] :=
    Block[ { uu = N[v], vv = Unit[N[n]] },
        uu = Cross[uu,vv];
        vv = Cross[vv,uu];
        Polygon[ { p + uu + vv, p + uu - vv, p - uu - vv, p - uu + vv } ]
    ]

dirunit[th_] := N[{Cos[th],Sin[th]}]

rect[{a_,b_},{c_,d_}] := ClosedLine[ { {a,c}, {a,d}, {b,d}, {b,c} } ]

Block[{
    vp = {3,.4}, vc = {.6,.4}, ev
},
    ev = vp + {.1,0};
    Show[Graphics[{
        rect[ {0,1}, {0,.7} ],
        rect[ {.1,.3}, {0,.4} ],
        Line[ { {-.1,.65}, {.5,1}, {1.1,.65} } ],
        Point[{.15,.2}], (* doorknob! *)
        rect[ {.4,.8}, {.2,.6} ], (* window *)
        Line[ { {.1,0}, {1.5,-.2} } ],
        Line[ { {.3,0}, {1.9,-.2} } ],
        Point[vc],
        Text[ "View",vc,{0,-3}],
        Text[ "Center",vc,{0,3}],
        Circle[ ev, .12, {5Pi/6,7Pi/6} ],
        Circle[ vp + {.5,0}, .5, {3Pi/4,19Pi/16} ],
        Line[ { ev, ev + 0.15 dirunit[5Pi/6] } ],
        Line[ { ev, ev + 0.15 dirunit[7Pi/6] } ],
        PointSize[.015], Point[vp],
        Text[ "Viewpoint", vp, {1.2,3} ],
        Text[ "Line of Sight", (vp+vc)/2, {0,-2} ],
        Text[ "View Vertical", {0,.3}, {2,0}, {0,1} ],
        Dashing[{.02,.02}], Line[{vc,vp}]
    },
    PlotRange->All, AspectRatio->Automatic,
    DefaultFont->{"Times-Roman",8}
]]];
```

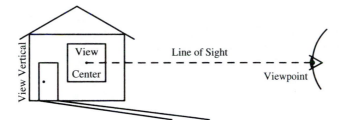

This figure can be found in Section 6.2.2 on page 192.

The next few figures illustrate the coordinate systems for perspective projection are quite similar.

```
Block[{
    vc = {.5,.5,.5}, vp = {3,.5,.5},
    vv = {0,0,.47}, vh = {0,.47,0}, pt = {.05,.1,.2},
    pp, ll
},
    ll = vc - vp;
    pp = pt - vp;
    pp = ((ll . ll) / (pp . ll)) pp + vp;
Show[Graphics3D[{
    { GrayLevel[1/3], Line[ { vc-vh, vc+vh } ], Line[ { vc-vv, vc+vv } ],
        Line[ { vc-vh, vc+vh } ], Line[ { vc-vv, vc+vv } ] },
    { Thickness[.008], Line[ { vc, vc+vv } ] },
    wirebox[ { {0,1}, {0,1}, {0,1} } ],
    {GrayLevel[.9],solidplane[ vc + .01(vc-vp), vp-vc, {0,0,.7} ]},
    PointSize[.02],
    Point[vc], Point[vp], Point[pt], Point[pp],
    { Dashing[{.01,.01}], Thickness[.001], Line[{vc,vp}], Line[{pt,vp}] },
    Text[ "VC", vc, {1.4,3} ],
    Text[ "VV", vc+vv, {0,-2} ],
    Text[ "VH", vc+vh, {0,-2} ],
    Text[ "VP", vp, {1.4,3} ],
    Text[ "P", pt, {0,3} ],
    Text[ "P'", pp, {0,3} ]
},
    Boxed->False, PlotRange->All, ViewPoint->10{3,-4,.7},
    Lighting->False, DefaultFont->{"Times-Roman",7}
]]];
```

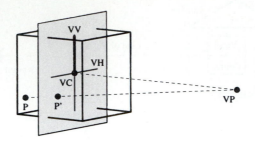

This figure appears in Section 6.2.2 on page 193.

```
Block[{
    vc = {.5,.5,.5}, vp = {3,.5,.5},
    vv = {0,0,.47}, vh = {0,.47,0},
    ls, x, vl
},
    ls = vc - vp;
    x = vc + 0.45 ls;
    vl = ( vc + vv + (# ls) )& /@ (.455 + Range[-2,2]/15);
Show[Graphics3D[{
    { Thickness[.008], Line[ { vc, vc+vv } ], Line[{ x, # }]& /@ vl },
    plane[ x, vh, {0,0,.7} ],
    plane[ vp + 0.75 ls, vh, {0,0,.7} ],
    {GrayLevel[.9],solidplane[ vc + .01(vc-vp), vp-vc, {0,0,.8} ]},
    PointSize[.02],
    Point[vc], Point[vp], Point[x],
    { Dashing[{.01,.01}], Thickness[.001], Line[{x,vp}], Line[{vc+vv,Last[vl]}] },
    Text[ "VV", vc+vv, {1.5,0} ],
    Text[ "VP", vp, {0,4} ],
    Text[ "VC", vc, {1.4,3} ],
    Text[ "X", x, {0,4} ]
},
    Boxed->False, PlotRange->All, ViewPoint->10{3,-4,.7},
    Lighting->False, DefaultFont->{"Times-Roman",7}
]]];
```

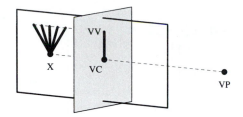

This figure appears in Section 6.2.2 on page 194.

```
Block[{
    vc = {.5,.5,.5}, vp = {3,.5,.5}, ls = {3,.9,.7},
    vv = {0,0,.47}, vh = {0,.47,0}
},
Show[Graphics3D[{
    { GrayLevel[1/3], Line[ { vc-vh, vc+vh } ], Line[ { vc-vv, vc+vv } ],
        Line[ { vc-vh, vc+vh } ], Line[ { vc-vv, vc+vv } ],
        Line[ { vp-vh, vp+vh } ], Line[ { vp-vv, vp+vv } ],
        Line[ { vp-vh, vp+vh } ], Line[ { vp-vv, vp+vv } ] },
    { Thickness[.008], Line[ { vc, vc+vv } ] },
    wirebox[ { {0,1}, {0,1}, {0,1} } ],
    {GrayLevel[.9],solidplane[ vc + .01(vc-vp), vp-vc, {0,0,.7} ]},
    plane[ vp, vp-vc, {0,0,.8} ],
    PointSize[.02],
    Point[vc], Point[vp], Point[ls],
    { Dashing[{.01,.01}], Thickness[.001], Line[{vc,vp}], Line[{vc,ls}] },
    Text[ "VC", vc, {1.4,3} ],
    Text[ "VV", vc+vv, {0,-2} ],
    Text[ "VH", vc+vh, {0,-2} ],
    Text[ "VP", vp, {1.4,3} ],
    Text[ "LS", ls, {0,-3} ]
},
    Boxed->False, PlotRange->All, ViewPoint->10{3,-4,.7},
    Lighting->False, DefaultFont->{"Times-Roman",7}
]]];
```

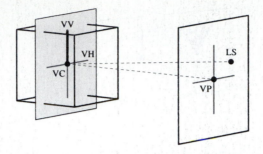

A.7 The Figure for Specular Reflection

Here is the code for illustrating how *Mathematica* models specular reflection:

```
Needs["Graphics`Arrow`"];
th = N[ 20 Degree ];
m1 = { {Cos[th],-Sin[th]},{Sin[th],Cos[th]} };
m2 = { {Cos[th],Sin[th]},{-Sin[th],Cos[th]} };
ph = N[ 40 Degree ];
n1 = { {Cos[ph],-Sin[ph]},{Sin[ph],Cos[ph]} };
n2 = { {Cos[ph],Sin[ph]},{-Sin[ph],Cos[ph]} };
hz = {5,0};
v1 = n1 . hz ;
v2 = n2 . (-hz) ;
pt = {5,0};
ls = pt + v2;
nm = pt + {0,5};
rf = pt + v1;
s1 = pt + (m1.(.8 v1));
s2 = pt + (m2.(.8 v1));
Show[Graphics[{
    Line[{ pt - hz, pt + hz }],
    Text["Reflecting Surface",pt,{0,2}],
    Arrow[ pt, nm ],
    Text["Normal",nm,{0,-2}],
    PointSize[.03], Point[ls],
    Text["Light Source",ls,{0,-2}],
    Arrow[ ls, pt ],
```

```
    Text["Primary\nReflection",rf,{-1,-1.5}],
    Arrow[ pt, rf ],
    Dashing[{.05,.02}],
    Line[{ pt, s1 }], Line[{ pt, s2 }],
    Text["Line of\n  Sight",s1,{-.2,-1.5}],
    Text[FontForm["q",{"Symbol",6}],pt,{-11.5,-9}]
},
    AspectRatio->Automatic, DefaultFont->{"Times-Roman",6},
    PlotRange->All
]];
```

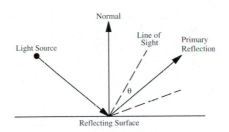

This figure appears in Section 7.4.2 on page 259.

Tables of Graphics Symbols

Here we present three tables of graphics commands, data types, and options. The first table lists all the graphics options and shows the commands and data types that accept each option. The second table lists all the graphics commands and data types and shows the options each one accepts. The third table breaks down *Mathematica*'s entire graphics vocabulary—commands, types, options, primitives, and directives—into categories and shows which graphics terms belong in each category.

Table 1: Functions Using Each Graphics Option

Option	Functions
AmbientLight	Graphics3D, ListPlot3D, ParametricPlot3D, Plot3D, SurfaceGraphics
AspectRatio	ContourGraphics, ContourPlot, DensityGraphics, DensityPlot, Graphics, Graphics3D, GraphicsArray, ListContourPlot, ListDensityPlot, ListPlot, ListPlot3D, ParametricPlot, ParametricPlot3D, Plot, Plot3D, SurfaceGraphics
Axes	ContourGraphics, ContourPlot, DensityGraphics, DensityPlot, Graphics, Graphics3D, GraphicsArray, ListContourPlot, ListDensityPlot, ListPlot, ListPlot3D, ParametricPlot, ParametricPlot3D, Plot, Plot3D, SurfaceGraphics
AxesEdge	Graphics3D, ListPlot3D, ParametricPlot3D, Plot3D, SurfaceGraphics
AxesLabel	ContourGraphics, ContourPlot, DensityGraphics, DensityPlot, Graphics, Graphics3D, GraphicsArray, ListContourPlot, ListDensityPlot, ListPlot, ListPlot3D, ParametricPlot, ParametricPlot3D, Plot, Plot3D, SurfaceGraphics
AxesOrigin	ContourGraphics, ContourPlot, DensityGraphics, Graphics, GraphicsArray, ListContourPlot, ListDensityPlot, ListPlot, ParametricPlot, Plot

Option	Functions
AxesStyle	ContourGraphics, ContourPlot, DensityGraphics, DensityPlot, Graphics, Graphics3D, GraphicsArray, ListContourPlot, ListDensityPlot, ListPlot, ListPlot3D, ParametricPlot, ParametricPlot3D, Plot, Plot3D, SurfaceGraphics
Background	ContourGraphics, ContourPlot, DensityGraphics, DensityPlot, Graphics, Graphics3D, GraphicsArray, ListContourPlot, ListDensityPlot, ListPlot, ListPlot3D, ParametricPlot, ParametricPlot3D, Plot, Plot3D, SurfaceGraphics
Boxed	Graphics3D, ListPlot3D, ParametricPlot3D, Plot3D, SurfaceGraphics
BoxRatios	Graphics3D, ListPlot3D, ParametricPlot3D, Plot3D, SurfaceGraphics
BoxStyle	Graphics3D, ListPlot3D, ParametricPlot3D, Plot3D, SurfaceGraphics
ClipFill	ListPlot3D, Plot3D, SurfaceGraphics
ColorFunction	ContourGraphics, ContourPlot, DensityGraphics, DensityPlot, ListContourPlot, ListDensityPlot, ListPlot3D, Plot3D, SurfaceGraphics
ColorOutput	ContourGraphics, ContourPlot, DensityGraphics, DensityPlot, Graphics, Graphics3D, GraphicsArray, ListContourPlot, ListDensityPlot, ListPlot, ListPlot3D, ParametricPlot, ParametricPlot3D, Plot, Plot3D, SurfaceGraphics
Compiled	ContourPlot, DensityPlot, ParametricPlot, ParametricPlot3D, Plot, Plot3D
ContourLines	ContourGraphics, ContourPlot, ListContourPlot
Contours	ContourGraphics, ContourPlot, ListContourPlot
ContourShading	ContourGraphics, ContourPlot, ListContourPlot
ContourSmoothing	ContourGraphics, ContourPlot, ListContourPlot
ContourStyle	ContourGraphics, ContourPlot, ListContourPlot
DefaultColor	ContourGraphics, ContourPlot, DensityGraphics, DensityPlot, Graphics, Graphics3D, GraphicsArray, ListContourPlot, ListDensityPlot, ListPlot, ListPlot3D, ParametricPlot, ParametricPlot3D, Plot, Plot3D, SurfaceGraphics
DefaultFont	ContourGraphics, ContourPlot, DensityGraphics, DensityPlot, Graphics, Graphics3D, GraphicsArray, ListContourPlot, ListDensityPlot, ListPlot, ListPlot3D, ParametricPlot, ParametricPlot3D, Plot, Plot3D, SurfaceGraphics

Option	Functions
DisplayFunction	ContourGraphics, ContourPlot, DensityGraphics, DensityPlot, Graphics, Graphics3D, GraphicsArray, ListContourPlot, ListDensityPlot, ListPlot, ListPlot3D, ParametricPlot, ParametricPlot3D, Plot, Plot3D, SurfaceGraphics
Epilog	ContourGraphics, ContourPlot, DensityGraphics, DensityPlot, Graphics, Graphics3D, GraphicsArray, ListContourPlot, ListDensityPlot, ListPlot, ListPlot3D, ParametricPlot, ParametricPlot3D, Plot, Plot3D, SurfaceGraphics
FaceGrids	Graphics3D, ListPlot3D, ParametricPlot3D, Plot3D, SurfaceGraphics
Frame	ContourGraphics, ContourPlot, DensityGraphics, DensityPlot, Graphics, GraphicsArray, ListContourPlot, ListDensityPlot, ListPlot, ParametricPlot, Plot
FrameLabel	ContourGraphics, ContourPlot, DensityGraphics, DensityPlot, Graphics, GraphicsArray, ListContourPlot, ListDensityPlot, ListPlot, ParametricPlot, Plot
FrameStyle	ContourGraphics, ContourPlot, DensityGraphics, DensityPlot, Graphics, GraphicsArray, ListContourPlot, ListDensityPlot, ListPlot, ParametricPlot, Plot
FrameTicks	ContourGraphics, ContourPlot, DensityGraphics, DensityPlot, Graphics, GraphicsArray, ListContourPlot, ListDensityPlot, ListPlot, ParametricPlot, Plot
GraphicsSpacing	GraphicsArray
GridLines	Graphics, GraphicsArray, ListPlot, ParametricPlot, Plot
HiddenSurface	ListPlot3D, Plot3D, SurfaceGraphics
Lighting	Graphics3D, ListPlot3D, ParametricPlot3D, Plot3D, SurfaceGraphics
LightSources	Graphics3D, ListPlot3D, ParametricPlot3D, Plot3D, SurfaceGraphics
MaxBend	ParametricPlot, Plot
Mesh	DensityGraphics, DensityPlot, ListDensityPlot, ListPlot3D, Plot3D, SurfaceGraphics
MeshRange	ContourGraphics, DensityGraphics, ListContourPlot, ListDensityPlot, ListPlot3D, SurfaceGraphics
MeshStyle	DensityGraphics, DensityPlot, ListDensityPlot, ListPlot3D, Plot3D, SurfaceGraphics
Plot3Matrix	Graphics3D, ListPlot3D, ParametricPlot3D, Plot3D, SurfaceGraphics

Option	Functions
PlotDivision	ParametricPlot, Plot
PlotJoined	ListPlot
PlotLabel	ContourGraphics, ContourPlot, DensityGraphics, DensityPlot, Graphics, Graphics3D, GraphicsArray, ListContourPlot, ListDensityPlot, ListPlot, ListPlot3D, ParametricPlot, ParametricPlot3D, Plot, Plot3D, SurfaceGraphics
PlotPoints	ContourPlot, DensityPlot, ParametricPlot, ParametricPlot3D, Plot, Plot3D
PlotRange	ContourGraphics, ContourPlot, DensityGraphics, DensityPlot, Graphics, Graphics3D, GraphicsArray, ListContourPlot, ListDensityPlot, ListPlot, ListPlot3D, ParametricPlot, ParametricPlot3D, Plot, Plot3D, SurfaceGraphics
PlotRegion	ContourGraphics, ContourPlot, DensityGraphics, DensityPlot, Graphics, Graphics3D, GraphicsArray, ListContourPlot, ListDensityPlot, ListPlot, ListPlot3D, ParametricPlot, ParametricPlot3D, Plot, Plot3D, SurfaceGraphics
PlotStyle	ListPlot, ParametricPlot, Plot
PolygonIntersections	Graphics3D, ParametricPlot3D
Prolog	ContourGraphics, ContourPlot, DensityGraphics, DensityPlot, Graphics, Graphics3D, GraphicsArray, ListContourPlot, ListDensityPlot, ListPlot, ListPlot3D, ParametricPlot, ParametricPlot3D, Plot, Plot3D, SurfaceGraphics
RenderAll	Graphics3D, ParametricPlot3D
RotateLabel	ContourGraphics, ContourPlot, DensityGraphics, DensityPlot, Graphics, GraphicsArray, ListContourPlot, ListDensityPlot, ListPlot, ParametricPlot, Plot
Shading	Graphics3D, ListPlot3D, ParametricPlot3D, Plot3D, SurfaceGraphics
SphericalRegion	Graphics3D, ListPlot3D, ParametricPlot3D, Plot3D, SurfaceGraphics
StringConversion	Display
Ticks	ContourGraphics, ContourPlot, DensityGraphics, DensityPlot, Graphics, Graphics3D, GraphicsArray, ListContourPlot, ListDensityPlot, ListPlot, ListPlot3D, ParametricPlot, ParametricPlot3D, Plot, Plot3D, SurfaceGraphics
ViewCenter	Graphics3D, ListPlot3D, ParametricPlot3D, Plot3D, SurfaceGraphics

Option	Functions
ViewPoint	Graphics3D, ListPlot3D, ParametricPlot3D, Plot3D, SurfaceGraphics
ViewVertical	Graphics3D, ListPlot3D, ParametricPlot3D, Plot3D, SurfaceGraphics

Table 2: Options Used by Each Graphics Function

Function	Options
ContourGraphics	AspectRatio, Axes, AxesLabel, AxesOrigin, AxesStyle, Background, ColorFunction, ColorOutput, ContourLines, Contours, ContourShading, ContourSmoothing, ContourStyle, DefaultColor, DefaultFont, DisplayFunction, Epilog, Frame, FrameLabel, FrameStyle, FrameTicks, MeshRange, PlotLabel, PlotRange, PlotRegion, Prolog, RotateLabel, Ticks
ContourPlot	AspectRatio, Axes, AxesLabel, AxesOrigin, AxesStyle, Background, ColorFunction, ColorOutput, Compiled, ContourLines, Contours, ContourShading, ContourSmoothing, ContourStyle, DefaultColor, DefaultFont, DisplayFunction, Epilog, Frame, FrameLabel, FrameStyle, FrameTicks, PlotLabel, PlotPoints, PlotRange, PlotRegion, Prolog, RotateLabel, Ticks
DensityGraphics	AspectRatio, Axes, AxesLabel, AxesOrigin, AxesStyle, Background, ColorFunction, ColorOutput, DefaultColor, DefaultFont, DisplayFunction, Epilog, Frame, FrameLabel, FrameStyle, FrameTicks, Mesh, MeshRange, MeshStyle, PlotLabel, PlotRange, PlotRegion, Prolog, RotateLabel, Ticks
DensityPlot	AspectRatio, Axes, AxesLabel, AxesStyle, Background, ColorFunction, ColorOutput, Compiled, DefaultColor, DefaultFont, DisplayFunction, Epilog, Frame, FrameLabel, FrameStyle, FrameTicks, Mesh, MeshStyle, PlotLabel, PlotPoints, PlotRange, PlotRegion, Prolog, RotateLabel, Ticks
Display	StringConversion
Graphics	AspectRatio, Axes, AxesLabel, AxesOrigin, AxesStyle, Background, ColorOutput, DefaultColor, DefaultFont, DisplayFunction, Epilog, Frame, FrameLabel, FrameStyle, FrameTicks, GridLines, PlotLabel, PlotRange, PlotRegion, Prolog, RotateLabel, Ticks

Function	Options
Graphics3D	AmbientLight, AspectRatio, Axes, AxesEdge, AxesLabel, AxesStyle, Background, Boxed, BoxRatios, BoxStyle, ColorOutput, DefaultColor, DefaultFont, DisplayFunction, Epilog, FaceGrids, Lighting, LightSources, Plot3Matrix, PlotLabel, PlotRange, PlotRegion, PolygonIntersections, Prolog, RenderAll, Shading, SphericalRegion, Ticks, ViewCenter, ViewPoint, ViewVertical
GraphicsArray	AspectRatio, Axes, AxesLabel, AxesOrigin, AxesStyle, Background, ColorOutput, DefaultColor, DefaultFont, DisplayFunction, Epilog, Frame, FrameLabel, FrameStyle, FrameTicks, GraphicsSpacing, GridLines, PlotLabel, PlotRange, PlotRegion, Prolog, RotateLabel, Ticks
ListContourPlot	AspectRatio, Axes, AxesLabel, AxesOrigin, AxesStyle, Background, ColorFunction, ColorOutput, ContourLines, Contours, ContourShading, ContourSmoothing, ContourStyle, DefaultColor, DefaultFont, DisplayFunction, Epilog, Frame, FrameLabel, FrameStyle, FrameTicks, MeshRange, PlotLabel, PlotRange, PlotRegion, Prolog, RotateLabel, Ticks
ListDensityPlot	AspectRatio, Axes, AxesLabel, AxesOrigin, AxesStyle, Background, ColorFunction, ColorOutput, DefaultColor, DefaultFont, DisplayFunction, Epilog, Frame, FrameLabel, FrameStyle, FrameTicks, Mesh, MeshRange, MeshStyle, PlotLabel, PlotRange, PlotRegion, Prolog, RotateLabel, Ticks
ListPlot	AspectRatio, Axes, AxesLabel, AxesOrigin, AxesStyle, Background, ColorOutput, DefaultColor, DefaultFont, DisplayFunction, Epilog, Frame, FrameLabel, FrameStyle, FrameTicks, GridLines, PlotJoined, PlotLabel, PlotRange, PlotRegion, PlotStyle, Prolog, RotateLabel, Ticks
ListPlot3D	AmbientLight, AspectRatio, Axes, AxesEdge, AxesLabel, AxesStyle, Background, Boxed, BoxRatios, BoxStyle, ClipFill, ColorFunction, ColorOutput, DefaultColor, DefaultFont, DisplayFunction, Epilog, FaceGrids, HiddenSurface, Lighting, LightSources, Mesh, MeshRange, MeshStyle, Plot3Matrix, PlotLabel, PlotRange, PlotRegion, Prolog, Shading, SphericalRegion, Ticks, ViewCenter, ViewPoint, ViewVertical

Function	Options
ParametricPlot	AspectRatio, Axes, AxesLabel, AxesOrigin, AxesStyle, Background, ColorOutput, Compiled, DefaultColor, DefaultFont, DisplayFunction, Epilog, Frame, FrameLabel, FrameStyle, FrameTicks, GridLines, MaxBend, PlotDivision, PlotLabel, PlotPoints, PlotRange, PlotRegion, PlotStyle, Prolog, RotateLabel, Ticks
ParametricPlot3D	AmbientLight, AspectRatio, Axes, AxesEdge, AxesLabel, AxesStyle, Background, Boxed, BoxRatios, BoxStyle, ColorOutput, Compiled, DefaultColor, DefaultFont, DisplayFunction, Epilog, FaceGrids, Lighting, LightSources, Plot3Matrix, PlotLabel, PlotPoints, PlotRange, PlotRegion, PolygonIntersections, Prolog, RenderAll, Shading, SphericalRegion, Ticks, ViewCenter, ViewPoint, ViewVertical
Plot	AspectRatio, Axes, AxesLabel, AxesOrigin, AxesStyle, Background, ColorOutput, Compiled, DefaultColor, DefaultFont, DisplayFunction, Epilog, Frame, FrameLabel, FrameStyle, FrameTicks, GridLines, MaxBend, PlotDivision, PlotLabel, PlotPoints, PlotRange, PlotRegion, PlotStyle, Prolog, RotateLabel, Ticks
Plot3D	AmbientLight, AspectRatio, Axes, AxesEdge, AxesLabel, AxesStyle, Background, Boxed, BoxRatios, BoxStyle, ClipFill, ColorFunction, ColorOutput, Compiled, DefaultColor, DefaultFont, DisplayFunction, Epilog, FaceGrids, HiddenSurface, Lighting, LightSources, Mesh, MeshStyle, Plot3Matrix, PlotLabel, PlotPoints, PlotRange, PlotRegion, Prolog, Shading, SphericalRegion, Ticks, ViewCenter, ViewPoint, ViewVertical
SurfaceGraphics	AmbientLight, AspectRatio, Axes, AxesEdge, AxesLabel, AxesStyle, Background, Boxed, BoxRatios, BoxStyle, ClipFill, ColorFunction, ColorOutput, DefaultColor, DefaultFont, DisplayFunction, Epilog, FaceGrids, HiddenSurface, Lighting, LightSources, Mesh, MeshRange, MeshStyle, Plot3Matrix, PlotLabel, PlotRange, PlotRegion, Prolog, Shading, SphericalRegion, Ticks, ViewCenter, ViewPoint, ViewVertical

Table 3: Words in Each Category

Category	Graphics Words
2D graphics data types	Graphics, GraphicsArray
3D graphics data types	Graphics3D, SurfaceGraphics
Mixed graphics data types	ContourGraphics, DensityGraphics
Graphics primitives for 2D and 3D	Line, Point, Polygon, Text
Graphics primitives for 2D only	Circle, Disk, PostScript, Raster, RasterArray, Rectangle
Graphics primitives for 3D only	Cuboid
Graphics directives for 2D and 3D	AbsoluteDashing, AbsolutePointSize, AbsoluteThickness, CMYKColor, Dashing, GrayLevel, Hue, PointSize, RGBColor, Thickness
Graphics directives for 3D only	EdgeForm, FaceForm, SurfaceColor
Display options for all graphics	AspectRatio, Axes, AxesLabel, AxesStyle, Background, ColorOutput, DefaultColor, DefaultFont, DisplayFunction, Epilog, PlotLabel, PlotRange, PlotRegion, Prolog, Ticks
Display options for 2D graphics	AxesOrigin, Frame, FrameLabel, FrameStyle, FrameTicks, RotateLabel
Display options for Graphics only	GridLines
Display options for GraphicsArray only	GraphicsSpacing
Display options for Graphics3D and SurfaceGraphics	AmbientLight, AxesEdge, Boxed, BoxRatios, BoxStyle, FaceGrids, Lighting, LightSources, Plot3Matrix, Shading, SphericalRegion, ViewCenter, ViewPoint, ViewVertical
Display options for Graphics3D only	PolygonIntersections, RenderAll
Display options for SurfaceGraphics, ContourGraphics, and DensityGraphics	ColorFunction, MeshRange
Display options for SurfaceGraphics and DensityGraphics	Mesh, MeshStyle
Display options for SurfaceGraphics only	ClipFill, HiddenSurface

Category	Graphics words
Display options for ContourGraphics only	ContourLines, Contours, ContourShading, ContourSmoothing, ContourStyle
2D graphics-making functions	ListPlot, ParametricPlot, Plot
3D graphics-making functions	ListPlot3D, ParametricPlot3D, Plot3D
Mixed graphics-making functions	ContourPlot, DensityPlot, ListContourPlot, ListDensityPlot
Algorithm options for all samplers	Compiled, PlotPoints
Algorithm options for 2D samplers only	MaxBend, PlotDivision
Algorithm options for 2D plotters only	PlotStyle
Algorithm options for ListPlot only	PlotJoined
Default variables	$DefaultFont, $Display, $DisplayFunction, $StringConversion
Values for options	All, Automatic, None
Option-processing functions	FullOptions, Options, SetOptions
Graphics-manipulation functions	Display, FullAxes, FullGraphics, Show
Modifiers for graphics primitives	FontForm, Scaled, ToColor
Obsolete words	ContourLevels, ContourSpacing, Framed, Plot3Matrix, PlotColor
Sound-related words	Sound, SampledSoundFunction, SampledSoundList, ListPlay, Play, PlayRange, SampleDepth, SampleRate, $SoundDisplay, $SoundDisplayFunction

Suggested Readings

This is a list of recommended readings.

About *Mathematica*

Blachman, Nancy. *Mathematica: A Practical Approach.* Englewood Cliffs, New Jersey: Prentice-Hall, 1992, ISBN 0-13-563826-7.

> This book offers a systematic introduction to *Mathematica* for people who want to get up to speed quickly. It provides the best presentation that I have seen. It covers all the important features of *Mathematica* thoroughly, with clear explanations, excellent examples, and challenging and instructive problem sets. *Note: this testimonial was written by Cameron and represents his sincere belief; Nancy didn't coerce him in any way!*

Blachman, Nancy. *Mathematica Quick Reference.* Reading, Massachusetts: Addison-Wesley,1992, ISBN 0-201-62880-5.

> This is a useful pocket reference to the built-in functions of *Mathematica* and the standard packages distributed with *Mathematica*. It is much more convenient for quick memory jogs than pulling out The *Mathematica* Book.

Boyland, Philip et al. *Guide to Standard Mathematica Packages*, Champaign, Illinois: Wolfram Research, Inc., 1993.

> This is the reference manual for the standard packages that are distributed with all versions of *Mathematica*. One copy is shipped with every copy of *Mathematica*, and additional copies can be ordered from Wolfram Research.

Gray, Theodore and Jerry Glynn. *Exploring Mathematics with Mathematica.* Redwood City, California: Addison-Wesley, 1991, ISBN 0-201-52809-6.

> This is a lighthearted and gentle introduction to some interesting mathematical topics, using *Mathematica* as the medium of presentation. The presentation

covers most of the basics of *Mathematica*, so a beginner can learn about the software while playing with mathematics.

Maeder, Roman. *Programming in Mathematica,* Second Edition. Redwood City, California: Addison-Wesley, 1991, ISBN 0-201-54877-1 (hardcover), 0-201-54878-X (paper).

This book focuses on good programming style in *Mathematica*. It includes detailed examples of how to write packages, how to use term rewriting as a programming paradigm, and other advanced programming topics. These examples result in packages that are not simply toy programs; many of them are included among the packages distributed with *Mathematica*.

Skiena, Steven. *Implementing Discrete Mathematics: Combinatorics and Graph Theory with Mathematica.* Redwood City, California: Addison-Wesley, 1990, ISBN 0-201-50943-1.

This book presents efficient implementations in *Mathematica* for many standard algorithms in combinatorics and graph theory. The packages that were written for this book, known collectively as *Combinatorica,* are distributed with *Mathematica.*

Wolfram, Stephen. *Mathematica: A System for Doing Mathematics by Computer,* Second Edition. Reading, Massachusetts: Addison-Wesley, 1991, ISBN 0-201-51502-4 (hardcover), 0-201-51507-5 (paperback).

About Computer-Assisted Typesetting

Eijkhout, Victor. *TEX by Topic.* Reading, Massachusetts: Addison-Wesley, 1992, ISBN 0-201-56882-9.

This is a concise but thorough treatment of TEX. It is definitely not for beginners, but it is a valuable wizard's guide.

Goossens, Michel, Frank Mittelbach, and Alexander Samarin. *The LATEX Companion.* Reading, Massachusetts: Addison-Wesley, 1994, ISBN 0-201-54199-8.

Knuth, Donald. *The TEXbook.* Reading, Massachusetts: Addison-Wesley, 1986, ISBN 0-201-13448-9.

This is the definitive book about TEX, by the creator of TEX. It is amusingly written, but not well organized as a reference book.

Lamport, Leslie. *LATEX: A Document Preparation System.* Reading, Massachusetts: Addison-Wesley, 1986, ISBN 0-201-15790-X.

This is the manual for the LaTeX macro package, which sits atop the TeX formatting engine and provides a more structured environment for document design. *The Mathematica Graphics Guidebook* was typeset with LaTeX.

About PostScript

Adobe Systems Incorporated. *PostScript Language Reference Manual,* Second Edition. Reading, Massachusetts: Addison-Wesley, 1990, ISBN 0-201-18127-4.

Nobody who does serious PostScript programming can get along without this book. It is to PostScript what Wolfram's book is to *Mathematica.*

Adobe Systems Incorporated. *PostScript Language Tutorial and Cookbook.* Reading, Massachusetts: Addison-Wesley, 1985, ISBN 0-201-10179-3.

This is a valuable collection of examples and techniques for the PostScript programmer.

Reid, Glenn. *Thinking in PostScript.* Reading, Massachusetts: Addison-Wesley, 1990, ISBN 0-201-52372-8.

This is a gentle introduction to the art of PostScript programming. It explains the PostScript model (in which all operations are performed on a stack) and shows what programming techniques do and do not work well with this model.

Roth, Stephen, ed. *Real World PostScript.* Reading, Massachusetts: Addison-Wesley, 1988, ISBN 0-201-06663-7.

About Computer Graphics

Glassner, Andrew S. *Three-Dimensional Computer Graphics,* Second Edition. New York, New York: Design Press, 1989, ISBN 0-8306-5501-8.

Glassner, Andrew S, ed. *Graphics Gems.* San Diego, California: Academic Press, 1990, ISBN 0-12-286165-5.

Gray, Alfred. *Modern Differential Geometry of Curves and Surfaces.* Boca Raton, Florida: CRC Press, 1993, ISBN 0-8493-7872-9.

Rogers, David F. *Procedural Elements for Computer Graphics.* New York, New York: McGraw-Hill, 1985, LC catalog T385.R63 1985, ISBN 0-07-053534-5.

This presents algorithms for graphics, such as hidden surface removal, illumination, and halftoning, together with mathematical justifications for the techniques.

About Data Graphics

Cleveland, William S. *The Elements of Graphing Data.* Monterey, California: Wadsworth, Inc., 1985, LC catalog number QA90.C54, ISBN 0-534-03729-1 (cloth), 0-534-03730-5 (paper).

This book is about graphing data for analysis. It discusses many kinds of data graphics presentations, pointing out the advantages and disadvantages of each in terms of ease of perception, clarity of detail, and other criteria of usefulness for data analysis. One of its strengths is that a single data set is frequently exhibited in several different presentations, allowing the reader to see which features are brought out and which are obscured by each type of data graphic. Chapter 4 on "Graphical Perception" is a valuable discussion of the perceptual and cognitive tasks involved in reading a graph. When a clear understanding of a data set is crucial to your argument, and you need the most effective possible illustration to make your point, the information in the sections on Weber's law of perception or the angle contamination of slope judgments will give a solid foundation for deciding whether to use a multiple bar chart, a scatterplot matrix, or other presentation of your data.

Tufte, Edward. *The Visual Display of Quantitative Information.* Cheshire, Connecticut: Graphics Press, 1983.

This book is an excellent introduction to statistical data graphics, explaining what presentations are and are not effective, and why. It enables the reader to see newspapers, journal articles, government reports, and other sources of data graphics in an entirely new light.

Index

Page numbers in **bold face** are primary references.

Colophon

This book was typeset by the authors, using Leslie Lamport's LaTeX macro package for Donald Knuth's TeX typesetting system. Cameron Smith wrote the typesetting macros, following advice on book design from Jan Benes and Juliet Silveri. The text and display typefaces are from Adobe, Inc.'s Stone Serif type family, and the typeface for labels of graphics is Adobe's Courier. The typefaces for *Mathematica* keywords and code listings are sans-serif adaptations of Donald Knuth's Computer Modern typewriter fonts; they were developed by Art Ogawa for use in *The Mathematica Journal*. The illustrations were created by the authors in *Mathematica*, and placed in the text by means of the psfig macro package by Trevor Darrell. The *Mathematica* programming and the TeX typesetting were executed on computers from NeXT, Inc. The device-independent typesetting files produced by TeX were converted PostScript form with the aid of Tomas Rokicki's dvips program and other TeX-related software from Rokicki's company, Radical Eye Software. Draft copies of the book were printed on a Hewlett Packard LaserJet4M at 600 dots per inch, a NeXT laser printer at 400 dots per inch, and an Apple LaserWriter IINT at 300 dots per inch, and the final form of the type was imaged directly on film by a Linotronic L330 phototypesetter at Canterbury Press in Berkeley, California. No manual stripping or paste-up was required to produce the book.